MANAGING HOSPITALITY HUMAN RESOURCES

EDUCATIONAL INSTITUTE BOOKS

UNIFORM SYSTEM OF ACCOUNTS FOR THE LODGING INDUSTRY
Eleventh Revised Edition

PLANNING AND CONTROL FOR FOOD AND BEVERAGE OPERATIONS
Ninth Edition
Jack D. Ninemeier

UNDERSTANDING HOSPITALITY LAW
Fifth Edition
Jack P. Jefferies/Banks Brown

SUPERVISION IN THE HOSPITALITY INDUSTRY
Sixth Edition
Jack D. Ninemeier

MANAGEMENT OF FOOD AND BEVERAGE OPERATIONS
Sixth Edition
Jack D. Ninemeier

MANAGING FRONT OFFICE OPERATIONS
Tenth Edition
Michael L. Kasavana

MANAGING SERVICE IN FOOD AND BEVERAGE OPERATIONS
Fifth Edition
Ronald F. Cichy/Philip J. Hickey, Jr.

THE LODGING AND FOOD SERVICE INDUSTRY
Eighth Edition
Gerald W. Lattin/Thomas W. Lattin/James E. Lattin

SECURITY AND LOSS PREVENTION MANAGEMENT
Third Edition
David M. Stipanuk/Raymond C. Ellis, Jr.

HOSPITALITY INDUSTRY MANAGERIAL ACCOUNTING
Eighth Edition
Raymond S. Schmidgall

MANAGING TECHNOLOGY IN THE HOSPITALITY INDUSTRY
Seventh Edition
Michael L. Kasavana

HOTEL AND RESTAURANT ACCOUNTING
Eighth Edition
Raymond Cote

ACCOUNTING FOR HOSPITALITY MANAGERS
Fifth Edition
Raymond Cote

CONVENTION MANAGEMENT AND SERVICE
Ninth Edition
James R. Abbey

HOSPITALITY SALES AND MARKETING
Sixth Edition
James R. Abbey

MANAGING HOUSEKEEPING OPERATIONS
Revised Third Edition
Aleta A. Nitschke/William D. Frye

HOSPITALITY TODAY: AN INTRODUCTION
Eighth Edition
Rocco M. Angelo

HOSPITALITY FACILITIES MANAGEMENT AND DESIGN
Fourth Edition
David M. Stipanuk

MANAGING HOSPITALITY HUMAN RESOURCES
Sixth Edition
Robert H. Woods, William Werner, Seonghee Cho, and Misty M. Johanson

RETAIL MANAGEMENT FOR SPAS

HOSPITALITY INDUSTRY FINANCIAL ACCOUNTING
Fourth Edition
Raymond S. Schmidgall/James W. Damitio

HOTEL INVESTMENTS: ISSUES & PERSPECTIVES
Fifth Edition
Edited by Lori E. Raleigh and Rachel J. Roginsky

LEADERSHIP AND MANAGEMENT IN THE HOSPITALITY INDUSTRY
Third Edition
Robert H. Woods/Judy Z. King

CONTEMPORARY CLUB MANAGEMENT
Third Edition
Edited by Joe Perdue and Jason Koenigsfeld for the Club Managers Association of America

HOTEL ASSET MANAGEMENT: PRINCIPLES & PRACTICES
Third Edition
Edited by Rich Musgrove, Lori E. Raleigh, and A. J. Singh

MANAGING BEVERAGE OPERATIONS
Second Edition
Ronald F. Cichy/Lendal H. Kotschevar

FOOD SAFETY AND QUALITY MANAGEMENT
Third Edition
Ronald F. Cichy and JaeMin Cha

SPA: A COMPREHENSIVE INTRODUCTION
Elizabeth M. Johnson/Bridgette M. Redman

REVENUE MANAGEMENT: MAXIMIZING REVENUE IN HOSPITALITY OPERATIONS
Second Edition
Gabor Forgacs

FINANCIAL MANAGEMENT FOR SPAS
Raymond S. Schmidgall/John R. Korpi

MANAGING HOSPITALITY HUMAN RESOURCES

Sixth Edition

Robert H. Woods, William Werner, Seonghee Cho, and Misty M. Johanson

LEGAL NOTICE

ISBN   978-0-86612-624-3 (print version)

Printed in the USA

1 2 3 4 5 6 7 8 9 10 26 25 24 23 22 21

CONTENTS

The content of *Managing Hospitality Human Resources*, Sixth Edition, has been updated throughout, including updated mini case studies and updates pertinent to the COVID-19 pandemic.

Improved Organization: The content has been reordered to focus on planning and staffing, human resources development, compensation and benefits, and unions and employment laws.

Expanded Coverage: In the Sixth Edition, students will find expanded coverage of the following topics:

- Recruitment, including characteristics and trends related to millennials and Gen Z-ers

- Diversity and inclusion

- Organizational culture

- Bias in evaluating employee performance

- Causes and remedies for turnover

- Competitive pay policies, compensation plans, and benefit plans

- Stress, emotional health, and employee assistance programs (EAPs)

- Right-to-work laws

- Discrimination, disability, and harassment

Robert H. Woods

Robert H. Woods, Ph.D., CHRE, ISHC, is a specialist in human resources and organizational behavior. He regularly consults with hospitality organizations and private clubs on management, strategic management, service management, human resources, and corporate culture issues. Dr. Woods is co-author of the textbook *Leadership and Management in the Hospitality Industry* and of *The Job Description Handbook*. He has written more than 150 refereed articles and has written chapters for various books, including *Ethics in Hospitality Management* and *Contemporary Club Management*. Dr. Woods received his master's and doctoral degrees from the Hotel School at Cornell University and is a former chair of the Hotel Management Department at UNLV. Before returning to academia, Woods owned and operated a successful chain of restaurants and a hospitality consulting firm. He still owns part of two restaurants in Portland, Oregon with one of his daughters.

William Werner

William Werner is a recovering attorney and associate professor in the William F. Harrah College of Hospitality at the University of Nevada, Las Vegas. He teaches courses in hospitality law, employment law, risk management, and labor-management relations, and has served two terms as Chair of the Hospitality Management Department. Prior to his appointment to the UNLV faculty in 2001, he practiced law in Las Vegas as in-house counsel for two major gaming resort companies. He has extensive hospitality industry experience in employment litigation, labor relations, and defending managers who don't know enough about human resources management. His experience drives his educational focus not so much on knowledge as on decision-making, risk management, and critical analysis.

Wage and hour laws, dispute resolution, and tips are the primary areas of Bill's research. His publications include articles in the Cornell Hotel and Restaurant Administration Quarterly and the Nevada Practitioners' Journal of Labor and Employment Law, and book chapters on labor relations, employment laws, and student rights.

Bill is a native Buckeye from Kettering, Ohio. He received his B.A. from The Ohio State University, where he played flugelhorn in the locally famous marching band. He moved to Las Vegas shortly after receiving his J.D from the University of Cincinnati College of Law in 1989. In their ample spare time, Bill and his wife Kathy enjoy hiking, fishing, and just being in southern Utah.

Seonghee Cho

Seonghee Cho, Ph.D., associate professor in the Hospitality Management Program at the University of Missouri, is a behavioral social scientist. She received a Master of Science degree from the Department of Restaurant, Hotel, and Institutional Management at Purdue University and a Ph.D. in Hotel Administration from the University of Nevada, Las Vegas (UNLV). Since 2004, she has been teaching in the Hospitality Management Program at the University of Missouri, where she has served as program chair since 2018. She has taught numerous courses such as Human Resource Management, Fundamentals of the Lodging Management, Strategic Management, Food, Beverage, and Labor Cost Control, Revenue Management, Hotel Financial Management, International Hotel Management, and others.

She has received United States Department of Agriculture (USDA) grants, including USDA-CSREES and USDA-ISE, for improving food safety. Her research has received several best paper awards from the Academy of Management and International Council of Hotel, Restaurant, Institutional Education. She serves on an editorial board of the *Journal of Hospitality and Tourism Research*. She is certified in hotel industry analytics.

Misty M. Johanson

Misty M. Johanson, Ph.D., Michigan State University, is a professor of hospitality leadership at the Driehaus College of Business at DePaul University, where she served as dean through June 2020. She joined DePaul in 2009 to establish the School of Hospitality Leadership, becoming its director in 2014. *The Journal of Hospitality and Tourism Education* has recognized DePaul's hospitality and leadership program as the best in Illinois.

An Executive-in-Residence Program, funded by Hyatt and Lettuce Entertain You Enterprises, brings executives into the School of Hospitality Leadership to network with faculty, advise students, and connect them with Chicago's world-class hospitality industry.

In addition to receiving multiple excellence in teaching awards, Johanson has published more than 50 top-refereed scholarly articles and two textbooks and served as executive editor of the *Journal of Hospitality and Tourism Research*.

She earned a BA, MS, and Ph.D. in hospitality business and tourism from Michigan State University and started her hospitality career with Marriott International, serving as a manager, management advisor, and consultant to international hospitality organizations.

1

JOB ANALYSIS AND JOB DESIGN

Chapter 1 Outline

Learning Objectives

1.   Explain the importance of job analysis and how to analyze jobs in the hospitality industry. (p. 4)

2.   Summarize the function of job design. (p. 4)

3.   Describe the seven steps of job analysis. (p. 6)

4.   Conduct a job analysis. (pp. 7–9)

5.   Design job descriptions and job specifications based on the results of job analysis. (pp. 10–14)

6.   Discuss legal issues related to job analysis and design. (p. 15)

7.   Explain the importance of job descriptions and job specifications. (pp. 10–16)

8.   Articulate five techniques for job design. (pp. 14–16)

9.   Explain the importance of a staffing guide and identify the steps involved in developing a staffing guide. (pp. 17–21)

10.   Apply trend line and moving average techniques to forecast business volume and labor needs. (pp. 21–24)

KEY TERMS

Job analysis

Job design

Hawthorne effect

Heisenberg effect

Position analysis questionnaire (PAQ)

Management position description questionnaire (MPDQ)

Critical incident

Job description

Job specification

Job summary

Job simplification

Job enlargement

Job enrichment

Job rotation

Team building

Permanent employees

Alternative employees

Staffing guide

Productivity

Productivity standard

Performance standard

Labor forecasting

Fixed labor expenses

Variable labor expenses

Trend line forecasting

Moving average forecasting

Seasonality

Imagine that you've been selected to open the first hotel for a new company. Among your earliest assignments is designing the jobs that people will do. You've had some experience in this area and know that before you can identify jobs, you have to identify some basics of hotel operation. You start writing questions you'll need to answer:

- What job titles do I need to create?

- What is the content of each job?

- How many jobs are necessary?

- How will the jobs fit together so that two people don't end up doing the same thing?

- What qualifications will people need to perform successfully in each job?

- What should each person be trained to do in the jobs?

- How will you know when people are doing a good job? How should you measure their performance?

- How much should you pay people for doing each job?

- How will you reward people for doing a better job?

What you've just done as an imaginary consultant is draw up questions you could answer through job analysis and job design. **Job analysis** is the systematic process of determining *what* will be done in a job. The process takes some time and effort. When completed, job analyses are rarely used in their entire form. Given these factors, many hospitality companies make the mistake of not completing a job analysis for each position, or only doing it half-heartedly. What these companies don't realize is that repeating job analysis often, at least every other year, improves administrative efficiency and financial performance. Although the analysis itself is rarely used, the information the analysis contains has a variety of uses. Job analysis reveals the tasks, duties, responsibilities, behaviors, and personal characteristics needed to do a job. In many cases, it tells a company *why* specific abilities, knowledge, and skills are required to successfully perform tasks and duties for a job. Job analysis generates job-related data needed for successful human resource (HR) management.

Whereas job analysis determines *what* will be done on a job, **job design** determines *how* the job will be done. Job design involves defining the combination of tasks, duties, and responsibilities associated with a job.

The importance of job analysis and job design should not be underestimated. Recruitment, selection, training programs, job evaluation, compensation planning, and performance appraisals all depend on a complete and comprehensive job analysis. The results of job analysis can be used in HR planning, recruitment, selection, placement, promotion, career path planning, and safety issues related to jobs. Job analysis can also be a company's frontline defense against charges brought by the U.S. Equal Employment Opportunity Commission (EEOC) or against frivolous lawsuits filed by job candidates, employees, or former employees. Job analysis may even reveal that the business has a bona fide legal reason for certain types of discrimination in selection and promotion decisions. Exhibit 1.1 illustrates many uses for job analysis.

Some managers believe that once a job is designed and described in an employee manual, it never changes. Good hospitality managers know that analyzing and designing jobs is a continual process. Regular job analysis is even more important now because of rapid technology and consumer expectation changes. *How* work is done and *what* is done at work changes constantly.

1.1 JOB ANALYSIS

As Exhibit 1.2 shows, managers must make several decisions when completing a job analysis. We discuss each of these decisions in the following sections.

Select Jobs for Analysis

A new hotel or restaurant requires a complete analysis of each job. But in an established operation, that might not be the case. Selecting which jobs to analyze is the first step in completing a thorough job analysis.

Some companies analyze each job in the organization once a year; others use a rotation system and analyze each job every

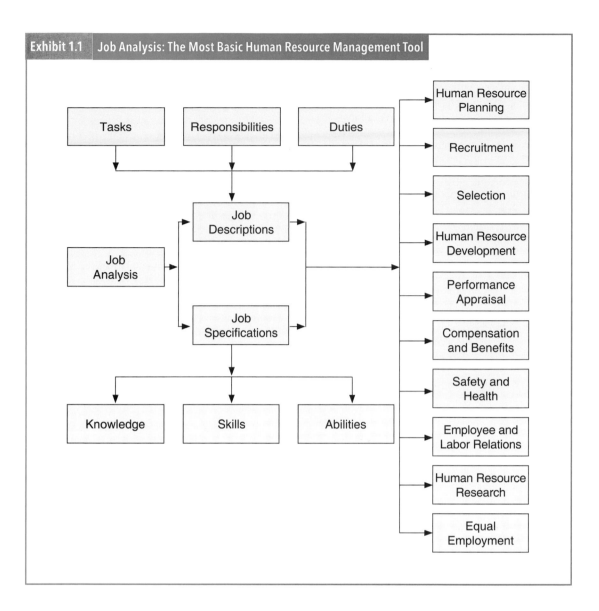

three years. Still others examine jobs only after major strategic changes within the organization. How often the job is analyzed depends primarily on the degree of change associated with the position.

Both internal and external factors can affect the frequency of analysis. For example, managers may need to analyze cooking jobs each time new items are added to a menu to ensure that no cook is overburdened. Adding or assigning new duties to a job or individual may also call for a thorough job analysis. A good manager will analyze the "new" job to make certain that duties are equitably distributed, and that productivity does not decline.

Assigning new duties is not the only internal factor that affects the frequency of job analysis. New technology in the work-

place likely will require job analysis. For instance, contactless check-in and check-out systems require that front desk positions be thoroughly analyzed to ensure the even distribution of work and efficient use of employees. Job analysis may be required even when a new employee comes on board. Consider the impact of hiring a new night auditor. If the auditor has substantial experience, the hotel could assign additional responsibilities to this position and redesign other duties and tasks. The opposite would be true if the night auditor has limited experience. Properties may wish to compare the skills of the new night auditor with those of previous night auditors.

Job analysis and design are more important when a hospitality company expands its business to foreign countries.

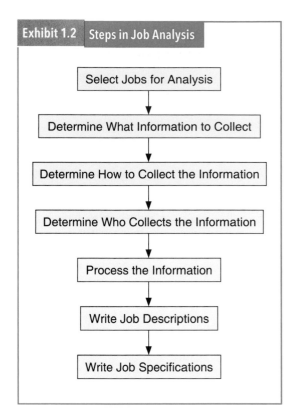

Exhibit 1.2   Steps in Job Analysis

Select Jobs for Analysis

↓

Determine What Information to Collect

↓

Determine How to Collect the Information

↓

Determine Who Collects the Information

↓

Process the Information

↓

Write Job Descriptions

↓

Write Job Specifications

For instance, in Canada, a server brings a credit/debit card machine to run the customer's card at the table. This slightly different procedure between the U.S. and Canada results in different duties and responsibilities for a server, especially for information security practice and consumer privacy issues.

External factors also create situations that require analysis of jobs. Increases and decreases in customer demand, seasonality (discussed later in the chapter), and new competition are examples of external factors that would require a hospitality operation to reanalyze its jobs. Certainly, many changes in jobs occurred during the Great Recession (which began in December 2007) and the COVID-19 pandemic (which started in early 2020) as companies cut back and consolidated work. During the pandemic, most hospitality businesses had to adopt new operating procedures for customer and employee safety. Restaurants had to reorganize their dine-in spaces or remain open only for takeout or delivery. Many hotels installed shields in their front-desk area to protect employees. All hospitality companies had to adapt more thorough and rigorous sanitizing practices.

Determine What Information to Collect

American corporations have a poor history of job design. Most managers think it's a good idea to break jobs down into their smallest components to understand them. This is probably a function of their desire for control over jobs and their employees more than an understanding of job analysis or design. Although analysis and design do provide managers with more control, that is not their primary purpose. Breaking a job down to understand what goes on and how it can be improved is much different than simply breaking it down to control employee behavior.

The following information needs to be collected in job analysis:

- Actual work activities
- Tools, equipment, and other necessary work aids
- Job context
- Personal characteristics
- Behavior requirements
- Performance standards

The kind of information collected depends on the ultimate use of the data, the time allowed for collection, and the budget. For instance, if information from the job analysis will be used to write new or updated job descriptions, the information gathered should focus on one of the first three categories: work activities, equipment used, or job context. If the information will be used to create job specifications, the focus should be on personal characteristics.

Determine How to Collect the Information

Several methods of collecting information are available and widely used. Some are more useful for specific purposes. Exhibit 1.3 suggests the most useful methods for certain areas.

Because hospitality jobs vary considerably from the front of the house to the back of the house and from property to property, managers should use several methods of data collection. The following sections dis-

| Exhibit 1.3 | Methods of Collecting Job Analysis Information |

Method	Method Useful for:				
	Job Description	Job Specifications	Interview Development	Performance Evaluation	Training
Observation	X	X	X		
Perform the Job	X	X	X	X	X
Interviews	X	X	X	X	X
Questionnaires	X	X	X	X	X
Critical Incidents	X	X	X	X	X
Performance Evaluations					
By supervisor		X	X		
Self-evaluation		X	X		
Diaries	X	X	X		

cuss each method as well as its advantages and disadvantages.

Observation. The simplest and least expensive method of collecting job analysis information is observation. With this method, managers simply watch employees at work and make detailed notes of the tasks and behaviors each employee performs. However, the observation method has its drawbacks:

- Managers may not be able to devote the time needed to use this approach.

- It is difficult to observe "normal" work performance since employees typically perform better when they know they are being watched.

This increased performance is known in management research circles as the **Hawthorne effect**. The Hawthorne effect got its name from a study conducted at the Westinghouse Hawthorne Relay Assembly Works Plant in Chicago. In this study, researchers observed employees at work to determine (among other things) whether changing lighting levels would improve employee productivity. Researchers found that productivity improved when the lighting level was increased. To their surprise, however, they detected similar improvements in productivity when the lighting was dimmed. After

much research, the researchers concluded that the improvements in productivity were related to the fact that someone was paying close attention to the employees.

The observation method has other problems:

- Observers may harbor certain biases toward specific employees.

- Observers may experience difficulty watching employees work without being obtrusive or getting in the way.

- Observers may have problems selecting which employees to observe. For instance, should they watch the best, the worst, or the average employee?

- Observers may find themselves in a quandary when deciding how to observe work that is not task-oriented.

The observation method is not very useful when analyzing a manager's job, simply because much of a manager's time is spent thinking and solving problems—duties that are difficult to observe. If observation is used, it is very important to watch several employees to arrive at an average level of work performance. The method is often improved when the person collecting the information actually does the job at some point to get a personal feel for what the work entails.

Perform the Job. One of the best ways to understand the intricacies of a job is to actually do the job. By performing the job functions, the person responsible for analyzing the job can better understand the skills, knowledge, physical requirements, and personality type required to do the job successfully. A major advantage of this method is that it gives the analyst credibility with employees, since they see the analyst as someone who has experienced the job and actually understands its demands. This can create better relationships with employees and can lead them to cooperate more with the analyst during the information-collection process. However, if the job is highly technical or requires a great deal of training, this method could be impractical, since the time required to learn and efficiently perform the job could be too great.

Interviews. Another popular method of compiling job analysis data is interviewing employees who do the job. Many researchers swear by interviews. They say that no one can know a job better than the person who does it. However, the employee's own view of the job can bias this method of gathering information. For instance, people naturally tend to overstate the importance of their work and their qualifications. And, when interviewed, most people are susceptible to what is known as the **Heisenberg effect**, which is the tendency of people to subconsciously give answers they think interviewers want to hear. Interviewers can reduce the impact of overstatement and the Heisenberg effect by simply being aware that these problems exist and conducting interviews carefully. Another safeguard for interviewers is to collect interview information from several employees.

Questionnaires. Questionnaires often ask employees to rate their work on a predetermined scale. These scales are generally designed to evaluate the difficulty, frequency, and importance of the job and the relationship of one job to another. The ratings provide a useful method of quantifying jobs if the questionnaire is completed by a large group of employees who do the same job. The **position analysis questionnaire (PAQ)** is a structured questionnaire that quantifies job elements. It is completed by employees familiar with the job being examined and then is studied by a job analyst. The PAQ consists of a list of 194 job elements divided into six job dimensions:

1. Information input (the employee gets information on how to do the job)
2. Mental processes (reasoning, planning, and problem-solving involved in the job)
3. Work output (physical activities associated with the job)
4. Interpersonal activities (relationships with other people)
5. Work situation and job context (physical working conditions and social aspects that affect the job)
6. Miscellaneous characteristics

Several standardized questionnaires are available to help managers develop job descriptions. One is the **management position description questionnaire (MPDQ)**, which collects information about management work in 13 categories. A second is the Minnesota Job Description Questionnaire (MJDQ), one of the more popular one-size-fits-all job design systems. However, a study on the practical applicability of this multi-method questionnaire has shown that the MJDQ does not do a very good job. The likely reason for this, and the reason most off-the-shelf systems fail, is that jobs, like the people who do them, are unique. This explains why transferring the requirements from a job at one company to a similar, but not the same, job at another company does not work.

Complete, thorough, and effective job analysis and design requires a company to consider itself and its jobs unique, and to analyze each appropriately. While this may take longer than using a standardized questionnaire, the results are much better. The federal government designed the Occupational Information Network system (or O*NET) to help employers with recruitment, training, and other workforce development programs. Information on O*NET is available at the U.S. Department of Labor Employment and Training website.

Critical Incidents. The **critical incident** method involves observing and recording actual events. A critical incident might read like this:

On June 27, Maurice Jones, a bellperson, observed guests fretting over how to get through a strong rain to their car, parked in a lot several hundred yards away. Without hesitation, Jones offered to walk the guests to their car using a company umbrella.

Over time, a large enough number of such critical incidents can form a fairly clear picture of a job's actual requirements. The disadvantage of this method is that it takes a considerable amount of time to compile the critical incidents needed to draw a complete picture of the job. The advantage is that this method is an excellent way to develop training materials that show employees how services should be provided.

Performance Evaluations. Performance evaluations provide an excellent opportunity to collect job analysis information. For instance, a manager conducting a performance evaluation with a room attendant might learn that the work could be completed more effectively if the employee were given the chance to clean the same rooms each day. Most performance evaluation methods include open-ended discussions between managers and the employee being evaluated. The discussion should be two-sided. Managers should give employees feedback on their performance and should listen to employee suggestions for improvement. Suggested improvements may relate to personal behavior or to the way a job is done.

Diaries. Some companies compile job analysis information by asking their employees to keep a diary or daily log of their activities during a specific period. This is a cost-effective, comprehensive way to gather information. Diaries encourage employees to think about the work they do and, theoretically, lead them to do a better job. This method has several drawbacks, however:

- It requires employees to dedicate a substantial amount of time to writing events in their journals.

- Employees may try to slant their supervisor's view of them by writing about incidents or actions that did not take place.

- Some employees may not read or write well enough to keep a diary.

- Job analysts must spend a substantial amount of time reading each journal and gathering information to completely portray the job.

Multiple Methods. As previously mentioned, the jobs within a hospitality firm can vary greatly. Therefore, it may be inefficient to use the same method of collecting information for every job within a property, or from property to property within a chain. Likewise, using a variety of methods may be the most efficient way to achieve a complete understanding of a single job. For example, to collect information for a front desk position, an analyst might use observation followed by interviews and/or questionnaires.

Determine Who Collects the Information

The purpose of the job analysis, time constraints, and the budget for the process generally determine who collects job analysis data. A trained professional is usually the best choice if the purpose is to design job specifications that will withstand close investigation by the EEOC. This professional can be from either inside or outside the company. Sometimes it is better to employ a third party, since (1) this person can often be more objective about the positions analyzed, and (2) the objectivity shown by an outsider can be important when presenting unusual or narrow job specifications to the EEOC. A disadvantage of using outside consultants is that they may be unfamiliar with the job requirements.

There are advantages to using current or past supervisors or current employees to conduct a job analysis. Current supervisors and employees have the most insight into what actually goes on in the job. As a result, their analysis may include subtle tasks and skills that others overlook. Using in-house personnel is usually more cost-effective than hiring outside analysts. One disadvantage of using current supervisors or employees is that the opportunity for bias increases. The degree of the interest the supervisors and employees have in their jobs influences the quality and quantity of the job analysis information provided by the job incumbents. Furthermore, job analysis information can be influenced by self-serving bias. Employees' own knowledge, skills, ability, and competency can bias the job analysis data. Also, employees sometimes refrain from reporting certain tasks, so they won't be required to perform them when new job descriptions are written.

By using former supervisors, the company may avoid the personal or job-related bias that is sometimes evident in analyses performed by people close to the job. Because former supervisors are no longer responsible for employee promotions, performance appraisals, and disciplinary action, there is less reason to suspect that personal issues might cloud their analysis.

Many organizations use teams to analyze jobs. Such teams are made up of employees who work in the position under analysis (or in lateral positions) and supervisors. This approach often provides the best overall view of a position. It is likely managers will need help developing such a team.

Chain operations have one more element to consider: consistency in job descriptions and specifications from unit to unit. As a general rule, a job analysis conducted by current supervisors or employees reflects local operational considerations. Such an analysis is less standardized and thus less useful to other operations in a chain.

One caution to managers before engaging in job analysis and design: unions are often opposed to job analysis and design programs. One of the main reasons for this is that re-design is often accompanied by changes in compensation. Another reason is that job analysis breaks the job down into the smallest components for analysis, and this threatens the unions' ability to negotiate and/or control what each job consists of. However, union opposition to job analysis is often only a case of fearing the unknown. Making it clear in advance that the objective is not reducing compensation or taking control from the unions—but, rather, helping workers and unions identify the important elements of a job and what exactly should be done in it—usually eliminates the opposi-

tion. In fact, unions may realize that completed job analyses and descriptions actually help by clearly establishing between management and employees exactly what work is to be done.

Managers often fail to empower their employees to consider job elimination when asking them to analyze a job. Since job analysis and design both strive to eliminate unnecessary parts of an employee's job, better results can be achieved if job analysts are considering job elimination while conducting the evaluation.

Process the Information

Data collection often yields more data than necessary. Using several methods of data collection doesn't mean you get different information; sometimes you simply get the same or similar information from different sources. In addition, data collection can yield data that is peripheral to the actual job. As a result, managers need to *process* information after it is collected.

Information processing is a simple but time-consuming task. The goal is to identify data that will be most useful in defining and describing the work and how to do the job. Content analysis—or the process of identifying topics and arranging information found in collected data—is one of the most effective methods of processing information. A thorough content analysis can be completed by first reading through the collected data and identifying important topics, then arranging this data in appropriate categories. Content analysis can help eliminate repetition of tasks or responsibilities.

Write Job Descriptions and Specifications

Job analyses are rarely used in their completed form. Instead, information contained in the job analysis is used to create other management tools used regularly in the travel and hospitality industry.

The two managerial tools most commonly derived from a job analysis are the job description and job specification. **Job descriptions** summarize the essential duties, tasks and responsibilities, working conditions, and activities of a specific job. **Job specifications** describe minimum qualifications and competencies such as knowledge, skills, and abilities needed in a prospective employee. For instance, a job description for an assistant director of human resources might include such responsibilities as recruiting and maintaining employee files.

In addition to describing the job, job descriptions are used for:

- *Recruiting.* Job descriptions and qualifications help hospitality managers develop recruitment ads.

- *Selection.* Job descriptions and qualifications help managers develop selection requirements and job interview questions.

- *Orientation.* Job descriptions serve as an excellent guide for familiarizing new employees with the requirements of the job.

- *Training.* Comparing an employee's job skills with the requirements outlined in a job description helps managers determine what kind of training an employee needs and how it should be accomplished.

- *Employee performance evaluations.* Performance appraisals are often developed directly from job descriptions, which provide a basis for evaluating employee performance.

- *Promotions and transfers.* Job descriptions provide information required for determining whether a current employee can perform the functions of a new job.

- *Defending tools in case of legal challenges.* Job descriptions and specifications become critical documents to show discrepancies between job standards and employee performance, if any.

Key Elements. Although specific formats used in job descriptions and specifications can vary substantially from company to company, content usually includes the following key elements:

- *Job identification data.* This consists of the job title, work unit, title of immediate supervisor, pay grade, last time the

job description was written or revised, and so on.

- *Job summary.* The **job summary** is usually a brief general statement that highlights the common functions and responsibilities of the job. In many job descriptions, the summary is called the *general statement of duties.* For instance, a job summary for a hotel's assistant director of human resources might read:

  Perform complex technical work in recruitment, examination, classification, wage and salary administration, training, and other functions of a human resources program.

  A job summary for a server might read:

  Responsible for gracious and proper service to all guests in their station during the assigned shift. Also responsible for appearance of entire station area, including tables, walls, floor, and so on.

- *Essential job functions.* This portion of the job description usually lists only essential duties, tasks, and responsibilities on which employees spend a significant amount (more than 20%) of their work time and perform regularly. The essential job functions affect other parts of the job as well as other jobs. Typically, each statement in this section begins with an action verb and briefly states what this portion of the job accomplishes. Examples of commonly used action verbs are *administer, assist, collect, conduct, prepare, furnish,* and *maintain.* For instance, the job duties of a buser in a food and beverage operation might be:

- Move dirty dishes to the dishwashing area.
- Assist servers in serving guests.
- Deliver beverages to guests.
- Set tables before opening and during operations.
- Maintain adequate supply of condiments at server stations.

Table 1.1 lists the differences between essential job functions and non-essential job functions.

- *Job environment.* A description of where the employee works and the surrounding environment.

- *Job specifications.* As noted earlier, job specifications describe the qualifications required to perform the job. Employers may outline qualifications related to training or education, skills, knowledge, abilities, and experience, as well as mental, physical, and personal characteristics. For instance, job specifications for a bell captain might include the ability to lift objects weighing up to 50 pounds repeatedly during an eight-hour shift, to coordinate other bell staff, and to learn room locations. Job specifications for an assistant director of human resources may include knowledge of personnel practices, experience with testing methods, and knowledge of EEOC guidelines. The knowledge, skills, and abilities employees or job candidates must have to perform the essential job functions are called *competencies.* Identifying the competencies based on the job description is important for a successful hiring process. For example, a front desk agent at a hotel must have a customer service orientation and good oral communication skills.

- *Minimum qualifications.* Minimum qualifications (or minimum requirements) are the fundamental qualifications a candidate must have to be considered for the position. To avoid legal issues such as discrimination, it is important that these requirements have a direct link to the candidate's ability to successfully perform the job. For example, five years of experience in food service and demonstrated leadership ability may be necessary requirements for the position of food and beverage director. On the other hand, it may be difficult to prove that a high school diploma is required for a janitorial position.

Exhibit 1.4 presents a sample job description.

Knowledge Check

1. If a job analysis is rarely used in its entirety, why is its completion so important?

2. How do job descriptions and job specifications differ?

3. List three reasons why companies perform job analysis.

Table 1.1	Essential and Non-Essential Job Functions

Characteristics	Essential functions	Non-essential functions
% of time	Significant (more than 20%)	5%–10%
Frequency	Regularly (daily, weekly, monthly)	Performed infrequently or substituted as part of another job
Importance	Affects other parts of the job as well as other jobs	Has little consequence to the job or other jobs if not performed

Title:	Assistant Director
Department:	Human Resources
Job Analyst:	Bob Smith
Date Analyzed:	12/01/20XX
Wage Category:	Exempt

Reports to: Director of Human Resources

Subordinate staff: 2–5 staff members of the Human Resources Department

Other internal contacts: CEO, Vice President, department managers, and staff members of other departments

External contacts: Government agents, vendors, staff members of strategic partners

Job Summary:

Perform complex technical work in recruitment, examination, classification, wage and salary administration, training, and other functions of a human resources department.

Job Duties:

1. Recruitment—25%
   a. Prepares open position announcements
   b. Screens applications for qualifications
   c. Prepares offer-of-employment documents
   d. Maintains recruitment and selection records

2. Classification of job and employees—20%
   a. Prepares employee exit documentation
   b. Processes employee-promotion paperwork
   c. Keeps records of employee-advancement activities

3. Wage and salary administration—20%
   a. Computes employee wage changes
   b. Maintains records of payroll activities
   c. Verifies proper execution of payroll procedures
   d. Creates reports of payroll activities

4. Training—35%
   a. Conducts general orientation program for new hires
   b. Obtains materials for special training sessions as need arises
   c. Assists with departmental training
   d. Conducts follow-up training reviews
   e. Maintains documentation of employee completion of orientation and training programs

Job Environment:

1. Primarily in an office setting

2. Recruitment conducted in locations such as:
   a. Schools, colleges, and universities
   b. Churches and synagogues
   c. Apartment complexes
   d. Youth, senior citizen, and community group environments

(continued)

Job Specifications:

1. Knowledge of the principles of human resource administration

2. Knowledge of examination processes and job evaluation methods and techniques

3. Knowledge of statistics

4. Ability to conduct statistical analysis

5. Ability to organize and present effective oral and written reports

6. Ability to establish and maintain effective working relations with employees, department heads, officials, and the general public

Minimum Qualifications:

Some experience in human resource management recruitment, examination, classification, and pay administration. Experience in training and other human resource functions of the professional level or equivalent also desired.

Source: Based on the layouts in Jeffrey S. Hornsby and Donald F. Kuratko, *The Human Resource Function in Emerging Enterprises* (Mason, Ohio: South-Western/Thomson Learning, 2002), pp. 70–72; and Luis R. Gomez-Mejia, David B. Balkin, and Robert L. Cardy, *Managing Human Resources*, 4th ed. (Upper Saddle River, N.J.: Prentice-Hall, 2004), p. 69.

1.2 JOB DESIGN

Jobs are one of the biggest stressors in many people's lives. Findings like this have led to a movement to redesign jobs so that they are less stressful. This does not mean eliminating necessary elements of a job; it simply means determining which elements are necessary and which are not—and making the necessary ones more palatable.

One way to accomplish thorough job design is through flowcharting. After breaking a job down into its basic components, managers should encourage employees to consider how each task or responsibility relates to other aspects of their workplace or to other people's jobs. Flowcharting also allows job analysts to more accurately determine what aspects of each job could be changed.[1]

Poor performance and low productivity are not always due to poor training, inadequate supervision, underdeveloped employee skills, or poor work habits. Sometimes employees are ineffective because the job itself is designed poorly. Job design and organizational design have perhaps the greatest influence on whether job holders do their jobs well. Poorly designed jobs can lead to unnecessary stress and low job satisfaction, which in turn can lead to low motivation, high employee turnover, and high rates of absenteeism.

Job design focuses on how work is to be done. Five techniques—job simplification, job enlargement, job enrichment, job rotation, and team building—are widely used in designing jobs.

Job Simplification. Job simplification involves breaking down jobs into their smallest components and assessing how work is done in each component. It is sometimes called *time and motion analysis*. Job simplification is useful when the skills required to perform the tasks are not extensive and/or do not require a great deal of managerial involvement. For example, a position in which the only tasks assigned to an employee are to load/unload a dishwasher and shelve the dishes may have resulted from job simplification. However, if a company simplifies job tasks too much, employees may not feel challenged enough,

The ADA, Job Analysis, and Job Design

In the past, many people would picture a person with a disability as someone who used a wheelchair, walker, or cane. Today, many people realize that disabilities cover a wide spectrum and may not be noticeable to a casual observer. The Americans with Disabilities Act is making people more aware of what constitutes a disability and what the rights of a person with a disability are.

Under the ADA, people with disabilities are considered qualified for a position if they can perform the essential functions of a job with or without reasonable accommodation. Essential functions are tasks that are fundamental to the position. For instance, cooking skills would be considered fundamental for a cook. However, the ability of a cook to hear orders called by servers (for a person with a hearing impairment) or of a room attendant to read written room-cleaning assignments (for a person with a developmental or cognitive disability) might not be fundamental. In such cases, operators must make reasonable accommodations to ensure that cooking and room attendant positions are open to people with such disabilities.

From a job analysis standpoint, employers need to identify the essential and non-essential activities of each job. Applicants who can perform the essential functions cannot be discriminated against because they cannot perform the non-essential functions. In addition, the ADA stipulates that employers may have to restructure jobs to eliminate the non-essential functions for these employees.

Unless it imposes an undue hardship, employers will also be required to make reasonable accommodations so that the workplace is accessible to people with disabilities. Among the accommodations considered reasonable by the Equal Employment Opportunity Commission are constructing wheelchair ramps, widening aisles, raising cashier stands, and modifying work schedules and equipment.

Both the essential functions provision and the reasonable accommodations provision of the ADA will dramatically affect how jobs are designed in some operations. For instance, employers may be required to rethink how work is done. Consider how a bellperson's position often involves carrying heavy bags to rooms for eight or more hours per day. That could change under the ADA. For example, hotels may be required to provide carts so that employees with disabilities would not be required to carry bags for long distances. In addition, frequent breaks for bell staff who cannot work for eight hours at a time may be viewed as a reasonable accommodation.

Managers need to take a number of actions to meet ADA requirements. At a minimum, managers should:

1. Review their methods of job analysis to ensure that essential and non-essential functions are appropriately designated.

2. Review job descriptions and specify the essential and non-essential aspects of each position.

3. Review job specifications to ensure that applicants are not being excluded on the basis of non-essential functions.

4. Maintain records of accommodations made to comply with the ADA.

5. Create and maintain records of people with disabilities currently on staff to ensure that reasonable accommodations are made for these people.

6. Review the application process—especially portions that include medical exams or other issues that may infringe on the rights of people with disabilities.

7. Revise application forms to exclude generic questions about disabilities and health issues. Many application forms commonly used in the past are not acceptable under the ADA.

8. Create and maintain records of personnel with disabilities; records should include the accommodations made for these individuals in compliance with the ADA.

9. Post compliance statements in prominent locations.

and the work can become mundane and not meaningful.

Job Enlargement. Job enlargement is the process of broadening jobs by adding tasks. Typically, tasks involving similar skills and abilities are combined. Adding similar tasks in this way is sometimes called *horizontal job expansion*. An example of job enlargement would be to add greeting customers and seating them at tables to the duties of a server. Job enlargement can help motivate employees who perceive increased responsibility as a step toward advancing their careers. However, some employees may be unwilling to take on additional tasks—especially if additional tasks are not accompanied by additional compensation. Others may simply feel that they are now performing two boring tasks instead of one.

Job Enrichment. In **job enrichment**, also called *vertical job expansion*, responsibilities are added to an employee's job that are not extremely similar to the tasks the employee performs. For example, the job of prep cooks may be enriched by making them responsible for rotating the stock they use, ordering the food products required for their job, or making finished salads with the products they chop.

The distinction between job enlargement and job enrichment can sometimes be blurred. Both require employees to perform additional tasks. The difference is that job enrichment gives employees additional levels of responsibility.

Job Rotation. Job rotation is often used to alleviate boredom that employees face when performing the same job over and over. With a job rotation system, the prep cooks responsible for cutting lettuce and tomatoes would do this job for a specific period. After this period, they would rotate to another kitchen position with different responsibilities. This system requires that employees be cross-trained in several jobs. Job rotation is often used in management-in-training and internship programs.

Team Building. Another widely used approach to job design is **team building**. At its heart, the team building approach views employees as members of work groups rather than as individuals. Goals and rewards are directed toward team efforts rather than toward individual efforts. For example, the California-based HMS Group has developed a team-building experience involving creating chocolate creations. Originally designed for the Culinary Institute of America, the "Chocolate Box Challenge" is an edible, hospitality-focused adaptation of the more familiar group-bungee-jump and shoot-your-boss-with-a-paint-pistol exercises.[2]

Team building encourages employees to work well together and to assist one another. A disadvantage is that it often requires several training sessions to get a team-building program started. Another disadvantage is that team building can sometimes lead to counterproductive competition among groups.

Knowledge Check

1. What is the difference between job enlargement and job enrichment?

2. Why is it important to design jobs properly?

3. What are the advantages to redesigning jobs so they are less stressful?

1.3 CLASSIFICATIONS OF EMPLOYEES

When the various jobs have been analyzed and designed with job descriptions written and the legal issues worked out, people actually need to be hired to perform the jobs. The question then arises as to what type (or classification) of employee best fits the organization's needs. The answer to this question is complex. Various issues must be considered, including the following:

■ What is the organization's size?

■ What is the organization's corporate culture?

■ What type of image does the organization wish to project?

■ What is the labor market like?

The labor force of an organization can be broken down into two main categories:

- **Permanent employees** are the main staff of the organization. They typically work at least 30 to 40 hours per week, are on the regular company payroll, and often receive benefits.

- **Alternative employees** often work part-time or on a temporary basis. These employees often do not have regularly scheduled shifts or are employed at the hospitality company only for a short period of time. Alternative employees can be grouped into three classifications: temporary employees, part-time employees, and outsourced employees.[3]

Temporary Employees. Temporary employees, often referred to as "temps," are not actually employed by the hospitality organization. They are employees obtained from an employment agency. The agency charges a fee to the hospitality company, the employee, or both, which can be thought of as a "finder's fee." Temporary employees work only for a designated time period, which can last only one day or as long as several months. Temporary employees are useful for occasional events such as banquets or during seasonal demands to fill positions for which hiring full-time employees would not be cost-effective.

Part-Time Employees. Part-time employees generally work 20 hours or less per week. In many organizations, they do not receive benefits, medical or otherwise. Although it varies from property to property, most part-time employees do not work regular shifts. They are extremely valuable for covering time periods of daily/weekly peaks in business, such as during check-out times at a hotel or on weekends at a restaurant.

Outsourced Employees. Like temporary employees, outsourced employees are not actually employed by the hospitality organization. They work for a separate company that the hospitality company pays for the services the outsourced employees provide. Outsourced employees usually do not perform their jobs while they are physically at the hospitality business. Most never even set foot on the hospitality property. While it is obvious that outsourced employees would not be useful at a hotel front desk, they can

quite effectively perform, for example, reservation call center functions or HR tasks.

Knowledge Check

1. What are the four categories of labor force in an organization?

2. What is the difference between permanent employees and alternative employees?

3. What is an advantage of hiring outsourced employees?

1.4 STAFFING GUIDES

A **staffing guide** is a scheduling and control tool that enables management to determine the number of labor hours and employees required to operate smoothly. They help managers control employee productivity and performance. Many managers also use staffing guides to estimate labor expenses for their labor budgets by multiplying the hours required by the pay rates of each employee. Staffing guides are very important tools for use in achieving profitability, which often depends on the degree to which managers control variable expenses such as labor.

To understand the development and use of staffing guides, managers must know the meaning of several key terms:

- **Productivity** is the amount of work output by an employee during a specific period of time.

- **Productivity standards** are the criteria that define the acceptable quantity of work to be completed by employees.

- **Performance standards** establish the required levels of quality in the work performed.

- **Labor forecasting** is any method used to anticipate the amount of work required in a specified period of time.

In addition, managers should recognize the two types of labor costs in hospitality companies: fixed labor expenses and variable labor expenses. **Fixed labor expenses** are those costs associated with the minimum number of employees required to operate a hotel or restaurant. **Variable labor expenses** are those costs that vary according to the amount of business. Managers have more control over variable labor expenses.

The following section provides a step-by-step example of how managers would develop a staffing guide. The example is based on a hypothetical operation—the Good Food Restaurant. Developing a staffing guide involves the following steps:

1. Set productivity standards.
2. Determine the total anticipated sales and guest volume.
3. Determine the number of employees required.
4. Determine the total labor hours.
5. Estimate the labor expense.

Set Productivity Standards

The first step in developing a staffing guide is to set productivity standards. Efficient staffing requires that productivity standards be met through scheduling. If productivity standards have not already been established for each position, managers can determine these standards by creating and evaluating

a historical profile of labor required over a period of time. Exhibit 1.5 provides an example of a portion of a productivity needs assessment form. Since single shifts can be influenced by a variety of factors, such a form should be completed over a period of time to thoroughly evaluate the operation's staffing needs.

Once a productivity standards assessment has been completed, managers can use the data to establish productivity standards for each position in the operation, as shown in Exhibit 1.5. Typically, such standards are based on labor hours required, although some operations base estimates on the number of employees required. The advantage of basing the standards on labor hours is that such standards more accurately portray exact scheduling needs.

The final step in determining the correct standard productivity levels for each operation is to compare the estimated needs to actual labor hours worked. Exhibit 1.6 provides a sample comparison form used by some managers. The comments section of this form is used to note extraordinary events that affect labor costs (weather, sales related to certain activities, and so on). This form also lets managers know how much the actual hours worked were over or under their

---

Exhibit 1.5	Productivity Needs Assessment Form

Shift: Dinner

Dates: Beginning 1/1   Ending 1/7

	Mon	Tues	Wed	Thurs	Fri	Sat	Sun	Average
Guest count	250	250	250	350	400	350	250	300

Position	Hours Worked							
Servers	18	18	18	24	28	24	18	21.1
Greeters	4	4	4	6	6	6	4	4.9
Bartenders	6	6	6	6	6	6	6	6.0
Buser	3	3	3	4	5	4	3	3.6
Prep cook	6	6	6	6	6	6	6	6.0
Broiler cook	6	6	6	6	6	6	6	6.0
Sauté cook	5	5	5	5	6	5	5	5.1
Dishwasher	5	5	5	5	6	5	5	5.1

Exhibit 1.6 Labor Comparison Form

Shift: Dinner

Dates: Beginning 1/1   **Ending** 1/7

Legend: Budgeted Hours (upper) / Hours Worked (lower)

	Mon	Tues	Wed	Thurs	Fri	Sat	Sun	Average
Servers	18 / 20	18 / 19	18 / 20	24 / 23	28 / 30	24 / 25	18 / 19	21.1 / 22.3
Greeters	4 / 5	4 / 4	4 / 4	6 / 6	6 / 7	6 / 7	4 / 3	4.9 / 5.1
Bartenders	6 / 6	6 / 6	6 / 5	6 / 7	6 / 6	6 / 7	6 / 6	6 / 6.1
Buser	3 / 2	3 / 2	3 / 3	4 / 4	5 / 5	4 / 4	3 / 3	3.6 / 3.3
Prep cook	6 / 7	6 / 7	6 / 6	6 / 7	6 / 7	6 / 7	6 / 7	6 / 6.7
Broiler cook	6 / 7	6 / 7	6 / 6	6 / 7	6 / 7	6 / 7	6 / 7	6 / 6.9
Sauté cook	5 / 5	5 / 4	5 / 4	5 / 6	6 / 6	5 / 5	5 / 5	5.1 / 5
Dishwasher	5 / 6	5 / 6	5 / 5	5 / 5	6 / 7	5 / 6	5 / 6	5.1 / 5.9

budgeted labor hours for a given period. In Exhibit 1.6, for example, budgeted labor hours were exceeded in six out of eight positions. To calculate how much this overage cost, managers multiply the average salary for each employee category by the number of hours over budget in each category. For example, if servers average $11.25 per hour, a total of $13.20 more per day was expended in this category than was budgeted.

When productivity standards are used to anticipate employee staffing levels, the result is a ratio of employees to guests. In other words, establishing productivity standards provides managers with one-half of the equation required to correctly schedule employees. The other half of the equation is derived by estimating the anticipated guest volume per shift.

Determine the Total Anticipated Sales and Guest Volume

Accurate labor use predictions require managers to anticipate business volume for each day of an upcoming period. The best

source of information is previous sales for similar periods. Usually, managers maintain records of the sales for each previous meal period. This forms a historical record of sales over time that managers can use to estimate potential sales in the future. Given this anticipated total sales volume, managers can determine the number of guests that the restaurant will serve by dividing the sales volume by the average per-person guest check.

> **LEGAL ALERT!**
>
> Much like the minimum qualifications and essential functions, the productivity expectations must be accurate and consistently followed to prevent a claim for discrimination or wrongful discharge.

For example, if the average sales on Friday nights at the 150-seat Good Food Restaurant is $6,000, and the average per-person guest check is $15, the average number of guests served is 400 ($6,000 ÷ $15).

Although this method is acceptable in many circumstances, more complex forecasting methods can better anticipate business volume. The most common forecasting methods are discussed later in the chapter.

Determine the Number of Employees Required

After forecasting potential sales, managers must determine how many employees are required to serve the estimated number of customers. Productivity standards are used to determine this requirement. Continuing with our example, let's assume that the productivity standard for the Good Food Restaurant calls for one server for every 20 guests per hour of operation. If the restaurant is open for four hours on Friday nights, this would tell us that five servers are required (400 guests ÷ 4 hours of operation ÷ 20 guests per hour). However, what this calculation does not tell us is that some periods will be busier than others. Exhibit 1.7 provides a breakdown of the number of guests served per hour on an average Friday night at the restaurant.

As Exhibit 1.7 indicates, because the business volume is not spread evenly throughout the evening, the restaurant will need six servers for one time period on Friday and only four or five for the others. Rather than schedule the entire night to meet the peak demand (six servers), the manager could reduce labor costs for this shift by staggering schedules. Note that some servers will need to arrive early to

set up and others will need to stay late to clean. In this example, scheduling all servers to arrive early and leave late would be the worst use of labor dollars.

Note that, while the employees' schedules in our example fit perfectly with the anticipated need, this is not always the case in actual practice. Factors such as variation from hour to hour in demand, employee availability, and labor laws can cause overlaps or gaps in the actual number of employees scheduled compared to the desired number. For instance, employees in Canada should not work more than 48 hours a week except for special circumstances such as emergency work or exceptional circumstances requiring a permit from the Minister of Labor. Employees who work more than 40 hours a week in Canada and the United States are entitled to overtime payment, which is a minimum of one and half times the regular rate of wages.

Determine the Total Labor Hours

To determine total labor hours, managers could multiply the number of hours each server is scheduled (an average of four hours in this case) by the number of servers scheduled (six). See the sample schedule worksheet presented in Exhibit 1.8.

Estimate the Labor Expense

Labor expense for the Good Food Restaurant for the Friday night in question can be estimated by multiplying the average hourly wage paid to each server by the total number of labor hours scheduled. Managers must consider the time that servers are scheduled to assist in setting up before the shift and/or cleaning after the shift. If we assume that each server is paid an hourly wage of $7.25, the total *estimated* cost for servers on Friday night is $174 (24 hours × $7.25). Not all servers will work the exact number of hours scheduled, of course, so this is an estimate. To complete the staffing guide for the Good Food Restaurant, managers must make similar calculations for each position with variable labor costs.

Many computer software programs can automatically calculate the anticipated labor hours and labor costs with minimal user

Exhibit 1.7	Labor Requirements per Hour		
Hours of Operation	Anticipated Covers	Labor or Staffing Requirements	
6:00 P.M. – 7:00 P.M.	80	4	
7:00 P.M. – 8:00 P.M.	120	6	
8:00 P.M. – 9:00 P.M.	100	5	
9:00 P.M. – 10:00 P.M.	100	5	

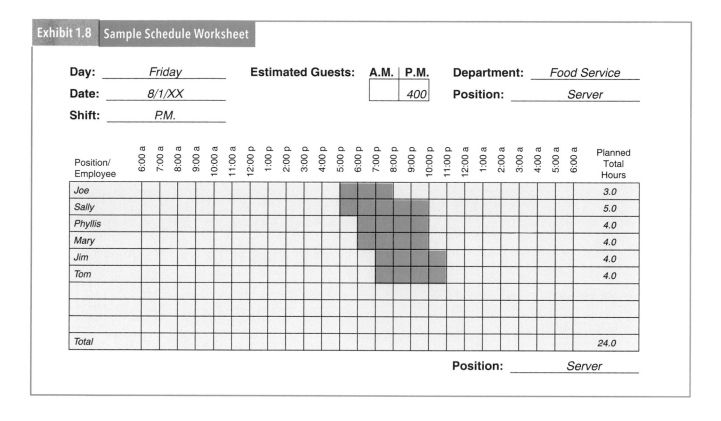

Exhibit 1.8 | **Sample Schedule Worksheet**

Day:	Friday							Estimated Guests:	A.M.	P.M.	Department:	Food Service
Date:	8/1/XX									400	Position:	Server
Shift:	P.M.											

Position/ Employee	6:00 a	7:00 a	8:00 a	9:00 a	10:00 a	11:00 a	12:00 p	1:00 p	2:00 p	3:00 p	4:00 p	5:00 p	6:00 p	7:00 p	8:00 p	9:00 p	10:00 p	11:00 p	12:00 a	1:00 a	2:00 a	3:00 a	4:00 a	5:00 a	6:00 a	Planned Total Hours
Joe													▓	▓	▓											3.0
Sally													▓	▓	▓	▓										5.0
Phyllis															▓	▓										4.0
Mary													▓	▓	▓											4.0
Jim														▓	▓	▓										4.0
Tom														▓	▓	▓										4.0
Total																										24.0

Position: _____ Server _____

effort as well as perform sales prediction functions (discussed in the next section). The output and user-friendliness of these programs vary greatly, along with the price. New consumer software is constantly being developed. If you're interested in using forecasting software, the best way to find products that fit your needs and budget is to use an Internet search engine.

Knowledge Check

1. What are the basic steps involved in developing a staffing guide for a hotel?

2. How would you establish productivity standards for a particular position?

3. Identify one fixed labor expense and one variable labor expense at a hotel or restaurant.

1.5 FORECASTING SALES VOLUME FOR STAFFING

The staffing guide just discussed is based on a sales forecast for a single Friday night;

this forecast is also based on past business levels on Fridays. Most hospitality organizations develop monthly, 10-day, and three-day forecasts of business volume.[4] Typically, managers develop monthly forecasts first and then revise the forecast for 10-day and three-day periods, depending on any special circumstances. These forecasts are used to determine the business volume component for upcoming scheduling periods. Exhibit 1.9 provides a sample form that food and beverage managers can use to develop a 10-day forecast. Exhibit 1.10 provides a sample three-day revised forecast form.

Trend Line Forecasting

The simple forecast used in the Good Food Restaurant example was based on business volume for previous Friday nights. This method of forecasting is known as **trend line forecasting**. Trend line forecasting involves graphing the sales from similar periods and fitting a line to the average sales projected for past periods. Fitting a line is much like connecting the dots, although the objective is to establish a straight line through the dots rather than a jagged one

Exhibit 1.9 Sample Ten-Day Volume Forecast–Food

TEN-DAY VOLUME FORECAST—FOOD

Date Prepared _____

Motor-Hotel _____   Week Ending _____
          (Location)

DATE																					
DAY	THUR		FRI		SAT		SUN		MON		TUES		WED		THUR		FRI		SAT		Totals	
Previous Week																						
FOOD DEPARTMENT	F	A	F	A	F	A	F	A	F	A	F	A	F	A	F	A	F	A	F	A	F	A
Dining Room																						
Breakfast																						
Lunch																						
Dinner																						
Total D.R. Covers																						
Coffee Shop																						
Breakfast																						
Lunch																						
Total C.S. Covers																						
Banquet																						
Breakfast																						
Lunch																						
Dinner																						
Total Banquet Covers																						
Room Service																						
Total R.S. Covers																						
TOTAL FOOD COVERS																						

SPECIAL COMMENTS
(i.e. types of groups—V.I.P. etc.)

F=Forecast
A=Actual

Source: David L. Balangue, "Payroll Productivity (Part IV: Staff Planning)," *Lodging* (November 1978): 39.

from dot to dot. Statistically, the "fitted line" is created by determining the midpoint between the jagged points.

Moving Average Forecasting

Although trend line forecasting is useful, it is often misleading because it does not account for unusual events that may have taken place during a given period. A forecasting method that helps avoid this problem is **moving average forecasting**.

Sales are never as consistent as managers hope they will be. Instead, sales in hospitality are characterized by a series of peaks and valleys. Some of these peaks and valleys

Exhibit 1.10 Sample Three-Day Revised Forecast—Food and Beverage

Three-Day Revised Forecast—Food and Beverage

	Yesterday	Today	Tomorrow
Day			
Date			
Guest Count			
Forecasted Guest Count			
Comments			

result from special events in the area that may increase or decrease business volume. Weather and other events also create peaks and valleys in sales volume.

Moving average forecasting smooths out the data collected from a specific time period. Mathematically, moving average forecast can be expressed as:

$$\text{Moving average} = \frac{\text{Activity in previous } n \text{ periods}}{n}$$

where n is the number of periods in the moving average.

As new weekly sales results become available, they can be added to the moving average forecast model; the oldest week is then dropped. In fact, the method is known as a moving average because it involves continually adding new results and dropping the oldest week off the model.

Seasonality

Many hospitality organizations are subject to variations in business depending on the season. **Seasonality** must be taken into consideration when forecasting anticipated business volume. Many restaurants, for instance, are busier just before and during the December holiday season and slower during summer months. Of course, restau-

rants in summer resort areas have the opposite experience.

Hotels are also subject to seasonal adjustments. Downtown hotels, which usually depend on business travelers for their business, often experience substantial dips during some periods of the month or year. For example, hotels in New York City and other large cities often see declines in business travel during January, February, and the summer; business travel is at its highest level in New York City during the spring and fall. Although some of the loss in business during the summer is made up by vacationers, hotels must adjust their schedules to reflect the needs of such travelers.

The simplest method of anticipating seasonal business variations is to use historical data from similar seasonal periods. For instance, when estimating sales for the month of June, operators will likely find that sales from June of the previous year provide the most accurate comparative data. A form of "seasonality" can also be used to prepare weekly business volume estimates. In fact, our Good Food Restaurant example used this format by basing sales estimates on previous Friday nights instead of on other days of the week.

Other Methods of Forecasting

Hospitality managers use a variety of forecasting methods to anticipate business levels; these levels, in turn, determine personnel levels. For instance, yield or revenue management is a system that attempts to manage the supply of rooms in a hotel over time by lowering and raising rates to maximize revenue. Exhibit 1.11 lists other methods popular with hospitality managers. Explanations of how to use these forecasting methods are beyond the scope of this chapter.

Exhibit 1.11   Summary of Lodging Industry Short-Term Sales Forecasting Methods

	Rooms	Food	Catering
Major purposes of forecast:	Staffing (98%) Motivating personnel (25%)	Staffing (100%) Order food (72%) Motivating personnel (19%)	Staffing (82%) Order food (72%) Motivating personnel (16%)
Methodology:	Room reservations plus estimated walk-ins (93%)	Prior period sales adjusted based on intuition (46%)	Booked catered events plus estimate of additional sales (90%)
	Prior period sales adjusted based on intuition (7%)	Meal reservations and estimate for walk-ins (28%)	Prior period sales adjusted based on intuition (10%)
		Capture ratios related to the rooms forecast (26%)	
Expression of S-T forecast:	Daily number of rooms sold (80%)	Total covers (79%)	Total sales dollars (70%)
	Daily sales dollars (55%)	Total sales dollars (61%)	Total covers (67%)
	Daily number of rooms by type (35%)	Food covers by meal period (60%)	Sales dollars by catered event (47%)
	Daily sales dollars by type of room (20%)	Sales dollars by meal period (44%)	Covers by catered event (47%)

Source: Raymond S. Schmidgall, *Hospitality Industry Managerial Accounting*, 7th ed. (Lansing, Mich.: American Hotel & Lodging Educational Institute, 2011), p. 425.

IN THIS CHAPTER, YOU LEARNED:

- Job analysis is a process of determining what will be done in a job, and job design shows how the job will be done.

- Organizations should conduct job analysis regularly because it reveals the tasks, duties, responsibilities, desired work behaviors, and personal characteristics needed to do a job.

- Job design can have great impacts on whether job holders do their jobs well.

- Job analysis can be done in seven stages: (1) select jobs for analysis, (2) determine what information to collect, (3) determine how to collect the information, (4) determine who collects the information, (5) process the information, (6) write job descriptions, and (7) write job specifications.

- Common methods of job analysis are the management position description questionnaire (MPDQ) or Minnesota Job Description Questionnaire (MJDQ). These questionnaires measure characteristics of a job.

- Job descriptions summarize the essential duties, tasks, responsibilities, working conditions, and activities of a specific job.

- Job specifications describe minimum qualifications and competencies such as knowledge, skills, and abilities of a prospective employee.

- Job simplification involves breaking down jobs into their smallest components and assessing how work is done in each component.

- Job enlargement is the process of broadening jobs by combining tasks. Typically, tasks involving similar skills and abilities are combined.

- With job enrichment, responsibilities are added to an employee's job that are not extremely similar to the tasks the employee performs.

- Job rotation is often used to alleviate boredom that employees face when performing the same job over and over.

- The team building approach views employees as members of work groups rather than as individuals.

- Staffing guides are scheduling and control tools that enable management to determine the number of labor hours and employees required to operate smoothly. Staffing guides are very important tools for use in achieving profitability, which often depends on the degree to which managers control variable expenses such as labor. Managers must have a good understanding of labor productivity, productivity standards, performance standards, and labor forecasting to develop proper staffing guides.

- Trend line forecasting involves graphing the sales from similar periods and fitting a line to the average sales projected for past periods. Fitting a line is much like connecting the dots, although the objective is to establish a straight line through the dots rather than a jagged one from dot to dot.

- Moving average forecasting smooths out the data collected from a specific time period.

KEY TERMS

alternative employees—Part-time or temporary workers. These employees often do not have regularly scheduled shifts or are employed at the company only for a short period of time.

critical incident—Job analysis technique based on capturing and recording actual events that occur at work that, when combined, form an accurate picture of a job's requirements. Useful in describing how services should be performed. Also used in training and as a measurement in certain performance appraisal systems.

fixed labor expenses—Labor costs associated with the minimum number of employees required to operate a business.

Hawthorne effect—Management theory describing the positive effect that paying attention to employees has on workplace productivity.

Heisenberg effect—Management theory stating that people being interviewed are likely to subconsciously give answers they think interviewers want to hear.

job analysis—Process of determining the tasks, behaviors, and characteristics essential to a job.

job description—A written summary of the duties, responsibilities, working conditions, and activities of a specific job.

job design—Process of defining how a job will be done.

job enlargement—Process of broadening the components of a job by adding similar tasks or responsibilities to the job. Sometimes called horizontal job expansion.

job enrichment—Process of improving a job by adding responsibilities that require different skills. Sometimes called vertical job expansion.

job rotation—Process of moving employees from one job to another or of changing employee responsibilities to enhance job interest or to cross-train.

job simplification—Process of breaking down jobs into their smallest components to assess how work is done in each of those components. Sometimes called time and motion analysis.

job specification—A written description of the personal qualities required to perform a job.

job summary—A brief general statement that highlights the common functions and responsibilities of a job.

labor forecasting—Any method used to anticipate the amount of work required in a specified period of time.

management position description questionnaire (MPDQ)—Structured questionnaire used to collect information about management work in 13 categories. Used in job analysis.

moving average forecasting—A forecasting method based on past sales that attempts to smooth out the peaks and valleys that businesses experience to project anticipated sales.

performance standard—A required level of worker performance.

permanent employees—The main staff of an organization. Permanent employees usually work at least 30 to 40 hours per week, are on the regular company payroll, and often receive benefits.

position analysis questionnaire (PAQ)—A structured questionnaire consisting of 194 job elements used to define work. Used in job analysis.

productivity—The amount of work an employee accomplishes in a specific period of time.

productivity standard—The criteria that define the acceptable quantity of work to be completed by employees.

seasonality—A concept used in forecasting that describes the highs and lows of business sales on the basis of seasonal demand for products or services.

staffing guide—A system used to establish the number of workers needed.

team building—A process of designing jobs that views employees as members of work groups rather than as individuals.

trend line forecasting—A simple forecasting method that estimates future sales on the basis of sales made during similar past periods.

variable labor expenses—Labor costs that vary according to the amount of business.

REVIEW QUESTIONS

1. What are the advantages and disadvantages of job enlargement?
2. What are the advantages and disadvantages of job enrichment?
3. What are the advantages and disadvantages of job rotation?
4. Why should companies be careful with listing an education as a minimum qualification?
5. Why is it important to identify essential job functions?
6. Why is it important for hospitality companies to have well documented job descriptions?
7. Discuss the importance of job specification.
8. What are drawbacks of "observation" method to collect job information?

Zippier Catering

Zippy Airline Catering—a small, independent company—was recently purchased by a large hospitality company in Guam. At the time, the operation had only eight full-time employees and a single manager and produced a single product: prepared meals for three airlines that flew out of the Guam airport. Each meal was prepared individually by a single employee. To package a meal, employees would sit at a long table where they would place a portion of meat, potato, and a vegetable in a ceramic tray. The ceramic tray was then covered with aluminum foil and placed in an oven. When finished, employees took the tray out of the oven and packed it into catering boxes for transfer onto an airline.

To meet the tremendously increased demand brought about by additional flights through the airport, the hospitality company that purchased Zippy Airline Catering decided to re-engineer the preparation process. A conveyor belt was installed, and each employee was assigned a single task in the meal preparation. Employees now sat along either side of the conveyor and placed only a single item—meat, potato, or vegetable—on the tray. Essentially, the individual preparation method had been thoroughly converted to a production-line approach. The speed of the conveyor belt had been calculated by the engineers who designed the system. The engineers estimated that employees would be able to put their item on a tray before it passed beyond reach.

To encourage teamwork, the company instituted a group bonus plan that rewarded employees for the total number of meals produced. According to this simple plan, the more trays produced, the more bonus earned.

DISCUSSION QUESTIONS:

1. Are the changes made by the hospitality company significant redesigns of the work done? Why or why not?

2. What do you think will happen as a result of this redesign? Explain your response.

3. What steps would you have taken before initiating substantial changes in the way work is done at Zippy Airline Catering?

ENDNOTES

1. Shari Caudron, "Job Stress Is in Job Design," *Workforce Management* 77, no. 9 (1998): 21–23.

2. "Training That Melts in Your Mouth," *Workforce Management* 78, no. 2 (1999): 34–35.

3. Luis R. Gomez-Mejia, David B. Balkin, and Robert L. Cardy, *Managing Human Resources,* 8th ed. (Upper Saddle River, N.J.: Prentice-Hall, 2014), 71–72.

4. Raphael R. Kavanaugh and Jack D. Ninemeier, *Supervision in the Hospitality Industry,* 5th ed. (Lansing, Mich.: American Hotel & Lodging Educational Institute, 2012), 149–154.

2
PLANNING AND RECRUITING

Chapter 2 Outline

Learning Objectives

KEY TERMS

Effective recruitment

Bottom-up forecasting

Top-down or engineering forecasting

Trend analysis

Skills inventories

Management inventories

Replacement chart

Succession chart

Management succession plan

Recruitment process

Internal recruiting

External recruiting

Job postings

Job bidding

Human resource information system (HRIS)

In hospitality, managers who don't know where they are going—that is, who don't plan—are choosing by default to take the road to high recruitment costs, high training costs, high turnover, and low productivity.

To staff a hospitality operation, you must know the critical steps in the human resource planning process, which include identifying potential employees, encouraging potential employees to apply for a position, and selecting the right applicants for your organization. Without completing these steps, hospitality operations leave their employee selection—and their success or failure—to chance.

Although the process of recruiting and selecting qualified employees is an expensive one, it is considerably less expensive than the alternative: processing and selecting unqualified staff. Ultimately, selecting unqualified employees results in repeating the same process over and over. What would happen, for example, if a new hotel didn't develop a strategic human resource plan before advertising positions, interviewing applicants, and hiring employees? Most likely, the hotel would not hire the right people—or even the right number of people—for the given positions. The same applies to any ongoing business. Unless management takes the time to establish a plan before recruiting, interviewing, and selecting employees, it leaves the results to chance.

2.1 PLANNING HUMAN RESOURCES

The human resource planning process involves anticipating an organization's business demands and providing the staff to meet those demands. Human resource planning involves two critical factors: the supply of and the demand for staff. *Supply* represents the number of potential employees available to a hospitality company; *demand* represents the number and nature of the jobs the company needs. Supply and demand are affected by conditions both inside and outside the organization. Planning for employee needs requires managers to investigate the particular factors influencing the supply of and

demand for employees in the workforce. Knowing as much as possible about the local available labor market is the first step in **effective recruitment**.

External and Internal Factors Influencing Supply of and Demand for Employees

Economic conditions such as overall job growth (or loss), especially in a given geographic area, have always been a key factor affecting the local labor market. The availability of substitute occupations (i.e., jobs for which similar backgrounds may qualify) as well as prevailing wage rates may also have an effect on the labor supply and demand. Globalization, mergers, and acquisitions within an industry segment and company policies such as promoting from within are additional examples of factors that may influence labor supply and demand.

Because these factors may be dynamic and are sometimes quite localized, it is imperative that the management of each hospitality firm pay close attention to and monitor their own specific labor market conditions. In addition to following reports from the news media, managers are typically well-served by staying engaged with national, regional, and local business/trade associations (e.g., the American Hotel and Lodging Association, the National Restaurant Association, their state hotel/lodging association, and the local convention and visitors' bureau/chamber of commerce) to learn and share observations and experiences with peers.

Finally, one of the most important factors influencing the supply and demand of workers is the reputation of a business among employees. Employees who are satisfied with their workplace tell friends and others they meet. Those who are unsatisfied often say negative things about their workplace. For this reason, employee satisfaction can determine potential employee supply. The impact of web-based platforms and social media has exponentially increased the exposure of such communication. Sites such as Glassdoor and others put millions of user-generated company reviews at the fingertips of any potential employment candidate with access to mobile technology. This has prompted some employers to take a more proactive approach to managing and responding to public postings by employees and applicants.[1] In fact, more than half of applicants pass on a company after reading negative reviews online, and 84 percent of job seekers say a company's reputation is important when they determine to which companies to apply.[2]

Before engaging in recruitment activities, managers should also consider the following internal factors that affect recruiting:

- What specific competencies are required?

- How are we going to address competency gaps?

- How should we develop our succession plan?

- What performance objectives do we need to establish, and how will they be measured?

- How will we reward employees?

- How will we communicate to employees their progress and success?

Knowledge Check

1. What is the first step in effective recruitment?

2. What two critical factors does human resources have to plan for?

3. How does the reputation of a business affect supply and demand for new employees?

2.2 FORECASTING DEMAND

The goal of forecasting is to accurately match the demand for employees and skills with the available supply. Hospitality managers use two general types of forecasting. The first type—called **bottom-up forecasting**—involves asking managers within an organization to estimate their upcoming staffing needs. This method of forecasting is intuitive; it is based on the experience of the managers. Although it is common, bottom-up forecasting is not necessarily the best method. Let's look at an example.

Managers in a typical hotel have various levels of expertise. Some managers—those with several years of experience—can anticipate and accurately estimate their labor needs. These estimates are based on their knowledge of what has happened in the past. Other managers—typically those with less experience—may not be able to anticipate all the factors that will influence their labor needs. For example, less experienced food and beverage managers may not realize that their department will lose a large number of people at the end of the school year when employees leave for summer jobs, family vacations, and so on. In addition, such managers may not intuitively know how a change in hotel technology will affect demand for employees. Consider what could happen when a hotel adopts a smartphone-based keyless room entry system. Could you expect new managers to be able to anticipate the effect the technology will have on front desk staff? Probably not. What you could expect, however, is that the human resources planning program may be jeopardized by the inaccurate estimates of such new managers.

Top-down or engineering forecasting eliminates inaccurate, intuitive estimates when forecasting demand for human resources because it relies on quantitative approaches. Factors influencing workforce demands are first identified, and specific data for those factors are entered in a statistical model to estimate workforce demand. Some examples of the factors are recent trends in turnover, national and regional unemployment rates, the current and forecasted economy, the number of high school and college graduates, regional economic development, and so on.

Generally speaking, bottom-up forecasting is suitable for temporary and short-term (less than a year) workforce forecasting whereas the top-down method is more appropriate for long-term (more than a year) forecasting.

Trend Analysis

Trend analysis is one method commonly used to forecast human resources demand because of its simple application. Competition, demographics, and changing government regulations can influence the demand for human resources. The key to trend analysis is selecting the single factor that most accurately predicts demand. This factor should relate directly to the nature of the business. No empirical evidence exists that a single factor totally predicts employee demand in the hospitality industry. However, evidence does suggest that *occupancy rate* can be a good predictor. Because this is the case, we'll use occupancy rate as our factor in Exhibit 2.1, which shows an example of trend analysis in the hospitality industry. The example is based on a hotel with 1,000 rooms.

Trend analysis consists of two types of forecasts, projecting a business factor and labor productivity ratio based on the estimated business factor. Each trend analysis has a total of eight steps. These steps are indicated by a number and boldface type; explanatory text appears directly below in the form of an example:

Forecasting the business factor:

Step 1: Identify the appropriate business factor that relates to the number of personnel required.

Example: Managers select occupancy rate as the single most important factor on which to base employee demand predictions.

Step 2: Chart the historical record of how that factor relates to the size of the workforce.

Example: Managers collect and itemize occupancy figures and number of employees on staff for previous years (see Exhibit 2.1). Use the years for the X-axis and the business factor, which is a room occupancy in this example, for the Y-axis.

Step 3: Chart the trend in room occupancy.

Example: Managers plot the gathered data for the previous years. The forecasted room occupancy is estimated by drawing a straight line along the plotted dots for the previous years and the historical occupancy rates and extending the line in a straight manner. This is called a straight-line forecast. Using the straight-line forecast, we can forecast the 2022 room occupancy rate is 67. See the Exhibit 2.2.

Step 4: Adjust the forecasted room occupancy.

Example: Adjust the forecasted room occupancy rate using the midpoint of the forecasted room occupancy and historical average. First, compute the average of the historical data by adding all historical occupancy rates together and dividing it by the number of years. In this example, the answer is 63 [(60+61+64+65+65)÷5]. Then, choose a midpoint between the projected and the historical average. The adjusted occupancy rate represents the midpoint between straight-line forecast (67) and average forecast (63) which is 65.

Forecast labor productivity:

Step 5: Project the labor productivity for each year.

Example: Compute the historical labor productivity ratio by examining historical employment records. The manager can establish a ratio of employees per hotel room sold (Labor Productivity Ratio) by dividing the number of employees by an average daily room sold. For 2017, the labor productivity ratio is

Exhibit 2.1	Sample Chart: Occupancy and Employee Demand	
Year	Occupancy Rate %	Number of Employees
2017	60	900
2018	61	824
2019	64	1,024
2020	65	943
2021	65	975

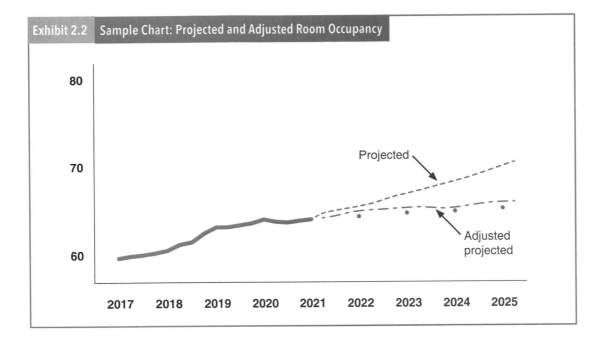

Exhibit 2.2 | **Sample Chart: Projected and Adjusted Room Occupancy**

1.5 (900÷600). Compute the projected labor productivity ratio by averaging the actual labor productivity ratio. For this example, the projected labor productivity ratio is 1.48 [(1.5+1.35+1.6+1.45+1.5)÷5]. See Exhibit 2.3.

Step 6: **Project the number of rooms sold.**

Example: Use the forecasted occupancy rates from the steps 1–3. Compute the number of rooms sold by multiplying the forecasted occupancy rate with the total number of rooms available. For this example, the number of rooms sold is 650 (65%×100).

Step 7: **Project the number of employees needed.**

Example: Compute the number of employees needed by multiplying a forecasted labor productivity

Exhibit 2.3 | **Sample Projection of Labor Demand**

Year	Average Daily Occupancy Rate %	Average Daily Rooms Sold	Number of Employees	Labor Productivity Ratio
2017	60	600	900	1.5 employees per occupied room
2018	61	610	824	1.35
2019	64	640	1,024	1.6
2020	65	650	943	1.45
2021	65	650	975	1.5
2022	65	650	975	1.5 } projected
2023	65	650	975	1.5
2024	65	650	975	1.5
2025	65	650	975	1.5

ratio with a forecasted number of rooms sold. For 2022, the number of employees needed is 962 (1.48×650).

Step 8: **Make adjustments in the trend based on unusual events—past or present—that may influence the estimate.**

Example: Managers may find that they need to adjust their trend forecast because of special events and conventions scheduled during the year. For example, if the city where the hotel is located will host a Super Bowl game, the hotel should adjust the occupancy rate, number of rooms sold, and the labor productivity ratio to reflect the high demand.

A real hotel might have many more adjustments to make. For example, if a counter-service coffee shop changes to a full-service restaurant, managers would need to add several servers—a factor the historical information would not anticipate. Other examples include the impact that changes in technology or conventions have on hotel services.

The adage "garbage in, garbage out" finds new life when describing trend analysis. If good information is provided for the computation, hospitality managers should expect estimates to be within 5 to 10 percent of real needs. On the other hand, if poor information is used, predictions are worthless.

Hospitality operations should make labor predictions for each department when predicting the labor needs for the entire property. As hospitality managers know, different departments have very different histories. For example, the housekeeping and food and beverage departments tend to have high employee turnover rates. The trend analyses for these departments must reflect the high turnover these areas experience.

Knowledge Check

1. What is bottom-up forecasting?

2. What is trend analysis?

3. Why is top-down forecasting more appropriate for long-term forecasting?

2.3 FORECASTING SUPPLY

Forecasting the supply of human resources involves analyzing the internal labor supply and an estimate of the external labor supply. Obviously, it is much easier to forecast the internal supply.

Internal Supply

Forecasting the internal supply of the workforce begins with an inventory of the present staff and their current skills, knowledge, and abilities. Managers should also anticipate the ability of current employees to acquire new skills through training. Even though a hotel has filled particular positions with qualified people, other employees may be able to acquire—through training—the necessary skills to do the job. What makes this relevant to the forecast is that employees may acquire these skills *within the time frame* of the prediction. This means that the hotel may actually have a higher number of skilled employees than it realizes. The use of skills inventories helps managers anticipate such eventualities.

Skills Inventories

Skills inventories list each employee's current skills, talents, ability to learn new skills, qualifications, and career goals. Companies use skills inventories for recruiting, training, and succession planning. Skills inventories can identify the skill gaps of current employees. These skill gaps can then guide the desired competencies job candidates should have for successful recruiting and selecting.

Many hospitality operations today compile and maintain skills inventories in computerized *human resource information systems* (discussed later in the chapter). Some businesses still maintain skills inventories manually. Using a computerized system allows inventories to be maintained and updated continually, which is more difficult to do using a manual system.

To be effective, skills inventories must meet two criteria: (1) they must be regularly updated, and (2) both managers and employees must agree on the information included in the inventory. Skills inventories for managers are often called **management inventories**. Unlike skills inventories, these inventories generally emphasize problem-solving skills and examine an individual's management track record.

Promotions, Layoffs, and Retirements

Predicting the supply of employees available to a hospitality operation is easier when policies are established for promotions, layoffs, and retirements. In unionized properties, these policies are typically included in the union contract to establish the relationship between employers and employees. Such policies also help properties forecast supply, because they establish what a property must do when an employee is promoted, laid off, or retires. Managers in non-unionized properties need to develop comparable policies.

Replacement and Succession Charts

Two types of charts are useful in predicting employee supply. Exhibit 2.4 shows a sample **replacement chart** that can help estimate the internal supply of employees in a particular position. This chart depicts the various human resources activities and decisions that affect the room attendant position in a hotel; it also itemizes the effect these activities and decisions have on the supply of employees.

A **succession chart** can be used to plot anticipated successions in an organization by position. The sample chart in Exhibit 2.5 demonstrates which kitchen employees the organization considers promotable if certain degrees of training and experience are achieved.

Succession Planning

The replacement and succession charts applied at the line level in Exhibits 2.4 and 2.5 can also be applied at the management level. To prepare succession charts for management positions, hospitality companies often begin by completing and regularly updating a **management succession plan** form. A sample succession form for managers is shown in Exhibit 2.6.

A management succession form quantifies the information in a management succession or replacement chart. Hospitality operations that use such charts can plan thoroughly for management turnover rather than simply guess about availability and future management staffing needs.

Exhibit 2.4	Sample Replacement Chart			
Classification: Room Attendant				
Source of Recruits	**Number**	**Current Level**	**Losses**	**Number**
Transfers	3	25	Resignations	6
Promotions	2		Discharges	2
New Hires	5		Demotions	1
			Retirements	0
			Transfers	4
			Promotions	2
Total	10		Total	15

Current level	25		
Recruits	+10	Needed 5	
Losses	−15		
Total	20		

Exhibit 2.5 Sample Succession Chart

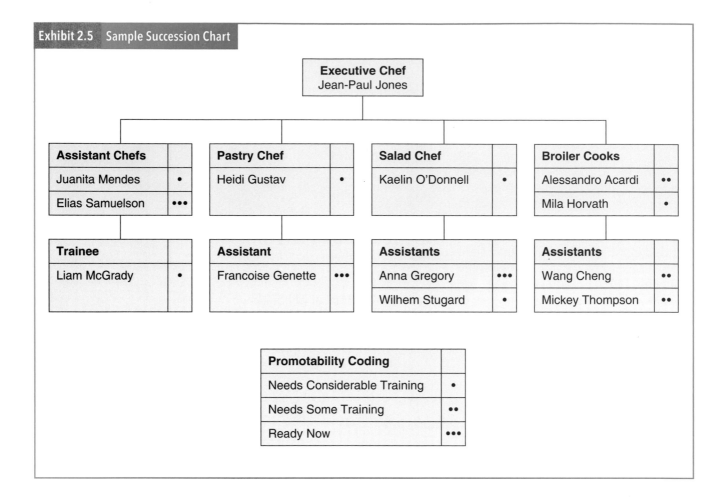

Executive Chef
Jean-Paul Jones

Assistant Chefs			Pastry Chef			Salad Chef			Broiler Cooks	
Juanita Mendes	•		Heidi Gustav	•		Kaelin O'Donnell	•		Alessandro Acardi	••
Elias Samuelson	•••								Mila Horvath	•

Trainee			Assistant			Assistants			Assistants	
Liam McGrady	•		Francoise Genette	•••		Anna Gregory	•••		Wang Cheng	••
						Wilhem Stugard	•		Mickey Thompson	••

Promotability Coding	
Needs Considerable Training	•
Needs Some Training	••
Ready Now	•••

Exhibit 2.6 Sample Succession Form for Managers

Date _____

Probability of Vacancy	
Within 6 months	•
Within 1 year	••
Within 18 months	•••
Within 2 years	••••

Name		Comments: Training, Experience Needed
Carlos Silva	••	Requires interpersonal skills, management training
Agatha Filo	•••	Housekeeping, front desk, valet service, room service
Neel Bedi	•	Seminar in accounts receivable, payable
Gloria Cavanaugh	••••	Hired without prior experience; kitchen, front desk, bell captain

2.4 EFFECTIVE RECRUITMENT PROCESS

Progressive properties recognize that recruitment is a process that involves identifying qualified employees and encouraging them to apply for open positions. An effective **recruitment process** attracts the right number of applications from the right applicants at the right time. In the past, attracting a large number of applications was the goal of recruitment. However, this goal is expensive for organizations.

As Exhibit 2.7 shows, a great deal of recruiting actually takes place before any ads are placed on recruitment websites and professional social media sites, in newspapers, or in notices posted on the company's intranet. The pre-recruitment process consists of a number of interrelated steps, beginning with defining job requirements and ending with evaluating recruiting methods. The following list summarizes important considerations of the recruitment steps outlined in Exhibit 2.7. (More detail will be provided on some of these steps later in the chapter.):

■ *Define job requirements.* To define the job and its requirements, a manager needs to understand the primary responsibilities and tasks involved in the job, the background characteristics needed to perform the job, the personal characteristics required, the key features of the organization's culture, and the manager's managerial style.

■ *Review job analysis information, job descriptions, and job specifications.* Managers should check that these tools are current, applicable, and complete. Changes and additions should be made when necessary.

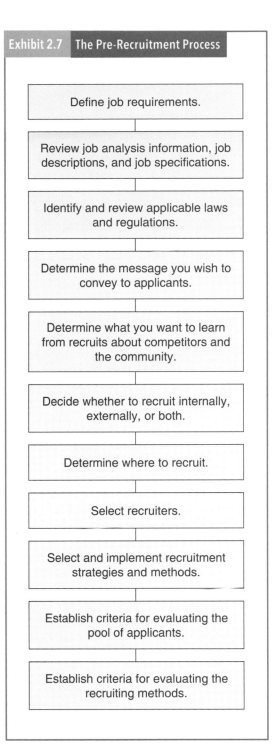

Exhibit 2.7   The Pre-Recruitment Process

- Define job requirements.
- Review job analysis information, job descriptions, and job specifications.
- Identify and review applicable laws and regulations.
- Determine the message you wish to convey to applicants.
- Determine what you want to learn from recruits about competitors and the community.
- Decide whether to recruit internally, externally, or both.
- Determine where to recruit.
- Select recruiters.
- Select and implement recruitment strategies and methods.
- Establish criteria for evaluating the pool of applicants.
- Establish criteria for evaluating the recruiting methods.

■ *Identify and review applicable laws and regulations.* Many claims of unlawful employment discrimination arise from recruitment practices, evaluation of applicants, and employee selection decisions.

■ *Determine the message you wish to convey to applicants.* The introduction of your business and the position is a critical part of recruitment. Many

Managers must be mindful of potential legal consequences at all stages of the employment relationship and must ensure the company's compliance with all applicable employment laws. The potential liabilities for discriminatory recruiting and hiring are summarized in Chapter 13.

applicants are attracted to companies by recruitment advertising only to find that there is a considerable difference between the job in the ad and the job in the actual workplace. Businesses that carefully consider the message they want to send, and present the situation realistically, establish conditions that encourage long-term success.

■ *Determine what you want to learn from recruits about competitors and the community.* Although identifying potential applicants is the primary purpose of recruiting, it is not the sole purpose. Recruiting also gives managers a great opportunity to learn about the outside world. Applicants from other companies can provide valuable information about how your operation compares with the competition—as well as about how your operation is perceived.

■ *Decide whether to recruit internally, externally, or both.* Some companies have successfully established programs in which only entry-level employees are recruited from the outside. In these companies, all supervisory and management positions are filled by internal applicants. Such internal recruitment programs are designed to create career ladders that encourage personnel to remain with the company longer. Other companies have successfully established programs for the external recruitment of both managers and entry-level personnel. The advantages and disadvantages

of internal and external recruitment are discussed later in the chapter.

■ *Determine where to recruit.* Managers should determine sources for both internal and external recruiting. For external recruiting, managers must determine the sites and media with the most potential to reach applicants. Using employee testimonials on social media and company websites has proven to be an effective way to promote recruitment of desired employees.[3] Managers must also identify productive sites for internal recruiting. For example, consider a chain hotel searching for housekeeping supervisors. This property might find more success recruiting from the housekeeping departments of other hotels in the chain than from departments within its own property.

■ *Select recruiters.* The impression that many applicants may form about your operation is based on how they perceive the recruiters. Selecting the right recruiters is critical to attracting the right applicants. In addition, managers should consider that the employees they choose as recruiters can be affected in a positive or negative way. For example, employees with doubts about their role may find that recruiting is exactly what they need to rekindle a flame for the organization. Unfortunately, the opposite also may be true. For these and other reasons, selecting the right recruiters is paramount to the recruitment process.

■ *Select and implement recruitment strategies and methods.* Recruitment can take many forms. In some cases, word-of-mouth may work best; in others, it may be better to recruit through mass media (radio, television, newspapers, magazines, Indeed.com, Hcareers.com) and/or web-based social media (Twitter, LinkedIn). Different approaches reach different markets. For that reason, the choice of approach is crucial to the recruiting process.

■ *Establish criteria for evaluating the pool of applicants.* Too often, managers simply toss out a wide recruiting net to see what they can catch. This approach can have two outcomes—both unproductive. First, although the right applicants may be caught in the net, others may be as well. These others may be unsuitable "catches" who waste management time on interviews. Second, this approach may not catch any applicants who really fit the criteria. In some cases, recruiters may think that they should select the most promising applicants from this pool, simply to justify the cost of recruitment. To avoid these pitfalls, managers should establish clearly defined evaluation criteria at the outset of recruiting.

■ *Establish criteria for evaluating the recruiting methods.* Costs, costs per hire, number of contacts made, acceptance-offer ratios, and salary-requested rates all vary depending on the type of recruiting method used. Before beginning a recruiting program, hospitality operations should establish acceptable rates for each of these and other evaluation criteria.

As part of the recruitment process, managers should also consider whether their personnel needs will be best met by internal or external sources of employees. An important goal for a human resources practitioner is to balance internal promotions and external hires.[4] The appropriateness of the recruitment source depends on an organization's strategy, needs, culture, and philosophy. Managers need to understand the advantages and disadvantages of the sources derived from internal and external recruiting.

Internal Recruiting

As noted earlier, many hotel and restaurant companies recruit only entry-level employees from external sources; all supervisory and management positions are recruited internally—or, as some say, are "hired from within." **Internal recruiting** has many advantages. It:

■ Improves the morale of the promoted employee by rewarding good work.

■ Improves the morale of other staff members who see opportunities for themselves.

■ Gives managers a better assessment of the abilities of internal recruits, since their performance has been observed over time.

■ Results in a succession of promotions for supervisory and management positions— meaning that one promotion is necessary to fill each job vacated by a promotion. These successions help reinforce the company's internal career ladder.

■ Costs less than external recruiting.

■ Is less risky because companies know the personality and attitude of the promoted employees.

Internal recruiting also has its disadvantages. For example, this method may:

■ Promote inbreeding; over time, the flow of new ideas into the company diminishes, and this is the biggest disadvantage.

■ Cause morale problems among those employees skipped over for promotion.

■ Have political overtones; some employees may attribute promotions to friendships with managers and supervisors.

■ Create a critical gap in one department when personnel are used to fill a gap in another.

■ Place a heavy burden on training and development. Promoted employees should receive proper training and development to obtain the necessary skills to perform their new tasks and responsibilities.

External Recruiting

External recruiting—or hiring from outside sources—is usually easiest at the entry level because managers can readily evaluate the skills and abilities required for such jobs. The factors that influence external recruitment strategies are strongly influenced by the labor market, which consists of individual candidates who possess the knowledge, skills, attitudes, and abilities that meet the standards for employment within the organization. External sources also include competitors. Experienced human resources practitioners are always looking for talented individuals employed at other companies.

Although it costs more than internal recruiting, external recruiting has some distinct advantages. Among its major benefits, external recruiting:

- Brings "new blood" and new ideas into the company.
- Gives recruiters an opportunity to see how things are on the outside by talking with applicants from both direct and indirect competitors.
- Provides a fresh look at the organization, which sometimes reinforces the reasons current employees work in the company. Consider, for example, the value of a recruit saying something like: "You keep your kitchen much cleaner than they do where I currently work," or "The light from the atrium certainly makes this a more pleasant place to work."
- Is sometimes cheaper than training current employees.
- Avoids many of the political problems associated with internal recruiting.
- Serves as a form of advertising for the company. Newspaper ads, posters, bulletin board notices, presentations, and so on remind the public of your products and services.

Like internal recruiting, external recruiting has its disadvantages. Hospitality managers should be aware of the following:

- It can be more difficult to find a good "fit" with the company's culture and management philosophy through external recruiting.
- Morale problems can develop if current employees feel they have no opportunity to advance in the organization.
- Job orientation for external recruits takes longer than it does for internal recruits, who already know the goals of the company, how the payroll system works, and so on.
- External recruiting can lower productivity over the short run, since, in some cases, new employees cannot produce as quickly or as effectively as internal recruits.
- Political problems and personality conflicts can result when employees believe they could do the job as well as the external recruit.
- Most external candidates are unknown entities and may not prove to be as they first appear. Managers typically know more about internal applicants.
- May result in misplacement because managers do not know about the job candidate.
- It is more costly. External recruitment takes four times as many applications to get to the interview stage and twice as many interviews for a job offer.[5]

2.5 RECRUITMENT SOURCES

All too often, managers recruit through the most common methods available. By doing so, they may reach few viable applicants. There are other options for creative managers to explore. This section discusses some of those options.

Internal Sources

Internal recruitment strategies often include career planning, skills inventories, and internal job-posting systems. Maintaining adequate skills inventories and replacement and succession charts makes internal recruiting easier. Doing so gives managers a better idea of who has the skills for an open position and who might be interested in taking the job. These inventories and charts should be viewed as critical—especially in organizations that stress internal recruiting.

To ensure that current employees know about openings, many businesses post notices or actual **job postings** on bulletin boards or announce current job openings via their recruitment websites and/or social media. Typically, postings or announcements include a job description and job specifications to inform employees of the responsibilities and skills required on the job. **Job bidding** results when employees sign a list indicating they are interested in applying for posted positions.

Another way to leverage internal sources to find new employees is to encourage current employees to refer people to the company. Employee referrals are considered as internal recruitment even though job applicants are not current employees. Friends and acquaintances of current employees often have more realistic views about the advantages and disadvantages of the organization. In addition, employees tend to refer only those friends they believe would make good employees; they realize that referring poor applicants reflects on their own judgment. Providing incentives, rewarding employees with promotions, and targeting employees for future promotions are all effective ways to make referral recruiting more effective.

Because of the benefits, employee referral has been a top source of recruitment and selection: about 30 percent of all hires and 45 percent of internal hires.[6] However, using referrals as the only source for recruiting can have unpleasant legal ramifications, because this method may be seen as discriminatory against rejected candidates. In addition, relying on employee referrals may not promote a diverse workforce.

External Sources

Local circumstances determine sources for external recruiting, but typical sources that may be of value to hospitality operations in general include the following:

- Online sources
  - Companies' recruitment websites: Most major hospitality companies have their own career websites. The major hotel chains' career websites (e.g., www.careers.marriott.com, www.careers.hyatt.com, www.jobs.hilton.com) include contemporary examples of well-done web-based recruiting, including written, photo, and video testimonials.
  - Social media sites: Social media sites have become a major source of recruitment in recent years. As of 2020, 91 percent of companies were using social media to recruit, compared to only 56 percent in 2011. The most popular social media sites for recruitment are LinkedIn, Facebook, and Twitter. Many recruiters say that LinkedIn is most effective for recruitment compared to many other social media sites such as Facebook.[7]
  - Third-party career sites and job search websites such as ZipRecruiter, Indeed, Monster, and CareerBuilder reach many people. ZipRecruiter claims that it has about half a billion job listings on its website.

- Employment agencies—state and private

- High schools and colleges: Sources for recruitment include high school and college job fairs, managers who serve as guest speakers in classes, notices with career and job placement counselors, personal contact with teachers and coaches, participants in work-study programs, contact with campus social and professional clubs, hospitality management programs, and dormitory counselors, among others.

- Previous candidates and former employees, employees at same-chain properties who may be laid off during seasonal slowdowns, and employees at other hospitality companies or service-oriented organizations that you meet while dining out, shopping, or doing other day-to-day activities. Retired employees of the operation may also be happy to help and can provide an immediate source of qualified workers during staff shortages or in other times of need. Likewise, former employees in good standing and current part-time employees might be available to fill in on a short-term basis.

- Youth groups and sports teams (for example, via sponsorships)
- Professional and trade journals
- Senior citizen groups and state units on aging
- Community events
- Urban League and other agencies that provide skills training and job placement, including the Vietnam Refugee Fund, the Mexican-American Opportunity Foundation, etc.
- Government rehabilitation, veterans, or military agencies
- Chambers of commerce
- Social/health organizations such as the Boys and Girls Club
- Social service organizations such as Goodwill
- Job fairs
- American Hotel & Lodging Association and any state or local restaurant associations

Advertising and Equal Employment Opportunity

Job advertisements must be created with care. In many locations, a property must obtain permission before distributing job notices, bulletins, and other forms of advertising. To avoid unlawful discrimination, properties must also pay special attention to how their job advertisements are worded.

Evaluating Recruitment Methods

Despite the importance of recruitment process evaluation, few companies measure the effectiveness of recruitment. However, just like any other business practices, organizations should determine whether their recruitment strategies are working. A critical determinant of recruitment success is the number of applicants recruited and the performance of new hires via each recruitment method per dollar spent on the process. The following data can be used to determine the success of different recruitment methods:

- Time to fill positions: Managers can calculate the time it took to fill each position.
- Total number of applicants: Managers can calculate the number of applicants from each recruitment source to measure the effectiveness of the specific source.
- Yield rate: Managers can calculate two yield rates for each recruitment source:
  - (Number of applicants invited to an interview ÷ number of total applicants) × 100
  - (Number of applicants hired ÷ number of total applicants) × 100
- Success rate: Managers can calculate the recruitment success rate beyond the yield rates by tracking high performers from each recruitment source:
  - (Number of high performers ÷ number of total applicants) × 100
- Performance success of new hires
- Costs of recruitment (including recruiters' salary, travel expenses to recruit applicants, technology expenses if companies use HR recruitment software, and advertising expenses)

- Number of hours managers spent on job interviews: Organizations can convert this to an hourly rate by multiplying the number of hours spent by the average hourly salaries of managers.

Knowledge Check

1. What are three online external sources that can be used for external recruiting?

2. How is job bidding different than job posting?

3. How can a company measure the effectiveness of their recruitment?

2.6 RECRUITMENT TRENDS

Some companies have found that keeping up with the times in recruitment can take on unique aspects today. For example, some companies use "open houses," much like open houses at homes for sale, to enable potential recruits to see the operation for themselves. Others network with their vendors (e.g., food and beverage suppliers) to identify top performers in the local hospitality market; sometimes these purveyors of good and services possess insights not so easily available to others. Some companies have specially prepared business cards for managers to use when they receive exceptional service as customers. These business cards include a special recruitment message on the back inviting an application and/or volunteering to answer questions about future employment opportunities at their business. Additionally, there is evidence that integrating persons with disabilities into the workforce improves business performance and business success in hospitality environments. Several companies, including large food and hotel chains, have active recruitment strategies targeted at hiring employees with disabilities.[8]

Artificial Intelligence

A more recent development in the realm of creative recruiting has been the implementation of artificial intelligence (AI) systems as "recruiting assistants" to qualify and engage applicants. These AI systems can be programmed to screen résumés or applications; ask prescreening questions; answer frequently asked applicant questions; provide tips, guidance, and application progress updates; as well as administer assessments and alert candidates when the position is filled—via text, social media, e-mail, or a chat client included on the company website.

Applicant Tracking Systems

Applicant tracking systems can help companies screen applicants, test job candidates, schedule interviews, and help managers complete the hiring process. Such systems can identify qualified candidates by using key words and/or job descriptions through machine learning algorithms.[9]

On-Demand Training

ERE Media has developed "on-demand training" for recruiters, which, while not hospitality-specific, is another example of a creative use of technology to improve recruiters' knowledge and skills—and ultimately recruiting results. This web-based training consists of a series of short videos targeting development of 14 competencies deemed essential for effective "talent acquisition." The training is packaged so that managers can earn continuing education credit/certificates from both the Society for Human Resource Management (SHRM) and the HR Certification Institute.[10]

Millennials and Gen Z Workforce

"Are millennials really that different? The answer is YES," says Jim Clifton, Chair and CEO of Gallup.[11] Millennials are those employees born between 1981 and 1996. In 2020, about 23 percent of the world population (1.8 billion people) were millennials, comprising half of all employees in the world. About one fifth of the millennial population (about 378 million people) reside in North America. Millennials are in their mid-20s and late 30s and are the largest labor market compared to any other generations preceding them. The millennial generation is also a greatly diverse group, with 44.2 percent identifying as people of color.[12]

Artificially intelligent recruiting assistants are chatbots that communicate directly with applicants looking for jobs via text, email, or through its own chat platform. Such AI assistants apply machine learning to auto-screen candidate résumés. In addition, special AI software can be used to analyze job descriptions to identify potentially biased language that the company can then correct. Examples of platforms experimenting in the AI recruiting space include Mya and Arya.

www.fastcompany.com/3061677/the-future-of-work/the-chatbot-who-can-make-sure-youll-never-get-radio-silence-after-applyin obtained 12/27/16); www.goarya.com

Millennials have unique characteristics that recruiters and managers should be aware of for better recruitment and training. Millennials have a high level of education compared to other generations. About half of millennials have a higher degree than secondary education; more female millennials (51 percent) have post-secondary education than male millennials (42 percent). Millennials tend to postpone having families and children and tend to invest in education, careers, and travel.[13]

The most important feature millennials look for when they apply for a job is development opportunities. A Gallup survey showed that 59 percent of the generation say opportunities to learn and grow are extremely important for the job search, and 87 percent rate "professional or career growth and development opportunities" as important to them in a job; this is far more than the 69 percent of non-millennials who say the same.[14] Millennials have great desire to advance in their career, but tend to be shy about discussing their career plans or goals with managers. Managers should therefore proactively reach out to them to talk about their career goals and provide opportunities to fulfill their needs. Millennials are often unfairly portrayed as the entitled generation; but they don't feel entitled, they feel empowered. They want to advance their knowledge and skills and be useful, and they want their work to be meaningful. Gallup summarizes the work-related characteristics of millennials in six categories:

1. Millennials don't just work for a paycheck—they want a purpose.
2. Millennials are not pursuing job satisfaction—they are pursuing development.
3. Millennials don't want bosses—they want coaches.
4. Millennials don't want annual reviews—they want ongoing conversations.
5. Millennials don't work to fix their weaknesses—they want to develop their strengths.
6. Millennials tend to think "It's not just my job—it's my life."[15]

Millennials are tech-savvy; they are the first generation born into technology. When they search for a job, websites of the organizations they are interested in are their number one source to find job opportunities, followed by online job sites, general web search, professional networking sites, social networking sites, and college career centers or websites. More than four out of five millennials use their smartphones to access the Internet, which implies that organizations should make sure their websites offer a seamless navigation experience on smartphones.[16]

As shown in Exhibit 2.8, the newest employees entering the job search arena are Generation Z. This generation consists of individuals born from 1997 onward. Because members of Gen Z are still young and their oldest members (age 24 in 2021) recently entered the labor market, not much data exists to define their attitudes toward work and careers. Some unique characteristics of this generation are that they are more diverse than any other preceded generations, with over half being non-Hispanic whites compared to about 40 percent of millennials. The U.S. Census Bureau projects that Gen Z will become majority non-white

| Exhibit 2.8 | The Generations Defined |

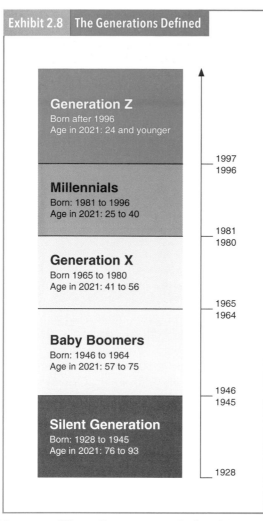

Exhibit 2.8   **The Generations Defined**

Generation Z
Born after 1996
Age in 2021: 24 and younger

1997
1996

Millennials
Born: 1981 to 1996
Age in 2021: 25 to 40

1981
1980

Generation X
Born 1965 to 1980
Age in 2021: 41 to 56

1965
1964

Baby Boomers
Born: 1946 to 1964
Age in 2021: 57 to 75

1946
1945

Silent Generation
Born: 1928 to 1945
Age in 2021: 76 to 93

1928

Source: "The Generations Defined," Pew Research Center, Washington, D.C. (January 14, 2019) https://www.pewresearch.org/social-trends/2019/01/17/generation-z-looks-a-lot-like-millennials-on-key-social-and-political-issues/psdt_1-17-19_generations-01/.

by 2026. They are also true digital natives; smartphones have always part of their lives. Gen Z is projected to be the best-educated generation yet. In 2019, about 57 percent of the Gen Zers ages 18 to 21 were enrolled in college, a number that is 5 percent higher than that for millennials.[17]

Knowledge Check

1. How can a human resource manager use artificial intelligence for recruitment?

2. What is the purpose of applicant tracking systems?

3. What are characteristics of millennials?

2.7 HUMAN RESOURCE INFORMATION SYSTEMS

The role of the human resources department has evolved over time, as have the systems that manage human resource data. Today, a good **human resource information system (HRIS)** can be a competitive advantage for companies. Some believe that HRISs are a means to control employees, others believe the objective is data control, while still others see such systems as developmental changes in the social psychology of organizations. Exhibit 2.9 shows the transformation of the human resources department since the beginning of the 20th century.

Back when human resources departments were called "personnel departments," the focus was on keeping records on employees. A lot has changed since then. By definition, an HRIS is a method of collecting, maintaining, organizing, analyzing, and reporting information about people and jobs. An HRIS is another recruiting tool because it provides so much useful information about supply, demand, specific needs and characteristics of employees, and so on. The types of data typically stored in an HRIS include the following:

- *Personal data.* Name; Social Security number; gender; date of birth; names, ages, and genders of dependents; marital status; racial/ethnic classification; address and telephone number; names of relatives or other persons to contact in case of emergency; and so on.

- *Recruiting data.* Date of recruiting contact, responsible recruiter, source of candidate, names of supervisors or managers referred to for interviews, dates of interviews, dates of offer and acceptance, outline of offer, and date added to payroll; if rejected, reasons for rejection or for candidate's rejection of employment offer; test scores; and so on.

- *Work experience data.* Names and locations of supervisors, employment history, job skills, training received, and dates and types of disciplinary action.

- *Compensation/work assignment data.* Salary or wage history, date of next forecast pay consideration, amount of

Exhibit 2.9   Transformation of the Human Resources Department

20th Century

- HR is a caretaker for employees
- Focus on employee records
- Personnel department

21st Century

- HR and employees are strategic partners
- Focus on cost effectiveness and employee development
- Human resources and development department

next forecast pay consideration, title, hours worked weekly/monthly, appraisal reports, and dates for next appraisal.

- *Benefit plan data.* Medical/life benefit plan information (self and family), pension plan information, vacation plan information, specialty benefit plan information, and so on.

- *Exit interview data.* Date removed from payroll, reason cited for removal, forwarding address, name and address of new employer, eligibility for rehire, reason for departure, and so on.

Data in an HRIS has many purposes. For example, information kept in a typical HRIS can be used in operational reports, regulatory reports, and analytic reports. Operational reports in a hotel might include such items as job vacancy information, wage reports, or recruiting reports. Preparing regulatory reports—such as required annual reports to the EEOC and OSHA—is much easier when information is collected, stored, and compiled in an HRIS. Many people feel one of the best applications of an HRIS is analytical reporting. For example, a hotel may wish to compare a method of recruiting to turnover activity. By using the information stored in an HRIS, the operation can prepare this report quickly and effectively. Without an HRIS, a similar report would take hours of manual labor to produce.

These systems do have problems. Hotels may tend to store "nice-to-know" information in the HRIS database and produce far too many "interesting" reports that have little usefulness. Because the information is readily available, some HRIS

managers may overuse the system's capability and mire the organization in information overload.

While the Federal Privacy Act of 1974 limits only information collected and stored in federal agencies, it provides some indication of where further limits may someday be placed in private industry. Operators employing HRISs should review and be aware of the three specific rights of individuals under this act:

(1) individuals have the right to review, copy, and amend reports about themselves kept in any personnel file—including an HRIS;

(2) individuals have the right to prevent information about them from being used for any purpose other than that for which it was collected; and

(3) individuals have the right to sue for damages as a result of any action that violates their rights.

For now, that law does not apply directly to private businesses; but from a hospitality manager's point of view, the best protection from this type of potential litigation is also threefold:

(1) set up specific policies regarding the collection and use of information,

(2) inform employees of these policies, and

(3) require employees to read and sign a statement acknowledging these policies.

By doing so, the organization protects both the individual and itself.

System Errors

Many of the mistakes associated with an HRIS are related to the system the business chooses. As a rule of thumb, total systems implementation costs approximately eight times the software and hardware costs. For example, if software and hardware costs are $10,000, the total implementation costs will approximate $80,000. Aside from cost considerations, any property considering an HRIS should keep the following points in mind:

- Managers and users should be active participants in installing the system. All too often, systems are installed, and installers leave before really teaching the staff how to use the system effectively.

- Data collection should focus on "need-to-know" information.

- Reporting needs should be analyzed thoroughly before choosing a system, and due diligence involving all key potential users of the system should be undertaken. The Society for Human Resource Management recommends the following steps when selecting an HRIS:

  1. Perform initial assessment (conducted either internally or by an outside consultant)

  2. Assess organizational needs (from a strategic company/property-specific perspective to determine needs vs. wants)

  3. Assess the project parameters (including budgetary, technological, and time constraints)

  4. Evaluate available packages against needs and project parameters (a rating matrix aligning needs/requirements with vendors/products and pricing can be useful for this stage)

  5. Select the project committee (ideally to include perspectives from IT, accounting/payroll, and HR)

  6. Send "request for proposals" (RFPs) to the top four identified vendors. (RFPs should include the specific requirements needed as well as a request to hold the pricing for 90 to 180 days while a decision is reached.)

  7. Demonstration and evaluation (select two to three finalists to come on-property and present a demonstration of the system; project committee members should ask questions and evaluate the system and services provided)

  8. Choose between the finalists (the finalists should provide reference checks from current users and HR should consider all available information before choosing a system and negotiating the final contract/service agreement.)

Knowledge Check

1. What is an HRIS?

2. What privacy issues should hospitality managers be concerned with when considering implementation of an HRIS?

3. What problems do you think may arise related to HRIS use?

LEGAL ALERT!

Many states have passed employment privacy laws in various forms. Some of them prohibit employers from distributing or disclosing confidential information about their employees, particularly concerning health conditions, disabilities, criminal histories, credit ratings, and information that could be used in identity theft. The best protection against claims for privacy violations is to adhere to a strict "need to know" policy for disclosing any employee information: only when necessary and limited to those who need it.

IN THIS CHAPTER, YOU LEARNED:

- Managers should consider several factors when they conduct HR needs plans, including economic conditions, wage rates, and the reputation of the organization.

- Hospitality managers use two types of forecasting for HR needs: bottom-up forecasting and top-down or engineering forecasting.

- Trend analysis is commonly used to forecast HR needs.

- Skills inventories are useful for HR needs forecast.

- Successful recruitment occurs when HR managers follow 11 pre-recruitment steps.

  1. Define job requirements.
  2. Review job analysis information, job descriptions, and job specifications.
  3. Identify and review applicable laws and regulations.
  4. Determine the message you wish to convey to applicants.
  5. Determine what you want to learn from recruits about competitors and the community.
  6. Decide whether to recruit internally, externally, or both.
  7. Determine where to recruit.
  8. Select recruiters.
  9. Select and implement recruitment strategies and methods.
  10. Establish criteria for evaluating the pool of applicants.
  11. Establish criteria for evaluating the recruiting methods.

- Internal recruitment gives managers a better assessment of the abilities of internal recruits but can promote inbreeding, which is the biggest disadvantage.

- External recruitment brings "new blood" and new ideas to the company but is more difficult to find a good "fit" with the company's culture and management philosophy.

- Organizations should measure the success of the recruitment by evaluating time to fill, total number of applicants, number of applicants invited to the interview, yield rate, performance of new hires, and costs of recruitment channels, among other factors.

- HR managers should understand characteristics of the workforce to attract qualified applicants.

- Professional or career growth and development opportunities are the biggest factors for millennials to stay with an organization.

KEY TERMS

bottom-up forecasting—Forecasting technique based on estimates made by managers in each department. These estimates are combined to create an estimate of human resources needs for the entire property.

effective recruitment—Process of attracting a pool of qualified job candidates from which an organization may select individuals to best meet its job requirements.

external recruiting—Process of seeking applicants from outside the property to fill open positions.

human resource information system (HRIS)—Computerized method of collecting, maintaining, organizing, analyzing, and reporting information on human resources and positions in an organization.

internal recruiting—Process of seeking applicants from inside the property to fill open positions.

job bidding—Process of posting a list internally for employees to sign when they are interested in open positions.

job posting—Internal or external notice of a job opening.

management inventory—A list of the problem-solving and management skills of current managers and management candidates that is used to identify candidates for internal recruitment.

management succession plan—A written plan that identifies readiness or skills required for managers to move up in the organization.

recruitment process—Sequence of recruiting steps that take place before advertising positions or posting notices.

replacement chart—A management tool that estimates the internal supply of employees for a particular position.

skills inventory—A list of skills, abilities, qualifications, and career goals of current employees that is used to identify candidates for internal recruitment.

succession chart—Management tool used to plot anticipated successions in an organization by position.

top-down forecasting—Forecasting techniques for human resources based on quantitative and statistical approaches.

trend analysis—Forecasting technique for predicting the future based on past performance.

REVIEW QUESTIONS

1. What are the steps in the recruitment process?
2. What are the basic steps involved in forecasting labor demands?
3. What are the purposes of replacement and succession charts?
4. What is bottom-up forecasting?
5. What is top-down forecasting?
6. What are the advantages and disadvantages of internal recruiting?
7. What are the advantages and disadvantages of external recruiting?
8. How can a company measure the success of recruitment?
9. What technology is used for the recruitment process?

Recruiting by Referral

During the 2000s, a hotel chain in the Midwest instituted a recruiting plan based on referrals from current employees. This system worked, primarily because the operation had a strong, competent staff during that period. However, problems began to develop in the 2010s as fewer and fewer people applied to fill the increasing number of positions at the hotel.

Despite a shrinking pool of applicants for an expanding number of jobs, the human resources manager continued to rely on the employee referral system for his labor supply. He justified this decision by saying, "Even though fewer employees are available, the employee referral method brings employees into our chain who know about our work and our expectations. That's because these people have friends working here. In the long run, this knowledge will help us keep training and orientation costs down."

Unfortunately, the manager's program is failing miserably. The hotel is desperately short of staff. To acknowledge the problem, the hotel chain developed a new position: director of recruiting. You have been hired for this position. You are asked to prepare a recruitment plan that taps labor supplies that your chain has failed to develop over the past several years. Your first problem, however, is convincing the human resources director of the need for such a recruitment program.

DISCUSSION QUESTIONS

1. What arguments can you use to convince the human resources director of the need to establish new recruiting methods and strategies?

2. Assuming you are given the go-ahead, what would your first step be?

3. What methods do you think would be most effective?

ENDNOTES

1. Susan Adams, "How Companies Are Coping With The Rise Of Employee-Review Site Glassdoor," last modified February 24, 2016, http://www.forbes.com/sites/susanadams/2016/02/24/how-companies-are-coping-with-the-rise-of-employee-review-site-glassdoor/#25d577dc8738

2. "Recruitment Statistics 2018: Trends & Insights in Hiring Talented Candidates," accessed February 23, 2020, https://empxtrack.com/blog/recruitment-statistics-for-better-hiring/

3. Roy Maurer, "Employee Referrals Remain Top Source for Hires," last modified June 23, 2017, https://www.shrm.org/resourcesandtools/hr-topics/talent-acquisition/pages/employee-referrals-remains-top-source-hires.aspx

4. Ibid.

5. "SHRM Survey Findings: Using Social Media for Talent Acquisition—Recruitment and Screening," *Society for Human Resource Management*, January 7, 2016, https://www.shrm.org/hr-today/trends-and-forecasting/research-and-surveys/Documents/SHRM-Social-Media-Recruiting-Screening-2015.pdf.

6. Roy Maurer, "Employee Referrals Remain Top Source for Hires," last modified June 23, 2017, https://www.shrm.org/resourcesandtools/hr-topics/talent-acquisition/pages/employee-referrals-remains-top-source-hires.aspx

7. "11 Top Social Media Recruitment Statistics to Ramp Up Your Hiring Strategy," *Profiles*, October 15, 2020, https://www.careerprofiles.com/blog/social-media-recruitment-statistics-for-hiring/

8. Valentini Kalargyrou and Anthony A. Volis, "Disability Inclusion Initiatives in the Hospitality Industry: An Exploratory Study of Industry Leaders," *Journal of Human Resources in Hospitality & Tourism* 13, no. 4 (2014): 430–454.

9. "Today's ATS Solutions Go Well Beyond Resume Storage," *Society for Human Resource Management*, last modified May 4, 2017, https://www.shrm.org/resourcesandtools/hr-topics/talent-acquisition/pages/ats-solutions-buyers-guide-shrm.aspx

10. John Ricciardi, "14 Skills to Save Recruiters from AI," last modified December 26, 2016, www.eremedia.com/ere/14-skills-to-save-recruiters-from-ai

11. "How Millennials Want to Work and Live," *Gallup*, accessed March 29, 2021, https://www.gallup.com/workplace/238073/millennials-work-live.aspx

12. "Millennials: Demographic change and the impact of a generation," *MSCI*, accessed March 29, 2021, https://www.msci.com/documents/1296102/17292317/ThematicIndex-Millenials-cbr-en.pdf/44668168-67fd-88cd-c5f7-855993dce7c4.

13. Ibid.

14. Amy Adkins and Brandon Rigoni, "Millennials Want Jobs to Be Development Opportunities," *Gallup*, last modified June 16, 2016, https://www.gallup.com/workplace/236438/millennials-jobs-development-opportunities.aspx.

15. Ibid.

16. "Race and Economic Opportunity Data Tables," *United States Census Bureau*, October 26, 2020, https://www.census.gov/programs-surveys/ces/data/public-use-data/race-and-economic-opportunity-data-tables.html

17. "Educational Attainment," *United States Census Bureau*, March 2017, https://www.census.gov/topics/education/educational-attainment/data.html

3
SELECTION

Chapter 3 Outline

Learning Objectives

1. Explain why it is important for selection methods to be reliable and valid. (pp. 56–58

2. Discuss the pros and cons of various selection methods. (pp. 58–67)

3. Discuss the pros and cons of unstructured and structured interviews. (pp. 69–70)

4. Develop interview questions to measure competency areas. (pp. 69–71)

5. Discuss types of selection errors and biases that managers must overcome when interviewing job applicants. (pp. 72–74)

6. Identify one time that interviewers must pay attention to applicants' nonverbal behavior during a job interview and explain why. (pp. 73–74)

7. Explain the STAR format of a job interview response. (p. 78)

KEY TERMS

Selection

Reliability

Validity

Predictor

Criterion-related validity

Content validity

Application blank

Weighted application blanks (WABs)

Test validity

Honesty test

Physical and motor ability test

Work sample test

Assessment center

Reference check

Negligent hiring

Credit reference check

Inter-rater reliability

Unstructured interview

Semi-structured interview

Structured interview

Panel or board interview

Stress interview

Similarity error

Contrast error

First impression error

Halo effect

Devil's horns

Recency error

Selection is one of the most critical tasks a manager undertakes. It is not something to delegate to untrained managers or employees. Management theorist Peter Drucker calls selection decisions "the most long-lasting decisions and the most difficult to unmake." The best managers make the right decisions only about 33 percent of the time. The other 67 percent of selections are either minimally effective or dismal failures.[1] Successful selection requires comprehensive planning. Effective job analysis and design, recruitment, job descriptions and specifications, and attention to legal and social requirements determine whether the right person is found and selected for the job.

Like managers everywhere, hospitality managers often hastily select employees in reaction to a crisis such as a personnel shortage. Managers who handle selection in this way do not become leaders in their field. Managers who take selection seriously are more likely to succeed.

This chapter focuses on effective techniques to use in the selection process. It discusses reliability and validity, selection steps and methods, employment and pre-employment tests, and interviewing skills and techniques. When done properly, selection is *legal* discrimination among job candidates. Its purpose is to choose candidates who are likely to succeed in the job.

3.1 FUNDAMENTAL CONSIDERATIONS

Selection practices should be both reliable and valid. Unreliable and invalid selection methods may be challenged in a court of law.[2] Selection methods should also predict work performance.

Reliability refers to the degree to which a selection method *consistently* produces the same results. A selection method is reliable if it consistently leads an employer to make the same decisions, regardless of who is applying the method. If it does not do this consistently, the method is not reliable. Whether the selection method is a test, an observation, or an interview, it must be reliable.

Validity is the degree to which a selection process actually measures or predicts what it is intended to measure or predict. The key in any selection process is to develop measures that validate the likelihood of success for each candidate. The selection process commonly uses two strategies to test for validity: criterion-related validity and content validity. The purpose of validation is to measure how well the predictor used in selection works. **Predictors** measure the relationship between performance during the selection process and performance on the job.

Criterion-Related Validity. **Criterion-related validity** is concerned with the relationship between the predictor and criterion scores. For the most part, the criterion in our discussions is job performance. There are two types of criterion-related validity: predictive and concurrent.

Predictive validity uses a predictor to ascertain whether *good* performance will be likely. Although many organizations base decisions on predictors, few validate whether predictors actually measure what they are intended to measure. As a result, there may be little correlation between performance on the predictor and performance on the job. To validate a predictor, managers should subject all applicants to the same predictor. Once tested using the predictor, applicants are selected on some other basis, such as on their résumé or experience. Once employees are hired, their performance can be tracked over time. After a certain period, performance can be compared to pre-hiring test scores. A strong correlation between scores on the selection process tests and actual job performance establishes validity for the predictor. Managers can then use this testing method as a predictor in future selection processes. Because predictive validity tests how employees will perform in the future, it is sometimes called the *future employee method.*

Concurrent validity—sometimes called the *current employee method*—differs from predictive validity in two ways: (1) the time frame in which the data are collected and (2) the choice of subjects. Concurrent validity compares the performance of newly developed selection tests to existing tests. For example, companies can administer a newly developed selection test to a group of job candidates and administer the existing test to the same group to determine whether the newly developed test is still valid. Then, organizations can test current employees. Another way to measure the concurrent validity is to test current employees and compare their scores on the selection test to their job performance. Concurrent validity is less effective than predictive validity in predicting future job performance. Also, if a company administers tests to current employees, they may give different answers than job candidates because of their work experience.

Content Validity. By using the criterion-related validity approach, a hospitality company can determine whether a test measures the performance required for a job, but the company still may not know whether an applicant can perform the entire job. **Content validity** measures the ability of applicants to perform the *entire* job. Unlike the predictive and concurrent methods, the content validity approach relies on the opinions of experts.

Content validity usually requires five steps:

1. Completion of a job analysis

2. Development of a test

3. Presentation of the test to a panel of experts for verification

4. Additions to or deletions from the test by the experts

5. Verification of validity and completeness of the modified test with current employees

To better understand this process, let's look at an example:

XYZ Hotels is advertising for a server position. The position requires servers to greet guests, suggest products, take orders, and serve guests. Four people have applied. Since Jenine makes a great first impression, she would be excellent at greeting guests. Kisha excels in describing products and taking orders. Jacques is great at serving guests and attending to their needs during the meal. Wang is good at each of these tasks but is not as good at any single task as any of the other three. Which one should you hire?

You create a test to measure the probability of success as a server. If that test emphasizes making a strong first impression, you will likely hire Jenine. If it measures the ability to sell products and take orders, you will probably hire Kisha. If it measures service during the meal, Jacques will likely get the best score. However, since each of these applicants has skills limited to certain parts of the job, they will probably be poor hires. Wang, on the other hand, whose skills are second-best for each individual part of the job, is the best overall. However, Wang will not be hired *unless* the test measures his overall ability. This measure of overall ability is known as content validity.

The validity of tests or assessment devices used in personnel selection is usually evaluated in terms of the correlation between scores on a test and scores on some performance measure. The key to usable validity is determining whether the device is a good determinant of performance. Although many forms of validity assessments are available, some are complicated, and many organizations do not have data to confirm the positive results associated with assessments they use when hiring.[3] The Mental Measurements Yearbook (MMY), which is published in three-year cycles, is widely regarded as an objective source for reviews of commercially available tests.[4]

Selection practices are particularly vulnerable to class-action lawsuits because they typically affect hundreds or thousands of applicants. If a selection method or standard has a disproportionate effect on applicants of a certain gender, race, color, national origin, or religion, it may result in legal liability for discrimination. The company's only defense in such a case is to prove that its standards or methods are valid and reliable.

LEGAL ALERT!

A Reminder

Although reliability and validity sound like academic concepts, in reality, they are not. Both are critical in determining the best selection procedures. Some companies are sophisticated in determining the reliability and validity of their selection methods; they make and regularly update statistical correlations to pinpoint the extent to which their techniques work. Companies that do little to ensure that their methods are reliable and valid may experience higher turnover and legal problems related to their selection process. Turnover can result from hiring the wrong person for the job; legal problems can develop from trying to terminate that wrong person.

3.2 SELECTION METHODS

After determining a selection philosophy, a company can begin to apply selection methods. Although the exact methods and applications of them vary from organization to organization, the most effective selection processes include several techniques. These methods involve application blanks, pre-employment tests, reference checks and recommendations, and job interviews.

Application Blanks

The purpose of an **application blank** is to learn what applicants have done in the past. Whether handwritten or online, application blanks typically ask a person to report on previous work experience, educational background, employment history, work references, personal references, and other personal data. By collecting information on an applicant's past, an organization assumes it can predict what an applicant will do in the future.

Two important points stand out in a discussion of application blanks. The first concerns the issue of *needed* versus *desirable* information. Application blanks can be too long or too short. Excessively long or complex applications can discourage potential applicants; they also raise concern over whether the issues on the form are truly job-related. On the other hand, application blanks that are too short can fail to collect the information needed to assess an applicant's qualifications to do the job.

Throughout the selection process, companies should limit questions to what are known as *bona fide occupational qualifications*. At issue is limiting questions to areas that are job-related. Generally speaking, questions about marital or family status, age, sex, sexual preferences, race, birthplace, religion, military records, convictions or arrests not related directly to the job, specific types of references (religious or military, for example), and requests for photographs are potentially illegal. According to the U.S. Equal Employment Opportunity Commission, there are different categories of potential illegal discrimination, including:

- Race
- Height and weight
- Financial information
- Unemployed state
- Background checks
- Religious affiliation or beliefs
- Citizenship
- Marital status or number of children
- Gender
- Disability
- Medical questions and examinations

The issue of bona fide occupational qualifications became particularly important when the Americans with Disabilities Act (ADA) became law. In the past, many application blanks included questions such as: "Do you have any handicaps?" or "Do you suffer from any permanent ailment or disease?" or "Have you ever suffered a serious accident while on the job?" Some application blanks included sections that asked applicants to identify any disabilities (loss of hearing, sight, and so on). These types of questions are not allowed under the ADA. Organizations may, however, ask about a person's ability to perform the essential functions of the job.

Many hospitality organizations rely on managers to subjectively evaluate the information contained on the application blank. However, technology may be employed via online applicant tracking systems to pre-screen candidates. Such systems select for the applicants who best meet the pre-programmed attributes typically identified by keywords or phrases pulled from the job description. Although online applicant tracking systems may streamline and possibly speed up the selection process, these systems are typically only as good as the coding/programming they are based on. These systems can also sometimes be perceived by applicants as being impersonal and cumbersome.

Weighted application blanks (WABs) are another tactic that employers may implement to identify issues that are important to performance on the job. Creating a WAB begins with a thorough analysis of each job. The purpose of this analysis is to determine which characteristics are required to effectively perform each job. After completing a job analysis to determine the characteristics and aptitudes an employee needs, a WAB is created that reflects the most desirable qualifications. After using the form for some time, a company tracks the work history of each new hire to determine the relationship between actual performance on the job and the performance predicted by the weighted application. In this way, the weighting on the application blank can be validated, and changes can be made on subsequent forms if necessary.

No matter the format, application blanks must conform to the guidelines of the Equal Employment Opportunity Commission (EEOC). The key test of these guidelines is how accurately the application blank predicts performance on the job. The organization must also ensure that applications do not cover issues that can be construed as illegally discriminatory. The Society for Human Resource Management has developed a list of acceptable and unacceptable questions for applications and interviews as shown in Table 3.1. Remember that unacceptable options are discriminatory.

Pre-Employment Tests

Tests are a popular selection method because they allow organizations to compare candidates easily. For example, a candidate who scores 90 on a paper-and-pencil test designed to evaluate applicants would appear more attractive than a candidate who scores 80. Recent research indicates that about three out of every four firms with more than 100 employees use aptitude and/or personality test results to inform their hiring decisions, and that figure is expected to climb over the coming years.[5] However, using tests to evaluate job applicants can lead to charges of discrimination.

Tests became the focus of many discrimination suits after the passage of the Civil Rights Act of 1964. Specific guidelines for testing were established through the *Uniform Guidelines on Employee Testing*, set forth as part of Title VII of the act. One important guideline pertains to **test validity**. All selection procedures must demonstrate a strong relatedness to the actual performance at work. Tests are no exception. Companies must be able to show that the tests they use are valid for the application. In many court cases, firms using tests as selection devices could not prove that the results were valid predictors of job success.

Discrimination is another issue in testing. Tests can inadvertently discriminate against certain protected groups. Hospitality employers should be particularly careful to avoid discrimination since women and people of color constitute a large percentage of hospitality job applicants.

Regardless of past problems, tests can sometimes be a practical way to legally determine the best applicant. The following sections describe tests that may apply in different hospitality settings.

Competency Tests. Competency tests may be administered via paper or online and typically require that job candidates respond to written or oral questions. Both multiple-choice and essay formats have been used successfully. Although some companies hire psychologists to develop and validate tests specifically for their work environments, many companies purchase standardized tests. The most popular standardized tests measure cognitive abilities: general intelligence, abstract reasoning,

Topic	Acceptable	Unacceptable
Age	If age is a legal requirement of the job, organizations can ask, "If hired, can you furnish proof of age?" or a statement that hires are subject to age verification.	What is your date of birth?
Attendance/reliability	What hours and days can you work?	How many children do you have?
Attendance/reliability	Are there specific times that you cannot work?	What religion are you?
Attendance/reliability	Do you have responsibilities other than work that will interfere with specific job requirements, such as traveling?	What are your childcare arrangements?
Attendance/reliability	Do you have a reliable method of getting to work?	Do you own a car?
Citizenship/national origin	Are you legally eligible for employment in the United States?	What is your national origin? Where are your parents from?
Citizenship/national origin	Have you ever worked under a different name?	What is your maiden name?
National origin	None	What is your family surname? What are the names of your relatives?
Arrest and conviction	Have you ever been convicted of a felony? * Please see note below for additional guidance.	Have you ever been arrested?
Disabilities	Can you perform the duties of the job you are applying for?	Do you have any disabilities?
Disabilities	None	Have you ever filed a workers' compensation claim?
Disabilities	None	Have you ever been injured on the job?
Emergency contact information	What is the name and address of the person to be notified of in case of an emergency? (Request only after the individual has been employed.)	What is the name and address of a relative to be notified of in case of an emergency?
Credit record	None	Do you own your own home?
Credit record	Credit references may be used if in compliance with the Fair Credit Reporting Act of 1970 and the Consumer Credit Reporting Reform Act of 1996	Have your wages ever been garnished?
Credit record	None	Have you ever declared bankruptcy?
Military record	What type of education, training, and work experience relevant to the job did you receive while in the military?	What type of discharge did you receive?
Language	What languages do you speak and write fluently? (if the job requires additional languages)	What is your native language? How did you learn to read, write, or speak a foreign language?
Organizations	Inquiry into membership in organizations that applicants consider relevant to their ability to perform the job.	List all clubs, societies, and lodges to which you belong.
Race or color	None	Complexion or color of skin.
Weight, height, eye color	Only if there is a bona fide occupational qualification.	
Religion	Only if there is a bona fide occupational qualification.	What is your religious denomination, religious affiliations, church, parish, or pastor? What religious holidays do you observe?
Gender	Only if there is a bona fide occupational qualification.	Do you wish to be addressed as Mr., Mrs., Miss, or Ms.?
Previous and current addresses	What was your previous address? How long did you reside there? How long have you lived at your current address?	Do you own your own home?
Education	Do you have a high school diploma or equivalent? Do you have a university or college degree? (if relevant to job performance)	What year did you graduate from high school or college?

*Note on arrest records: Using arrest or conviction records as an absolute bar to employment disproportionately excludes certain racial groups. Therefore, such records should not be used in this manner unless there is a business need for their use. Thus, an exclusion based on an arrest record is justified only if the conduct is job-related and relatively recent and also if the applicant or employee actually engaged in the conduct for which he or she was arrested. According to the EEOC, whether there is a business need to exclude persons with conviction records from particular jobs depends on the nature of the job, the nature and seriousness of the offense, and the length of time since the conviction or incarceration. In addition, some states bar the use of arrest records in employment decisions.

Source: https://shrm.org/ResourcesAndTools/tools-and-samples/toolkits/Pages/interviewandemploymentapplicationquestions.aspx numerical ability, verbal ability, clerical ability, and mechanical aptitude. Because courts have focused on such selection devices in the past, hospitality companies should pay careful attention to the tests they use and how they use them. Also, some states prohibit or regulate the use of these tests. Companies can evaluate the characteristics of a published test by answering five questions.[6]

1. Does the test measure aptitudes and abilities need for the job?
2. Are the tests reliable?
3. Are proper test development procedures used in the design?
4. Are the tests easy to administer?
5. What is the past success of the test (especially regarding EEOC proceedings)?

Honesty Tests. Because workplace theft amounts to tens of billions of dollars per year, many employers are interested in testing the honesty of job candidates. This is especially true in industries where ample opportunity exists for employee theft. Many consider hospitality a theft-prone industry because employees have chances to steal both products and money almost every day. Some **honesty tests** measure attitudes about honesty by posing a hypothetical situation in which the potential employee makes a value judgment. For instance, a common follow-up question to a situation involving money that is lost by a guest and then found by an employee might be: "Do you think it is wrong to keep the money?" Another form of honesty testing evaluates a candidate's candor—or, more appropriately, lack of candor—and propensity to lie. In some tests, the principal method involves posing either negative statements that are true about most people or positive statements that are false about most people; then, the candidates are asked to identify how often their behavior mirrors that described. For instance, a question might be: "Do you ever have bad thoughts that you would not want to tell others about?" Statistically speaking, most people do. The theory is that a candidate who responds "no" is probably lying and has a low propensity toward candor. However, an honesty test means little if it is not job-related.

Another form of honesty testing is the polygraph exam, also known as the lie detector test. This exam is considered to be reliable in 60 to 70 percent of its applications.

Physical and Motor Ability Tests. In the past, employers could subject applicants

Polygraph tests were popular in the hospitality industry in the mid-1980s. Their popularity has since waned due to their unreliability and possible legal ramifications. Much of the debate surrounding polygraphs was muted when the U.S. Congress passed the Employee Polygraph Protection Act in 1988. This act prohibits polygraphs in about 85 percent of employment situations. Generally speaking, polygraph tests are now allowed only when applicants are applying for state, local, or federal government positions or for positions with companies under contract with the Department of Defense, the FBI, or the CIA. Employers may still request polygraph tests under a very narrow exception that permits employers to investigate economic loss or injury in cases when reasonable suspicion of an employee is involved and the employee is afforded other protections. Even under these conditions, examinees have the right to refuse tests and to discontinue a test after it has begun; they also have the right to prohibit the disclosure of test results to unauthorized persons.

DID YOU KNOW?

to physical exams as a part of the selection process. However, due to potential discrimination against people with disabilities, the ADA eliminates most of the conditions in which exams are allowed. Some **physical and motor ability tests** that are specifically job-related (for example, the ability to lift objects for bell staff) may still be admissible.

Drug Tests. Many people believe that the government requires companies to test for drug use. This is not true. According to the U.S. Department of Labor, the Drug-Free Workplace Act of 1988 requires some federal contractors and all federal grantees to agree to provide drug-free workplaces as a condition of receiving a contract or grant from a federal agency. The act does not apply to those who do not have, nor intend to apply for, contracts or grants from the federal government, including subcontractors. If a company is going to ask its applicants and/or employees to submit to drug testing, it must make sure the program is as fair and well-run as possible with consideration of federal and state laws.

At the federal level, the ADA permits employers to deny jobs to current users of illegal drugs, to prohibit the use of drugs and alcohol in the workplace, and to prohibit employees from being under the influence of drugs or alcohol while on the job. Under the ADA, alcohol testing is currently regarded as a medical test; therefore, a conditional job offer must be extended before alcohol testing may legally occur. However, a drug screen is not considered a medical test, and an employer may require applicants to take pre-employment drug tests. Many states have laws applying to drug use and drug testing in the workplace. Some employers only allow testing done by state-approved labs; others require that a second, confirming test be done before allowing any disciplinary actions against employees who test positive. Employers are well served to pay close attention to the laws in the states where they do business before implementing drug testing programs because the approaches to the issues around these tests vary from state to state.

A special note about medical marijuana laws: at the time of this publication, 28 states and the District of Columbia have passed laws permitting residents to use marijuana for medical purposes. These laws usually include some requirement that the user have a written note from a licensed physician, often noting a specific disability or disease. If the resident (patient) possesses such a note, they cannot be prosecuted under state law for the use, possession, or cultivation of specific quantities of marijuana. However, under the Controlled Substances Act of 1970, marijuana is still federally classified as a Schedule 1 substance (i.e., a drug with no currently accepted medical use and a high potential for abuse). Although federal law supersedes state laws, the U.S. Drug Enforcement Agency to date has not taken aggressive action in states that have opted to legalize medical marijuana. In the meantime, employers who administer drug tests are left with the dilemma of what to do with a candidate with a legal prescription for marijuana who tests positive. Cases exploring this and related questions are currently being litigated in state courts, and the contradiction in these laws will no doubt be legally reconciled over time. Until such time, employers must be diligent in maintaining a high level of awareness around the dynamic legal environment in the states in which they do business.

Work Sample Tests. By definition, **work sample tests** measure a candidate's ability to perform the skills and tasks associated with a job. For example, a candidate for a clerical position may be asked to take a typing test. Work sample tests are one of the most reliable predictors of job success because applicants perform or simulate tasks they would do on the job. Such tests can be useful in many areas of the hospitality industry. Consider the case of a lodging facility. In its advertisement for a chef, the facility specified that the applicant would need to demonstrate cooking skills. Later, each applicant was asked to prepare a meal for the search committee.

Companies must consider two issues when using work sample tests. First, the test must have content validity. That is, the test must measure job performance for skills that are actually useful on the job. Second, it can be difficult to establish acceptable standards for work sample tests. Companies should conduct a thorough job analysis to determine the level of competence required on the job before subjecting applicants to a test.

Assessment Centers. Assessment centers were originally designed by the U.S. Office of Strategic Services and the British War Office during World War II to assess candidates for high-stress assignments. Because of their cost, assessment centers are typically used to predict managerial performance rather than line-level employee success.

The idea behind assessment centers is to place applicants in a series of real-life situations in which they make decisions and take action. Typically, observers watch the performance of each candidate and make subjective evaluations of their performance. In most cases, the assessment center approach takes between one to two-and-a-half days to conduct. This is part of the reason for the high cost. Applicants complete in-basket exercises (exercises that ask applicants to rank, order, and respond to items in a "to-do" file), work in leaderless groups, complete computer simulations, role play, attend problem-solving meetings that emphasize creativity and other leadership traits, and so on—much as they would do at work.

Three to five observers are usually required to implement an effective assessment center. These observers take notes on the performance of each person. After the participants finish, the observers meet and compare their notes. Many times, observers work as a group to rank attributes they observe in each candidate.

Each term, the School of Hotel Administration at Cornell University puts a group of graduate students through the assessment center approach to identify both good and bad qualities in these future managers. Students find the method effective—even if they do not perform well—because they each receive individualized feedback. Even if a student is not chosen for a particular management assignment, the evaluation process itself provides helpful goals to work toward. Once again, job-relatedness and validity are important issues to consider when using assessment centers to evaluate applicants.

Reference Checks and Recommendations

Reference checks and recommendations are integral parts of the selection process.

Organizations collect and verify information for numerous reasons. For example, some sources claim that over 50 percent of U.S. hiring managers have caught applicants lying on their résumés.[7] Many of these fabrications involve applicants embellishing their skills or work experiences. Clearly, the onus is on the employer to perform due diligence when it comes to verifying job candidates' credentials.

References can be personal or professional. Although many companies still collect personal references, some see it as a waste of time. These companies feel that because little is known about the references, information from them would likely be of minimal value. However, professional and educational references are a different story. Professional references relate directly to the applicant's work history. Although most of these references report only employment dates and position responsibilities, this information is often valuable in creating a profile of the applicant.

Background Checks. In the wake of the 9/11 terror attacks and negative publicity surrounding what seems like a never-ending variety of corporate and political scandals, background checks of job applicants have become commonplace as employers attempt to avoid a range of issues from workplace attacks to employee theft.

Failure to conduct a thorough background check can leave an employer open to litigation for **negligent hiring**—commonly defined as an employer's failure to exercise reasonable care in the selection of its employees. Although the pain and suffering of victims of negligent hiring would be the foremost concern, the risks for employers to be sued for not taking reasonable precautions to protect guests from the actions of employees are very real. Restaurant delivery companies have been sued, for example, for criminal acts committed by delivery drivers. Hotels have been successfully sued for actions taken against guests by maintenance and other employees with access to guestrooms and other secluded settings. Such cases can be very costly.

Typical checks include criminal background records, previous employment, educational degrees/credentials, Social Security verification, and driving records for work involving driving. Additional checks may be included depending on the job in question. According to the Society for Human Resource Management, nine out of 10 employers run criminal background checks as a component of the selection process.[8] An employer's consideration of an applicant's criminal record is allowed under federal law so long as an individual assessment is made based on the nature of the job being sought, the type of offense committed/repeat offender status, and the time since the conviction(s). There is recent evidence that more employers are letting applicants explain conviction records, and fewer employers are asking about criminal history at the application stage.[9] Some states have also passed laws that restrict employers from asking applicants about criminal records on initial application forms instead of delaying this line of questioning until later in the selection process.

Exhibit 3.1 shows an example of a sample release form for reference checks.

Regardless of these problems, companies should ask applicants to sign waivers that grant permission to contact references, check court records, and verify educational

LEGAL ALERT!

When asked to provide verification of a past employee's work record, many employers are reluctant to report on an employee's past performance for fear of someday ending up in court with that person. There is nothing inherently unlawful about honestly responding to a reference request, but employers must remain mindful of potential liability for defamation, blacklisting, and violation of privacy. Many employers refuse to provide information such as reasons for termination out of concern for these risks.

Some suggest that the safest route to take is to report information only on dates of employment, job title, absentee record, promotions, and demotions, and stated reasons for termination—and only if the express written permission from the former employee is on file. Unfortunately, even such factual information can lead to unforeseen legal entanglement.[10]

Exhibit 3.1 | Sample Employment Reference Release

Employer Tip Sheet

I acknowledge that I have been informed that it is [Your Business's] general policy to disclose in response to a prospective employer's request only the following information about current or former employees: (1) the dates of employment, (2) descriptions of the jobs performed, and (3) salary or wage rates.

By signing this release, I am voluntarily requesting that [Your Business] depart from this general policy in responding to reference requests from any prospective employer that may be considering me for employment. I authorize employment-related information that [Your Business], in its sole discretion and judgment, may determine is appropriate to disclose, including any personal comments, evaluations, or assessments that [Your Business] may have about my performance or behavior as an employee.

In exchange for [Your Business's] agreement to depart from its general policy and to disclose additional employment-related information pursuant to my request, I agree to release and discharge [Your Business] and [Your Business's] successors, employees, officers, and directors for all claims, liabilities, and causes of action, known or unknown, fixed or contingent, that arise from or that are in any manner connected to [Your Business's] disclosure of employment-related information to prospective employers. This release includes, but is not limited to, claims of defamation, libel, slander, negligence, or interference with contract or profession. I acknowledge that I have carefully read and fully understand the provisions of this release. I further acknowledge that I was given the opportunity to consult with an attorney or any other individual of my choosing before signing this release and that I have decided to sign this release voluntarily and without coercion or duress by any person.

This release sets forth the entire agreement between [Your Business] and me, and I acknowledge that I have not relied upon any representation or statement, written or oral, not set forth in this document.

Signed: _____ Date: _____
(Employee)

Reference Check Control Form

Applicant Name: _____ Position: _____

Personal references checked:

Name: _____ Relationship: _____

Address: _____

Telephone: _____ Date Contacted: _____ Method of Contact: _____

Notes: _____

Name: _____ Relationship: _____

Address: _____

Telephone: _____ Date Contacted: _____ Method of Contact: _____

Notes: _____

(continued)

Exhibit 3.1 Sample Employment Reference Release *(continued)*

Employment references checked:

Name: _____ Employer: _____

Relationship: _____ Dates of employment: _____

_____ Pay: _____

Address: _____

Telephone: _____ Date Contacted: ____ Method of Contact: _____

Would you rehire: _____ Reason for termination: _____

Notes: _____

Name: _____ Employer: _____

Relationship: _____ Dates of employment: _____

_____ Pay: _____

Address: _____

Telephone: _____ Date Contacted: ____ Method of Contact: _____

Would you rehire: _____ Reason for termination: _____

Notes: _____

Records Checked:

School records (date requested: _____) Notes: _____

Criminal records (date requested: _____) Notes: _____

Driving records (date requested: _____) Notes: _____

Credit records (date requested: _____) Notes: _____

Source: http://client.lycos.com/cch/tools/rfrncrel.rtf.

histories and other credentials. These waivers should include a statement about releasing all involved from any liability. Although they may not be lawsuit-proof, such waivers can be helpful and are often included as a final paragraph on employment applications. Yet again, it is essential that employers be aware of the state laws in the locations they do business as some states have passed laws to help protect employers who disclose information about a former employee in good faith. These laws usually detail what is considered protected information.

Credit Reference Checks. Many companies have historically used **credit reference checks** to evaluate the character of job applicants. However, several states have recently passed laws restricting the use of credit reports in employment selection, and federal law otherwise holds that any selection "test" such as credit checking be relevant to the position being applied for—effectively restricting credit checks to jobs directly involving cash handling or having authority over spending significant sums of money. According to the Society for Human Resource Management, before using credit histories in the employment selection process, employers should be able to show the business necessity and job relevancy of credit history information and follow appropriate Fair Credit Reporting Act (and any state) notice and documentation requirements (i.e., the subject of the credit check must be notified, given a copy of the credit reference report, and allowed a chance to correct any discrepancies).[11] When performing credit checks is deemed appropriate, a detailed policy should be adopted.

Third-Party Reference Checks. Some companies use outside agencies to check applicant references. Most reference checks can be completed within 24 hours for a reasonable sum. Although many hotel managers view reference checking as a necessary evil, such work is the principal function of these agencies, which conduct reference checks with professional expertise.

Social Media Profile Checks. According to a recent survey of HR professionals, 84 percent use social media for recruiting, and 43 percent screen applicants' social media profiles.[12] Recruiters use social media in several ways to vet candidates. Depending on the position (e.g., marketing or public relations jobs), it may be appropriate for an employer to seek out writing samples and/or the social media presence of a candidate. Reviewing a candidate's LinkedIn profile might allow an employer to view comments and endorsements offered by current and past coworkers or clients.

The risks associated with online vetting of candidates include discovering information unrelated to the job, which, if used to reject a candidate, would be illegal. To shield against any potential discrimination charges, employers who choose to use social media and online searching to screen candidates should document the timing of the screen (later in the hiring process is typically less risky), the specific job-related information sought and considered, as well as the sites viewed (e.g., Facebook, YouTube, Instagram, Tumblr, Pinterest) and how the employment-related information obtained influenced hiring decisions.

Personal Interviews. The most infrequently used method of collecting information about an applicant is personal interviews with an applicant's references. Although some government agencies use this method extensively, the time and cost of such an approach prevent many private sector employers from using this method except in important or unusual circumstances.

The Right to Privacy

Throughout a reference check process, employers should maintain a genuine concern for the applicant's privacy. In fact, a number of states have buttressed this concern by attempting to protect an employee's or potential employee's right to privacy. As a general rule, employers should review the appropriate state legislation regarding privacy before undertaking any action.

Employers should always obtain permission from former employees before releasing any information about them. The best rule of thumb is to secure written permission from individuals for the release of specific information and to limit responses to those areas for which permission has been granted. Individuals have gained the right to know what is contained in their personnel files maintained by the federal government (Privacy Act of 1974), as well as the nature and substance of their credit reports (Fair Credit Reporting Act). In addition, students may inspect their education records, and universities are prohibited from disclosing information about students without their written consent. As a result, postsecondary institutions release student information (grades, etc.) only to the student unless the student instructs them otherwise in writing.

Trends clearly point toward more open disclosure laws. In the near future, it is likely that employees will have the right to inspect any files kept on them by employers in the private sector and will be able to respond to negative or derogatory information contained in them. Many states already have statutes to this effect. If the private sector becomes subject to legislation similar to current federal laws, employers will be prohibited from collecting any information that is not directly related to job performance.

1. Is "What is your date of birth?" an acceptable question to ask applicants? If not, how should you determine whether an applicant meets the age requirement?

2. Is "Have you ever been arrested?" an acceptable question to ask applicants? If not, how should you determine whether an applicant has been convicted of a felony?

3. What is an example of a work sample test in the hospitality industry?

3.3 JOB INTERVIEWS

The overall goal of an employment interview is to attract, select, and retain a highly competent employees. Attraction is achieved when the organization creates or enhances a positive image of the company. Selection is carried out when the company predicts who is and who is not likely to succeed in a job. Retention is enhanced when a company projects an accurate first impression of the position, including a clear description of job objectives and responsibilities.

Although employment interviews are the most common method of evaluating applicants—and for predicting success—there is also reason to believe that they are the most unreliable. Several problems are associated with interviews, the most notable of which is lack of **inter-rater reliability**. What this means is that if two people interviewed the same candidate, they would probably not reach the same conclusions. Both might agree on general issues, on overall assessments such as "outstanding" or "poor," and on factual issues such as past performance, but they probably would not agree on more subjective issues such as the likelihood of job success.

Not all experts agree on this appraisal of employment interviews. Some researchers believe that the reliability of the interviewing process has increased significantly now that managers are more aware of and educated about how to interview properly and effectively. In addition, some contend that if companies use well-developed interview questions that predict work performance, interviews can identify the right employees.

Preparing for Job Interviews

The collection of information during an interview can be enhanced substantially by following a few simple rules. The four basic rules are:

1. *Do your homework before meeting with applicants.* Nothing is more distracting than reading from a candidate's résumé during an interview. Lack of knowledge about the candidate sends signals that you either did not care enough to prepare or that you are unorganized.

2. *Establish the appropriate setting.* Generally, interviewers should block out whatever time is needed to conduct the interview and create an environment in which the focus is solely on the candidate and the interview. Interruptions (phone calls, walk-ins) are distracting and inappropriate during an interview.

3. *Establish rapport.* By putting the candidate at ease, the interviewer will learn more during the process.

4. *Know the job.* Interviewers should conduct a thorough review of the job analysis before an interview. Many might argue that this rule is the most important because it is impossible to find the right candidate unless the interviewer understands the requirements of the job.

Interview process. Job interviews have three basic parts: the pre-interview, the interview itself, and the post-interview. Prior to job interviews, managers and interviewers should review the job description, clarify the performance expectations, examine the list of desired competencies, and review candidates, résumés, and applications. During the job interview, interviewers ask questions to measure the suitability of the candidates for the position and their ability to perform the essential job functions. At this time, they take notes about the candidate's responses. Interviewers should also pay attention to the non-verbal communication of the candidates (e.g., sitting up straight, etc.). After the interview, interviewers should follow up with candidates about the hiring decision. Many job seekers complain about lack of communication from recruiters and interviewers. Companies should ensure timely communication with job candidates, even if they are not hired, because it is the right thing to do—and because candidates are potential customers.

Types of Interviews

Interviews fall into three categories: unstructured interviews, semi-structured interviews, and structured interviews. These types are also known as non-directive, mixed, and patterned interviews, respectively.

Unstructured Interviews. In an **unstructured interview**, questions are not planned in advance. Instead, the interviewer directs the interview down whatever path seems appropriate at the time. By doing so, the interviewer achieves little similarity between interviews. This means that interviews with different candidates will likely cover different subjects.

Opinions vary on the value of unstructured interviews. Some experts believe that such interviews have little merit because of the low inter-rater reliability they achieve. These same experts believe that the unstructured method is most likely to skip over important job-related issues and to result in illegal questions. Other experts believe that skilled interviewers can use this method to achieve a better understanding of the candidate since areas can be explored that both structured and semi-structured approaches would miss. Proponents of both perspectives agree that training is essential for interviewers who use a non-directive approach.

Although question exists as to the validity of unstructured interviews, they are common. Sometimes, interviews are unstructured for the wrong reasons; managers who are poorly prepared often take an unstructured approach to interviews.

Semi-Structured Interviews. A **semi-structured interview** involves preparing or planning the issues to be explored but allowing for flexibility during the process. This structure has been called a *cone approach*—meaning that the interviewer prepares very *broad* questions that relate to *specific* important issues. For example, interviewers might explore a candidate's beliefs about the team approach to work performance versus the individual approach, or about performance on a recent job. Once these "cones" are introduced, the interviewer encourages the candidate to speak more freely about each topic. In this way, the semi-structured interview allows for elaboration as well as structured responses.

A feature of both unstructured and semi-structured interviews is the use of open-ended questions to elicit responses from candidates. For example, the question, "Did you enjoy your previous job?" requires only a yes or no response. The open-ended question, "What aspects of your previous job did you like best?" engages the interviewee and promotes a more comprehensive response.

Structured Interviews. In a **structured interview**, questions are prepared in advance and are asked in the same way and at the same time during the interview. Very little flexibility is allowed. Flexibility is reserved for a period of follow-up questions that an interviewer can ask if a candidate fails to fully address patterned questions.

Structured interviews result in answers that are comparable between candidates. As a result, some experts believe that structured interviews provide more reliable and valid information. On the other hand, this approach tends to produce information that is arguably narrower or shallower. Some experts believe that this type of interview is less worthwhile because an interviewer can fail to learn important strengths and weaknesses about a candidate.

Other Types of Interviews. Other types of interviews used in certain circumstances include **panel or board interviews** (also known as group interviews) and **stress interviews**. The first type requires a candidate to be interviewed by a panel or group of interviewers. Group members later compare notes to arrive at a group decision about the applicant. Stress interviews create a highly charged emotional setting in which a candidate is literally challenged by the interviewer. When using this approach, an interviewer might challenge an applicant's response to a seemingly standard question.

Chastisement, belittlement, and even contradiction on the part of the interviewer are common in stress interviews. This approach is useful only for simulating the type of stress applicants might face on the job, for it provides an example of how they may respond under pressure.

Types of Interview Questions

Three types of job interview questions exist:

- *Self-appraisal questions* evaluate job candidates themselves. These questions tend to focus on past work experiences, goals, education, and so on. Self-appraisal questions include "What are your long-term plans?" "What are your strengths and weaknesses?" "What do you hope to be doing five years from now?" "Why would you be effective in this job?"

- *Situational questions* measure how candidates might react to a hypothetical situation. Situational questions include "What would you do if your cook failed to show up on a Friday night?" or "What would you do if a guest complained that their room was not acceptable?"

- *Behavioral questions* ask candidates about their past behavior. Behavioral questions may be useful than other types of questions because individuals tend to behave in a similar way to how they behaved in the past. Behavioral questions include "Can you describe a time when you had difficulty achieving a goal or deadline?" Interviewers can follow up by asking, "Can you describe the goal, what obstacles were in your way, and how you overcame the obstacles?"

Interview questions should be designed in a way to identify candidates' behavioral patterns. Many job interviews are considered ineffective because interview questions are not properly designed. Interviewers and recruiters often ask questions to reveal candidates' attitudes and beliefs which hard to predict future behavior at work. In addition, job applicants try their best to provide the expected and desired responses. It is relatively easy for applicants to lie about what they believe and think but it is more difficult to come up with fake stories about their own experiences, which behavioral questions focus on.

Development of Job Interview Questions

There are three steps to developing proper interview questions:

1. *Identify the competencies desired and rank them in order of importance for successful job performance.* Organizations should use the essential job functions listed on job descriptions to identify the desired competencies.

2. *Define competencies.* For example, if a company is looking for an applicant who is a good communicator, good communication is the desired competency. Good communication is a vague concept. Companies should define the meaning of good communication. Does it mean verbally or in writing? Is the person expected to communicate within the organization and/or with those outside it? Will the person communicate with customers face-to-face? Defining the meaning of the competency provides a good starting point to develop interview questions.

3. *Develop interview questions to determine whether the candidate has the desired competencies.* For example, if a company is looking for a candidate who is motivated, motivation is the desired competency. The motivation can be redefined as "interest in this type of work," "works with a minimum of supervision," "willing to go beyond what's in the job description," and "interested in becoming better at what they are doing." Based on the definitions, possible questions are:

   - What are the three reasons you are considering leaving your present job?

   - If hired, what would you want to do in this job in six months? In one year?

   - What special assignments have you handled that were outside your regular responsibilities?

- What situations have you faced where additional responsibilities were thrust on you unexpectedly?
- What have you done to become more effective in your present job?

Approaches to Interviewing

As well as choosing the general structure of an interview, managers must decide on the tone they want to set for an interview. There are three common approaches to interviewing. Each might be best in different situations.

Direct Approach. In the *direct approach*, interviewers typically ask specific questions that require only yes or no responses. Although useful in situations where an exact response is required, this approach leaves little room for learning much about a candidate. Interviewees may also tend to use only rehearsed responses that they know interviewers want to hear.

Non-Direct Approach. With a *non-direct approach*, the interviewer encourages applicants to talk freely about their experience in former jobs, goals for the future, expectations at work, and so on. The objective is to gain more personal information about candidates. Open-ended questions are used exclusively.

Eclectic Approach. The *eclectic (or mixed) approach* emphasizes both yes/no and open-ended questions. Yes/no questions are used to learn specific background information, while open-ended questions are used to allow the candidate to expound on certain topics or areas of interest. The eclectic approach requires interviewers to have more skill than the direct approach since it relies on some open-ended questions. Conversely, less skill is required in the eclectic approach than in the non-direct approach because the latter uses only open-ended questions.

Contemporary Approaches. A note about technology developments and interviewing: to reduce travel and related expenses, it is not uncommon for employers to utilize live video technologies to conduct pre-screening/initial employment interviews. According to a survey of over 700 executives from a variety of industries conducted by Future-step (a company specializing in recruitment

Regardless of the interview method, interviewers must know what topics and questions to avoid. Table 3.1 lists sample lawful and unlawful pre-employment inquiries. Because laws and their interpretation vary from state to state, an attorney should review a property's application and interview procedures to ensure that discriminatory practices do not occur.

outsourcing), 50 percent of respondents indicated they use video interviewing as a way to shortlist their candidate pools.[13] Additionally, firms such as Big Interview provide tutorials and virtual interviewing practice software.

Given the contemporary prevalence of text messaging, it may be only a matter of time before this technology plays a larger role in the recruitment and selection process. Although there is evidence that employers and candidates use text messaging for general communication (in lieu of emailing and or telephones, which may not be best for communicating with candidates who are currently employed), at least one researcher has suggested that text interviewing may become the next big thing—or at least a supplement to telephone and/or live video interviewing. The rationale is that text interviewing provides advantages such as convenience (most everyone carries their smartphone 24/7), reduction in unconscious bias, lower costs, and the potential "cool factor" associated with what may be (at least for a time) a unique selection method.[14]

Making the Right Impression

Interviewers represent their companies. An interviewer is frequently an applicant's sole contact with a company. In this case, the interviewer represents the type of people who work for a company, their behavior, actions that are acceptable and not acceptable, and so on. As a result, a company should carefully choose an interviewer.

Two schools of thought exist on this subject. The first—and most obvious—suggests that because an interviewer establishes the image of success for a candidate, only the *best* representatives should be interviewers. However, the second school of thought suggests that interviewing can encourage employees to improve their performance. This theory suggests that, because interviewers are required to project a positive impression of the company, the interview process can prompt employees to rethink why they joined the company. Because interviewers often learn as much about the "outside" from applicants as they provide to applicants about the "inside," the comparison can help employees whose performance is mediocre to recognize the value of their jobs and improve their performance.

Establishing a realistic impression is another important role of interviews. Because interviews are the initial stage of orientation for applicants who are hired, it is critical to communicate what the job really entails. For example, telling an applicant that a front desk agent's position can lead to exciting opportunities to travel and see the world does *not* establish a realistic perspective of the job. Nor would telling applicants for a management trainee position that they would make important decisions about room rates, property locations, or other higher management issues.

We've examined several approaches to selection and interviewing in this chapter. Some companies may find that they can best identify successful employees by using a combination of skills tests and direct interviews. Others may find that combining paper-and-pencil tests with non-direct interviews works best. Regardless of which methods are used, managers must ensure that the methods they choose accurately predict which applicants will perform best on the job.

Human Errors During Interviews

Even well-trained interviewers can make biased hiring decisions because of the following common errors. Many of the errors can be prevented if interviewers use interview evaluation forms. An example is presented in Exhibit 3.2.

Similarity Error. Interviewers make **similarity errors** when they show preferential bias to candidates who are similar to them in terms of outside interests, personal background, and even appearance. In addition, interviewers are often negatively disposed to people who are different from them. Even similarities and dissimilarities that are not job-related can result in an interviewer's selective opinions about candidates.

Contrast Error. It is common to interview several candidates for the same position and to compare the candidates with one another, either consciously or subconsciously. However, candidates should be compared not to one another, but to the standards a company has established for successful candidates. Assume that two weak applicants are followed by an average candidate. Because of the contrast between candidates, the average applicant may incorrectly be viewed as excellent. This type of misevaluation is called a **contrast error**.

Overweighing Negative Information. Unfortunately, we are more likely to note negative rather than positive information. This means that when we examine a résumé or an application, we tend to look for the negative—not the positive. This also occurs in interviews; an interviewer is more likely to notice and remember the negative than the positive.

Race, Sex, and Age Bias. Because of the similarity error, in some cases, interviewers are more likely to be positive toward candidates who are the same race, sex, and age as themselves. This can reflect *unconscious bias.*

Making choices that are unconsciously rooted in bias is detrimental to individuals and the organization as a whole by creating a workplace lacking in diversity. Diversity brings together individuals who each contribute unique experiences and perspectives. This diversity within organizations fosters better problem-solving, innovation, and thoughtful strategic planning.[15]

Exhibit 3.2 Sample Employment Reference Release

APPLICANT RATING FORM

This form can be used to more effectively compare one applicant to another. It is important to capture your impressions of a candidate immediately after interviewing.

Candidate's Name _____ Date _____

Job Title _____ Rating _____

Selection Criteria	Below acceptable level					Acceptable	Good	Outstanding			Weighted score	
	10	20	30	40	50	60	70	80	90	100	weight	total
1. Physical appearance, neatness, grooming												
2. Salary needs												
3. Composure												
4. Dependability —Attendance												
—Work habits												
5. Communication ability												
6. Cooperation												
7. Responsibility and initiative												
8. Work experience —Experience with similar work												
—Knowledge of tools												
—Knowledge of procedures												

Total _____   Weighted Total _____

First Impression Error. Many interviewers form a strong first impression of a candidate that they maintain throughout the interview. This **first impression error** can be based on the candidate's first appearance and even on the information interviewers have about a candidate before they actually meet.

Halo Effect. Sometimes an interviewer's impression of a single positive dimension about a candidate—such as appearance, performance in a single task, or background—can substantially affect the interviewer's overall impression. The **halo effect** occurs when an interviewer views everything that a candidate says or does in a favorable light.

Devil's Horns. The opposite is true with **devil's horns**. A single negative trait or impression often causes interviewers to see everything a candidate says or does in an unfavorable light.

Faulty Listening and Memory. Interviewers do not always hear what is said in the way that it was intended, nor do they remember everything that was said. In fact, even immediately after an interview, the interviewer may have forgotten as much as 75 percent of what was said. This phenomenon is generally rooted in poor listening habits, failure to take notes during the interview, and preoccupation with what comes next. Taping an interview can reinforce memory but should be done only with the applicant's permission.

Recency Errors. Recency errors relate to the most recent actions of an applicant. An interviewer is likely to remember the most recent behavior or responses of an applicant rather than the behaviors or responses that occurred earlier in the interview. Recency can be a particular problem when interviewing a current employee for a different position within the company. Because interviewers often have personal knowledge of the applicant, they often remember certain behaviors the candidate displayed. Typically, the more recent the behavior, the more likely it will be remembered.

Interviewer Domination. Information should flow both ways in an interview. In some cases, the interviewer so dominates the process that applicants fail to collect the information they need to remain interested in a job.

Nonverbal Communication

Nearly 90 percent of communication is nonverbal. About 55 percent of messages are delivered through body language, 38 percent by voice, and 7 percent through words. It is therefore important that interviewers pay close attention to applicants' body language during interviews. If applicants like an interview question, they tend to show positive body language, which leads to a positive response. If applicants do not like an interview question, they tend to show negative body language, which leads to a negative response.

The trouble occurs when applicants show negative body language but a positive response. For example, say the interviewer asks: "We train our customer service reps to resolve all customer complaints on their own. How does this align with your previous experience?" The applicant may avert their eyes, look down and then out the window, and say "I've had lots of experience making those kinds of decisions." In this example,

the applicant showed negative body language but gave a positive response. When interviewers see such discrepancies, they should follow up in some way to determine whether the applicant is capable of performing the required tasks.[16]

Exhibit 3.3 shows typical interpretations of some common nonverbal messages.

Note: Remember that nonverbal communication can reflect cultural preferences; for example, lack of eye contact is considered a form of respect in some cultures.

Interviewing is the most common selection method and will likely remain popular because it is easy to do. So, it makes sense to attempt to improve the reliability of this process. The next few sections provide suggestions for improving the reliability of interviews by addressing how managers can prepare for, choose, and approach various types of interviews.

Knowledge Check

1. What are direct questions and why are they sometimes not helpful in job interviews?

2. Why are behavioral and situational questions asked during job interviews?

3. What are three nonverbal messages that applicants should and should not send during an interview?

3.4 SELECTION FROM THE APPLICANT'S VIEWPOINT

Managers should understand recruiting from the applicant's viewpoint for several reasons. First, an applicant's point of view can provide managers with information about how other recruiters function. Second, managers themselves have been—or may be—recruits at some point in time. Third, applicants can provide valuable information about competitors. Finally, this helps companies understand what potential employees want so the organization can attract and retain the best employees.

Exhibit 3.3 Common Interpretations of Nonverbal Communication Cues

What You Do and What It Says

Nonverbal Message	Typical Interpretation
Making direct eye contact	Friendly, sincere, self-confident, assertive
Avoiding eye contact	Cold, evasive, indifferent, insecure, passive, frightened, nervous, concealing something
Shaking head	Disagreeing, shocked, disbelieving
Patting on the back	Encouraging, congratulatory, consoling
Scratching the head	Bewildered, disbelieving
Smiling	Contented, understanding, encouraging
Biting the lip	Nervous, fearful, anxious
Tapping feet	Nervous
Folding arms	Angry, disapproving, disagreeing, defensive, aggressive
Raising eyebrows	Disbelieving, surprised
Narrowing eyebrows	Disagreeing, resentful, angry, disapproving
Wringing hands	Nervous, anxious, fearful
Leaning forward	Attentive, interested
Slouching in seat	Bored, relaxed
Sitting on edge of seat	Anxious, nervous, apprehensive
Shifting in seat	Restless, bored, nervous, apprehensive
Hunching over	Insecure, passive
Erect posture	Self-confident, assertive

Source: Diane Arthur, "The Importance of Body Language," *HR Focus* 72 (June 1995): 23.

What Recruiters Look For

For decades, researchers have been conducting studies of hospitality recruiters on college campuses to identify the factors that most influenced their choice of graduates. Not surprisingly, researchers discovered that recruiters were influenced the most by personal factors. Appearance, first impressions, and personality were all rated very high by recruiters.[17]

Rest assured: contemporary recruiters are interested in factors other than personality and appearance. More recent studies have indicated that recruiters on college campuses are interested in a candidate's leadership qualities, career preparedness, professionalism, relevant job experience, and how well the candidate's personality and values align with the organization's values and culture (sometimes referred to as organizational fit).[18]

Exploring applicants' social media profiles as well as using social media to attract talent is now common practice among recruiters.[19] Recruiters also scan the Internet for information about applicants' lives. That freely shared video of an applicant tapping a keg with a bunch of friends may have created the right image for a college student, but not for a job applicant. Applicants who are worried that their activities posted online will come back to haunt them have some choices. First, they can try to simply overwhelm the negative impression by posting a lot of new information that casts the applicant in a more favorable light. They can also attempt to delete information, but this is not easy because of the viral nature of the Internet. Applicants can also hire professionals to cleanse their Internet presence, with varying degrees of success.

Preparing for Job Interviews

Many candidates go to job interviews with little information about the company. More often than not, this is a mistake. For a first interview, it benefits a candidate to do some preliminary research. Candidates should find out basic facts about the company, recent developments within the company, the direction in which the company is headed, and how it is perceived by stock analysts.

The convenience of the Internet has allowed candidates to easily access a wide variety of company and industry information. Candidates can find the latest hospitality industry news on websites such as Hotel News Now. They can also follow a company via social media and go to a company's website for specific information.

As a candidate's list of companies narrows, the research should become more intensive. Resources such as LinkedIn allow candidates to access a specific recruiter or hiring manager's background, including professional affiliations, academic credentials, and schools attended.

Exhibit 3.4 gives interview preparation tips from the perspective of a job applicant.

What Questions Will Be Asked

Although their delivery may vary, recruiters and interviewers typically ask the same types of questions. These questions are geared to ensuring that the company and applicant fit well together.

The following lists some common questions posed by recruiters:

- Tell me about yourself.
- How did you hear about this position?
- Why do you want to work at this company?
- Why do you want this job?
- Why should we hire you?
- What can you bring to the company?
- What are your greatest strengths?
- What do you consider to be your weaknesses?
- What is your greatest professional achievement?
- Tell me about a challenge or conflict you've faced at work, and how you dealt with it.
- Tell me about a time you demonstrated leadership skills.
- What's a time you disagreed with a decision that was made at work?
- Tell me about a time you made a mistake.
- Tell me about a time you failed.
- Why are you leaving your current job?
- What other companies are you interviewing with?
- What makes you unique?
- What should I know that's not on your résumé?
- What would your first 30, 60, or 90 days look like in this role?
- What are your salary expectations?
- What do you think we could do better or differently?
- Why was there a gap in your employment?
- Can you explain why you changed career paths?
- What's your current salary?
- What do you like least about your job?
- What are you looking for in a new position?
- What type of work environment do you prefer?
- What's your management style?
- How would your boss and coworkers describe you?
- How do you deal with pressure or stressful situations?
- What do you like to do outside of work?
- What motivates you?
- What are your pet peeves?
- How do you like to be managed?
- Where do you see yourself in five years?
- How many tennis balls can you fit into a limousine?
- If you were an animal, which one would you want to be and why?
- Sell me this pen.
- Are you willing to relocate?
- What's your dream job?
- Is there anything else you'd like us to know?
- Do you have any questions for us?

What follows are 10 tips for job applicants before and during the interview:

1. *Do your homework.* Research the company beforehand so that you can showcase that knowledge during the interview. This will boost your credibility with the interviewer and will help you formulate intelligent questions to ask him or her.

2. *Know where you're going.* Make sure to find out where you are going and how to get there. Do you know how long the trip will take? Do you have the name and phone number of the person you'll be meeting with? Do you know how easy it is to park?

3. *Look the part.* Your clothing should be neat, pressed, and professional-looking. Since it can be difficult to know the culture of the office environment beforehand, err on the conservative side. Even if everyone is wearing jeans when you arrive, you are still probably better off having shown up in a suit. However, don't be afraid to inject some personality into your look, and don't neglect the details. Make sure to have a fresh haircut and clean, manicured nails.

4. *Rehearse beforehand.* Prior to your interview, prepare answers to common questions the interviewer is likely to ask, such as, "What are your strengths and weaknesses?" "Why do you want to work here?" "Why should we hire you?" and the ever-popular, "Tell me about yourself." To practice, go through a mock interview with a trusted friend.

5. *Secure your references.* Find at least three key people – former supervisors, colleagues, or instructors – who are willing to serve as your professional references. Be sure to secure their permission beforehand, and be certain that they will speak highly of you if contacted by a potential employer.

6. *Arrive early.* Be sure to arrive at least fifteen minutes before the interview. Visit the restroom and check your appearance in the mirror. Announce yourself to the receptionist to let him or her know that you have arrived and that you have an appointment. Turn your cell phone off so it doesn't ring during your meeting.

7. *Bring necessary documentation.* Make a checklist of documents that you will need for the interview, and make sure you have them in your briefcase before leaving home. These documents may include extra copies of your résumé, a passport, driver's license, Social Security card, and portfolio of writing samples or other professional work. If you are a recent graduate, you should also bring along your college transcripts.

8. *Sell yourself.* The interview is your chance to shine, so now is not the time to be humble. Develop a 25-second sales pitch that sings your praises. In the business world this is called an "elevator speech," a compelling overview of "Why you?" that can be recited in the time it takes to ride the elevator. It should include your strengths, your abilities, and what sets you uniquely apart from other applicants.

   ■ You should attempt to position yourself in the interviewer's mind as an individual with a particular set of skills and attributes. Remember that employers have problems that need to be solved by employees with particular skills.

9. *Don't neglect to ask questions.* Based on your earlier research of the company, ask how the responsibilities of the open position relate to the company's goals and plans for the future. Interviewers are often favorably impressed by candidates who show that they are knowledgeable about the organization.

10. *Follow up.* After the interview, don't forget to send a handwritten note or friendly e-mail thanking the interviewer for his or her time and consideration, as well as restating your interest and commitment to the position. If you don't hear anything after one week, call to politely inquire about when a final decision will be made.

Source: "Ten Tips for Preparing for a Job Interview," www.allbusiness.com/human-resources/careers-job-interview/11120-1.html (2010).

The hospitality industry is a unique field because it relies on a complex system of different businesses and employees and guests from different backgrounds. While this can present some challenges, it also creates opportunities to build a productive, creative, and innovative organization that caters to all guests. Making cultural diversity a priority and building it into the company culture can result in significant rewards. At a time when companies are emphasizing diversity, employee selection offers an opportunity to create a multicultural workforce. Remember, the "right employee" can sometimes be lost through interviewer bias.

How to Answer Interview Questions

Job applicants should think about how to answer anticipated questions and how to behave during job interviews. The following list will help candidates prepare for an interview:

- Candidates should speak clearly and enthusiastically about their job experiences and skills. They should be professional but unafraid to show their personality.

- Candidates should listen carefully. They will want to remember the information the interviewer provides about the job and will want to answer questions the interviewer asks.

- Candidates should be positive. Employers do not want to hear excuses or bad feelings about negative experiences. If the interviewer asks job candidates about a sudden job change or a weakness in their background, candidates should not become defensive. Instead, they should focus on the facts and what they learned from the experience.

- Candidates should pay attention to their nonverbal communication, looking the interviewer in the eye, sitting up straight with both feet on the floor, controlling nervous habits (e.g., cracking knuckles, drumming fingers, etc.), and smiling.

- Candidates should not be afraid of short pauses. They may need a few seconds to formulate answers to ques-

tions, or the interviewer may need time to phrase an appropriate question. It is not necessary to fill up every second with conversation.

One popular format used to answer behavioral interview questions is the STAR format, which stands for:

- Situation
- Task
- Action
- Result

The *situation* describes the context within which an applicant performed a job or faced a challenge at work. The *task* refers to responsibility in that situation. The *action* is about how the applicant completed the task or endeavored to meet the challenge. The *result* is the outcome or result generated by the action taken in the situation.

Applicants Are Doing Their Homework, Too

Applicants size up companies with which they interview just as the company sizes them up. Often, they look for reasons they might want to work for the company. These reasons are as varied as the applicants themselves. Because applicants increasingly turn to the Internet for information, it is important that hospitality companies not only have a presence on the Internet but that they monitor what people say about them online. Videos posted by both satisfied and disgruntled employees are easy to find. Because many applicants will look at this type of information, companies need to be on the alert for damaging information on the Internet and take steps to counteract it.

Knowledge Check

1. What does STAR stand for?

2. Why should companies encourage applicants to respond in the STAR format?

3. What can an applicant do to prepare for a job interview?

IN THIS CHAPTER, YOU LEARNED:

- Reliability and validity are important because selection methods and processes should produce the same outcomes regardless of applicants and should measure what they are supposed to measure.

- Companies can adopt many selection methods. Most companies use applicant blanks, reference checks, pre-employment tests, and job interviews.

- Applicant blanks are helpful in screening qualified candidates. However, applicant blanks do not show applicants' attitudes or behaviors, which can predict their work performance.

- Pre-employment tests must show test validity.

- Companies should be careful when they use social media to check candidates because it can lead to unintended discrimination.

- Open-ended questions engage interviewees and promote a more comprehensive response.

- Self-appraisal questions, situational questions, and behavioral questions are three variations of structured interview questions.

- Common interviewing errors include similarity errors, contrast errors, first impressions errors, and others.

- Interviewers can avoid common errors by using an interview evaluation form with response ratings.

- Interviewers should pay special attention to applicants' body language right after asking an interview question because applicants may show a discrepancy between their true feelings and their response.

- Interviewers should encourage applicants to respond to interview questions using the STAR response format because it encourages candidates to share information about their past work behavior.

KEY TERMS

application blank—A form used by companies to solicit information from prospective employees about their work experience, educational background, references, and other information.

assessment center—A selection tool that places applicants in simulated real-life situations where observers watch their performance to determine the extent to which the applicants would fit the company's needs.

content validity—A test to determine whether the selection measure used assesses the overall ability of an applicant to perform a job.

contrast error—An error in a performance appraisal or interview that results when a manager or interviewer consciously or subconsciously compares one employee or applicant to another.

credit reference check—A selection test that examines an applicant's credit history. Some experts feel that an applicant's credit history is a good predictor of job performance.

criterion-related validity—The degree to which the predictor relates to the criterion (such as job performance).

devil's horns—An impression based solely on one undesirable quality that an applicant may possess. Opposite of the halo effect.

first impression error—An error made by managers or interviewers who bases their entire opinion of an applicant on the first impression that person makes.

halo effect—An impression based solely on a single positive dimension of an applicant such as appearance or performance. Opposite of devil's horns.

honesty test—A type of test that measures attitudes toward honesty by posing hypothetical situations about which a potential employee makes a value judgment.

inter-rater reliability—The degree to which observations made by different interviewers about the same applicant agree.

negligent hiring—A practice commonly defined as an employer's failure to exercise reasonable care in the selection of its employees. Lawsuits over actions by employees are often based on an employer's failure to protect guests because of negligent hiring practices.

panel or board interview—Requires a candidate to be interviewed by a panel or group of interviewers. Group members later compare notes to arrive at a group decision about the applicant.

physical and motor ability test—Selection tests that subject applicants to physical exams. Only those physical and motor tests that measure specific job-related skills or abilities are acceptable under the American with Disabilities Act.

predictor—A measure used to predict performance on the job.

recency error—A type of error in a performance appraisal or interview that results when managers or interviewers base employee ratings primarily on the most recent events or behaviors.

reference check—An inquiry made by prospective employers of past employers to learn about and verify an applicant's work history.

reliability—The degree to which a selection method consistently produces the same results.

selection—The process of choosing the right person for a job out of a pool of recruited candidates.

semi-structured interview—An interview style that allows both planned and unplanned questions. Typically, the unplanned questions allow interviewers to ask more specific questions about broad issues raised by structured questions.

similarity error—A type of error in a performance appraisal or interview that results when a manager or interviewer is preferentially biased towards an applicant because of personal or professional similarities.

stress interview—An interviewing style that creates an emotionally charged setting in which the applicant is challenged by the interviewer to see how the applicant performs under stress.

structured interview—An interview style in which questions are totally prepared in advance and are asked of each applicant in the same order.

test validity—The degree to which a selection process really measures what it is supposed to measure.

unstructured interview—An interviewing style in which no questions are planned in advance. Instead, an interviewer directs the interview down whatever path seems appropriate at the time.

validity—The degree to which a selection process really measures what it is supposed to measure.

weighted application blank (WAB)—An application form in which points are accumulated for different types of work experience. Typically, weighted application blanks emphasize the most desirable qualifications of applicants.

work sample test—A selection test that measures a candidate's ability to perform the skills and tasks associated with a specific job. For example, an applicant for a chef position may be asked to prepare a meal.

REVIEW QUESTIONS

1. What is reliability and why is it important for employee selection?

2. What is validity and why is it important for employee selection?

3. Why should companies use multiple selection methods instead of one?

4. What are the three steps in interview question development?

5. Develop two behavioral and situational interview questions that measure customer service skills. Use the three steps to develop the questions.

6. How can applicants best prepare for an interview?

7. How can social media impact a candidate?

Turning Around the Turnaround

Ashcroft Hotels Inc., a mid-sized chain with an outstanding track record of turning around underperforming properties, recently acquired the Lincoln Hotel. The Lincoln posed a considerable challenge—even for the Ashcroft chain. The transition began with corporate executives deciding to replace the Lincoln's general manager with Martin Wood, the most experienced and successful manager of the chain's turnaround team. Martin would be responsible for assessing the current Lincoln staff and making changes to improve the property's performance.

The only restriction was that Martin had to replace the current food and beverage director with Theo Waters, a rising star at the corporate flagship hotel. Inez Camanno, Ashcroft's vice president of food and beverage, insisted that now was the time for Theo's big test.

Martin expressed concern. He felt that turning around the Lincoln posed enough of a challenge. He didn't need the additional burden of mentoring someone who never faced serious problems and had always had the resources available to help him succeed.

Inez understood Martin's concerns and took full responsibility for Theo's placement. "You'll see," Inez said. "Just turn him loose, and he'll turn it around." Unconvinced, Martin gave in to the demand but insisted that Theo be part of the management team at Lincoln. Inez readily agreed that Theo, like the other managers, would be accountable to Martin. Her last comment was, "I don't want to interfere with your responsibilities, Martin. I only want to give Theo a chance to shine at another property. I'll have HR send you a copy of his file this afternoon."

Theo was indeed a rising star at Ashcroft. He had bused tables and was a server in college while he earned his hospitality degree. After graduation, he entered Ashcroft as a management trainee at the flagship hotel. He was soon promoted to assistant restaurant manager. His first department head position was as room service manager.

Most recently, he was the fine dining restaurant manager. He learned the chain's standards and procedures at the finest and best-run hotel in the chain. Even in this environment, he helped fine-tune an already profitable, smoothly running operation into an even more profitable one. In addition, he was instrumental in launching the company's new award-winning fine dining concept, which the company planned to roll out to other properties, including the Lincoln.

The next week, Theo arrived at the Lincoln. At an hour-long meeting, Martin welcomed Theo as a member of the high-performance team that would turn the hotel around.

"Theo," Martin began, "it's important that we start things off right. Change is always difficult, but at underperforming hotels, like the Lincoln, change is often resisted, especially if managers and employees perceive changes as personal attacks."

"I understand," responded Theo. "Changing procedures at the flagship wasn't easy either. But once we let the staff know how serious we were, people straightened up and we moved ahead."

Martin paused and momentarily regretted giving in to Inez. "Yes, Theo. You did a fine job there. But we're not just changing procedures here—we're challenging and changing a whole culture of work."

"Sure. It's a bigger job. What are some of the immediate problems?" asked Theo.

Martin handed Theo a list of several areas that needed immediate attention:

- The restaurant is operating at a loss. Profitability must be restored as soon as possible.

- Inventory levels are too high, as are costs, but the staff complain of frequent stockouts of critical items.

- Food production is often of inconsistent quality and portion size, and food is late coming out of the kitchen for guests.

- Sanitation levels are often unacceptable in the kitchen and dining areas.

- Table linens sometimes come back from in-house laundry with stains still on them, and employee uniforms are dated and poorly maintained.

- Two ovens in the kitchen are not working properly, and most appliances are old and need maintenance, but complaints to engineering just pile up.

- ■ Guests often complain about poor service. The hotel's director of sales is reluctant to bring potential clients to the hotel's restaurant because of the service, which has embarrassed her in the past.

- ■ There are scheduling problems, especially (but not only) during high occupancy periods, when the restaurant is often understaffed.

Martin continued, "As you can see, there are problems with the management team as well as with line staff. I suspect that the director of sales and the rooms director understate forecasts so they can exceed them. This puts staffing in the restaurant at risk—you're always short-handed. I don't know what the deal is with engineering, but I'll find out."

"I'm sure I can tackle my area's problems right away," Theo offered.

Martin continued: "For the next 30 days, I'm going to focus on several critical areas of the hotel. But don't be the Lone Ranger, Theo. I'm here for support and advice, so don't hesitate to meet with me. This has to be a team effort."

Theo began by calling a restaurant department meeting, during which he made it clear that the level of performance that had been acceptable in the past would no longer be tolerated. "I intend to make this restaurant's service rival that of our flagship property," he announced.

He distributed a new procedures manual that he had helped revise in his previous position and insisted that everyone read it thoroughly and follow its contents. Theo pointed out, "There will be no more eating in production or service areas of this restaurant—that's why we have a break area."

Theo continued, "I'm bringing in a leading customer-service training program that guarantees to increase the restaurant's average check and total revenue. This program will also address the top 10 guest complaints and give the servers responses and tools that will help them satisfy unhappy guests." He banned the servers' current practice of pooling tips: "I don't believe that pooling tips encourages the kind of service we want at this restaurant," he declared.

A few days later, Theo unveiled a new work schedule with major changes on it in a deliberate attempt to upset underperformers. When some staff members complained, he responded, "There are a lot of restaurants in this town. If you don't like it here, a person has to do what a person has to do."

Over the next couple of weeks, Theo put out one fire after another. He disciplined the chef for allowing cooks to give servers food prepared by mistake. He found a group of servers still pooling tips and threatened to fire them. It seemed like every time he turned around, the staff was doing all it could to ignore his directives and undermine his authority.

One day, near the end of the month, things blew up. The restaurant was very busy because of high occupancy at the hotel. As Theo walked through the dining room, he heard a guest complain that his food was taking forever to arrive. Theo went to the kitchen and asked the chef what was causing the delay. The chef explained that he was not prepared for this business volume. "My cook was swamped and burned the first plate, which had to be redone."

Theo returned to the guest and, as he comped the meal, another guest at the next table complained that she had been sitting for several minutes and no one had even brought her water. Theo rushed to the kitchen and accused Hans, the table's server, of failing to take a guest's order within the time frame set out in the procedure manual. Hans lost his composure and let Theo have it. "I'm working a double station. How am I supposed to keep up according to your standards? Why don't you get off people's backs? We're working hard to cover up for your stupid new schedule. What do you expect when we're always understaffed?"

Theo began helping servers get food out. In the dining room he noticed the director of sales leaving with a client. She called him over privately and said, "This is exactly the kind of service that always embarrasses me when I'm with clients." Theo snapped back, "If you didn't sandbag your occupancy projections, we could schedule staff appropriately and this wouldn't happen!" As Theo walked away, another server rushed up to him and said he couldn't get the cappuccino machine to work properly. After comping another meal, Theo struggled to control his emotions. "Engineering has known about the cappuccino problem for days. Why doesn't anything ever get done right?"

By the end of Theo's first month, despite increased customer counts, the restaurant's revenue performance had not improved. Moreover, Theo had alienated not only the restaurant staff, but also most of the hotel's management team. Even the controller, who had cautiously supported Theo, started to doubt him when she saw many comped checks and no increase in net revenue. Her willingness to cooperate with Theo was beginning to ebb.

Martin called Theo into his office for an end-of-month progress report.

DISCUSSION QUESTIONS

1. Do you agree with corporate's decision that Theo was an excellent candidate for this position? What about his background and experience would prepare him to succeed at the Lincoln? What about Theo's background and experience would hinder his ability to succeed at the Lincoln?

2. What did Theo do well in approaching his new assignment? Why did Theo's efforts to create change fail?

3. What could Martin have done to avoid the end-of-month situation? At the end-of-month meeting, what is Martin likely to say to Theo? How might Theo respond? What are the next steps Theo should take to turn his department around?

Case number: 3564C

The following industry experts helped generate and develop this case: Philip J. Bresson, Director of Human Resources, Renaissance New York Hotel, New York, New York; and Jerry Fay, Human Resources Director, ARAMARK Corporation, Atlanta, Georgia.

ENDNOTES

1. Peter Drucker, "Getting Things Done: How to Make People Decisions," *Harvard Business Review* 63 (July–August 1995): 22.

2. Gemma S. Milligan, Tara J. Reilly, Bruno D. Zumbo, and Michael J. Tipton, "Validity and reliability of physical employment standards," *Applied Physiology, Nutrition, and Metabolism.* 41 no. 6 (2016): S83-S91.

3. Whitney Martin, "The Problem with Using Personality Tests for Hiring," last modified August 27, 2014, https://hbr.org/2014/08/the-problem-with-using-personality-tests-for-hiring.

4. Society for Human Resource Management, "Screening by Means of Pre-employment Testing," last modified September 10, 2018, https://www.shrm.org/resourcesandtools/tools-and-samples/toolkits/pages/screeningbymeansofpreemploymenttesting.aspx.

5. Tomas Chamorro-Premuzic, "Ace the Assessment," last modified July-August 2015, https://hbr.org/2015/07/ace-the-assessment.

6. Cynthia Fisher, Lyle D. Schoenfeldt, and James B. Shaw, *Human Resource Management* (Boston: Houghton Mifflin, 1990), 253.

7. Nicole Lyn Pesce, "These are the most outrageous lies people have put on their résumés," last modified August 30, 2019, https://www.marketwatch.com/story/these-are-the-most-hilarious-lies-people-have-put-on-their-resumes-2018-08-24.

8. Roy Maurer, "When Background Screens Turn Up Criminal Records," last modified May 5, 2014, https://www.shrm.org/ResourcesAndTools/hr-topics/risk-management/Pages/Background-Screens-Criminal-Records.aspx.

9. Roy Maurer, "More Employers Letting Candidates Explain Conviction Records," last modified May 15, 2015. https://www.shrm.org/ResourcesAndTools/hr-topics/talent-acquisition/Pages/Candidates-Explain-Conviction-Records.aspx.

10. Julia Levashina and Michael C. Campion, "Expected Practices in Background Checking: Review of the Human Resources Literature," *Employees Responsibility and Rights Journal* 21, no. 3 (2007): 231–249.

11. Society for Human Resource Management, "Can we run credit reports and use them as part of our employee selection process?" last modified August 17, 2016, https://www.shrm.org/resourcesandtools/tools-and-samples/hr-qa/pages/creditreports.aspx.

12. Society for Human Resource Management, "SHRM Survey Findings: Using Social Media for Talent Acquisition–Recruitment and Screening" last modified January 7, 2016, https://www.shrm.org/hr-today/trends-and-forecasting/research-and-surveys/Documents/SHRM-Social-Media-Recruiting-Screening-2015.pdf.

13. BusinessWire, "Futurestep Executive Survey: Video Interviewing Becomes a Mainstay," last modified July 15, 2015, https://www.businesswire.com/news/home/20150715005532/en/Futurestep-Executive-Survey-Video-Interviewing-Mainstay-Companies.

14. John Sullivan, "Text-Interviewing: The Next Big Thing In Recruiting," last modified September 12, 2016, www.eremedia.com/ere/text-interviewing-the-next-big-thing-in-recruiting.

15. Becca Carnahan and Christopher Moore, "Unconscious Bias in Recruiting," *Harvard Business School*, https://www.hbs.edu/recruiting/blog/post/actively-addressing-unconscious-bias-in-recruiting.

16. Deanne Rosenberg, Hiring the Best Person for Every Job, (New York: Pfeiffer, 2002).

17. L. Kwok, C. Adams, and M. Price, "Factors Influencing Hospitality Recruiters' Hiring Decisions in College Recruiting," *Journal of Human Resources in Hospitality & Tourism* 10 (2011): 372–399.

18. L. Kwok, C. Adams, and D. Feng. "A comparison of graduating seniors who receive job offers and those who do not according to hospitality recruiters' selection criteria," *International Journal of Hospitality Management* 31 (2012): 500–510.

19. K. Morrison, "Social Media Survey: 92% of Recruiters Use Social Media to Find High-Quality Candidates" last modified September 22, 2015, www.adweek.com/socialtimes/survey-96-of-recruiters-use-social-media-to-find-high-quality-candidates/627040.

4

ORIENTATION, SOCIALIZATION, AND CULTURE

Chapter 4 Outline

Learning Objectives

1. Explain the purpose of an orientation program. (pp. 88–90)

2. Distinguish between a general property orientation and a specific job orientation. (pp. 91–92)

3. Identify approaches to orientation that managers should take, and others that they should avoid. (pp. 92–93)

4. Explain the purpose of a socialization and culture program and identify specific socialization strategies and approaches. (pp. 95–100)

5. Describe the importance of diversity, equity, and inclusion in an organization. (pp. 100–101)

KEY TERMS

Turnover

Orientation

Orientation kits

General property orientation

Specific job orientation

Values

Norms

Behaviors

Socialization

Organizational culture

Diversity

Equity

Inclusion

In Wonderland, Alice turned to the Cheshire Cat for direction.

"Would you tell me, please, which way I ought to walk from here?"

"That depends a good deal on where you want to get to," said the Cat.

"I don't much care where—" said Alice.

"Then it doesn't matter which way you go," said the Cat.

"—so long as I get somewhere," Alice added as an explanation.

"Oh, you're sure to do that," said the Cat, "if you only walk long enough."

—Lewis Carroll, *Alice's Adventures in Wonderland*

Hospitality employee **turnover** is a well-documented problem. In fact, turnover in the U.S. hospitality industry is reported to be nearly double the average rate of other business sectors. It often averages as much as 200 to 300 percent each year. Statistically speaking, this means that the entire staff of a hospitality operation turns over two to three times per year! Fortunately, this rarely happens. Instead, the percentages reflect extremely high turnover rates for employees in their first 30 days.

Costs of such turnover can range between 100 and 200 percent of the total remuneration of an employee, depending on the level of job responsibilities. In addition to financial costs is the loss of consistency in service. Research has found that turnover rates must be controlled to improve service, to retain high levels of customer satisfaction, and to gain the economic benefits associated with increased competitiveness, which is driven in part by brand consistency and resulting loyalty.

More times than not, employees who resign within 30 days of being hired just got off to a poor start. For many, the stress of starting a new job is simply too great. On the first day of a new job, employees face new surroundings, rules, responsibilities, bosses, and coworkers. At best, this combination may make an employee feel insecure; at worst, it may provoke anxiety that compels the employee to resign. In such cases, the time and money spent by the company to recruit, select, and hire that employee is lost. **Orientation** provides companies with an opportunity to welcome new employees into the organization, allowing new hires to feel comfortable about their job and work environment. Orientation is well worth the time and money spent in the hospitality industry, yet often it is a neglected function. Orientation is tied directly to decreasing turnover and increasing employee commitment, engagement, service quality, and productivity. Orientation also reduces the negative effects of any drastic change of environment and lifestyle and accelerates adaption to conditions that employees encounter on the new job. If done well, orientation can enable hospitality organizations to make a good initial impression about both the organization itself and the work environment.[1]

4.1 ORIENTATION PLANNING AND GOALS

It is critical that orientation programs are planned carefully, providing general organizational and job-specific information to employees, connecting them to the organization's culture and goals, and allowing them to become productive quickly in their jobs.

The information included in orientation programs falls into three general categories:

- Information about job-related issues such as company standards, management expectations of employees, and policies and procedures.

- Information about management philosophies such as acceptable conduct, definitions of acceptable and unacceptable behavior, traditions, and strategic beliefs.

- Information about specific job responsibilities and technical aspects of the job, such as what is contained in the job description, what kind of equipment is required to perform the job, and how performance is evaluated.

Orientation programs are designed to reduce the stress that employees feel when beginning a new job. However, many orientation programs compress huge amounts of information about managerial philosophies, company history, policies, and procedures into a very brief period, leaving new employees feeling overwhelmed. Proper planning of an orientation program ensures that all pertinent topics are covered without duplication. Exhibit 4.1 lists key considerations in effective orientation planning.

Research has found that it is natural for new employees to want to engage in orientation activities such as information and feedback seeking, relationship building, and positive framing of new surroundings and circumstances. New employees naturally have many questions about their jobs and their new organization. It is up to hospitality companies to develop well-designed orientation programs that address the questions employees have about their roles. These questions must be answered quickly and effectively to get employees off to a good start. Exhibit 4.2 provides some common questions new employees might ask.

Knowledge Check

1. What are orientation programs designed to reduce?

2. What topics should be covered during an orientation program?

3. What are some ways to engage new employees at orientation?

4.2 ORIENTATION PROGRAMS

In theory, orientation provides new employees with the information they need to succeed in the company. But in practice, unless orientation programming and delivery are carefully managed, too much new information at one time increases the anxiety new employees experience. We know that new employees who receive quality orientation training tend to stay longer.[2] This is especially true when an orientation program stresses what is important to the newcomer, not what is important to the company. Inadequate orientation programs can be financially damaging to a company because they may reduce new employees' effectiveness for the first few weeks on the job and may contribute to job dissatisfaction and turnover.[3]

Well-organized managers prepare **orientation kits** that new employees can take home or access online after program attendance. Orientation kits enable employees to review material discussed during the day and share information with their families or

---

Exhibit 4.1	Key Considerations in Orientation Planning

- Program goals

- Range of topics to be considered

- Timing and duration of orientation sessions

- Company topics vs. departmental and job topics

- Identification of specific training to be conducted by the human resources (HR) department

- Technical vs. social aspects of orientation

- Methods for encouraging employee discussion sessions and feedback

- Training required for HR representatives before the orientation program

- Training required for managers and supervisors before the orientation program

- Checklist of topics to ensure follow-up by the HR department and managers

- Any necessary updates to the employee handbook

- Program flexibility to accommodate differences in employee education, intelligence, and work experience

Source: Adapted from Wayne F. Cascio, *Managing Human Resources: Productivity, Quality of Work Life, Profits* (New York: McGraw-Hill, 1989), p. 228.

Exhibit 4.2   Common Questions New Employees Might Ask

1. What are the duties of my job?

2. Where do I fit in the organization?

3. What are the limits to what I can and cannot do without getting permission?

4. What performance standards must I meet to succeed in the job and the organization?

5. Who will I work for?

6. How will I fit in with coworkers?

7. What general and specific benefits am I eligible for?

8. What positions can I advance to within the organization?

9. What type of training will I receive, both immediately and later, to help me prepare for this and future jobs within the organization?

10. What are my rights as an employee?

11. What is the organization's mission?

12. Why does the organization exist?

Source: Adapted from Raphael R. Kavanaugh and Jack D. Ninemeier, *Supervision in the Hospitality Industry*, 4th ed. (Lansing, Mich.: American Hotel & Lodging Educational Institute, 2007) pp. 127–130.

friends. Further, they enable new employees to reflect on the information and think about questions to ask the HR department or manager the following day. Exhibit 4.3 lists items commonly found in orientation kits.

Hospitality companies should consider including the following items in their orientation kits in addition to those listed in Exhibit 4.3:

- Copies of EEOC notices and company policies regarding compliance
- Recent company newsletters
- Names and telephone numbers of other employees in the department
- Contact information for an anonymous hotline to report harassment or illegal activities
- Schedule for the remaining portions of orientation and training
- Information regarding social activities of the department and/or company
- Current organization chart
- Projected organization chart (illustrating succession)
- Map of the facility
- Key terms unique to the industry, company, and job
- Copy of specific job goals and descriptions

Some properties divide orientation into two programs: *general property orientation* and *specific job orientation*.

LEGAL ALERT!

Many state and federal laws require employers to provide certain information and notices to new hires and to post various notices of employees' legal rights. Someone with knowledge of these requirements should review the orientation kit or packet contents to ensure compliance.

Exhibit 4.3	Items Commonly Found in Orientation Kits

- Employment and benefit enrollment forms to be completed
- Explanations of:

  - Hours of work
  - Meal and break periods
  - Attendance policy
  - Safety procedures
  - Uniform or dress code requirements
  - Personal appearance and grooming standards
  - Emergency procedures
  - Performance evaluations
  - Disciplinary rules and actions
  - Promotion policy
  - Harassment policy

  - Payroll procedures
  - Vacation, sick, and other leave policies
  - Holiday schedule
  - Group health insurance policy
  - Pension/savings plan
  - Important telephone numbers and when to use them
  - Available or required training programs
  - Employee assistance programs (if applicable)
  - Union policies (if applicable)

General Property Orientation

One of the first steps a property takes to orient new employees is to acquaint them with the organization and with the property as a whole. **General property orientation** covers topics such as the organization's mission statement and management philosophy, general policies and procedures, insurance and benefits, personnel forms, guest and employee relations, and the role employees play in meeting organizational goals.

At large properties, general property orientation is typically conducted by an HR representative. At smaller properties, the general manager usually presents the information.

As noted earlier, orientation plays a valuable role in reducing turnover, which saves organizations money. Exhibit 4.4 lists other benefits that employees and the organization can derive from general property orientation.

One researcher who has studied orientation measured the extent to which those employees who attended voluntary programs were more or less acculturated to the company. What he learned was that, even though the program was voluntary, employees attending the orientation were significantly more socialized on the goals, values, history, and people of the company. Those attending orientation programs also showed significantly higher levels of organizational commitment than non-attendees.[4] The results of such research have been reviewed and tested, and these findings have continually been supported over the past 15 years.

Specific Job Orientation

During **specific job orientation**, the focus shifts from organizational and departmental topics to those directly related to job performance. Employees are introduced to the responsibilities outlined in their job description, portions of the handbook relating to their job, the work environment and location of equipment, and their department's relationship to other departments. New employees are taken on a tour of the property and their department and are introduced to people with whom they will work and interact. The department's policies and procedures are discussed, including those related to work hours, time clock operation and payroll, breaks, smoking, employee dining, and so on. Managers and supervisors involved in a specific orientation program identify potential career tracks so

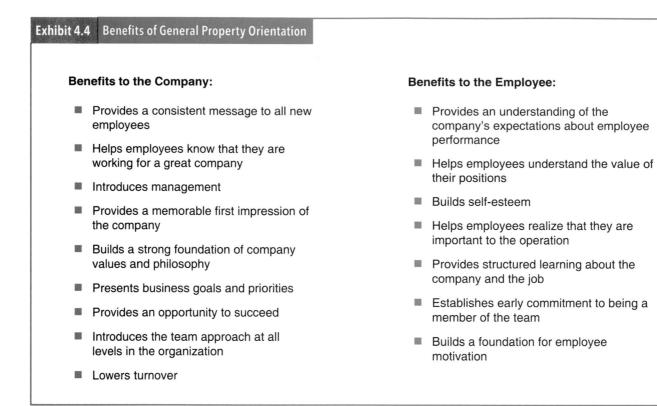

Exhibit 4.4 Benefits of General Property Orientation

Benefits to the Company:

- Provides a consistent message to all new employees

- Helps employees know that they are working for a great company

- Introduces management

- Provides a memorable first impression of the company

- Builds a strong foundation of company values and philosophy

- Presents business goals and priorities

- Provides an opportunity to succeed

- Introduces the team approach at all levels in the organization

- Lowers turnover

Benefits to the Employee:

- Provides an understanding of the company's expectations about employee performance

- Helps employees understand the value of their positions

- Builds self-esteem

- Helps employees realize that they are important to the operation

- Provides structured learning about the company and the job

- Establishes early commitment to being a member of the team

- Builds a foundation for employee motivation

Source: Raphael R. Kavanaugh and Jack D. Ninemeier, *Supervision in the Hospitality Industry*, 4th ed. (Lansing, Mich.: American Hotel & Lodging Educational Institute, 2007) p. 131.

that new employees understand their promotional opportunities and limits. Specific job orientation programs are designed to familiarize employees with their job responsibilities and work environment. Exhibit 4.5 outlines some additional benefits of specific job orientation.

Approaches to Take

The following orientation approaches help new employees start work in a positive way:

- *Welcome new employees.* Arranging a welcome party may be a good way to reinforce excitement in new hires.

- *Help employees develop positive impressions about the employer.* The supervisor's direct involvement, such as at lunch on the employees' first day, suggests to new hires that the employer cares.

- *Confirm the employees' decision to take the job.* Help employees see that they made the right choice about the job and the company.

- *Put new employees at ease.* Make them comfortable with the workplace and new colleagues.

Exhibit 4.6 lists 10 steps in an effective new-employee orientation.

Approaches to Avoid

Unfortunately, some managers do not take orientation programs seriously. Instead of seizing the opportunity to get new employees off to a good start, many managers simply delegate orientation to the closest available employee. Although it is important to include current employees in the process, managers may lose one of their best opportunities to directly influence new employee behavior if they put orientation solely in others' hands.

Managers should avoid the following five approaches to orientation:[5]

1. *Emphasis on paperwork.* When too much emphasis is placed on HR paperwork, employees may feel like they are not really part of the company.

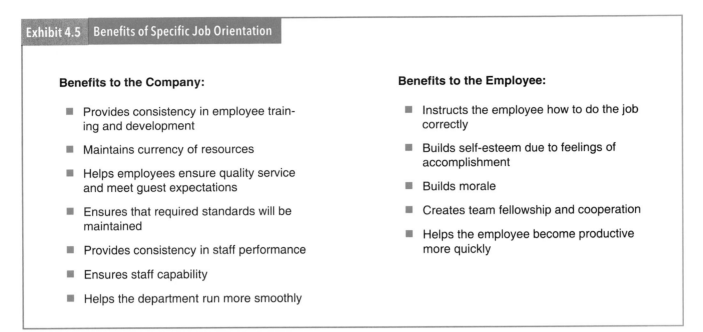

Exhibit 4.5   Benefits of Specific Job Orientation

Benefits to the Company:

- Provides consistency in employee training and development

- Maintains currency of resources

- Helps employees ensure quality service and meet guest expectations

- Ensures that required standards will be maintained

- Provides consistency in staff performance

- Ensures staff capability

- Helps the department run more smoothly

Benefits to the Employee:

- Instructs the employee how to do the job correctly

- Builds self-esteem due to feelings of accomplishment

- Builds morale

- Creates team fellowship and cooperation

- Helps the employee become productive more quickly

Source: Raphael R. Kavanaugh and Jack D. Ninemeier, *Supervision in the Hospitality Industry*, 4th ed. (Lansing, Mich.: American Hotel & Lodging Educational Institute, 2007) p. 133.

2. *Mickey Mouse approach.* When new employees are assigned easy jobs so they can "get the feel for the work," they may believe that they are not really considered capable or important. (This is so-called because of the laxity of the program; it does not refer to the Disney approach.)

3. *Sketchy overviews.* When new employees are given vague or incomplete information and then are tossed into jobs to sink or swim, they often sink.

4. *Suffocation.* When new employees are given too much information, they often feel overwhelmed.

5. *Unrealistic job previews.* Research has shown that employees who receive realistic job previews that communicate the real advantages and disadvantages of a position are much more likely to remain with a company.

We could add one more approach to this list that is particularly common in the hospitality industry. The "follow-Mary-around" approach turns the entire orientation over to an employee. Although it is a good idea for current employees to take new employees on tours and introduce them to coworkers, turning orientation over to an employee is not a good idea, because the new employee will learn both the good *and* bad habits of the employee conducting the orientation.

Rather than having a current employee be the sole source of orientation for a new hire, managers instead should ask an experienced employee to act as a role model when newcomers first arrive to affirm the identity and personal characteristics of the newcomers and show how the newcomers fit into the organization and its culture.

Orientation Follow-Up

Orientation should be followed by a period of close supervision. During this time, managers should observe and assist new employees in learning the new job. Managers can spend less time watching and helping new employees as their performance improves.

Orientation should have an end point. For example, new employees of an upscale hotel and resort chain are given an intensive orientation in the basics of the company's philosophy and culture and participate in a seven-part orientation program spread over 12 weeks. The program culminates with an overnight stay in the hotel, which allows newcomers to experience all aspects of service as a guest would.[6]

Exhibit 4.6 **10 Steps in an Effective New-Employee Orientation**

The following steps should be part of any successful orientation:

1. **Introduce the company.**

   The key is to make new employees feel good about the company, instilling pride in their being part of the organization.

2. **Review important policies and practice.**

   This includes such things as standards of conduct, performance standards, the introductory period of employment, the discipline policy, and safety.

3. **Review benefits and services.**

   Employees need to appreciate the cost of benefits. Also, discuss services that employees might not consider benefits, such as a credit union, parking, food, medical care, discounts, and social and recreational services.

4. **Complete necessary benefit enrollment forms.**

   Allow employees time to discuss plan options with a spouse or partner before making a commitment.

5. **Complete other employment documents.**

   Complete any other necessary employee documents that pertain to the particular job.

6. **Review employer expectations.**

   A performance appraisal form serves as a good topical outline for a discussion of employer expectations on teamwork, working relationships, attitude, and loyalty.

7. **Set employee expectations.**

   If employees meet the employer's expectations, what can they expect in return? Detail training and development, scheduled wage and salary reviews, security, recognition, working conditions, opportunity for advancement, educational assistance programs, counseling, grievance procedures, and other relevant expectations.

8. **Introduce the employees to fellow workers.**

   Using nametags and adopting a buddy system are helpful.

9. **Provide a standard tour of the facility.**

   It may be more effective to break the tour into several tours, starting with the immediate work area on the first day.

10. **Introduce the job.**

   Be prepared to have the new employee involved in the workflow.

Source: Ronald Smith, "Employee Orientation: 10 Steps to Success," *Personnel Journal* (December 1984), p. 48.

Managers may define an orientation end point by setting a date to meet with a new employee to answer questions. This meeting usually is scheduled a few days to a week after orientation and training begin. During this meeting, the manager can appraise the employee's progress and establish goals and objectives for the employee to meet before the first formal performance appraisal. Some companies also schedule one-, two-, and three-month reviews with employees for similar purposes. Others, like a popular hotel chain, have developed mentoring or "buddy" programs for new employees that provide continual close contact with experienced employees for the first few months on the job. Mentoring approaches to socialization are extremely effective during the first six months after hiring.

To determine whether newcomers are adequately oriented (or socialized) to their new surroundings, managers may want to give a short test. One technique involves taking a recent speech delivered by the CEO of the company and blocking out 10 to 12 key words in the text of the speech. New employees are then asked to insert each correct word. One researcher who studied this method found that employees who were adequately oriented and socialized were, in fact, able to supply each word correctly, while those who were not were unable to do so. Managers may want to replicate this type of test to make sure that the messages they intended to deliver during orientation and/or socialization have been completely mastered by new employees.

Knowledge Check

1. What type of information is included in an orientation kit?

2. What is the difference between general property orientation and specific job orientation?

3. What are some ways a manager can make new employees feel welcome?

4.3 SOCIALIZATION AND CULTURE

Orientation programs are important in part because they can help relieve the anxiety many new employees experience. However, simply orienting employees to their new environment is not enough. New employees also must be introduced to the **values**, **norms**, and **behaviors** consistent with success in the organization. This process is known as **socialization** or cultural orientation.

Socialization is an *ongoing* process of learning the culture of the organization and how to get along with others in it.[7] Although orientation typically occurs in a new employee's first week to month on the job, socialization takes much longer. Rushing new employees into their work without attending to the socialization process is not effective. Moreover, it makes employees feel unprepared, unsupported, overwhelmed, and less than appreciated.

Socialization of new employees can be difficult, in part because of their anxiety ("Will I be able to handle it?" "How will I get along with my boss?" "Where do I start?"). With these issues in mind, Texas Instruments conducted a classic experiment in which one group of new workers (the control group) was given the normal first-day orientation, consisting of a two-hour briefing by the personnel department on hours of work, insurance, parking, and the like. Then, as was customary, the new employees met a friendly but very busy supervisor, who provided further orientation and job instruction. A second (experimental) group received the same two-hour personnel department orientation followed by a six-hour anxiety reduction session. There, individuals were told that there would be no work the first day, and that they should relax, sit back, and use the time to get acquainted with the organization and each other and ask questions. The following points were emphasized during this phase:

(1) the high probability of success on the job, as evidenced by statistics disclosing that 99.6 percent of all new employees are successful;

(2) what new employees should expect in the way of hazing and unfounded rumors from older employees designed to intimidate them about their chances of success;

(3) encouragement of new employees to take the initiative in asking supervisors questions about their jobs; and

(4) information about the specific personality of the supervisor to whom they would be assigned.

This innovative orientation program had a remarkable impact: The experimental group exceeded the control group in terms of learning rate, units produced per hour, absentee rate, and tardiness. Although this research was conducted years ago, it clearly shows the beneficial effects of reducing the anxiety of new workers.[8]

As noted earlier, organizational socialization is the process by which newcomers come to understand and appreciate the values, abilities, expected behaviors, norms, and social knowledge essential for assuming an organizational role and for participating as an organizational member.[9] Although socialization to the company culture may take months, newcomers tend to experience and incorporate the more perceptible and concrete parts of the culture, like acceptable behavior or norms, immediately. Research indicates that new employees who are effectively socialized to the organization are more productive more quickly than those who are not. Researchers contend that socialized employees quickly learn the values that are critical to the organization and can integrate those values into their jobs.[10] For example, new employees who learn that service is a key value of their hotel are more likely to reflect that value in their work. In addition, employees who are effectively socialized are more productive for longer periods than employees who are not.

Successful socialization is related to important outcomes including job performance, and it has also been found to positively affect organizational commitment and retention. The impact of socialization on retention of new hires is particularly important because, as noted earlier, turnover is often highest in the first 30 days and can be particularly high in many hospitality organizations.

Recent research has suggested that relationships be considered at the forefront to retaining newcomers. By shifting the focus to relationships, researchers have provided a novel way of thinking about how socialization affects retention that is grounded in the fundamental human need to connect with others. Researchers suggest that this may help explain the link between socialization and turnover in a way that focusing on role clarity, task mastery, and information seeking has not.

In practice, hospitality organizations may need to explore how to provide common learning experiences with opportunities to interact with others even in situations where large numbers of new hires do not enter the organization simultaneously and in the face of increasing use of self-paced electronic orientation materials. One possibility that research has suggested is to take advantage of social networking technology to connect newcomers with others who may be at different stages of the socialization process or even at different locations.[11]

In short, proper orientation and socialization can help reduce unwanted turnover—especially turnover that occurs within an employee's first 30 days. Effective orientation and socialization programs can also help organizations in other ways. For instance, effective cultural socialization can contribute to reduced absenteeism and higher productivity. Finally, researchers have linked effective cultural socialization to other benefits, including profitability, employee performance, and loyalty.

Further, failing to develop and deliver good orientation and socialization programs can have an opposite effect. In a study conducted on socialization, newcomers reported on how many negative versus positive impressions they received. During the first day, negative impressions outweighed positive impressions 71 percent to 29 percent. Over the first week, 59 percent of the impressions newcomers received were negative, and over the first month, 54 percent were negative. After six months, newcomers reported that, overall, 56 percent of the impressions they received about the company and their coworkers were negative. When newcomers took orientation and socialization programs, on the other hand, the figures were reversed; nearly 70 percent reported positive impressions about the first month. These positive impressions still held true six months later.[12]

Stages in Socialization

The socialization process generally consists of four stages:

(1) welcoming activities;

(2) understanding the organization's culture, including its history, values, and purpose;

Making a chart that depicts how you use your time at both the start and the end of planning your life helps you discover better ways to socialize.

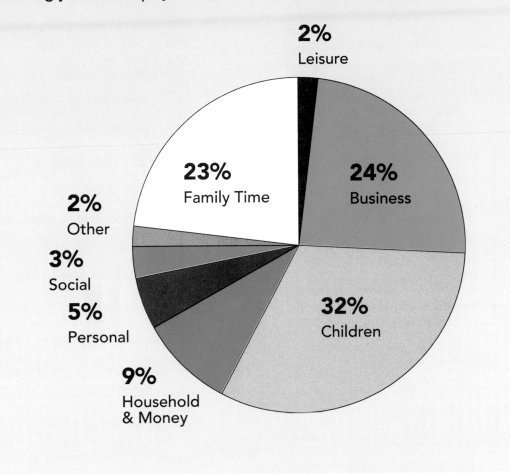

- 2% Leisure
- 24% Business
- 23% Family Time
- 2% Other
- 3% Social
- 5% Personal
- 9% Household & Money
- 32% Children

(3) implementation of a realistic onboarding program that addresses the stress new employees feel; and

(4) immediate connection to a person in a similar role or to a mentor.

Welcoming activities can help employees feel appreciated at work. Some organizations create welcome baskets for this purpose. The baskets may include items with the organization's logo and mission (such as T-shirts, coffee mugs, pens, and balloons); survival items (such as chocolate bars, coffee, and gift cards); or items, such as a bouquet of flowers, that are designed to say "We are glad you are here" and "You are now part of our team." It is also common for organizations to plan a welcome dinner or lunch for new employees.

New employees need to feel connected to the organization to act in accordance with the organization's purpose and mission. During the introduction to their new job and roles, it is important that new hires learn about the organization's history, values, and purpose. Thus, managers need to understand the critical cultural values of their organizations before beginning a socialization program.

Few managers or employees can simply describe the key values of their **organizational culture** to an outsider. Organizational cultures are usually complex and, for that reason, difficult to articulate. In addition, organizational members are generally too close to their cultures to easily identify the critical values, beliefs, and norms.

Many organizations hire culture consultants to help identify the critical values of their companies. This is the first step in teaching values to employees, with the hope that they will project these values on the job. Insiders find it difficult to be effective consultants because they cannot divorce themselves sufficiently from the culture to be objective. Sociologists might describe this phenomenon by suggesting that insiders are "too native to study the local customs."

Companies wishing to identify their organizational culture should follow these 10 rules to find an effective culture consultant:[13]

- *Rule 1:* Find a consultant who will treat your company as unique. Each company has a unique culture; that's what makes it different. Generic questionnaires do not help managers find out what is important in their company.

- *Rule 2:* Find a consultant who will not stereotype your company. This follows the advice in Rule #1: each company is different. Your company culture does not fit a mold (entrepreneurial, chauvinistic, or bureaucratic) of any kind.

- *Rule 3:* Hire a consultant who will admit that you—the manager or owner—cannot "control" your culture. You *can* facilitate, manage, and direct your culture, but you *cannot* control it.

- *Rule 4:* Find a consultant who believes that what your employees think and do is important. There is often a big difference between "the way things should be" and "the way things are" in a company. What you want to know is what your employees believe in and will work to support.

- *Rule 5:* Do not listen to someone who suggests that you either need to or can "get," "buy," "create," or "borrow" a culture. You already have a culture. You do not want someone else's. No amount of money can buy one.

- *Rule 6:* Hire someone who thinks that cultures are hard to learn about and

doesn't generalize. Certain things are easy to see about your culture. For instance, symbols, ceremonies, stories, rites, rituals, and norms are all part of a culture, but are not as important as the shared values, beliefs, and assumptions.

- *Rule 7:* Hire someone who refuses to label your culture as "weak," "strong," "good," or "bad." Cultures can be all these things at different times.

- *Rule 8:* Take a long-term view. There is no such thing as a quick fix for cultural ineffectiveness. Cultural change takes time, and it can be painful, both personally and for the corporation.

- *Rule 9:* Make sure you find a consultant who thinks of your culture as many-faceted. Companies generally have many subcultures, each playing a role in the whole.

- *Rule 10:* Find a consultant who will teach your managers how to manage your culture effectively. Managers should play three important cultural roles: assessor (find out what the culture stands for), spokesperson (spread the culture), and change agent or facilitator (effect cultural changes). Good consultants teach managers how to play these roles in the long term. Otherwise, you will have to hire a consultant to perform these tasks repeatedly.

Once the culture has been effectively identified, managers can develop a socialization program to teach these values to new employees.

It is critical in the socialization process to offer a realistic onboarding program designed to reduce new employee stress. Research suggests that hospitality organizations should develop socialization programs to strengthen interpersonal relationships and mutual understanding among employees in a work group. This enables newcomers to feel more open to discussing job-related matters at work. For example, a research-based program called ROPES (Realistic Orientation Programs for new Employee Stress) is designed to provide realistic information about the job to new employees and to encourage them to stay in their jobs.

It is important to let new employees know that they will likely encounter experiences that cause stress, but that this is normal. Crossing any organizational boundary, whether entering or leaving a job, causes stress. It is important that new employees know that feeling fear, frustration, disappointment, and even anger in their new positions is common and in fact is expected, and that these feelings will likely disappear. Giving new employees opportunities to discuss such issues with current employees can help reduce feelings of fear and anxiety that new employees might have.

Approaches to Socialization and Culture

There is no single best way to socialize employees. Managers must choose from a variety of socialization approaches and decide which are best for the company and its employees. Exhibit 4.7 lists the seven choices managers must make when designing socialization programs.

At first glance, these strategies might sound too academic or theoretical to actually work. However, the strategies listed in Exhibit 4.7 are currently used in many organizations. For example, organizations practice sequential socialization by training employees to perform many functions before allowing them to manage. Hospitality companies often use the sequential method. Similarly, most U.S. high schools "track" students by preparing them to enter either college or the work force immediately after high school. This is an example of a "tournament" socialization strategy; once students score poorly on an achievement test, they are tracked out of college prep courses. If it were a "contest" socialization strategy, all students would be allowed to try all courses. The Marine Corps, fraternities, and many elite schools practice divestiture to eliminate newcomers' unwanted or bad habits. Many companies divest newcomers of what they know so they begin with a "clean slate."

Different strategies work for different companies, depending on the organizational goals. If a company wants to produce a relatively high degree of similarity in the thoughts and actions of newcomers, then a combination of formal, serial, and divestiture strategies works best. If a company believes that dissimilarity is best, then informal,

---

Exhibit 4.7   Socialization Strategies

1. *Formal vs. Informal.* In formal strategies, newcomers are segregated from other organizational members. In informal strategies, newcomers are included with organizational members; much of the learning takes place in their natural environments.

2. *Individual vs. Collective.* Newcomers either go through socialization alone or as part of a group.

3. *Sequential vs. Non-sequential.* Newcomers either go through identifiably different stages or the process is one single transitional stage.

4. *Fixed vs. Variable.* Fixed strategies have specific timetables for certain types of training; variable strategies have no timetables.

5. *Tournament vs. Contest.* In tournaments, newcomers win to move on to next stage; in contests, newcomers are given multiple opportunities to succeed.

6. *Serial vs. Disjunctive.* Serial strategies involve current members teaching newcomers to "act as we act;" disjunctive strategies allow for new behaviors.

7. *Investiture vs. Divestiture.* In investiture, the process is one of "giving" information to newcomers; in divestiture, the process is one of taking old habits away.

Source: Adapted from John Van Maanen, "People Processing: Strategies of Organizational Socialization," *Organizing Dynamics* (Summer 1978): 240–259.

disjunctive, and investiture strategies may work well.[14] A hospitality company that wishes to teach newcomers to behave and perform like current employees within a specific time frame should choose a formal-sequential-fixed-serial combination. Companies that want employees to learn more on their own should choose an informal-variable strategy.

Research has shown that different approaches influence different socialization factors. For instance, the investiture-divestiture tactic has been found to have significant impact on self-change in individuals. On the other hand, fixed-variable tactics have a significant impact on whether newcomers attempt changes in the mechanics of their jobs early on.[15]

Who Should Socialize Newcomers?

Most managers would say that the best managers and employees should teach newcomers what is important in an organization because these employees best exemplify the behaviors that managers like. This may be true in many cases, but not in all cases. Socializing newcomers can also be done by marginal employees. In fact, research suggests that it may be better to have marginal employees socialize newcomers. Often, the performance of marginal employees improves at the same time new employees are socialized.[16] This happens because the underachievers must prepare for the job of socialization; and doing so sometimes helps reinvigorate their attitudes about the organization. Newcomers can also provide employees with positive views of the organization by comparing their new job to their past jobs. For instance, consider the effect of a newcomer who notes that the kitchen has much better lighting than the one he or she worked in before, or who says that he or she heard a lot of nice things about the people who work here, or who claims that the employee meals seem much better than at other companies. Such feedback helps refresh current employees' perspectives on their own jobs. Research also has indicated that newcomers socialized by teams are more likely to learn the ropes faster.

Years ago, Stanford professor Joanne Martin assessed the socialization of a large lot of new employees in one exercise. Each employee attended, en masse, the annual "how are we doing?" speech given by the president. That speech purportedly advises employees of the direction of the company for the next year. The speech was the first impression of the company as a whole for the new employees. Later the researcher asked each new employee to complete a form about what the president said. Even though the new employees did not understand a lot of the speech, they still understood what the company stood for and more or less where they were going. Some organizations today have forgotten this lesson.

Both orientation and socialization are becoming much harder. It is important to make ALL new and current employees feel welcome. Therefore, organizations work hard to identify ways in which their varied employees (varied by race, gender, age, life choices, family responsibilities, and so on) ALL have a path to learn and improve. One popular hotel chain has long called these the "Vital Few," translated to mean the few things an organization MUST do to allow employees to feel wanted.

Knowledge Checks

1. What is the difference between values and norms?

2. What are the four stages of the socialization process?

3. How can organizational culture affect a company?

4.4 DIVERSITY, EQUITY, AND INCLUSION

For Human Resource departments, diversity, equity, and inclusion (DEI) are no longer just a mandate for compulsory annual training. When DEI is a priority, it makes a difference throughout the organization.

Diversity reflects an organization in which a variety of social and cultural characteristics exist. It entails the presence of different types of people from a wide range of identities with different perspectives, experiences, etc.

Equity means everyone is given fair treatment, opportunities, and advancement. Not to be confused with equality, equity aims to identify and eliminate barriers that prevent the full participation of some groups. It also means removing any correlation between success or failure and social or cultural factors.

Inclusion suggests that employees feel a part of their team and the larger organization, no matter what their identity. Inclusion is actually diversity in action. It creates an environment of acceptance and respect and shows the impact of different ideas, experiences, and perspectives.

A study by McKinsey & Company and The Society for Human Resource Management (SHRM) evaluated the performance of organizations with different levels of workplace diversity. They found that organizations that exhibit gender and ethnic diversity are, respectively, 15% and 35% more likely to outperform less diverse organizations. Similarly, organizations with more gender and racial diversity bring in increased revenue, more customers, and higher profits.[17]

There are eight considerations when a company creates a DEI development plan:

1. Emphasize the need for DEI.

2. Emphasize that the DEI initiative is a core value rather than a peripheral task.

3. Be conscious of unconscious bias.

4. Practice empathetic leadership.

5. Create sponsorship programs.

6. Identify employees willing to serve as DEI sponsors.

7. Make DEI goals actionable and measurable.

8. Communicate expectations and hold leaders accountable for results.[18]

DEI in the Hospitality Industry

According to the Cornell SC Johnson College of Business, the American Hotel & Lodging Association Foundation (AHLA Foundation) announced a new $5 million, multi-year commitment and action plan to advance diversity, equity, and inclusion (DEI) in the hotel industry.

Over the next five years, the foundation will focus on three strategic priorities:

- driving DEI at the leadership level,

- driving DEI across all talent levels, and

- developing a DEI blueprint for the industry.

Some specific examples of DEI initiatives in hospitality come from two popular hotel chains:

"The foundation for diversity and inclusion is promoting 'UNITY and Family.' Through UNITY, we create an inclusive environment that supports the recruitment, retention, and advancement of all employees, and actively engages in efforts to develop a diverse and inclusive workforce, owner, guest and supplier base."

"Diversity is at the core of our Vision, Mission, and Values. We are committed to an inclusive workforce that fully represents many different cultures, backgrounds and viewpoints. Our global brands provide meeting places for people to connect, creating a welcoming environment for all."

Knowledge Checks

1. What are the differences between diversity, equity, and inclusion?

2. What are some of the considerations when implementing a DEI initiative?

3. What is the impact of DEI on organizations?

IN THIS CHAPTER, YOU LEARNED:

- Orientation provides new employees the information they need to succeed in a company.

- Orientation programs are designed to reduce the stress that employees feel when beginning a new job.

- Orientation kits enable employees to review material discussed during the day and to share information with their families or friends.

- General property orientation covers topics such as the company's mission statement, general policies, insurance and benefits, and company goals.

- During specific job orientation, employees are introduced to the responsibilities outlined in their job description.

- Orientation approaches include welcoming new employees, helping the employees develop positive impressions about the employer, confirming their decision to take the job, and putting them at ease.

- Orientation approaches to avoid include emphasizing paperwork, the Mickey Mouse approach, sketchy overviews, suffocation, and unrealistic job previews.

- Orientation should have an end point.

- New employees must be introduced to the values, norms, and behaviors consistent with success in the organization.

- The socialization process has four stages: (1) welcoming activities; (2) understanding the organization's culture, including its history, values, and purpose; (3) implementation of a realistic onboarding program that addresses the stress new employees feel; and (4) immediate connection to a person in a similar role or to a mentor.

- When DEI is a priority, it makes a difference throughout the organization. Organizations that exhibit gender and ethnic diversity are more likely to outperform less diverse organizations.

KEY TERMS

behaviors—The manner in which people conduct themselves; the responses of an individual or group to an action, stimulus, or environment.

diversity—Reflects an organization in which a variety of social and cultural characteristics exist.

equity—Everyone is given fair treatment, opportunities, and advancement.

general property orientation—A formal program presented by an employer to introduce the organization's mission and values to employees, which is usually conducted shortly after hiring.

inclusion—Suggests that employees feel a part of their team and the larger organization, no matter what their identity.

norm—A pattern or trait that is considered typical behavior of an individual or group.

organizational culture—The dominant culture or personality of the organization.

orientation—The process of introducing new employees to their work and the environment in which their work will be completed.

orientation kit—The package of information provided by employers to new employees during orientation to help them understand and get acquainted with the organization's policies, procedures, and facilities.

socialization—The process in which employees learn what is expected of them at work, which includes both written and unwritten rules of behavior.

specific job orientation—The process of introducing new employees to the specific tasks and behaviors of their job.

turnover—The rate at which employees leave a company or work unit.

values—A set of beliefs, often socially and culturally defined, that attempt to guide the behavior of an individual or group.

REVIEW QUESTIONS

1. What are the broad goals of an orientation program?

2. What are the three general categories of information provided in orientation?

3. How does general property orientation differ from specific job orientation?

4. What items should be included in an orientation kit?

5. What approaches to orientation should managers avoid?

6. How does orientation differ from socialization?

7. What is the purpose of socialization and what are its benefits?

8. What is organizational culture? Why is it important in designing socialization programs?

9. What are the 10 rules involved in hiring culture consultants?

10. Who should socialize newcomers? Why?

11. What is DEI?

Restaurant Balancing Act

Before opening his new restaurant, Bob Borich spent two weeks training his personnel. Although the money spent on employee salaries and other training costs added substantially to the pre-opening costs, Bob justified the expense by noting the large number of restaurants that failed in their first year because of inadequate service. Bob believed that in the long run, his training costs would be viewed as money well spent.

Six months after opening, Bob experienced a turnover of about 50 percent. As a result, he found himself hiring new employees weekly. Because Bob was busy with the operation of the restaurant—particularly since he had started cooking three shifts a week to ensure food quality—he turned orientation over to a group of employees who had been with him from the start. He reasoned that since these employees had been through the full training program and had displayed their loyalty, they would provide the type of orientation that he would—if he had the time.

Unfortunately, although the new employees seemed perfectly suited for their jobs, turnover increased dramatically. Within three months after starting the orientation program, Bob was experiencing turnover in excess of 100 percent annually. While this was still below the national average for his industry, Bob was dissatisfied with the high rate of turnover. Sitting down with a cup of coffee, Bob thought over his problems at the end of a particularly frustrating week.

DISCUSSION QUESTIONS

1. What advice would you give Bob?

2. How unique do you believe Bob's current situation is?

3. What parts of orientation should be turned over to employees to conduct?

ENDNOTES

1. Understanding and Developing Organizational Culture, SHRM toolkit, accessed online on February 27, 2021. https://www.shrm.org/resourcesandtools/tools-and-samples/toolkits/pages/understandinganddevelopingorganizationalculture.aspx.

2. Robert J. Taormina, "Organizational Socialization: The Missing Link Between Employee Needs and Organizational Culture," *Journal of Managerial Psychology* 24, no. 7 (2009): 650–676.

3. David G. Allen, "Do Organization Socialization Tactics Influence Newcomer Embededdness and Turnover?" *Journal of Management* 32, no. 2 (2006): 237–256.

4. Allen. ibid. 242.

5. Edgar H. Schein, "Organizational Socialization and the Profession of Management," *Sloan Management Review* (Fall 1988): 53–65. (A reprinted version of an article that originally appeared in the *Sloan Management Review* in 1968.)

6. Karen H. Tidball, "Creating a Culture that Builds Your Bottom Line," *Cornell Hotel and Restaurant Administration Quarterly* 29 (May 1988): 63–69; Richard D. Normann, *Service Management: Strategy and Leadership in Service Businesses* (New York: Wiley, 1984); Jay Barney, "Organizational Culture: Can It Be the Source of Sustained Competitive Advantage?" *Academy of Management Review* 11 (1986): 656–665.

7. Craig C. Lundberg and Cheri A. Young, "Newcomer Socialization: Critical Incidents in Hospitality Organizations," *Journal of Hospitality and Tourism Research* 21, no. 2 (1997): 58–74.

8. Sheryl Ann Larson, Amy S. Hewitt, (2005) *Staff Recruitment, Retention, & Training Strategies for Community Human Services Organizations*, Paul H. Brookes Publishing Company. P. 112.

9. Robert Hackett, (2015) "Five Great Reasons to Work for Four Seasons Hotels," *Fortune*, February 1, 2015.

10. The rules for choosing a culture consultant are adapted from Woods, "Ten Rules for Culture Consultants," *The Consultant (FCSI)* 23 (Summer 1990): 52–53.

11. Jen-Te Yang, "Facilitating or Inhibiting Newcomer Socialization Outcomes in International Hotels," *Tourism and Hospitality Research* 9, no. 4 (2009): 325–339.

12. Eleanor E. Maccoby (1961) "The Choice of Variables in the Study of Socialization," *Sociometry*, 13, 4, 357-371. www.jstor.org/stable/2785918.

13. Elizabeth Wolfe Morrison (2002) "Newcomer's Relationships: The Role of Social Network Ties During Socialization." *Academy of Management Journal* (November, 2002).

14. John Van Maanen, "People Processing: Strategies of Organizational Socialization," *Organizational Dynamics* (Summer 1978): 258.

15. J. Stewart Black and Susan J. Ashford, "Fitting In or Making Jobs Fit: Factors Affecting Mode of Adjustment for New Hires," *Human Relations* 48 (April 1995): 425.

16. Robert I. Sutton and Meryl Reis Louis, "How Selecting and Socializing Newcomers Influences Insiders," *Human Resource Management* 26 (Fall 1987): 347–361.

17. McKinsey & Co., May 2020 Study, https://www.shrm.org/hr-today/news/hr-magazine/fall2020/pages/a-new-approach-to-diversity-and-inclusion.aspx.

18. Ajay Kaul, "The Importance and Benefits of Bringing Diversity, Equity, and Inclusion (DEI) Initiatives into Your Workplace," https://staffinghub.com/.

5

TRAINING AND DEVELOPMENT

Chapter 5 Outline

Learning Objectives

1. Discuss training expenditures and explain the stages of the training cycle. (pp. 108–110)

2. Explain how a training needs assessment is developed and conducted. (pp. 110–115)

3. Discuss the first steps in designing a training program. (pp. 115–117)

4. Describe various training methods and how to select one. (pp. 117–122)

5. Explain how to implement and evaluate training programs and activities. (pp. 122–126)

6. Discuss career development for managers. (p. 126)

KEY TERMS

Training cycle

Training objective

Training criteria

Selection

Pretesting

Training evaluation

Needs assessment

Organizational analysis

Task and behavior analysis

KSA

Individual analysis

Advisory committee

Work sampling

Job performance measurement

Attitude survey

Performance document

Exit interview

Critical incidents

Case study

Control group

E-learning

Computer-based training

In-basket training

Conference training

Modeling

On-the-job training (OJT)

Job instruction training (JIT)

Off-the-job training

Programmed instruction

Job rotation

Role-playing

Vestibule training

Business games

Sensitivity training

Jobs are evolving at an increasingly rapid pace. In fact, it is estimated that over 50 percent of the jobs currently performed in the United States did not even exist half a century ago. Hospitality is not exempt from this evolution. If anything, the rate of job growth and change in the hospitality industry is among the most rapid in any field.

Consider how much guest registration has changed. Many hotels used manual check-in and check-out systems well into the 1980s. Today, most hotels offer automated check-in and check-out options, often through guests' phones. Hospitality employees must therefore develop skills to keep up with advancing technologies.

Other positions may actually become obsolete. How long will be it before all quick service restaurant operate without cooks? Back in 2013, a survey revealed that 8 percent of the population thought cooking in quick service restaurants would be automated soon.[1] A California burger chain with locations in countries around the world is already testing an automated workforce, using all driven, burger-flipping assistants.[2] Workers who lose their jobs to automation may wish to be trained to perform different jobs at the organization.

Employee recruitment and selection are crucial to an organization's success, but they do not guarantee that employees will perform well. Organizations must provide training for employees to transform their high potential into high performance. In the hospitality industry, service and quality determine the success or failure of a property. Not surprisingly, employees determine the level of service provided, and, thus, the quality of the guest experience. Therefore, well-considered, adequate training should be provided to ensure guest satisfaction and, ultimately, increase profits. Teaching managers and employees how to adjust to the new jobs they do is the primary focus of this chapter.

5.1 TRAINING EXPENDITURES TODAY

It is clear that 2020 was not a great year for the hospitality industry. More than 110,000 restaurants closed in 2020 due to the coronavirus pandemic.[3] Two large hotel chains tell the story of 2020: one reported a net loss of $225 million for the fourth quarter alone and $720 million for the year 2020 while another lost $164 million in the fourth quarter alone. In contrast, in the fourth quarter of 2019, the latter company earned $279 million—in other words, the difference between its profits in 2019 and its loss in 2020 was over $400 million.[4] At the end of 2020, STR reported that occupancy in U.S. hotels was 38.3 percent nationally, while occupancy was 66.1 percent in 2019 for the industry as a whole.[5] Obviously, the hotel industry has been hurt.

In addition, the average turnover rate for the restaurant industry is 73 percent. So, in a year, about three out of four employees will leave and be replaced. Turnover costs in the hospitality industry average $5,864 per employee.[6] However, according to the 2019 Linkedin Workplace Learning Report, 94% of employees say they would stay at a company longer if it invested in their learning and development. The report states that one solid way to retain employees is to "have a clear path to higher positions and make sure employees know what they need to accomplish in order to get there."[7]

Meanwhile, research continues to show the link between training and increased productivity and supports the theory that employees who receive training reach their full productivity levels sooner than employees who don't receive such training.

Return on investment (ROI) for training is calculated by dividing the net financial gain of a training program by the program's total cost. However, the process of identifying proper variables and gathering valid data can make calculating ROI complex and confounding. Despite these difficulties, it is widely accepted in hospitality industry literature that tracking the costs and benefits associated with training improves management knowledge and can enhance the delivery of training activities.

Knowledge Check

1. Why have training expenditures decreased in recent years?

2. How is return on investment for training calculated?

3. What does research show about the correlation between training and productivity?

5.2 THE TRAINING CYCLE

It is not enough for hospitality employees to know how to perform the tasks required in their jobs. Because most hospitality employees work with guests, they must also know how to demonstrate behavior associated with quality service, or at least the service that guests expect. Of course, satisfying all customers is extremely difficult. That is why training is key.

Most experts agree that training should be viewed as a continuous cycle instead of a single event. As Exhibit 5.1 shows, the **training cycle** begins with identification of a problem (also referred to as a needs assessment). The problem usually results from a discrepancy between a *desired* outcome and the *actual* outcome.

In hospitality companies, the discrepancy between desired and actual outcomes can take many forms. Guest complaints about service, room cleanliness, or the amount of time it takes at check-in are all examples of discrepancies between the desired outcome and actual outcome. However, because many guests do not lodge specific complaints, most training programs are based on problems identified by managers or employees.

Some years ago, author Bob Woods and two colleagues from Michigan State University developed a study to determine the most common types of restaurant customers.

To conduct this research, they asked about 100 servers to identify the customers they had. We put these customers into groups and gave each group a name. The name of one group, referred to as "customers from Hell," indicated how difficult the servers thought it was to constantly satisfy guests both technically and behaviorally.[8]

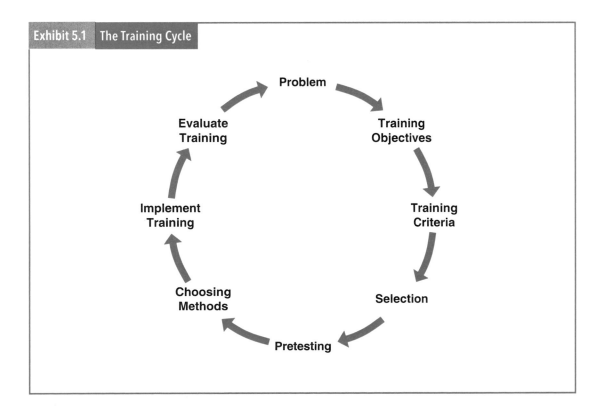

Exhibit 5.1 The Training Cycle

Problem → Training Objectives → Training Criteria → Selection → Pretesting → Choosing Methods → Implement Training → Evaluate Training → (back to Problem)

The second stage in the training cycle is the identification of **training objectives**. In this stage, managers establish the goals of the training program based on their particular circumstances. Some objectives aim to improve the service delivered to customers; others aim to improve productivity or reduce costs.

The third stage in the training cycle is the establishment of **training criteria**—the benchmarks hospitality managers set to measure effectiveness. In effect, these benchmarks become the standards that participants should reach in their training. Once achieved, these benchmarks indicate when the learning of a particular training topic is complete.

The fourth stage in the training cycle is the **selection** of trainees. Trainees may be new, potential, or current employees. In any case, managers should carefully select employees who will benefit from the training.

The fifth stage in the training cycle is **pretesting** employees to establish a baseline of knowledge, skills, and abilities. By testing the employees' current knowledge, skills, and abilities before beginning a training program, managers have a baseline for evaluating the program's effectiveness later.

The sixth stage in the training cycle is choosing the proper training methods and techniques. As shown later in the chapter, methods and techniques vary substantially depending on the objectives of the training program, the criteria developed for evaluating learning, and the current level of employee performance. Note that managers should take care to develop training programs that are neither too simple nor too complex as both extremes result in ineffective training.

The seventh stage in the training cycle is implementation of the training program itself. Managers should follow the methods identified in previous stages of the training cycle during this stage.

The eighth, and final, stage in the training cycle is **training evaluation**. Unfortunately, many hospitality managers—even those who are good at identifying training needs, selecting the proper approach to training, and conducting training—fail to effectively evaluate whether training goals have been achieved.

5.3 DEVELOPING NEEDS ASSESSMENTS

The first step in any training program is to assess the need for training—to identify the problem. In human resources circles, this is known as a **needs assessment**. When developing needs assessments, experts typically identify three factors to analyze: the organization, tasks and behaviors, and individuals.

Organizational Analysis

Every training program affects both the specific unit receiving the training and the organization as a whole. An example often used to explain **organizational analysis** is drawn from the manufacturing industry. Consider what might happen when one team on an assembly line is trained to perform its task at a 25 percent faster pace. Although this change might improve the productivity of this single unit, it does not help the organization as a whole because the rest of the assembly line is not prepared to meet the increased production pace.

The same holds true for hospitality. Consider what might happen if servers are trained to write guest checks in a new way. Although training might teach servers a more effective way to write guest checks, this could be detrimental instead of helpful unless the cooks who read the checks are also trained in this new method. The same would be true if front desk agents were trained to prepare guest folios (bills) in a new way. Unless the night auditor received the same training, the program would not be effective because the auditor must prepare reports accurately.

These examples illustrate task-oriented training approaches. However, organizational analysis also exists on another level. Consider issues such as management philosophy and organizational culture. To be effective, each company must incorporate its own management philosophy into its training programs. Consider the suitability of a training program that teaches employees to make decisions for themselves in a company that encourages employees to turn problems over to managers. Training programs are unsuccessful when they conflict with the management philosophy and organizational culture of a company. For example, assume that an important ingredient in your organizational culture is teamwork. A training program that teaches employees to work better individually would be incompatible.

These examples illustrate the need for consistency among training objectives and organizational goals. In the 1960s, many organizations experimented with sensitivity training to help employees grow as individuals, become better listeners, and generate new ideas. The training was effective, but many organizations that these employees returned to after training did not embrace these goals. Reward systems did not support the goals and management styles at the time promoted a more dictatorial approach. Consequently, the training was wasted and along with it the cost. Sensitivity training would work better today.

Task and Behavior Analysis

Every job consists of several different tasks and behaviors. The objective in **task and behavior analysis** is to determine which tasks and behaviors are required for each specific job. The first step in this process is to conduct a thorough job analysis. The second step is to prepare complete job descriptions and job specifications.

Job analyses, job descriptions, and job specifications identify three critical elements for managers to consider before beginning any training program. These elements encompass the knowledge, skills, and abilities necessary to complete the various tasks and behaviors associated with a job. These three—often called **KSAs** (knowledge, skills, and abilities)—provide the information managers need to determine which duties and responsibilities to feature in training programs.

Individual Analysis

An **individual analysis** identifies the strengths and weaknesses of each employee performing the job. The purpose of individual analysis is to determine which employees require which types of training. Sometimes, training programs are designed for entire departments. Other times, only individual employees receive training. Recognizing this fact is important for managers. It is often necessary to train only one or a few employees.

For example, restaurant managers may conduct a thorough needs analysis and find that their employees need training in wine sales and service. The managers should then assess whether all restaurant employees should receive the same training. Some employees will know nothing about wine, while others will know quite a lot. Under such circumstances, a training program on the basics of wine identification and service would be useful to some employees, but unnecessary for others. From a managerial perspective, training employees who already have this knowledge represents a waste of training dollars. To prevent such waste, managers should assess the individual KSAs of each employee before beginning any training program.

Some aspects of job safety training are required by law. For example, employees who use harmful chemicals must receive detailed information about their potential dangers and training for using them safely. More intense training is required for machine operators and facilities engineers.

LEGAL ALERT!

5.4 CONDUCTING NEEDS ASSESSMENTS

Multiple methods can be used to conduct needs assessments, as noted in Exhibit 5.2. Unfortunately, no single method can be recommended for all circumstances or environments. Instead, each method may be effective in different situations. When choosing a method or combination of methods, it can be helpful to review the skill levels of job applicants and employees to determine whether the method is appropriate.

Advisory Committees

Typically, an **advisory committee** consists of managers who review job skill and behavior

Exhibit 5.2	Needs Assessment Methods

1. Advisory committees

2. Job descriptions and job specifications

3. Work sampling

4. Job performance measurements

5. Attitude surveys

6. Performance appraisals

7. Skills tests

8. Performance documents

9. Guest feedback

10. Questionnaires

11. Exit interviews

12. Critical incidents

demands and compare these to the current level of employee performance. This method of needs assessment often benefits from employee representation on the committee (i.e., it is common to include both managers and employees on the advisory committee). An effective advisory committee in a housekeeping department may include the assistant housekeeping manager, a manager from the front desk, a manager from reservations, a housekeeping employee, and employees from each department. One advantage of advisory committees is that they can often establish desired outcomes that are well suited to organizational needs. A disadvantage is that employee participation is sometimes limited by a reluctance to disagree with managers. This obstacle can be overcome by establishing an open-meeting, full-participation policy from the outset. Good managers do not have this problem because they have established trust and rapport with employees.

Job Descriptions and Job Specifications

A second method of conducting an effective training needs assessment is to compare the KSAs identified in current job descriptions and specifications to current job performance. The effectiveness of this type of needs assessment, typically conducted by managers in charge of a given unit, can be enhanced by an advisory committee.

Work Sampling

Work sampling is conducted by trained analysts who systematically observe and review actual work performance. Analysts only observe the work; they do not participate. A typical work sampling in a restaurant setting might occur when a manager sits in a specific server's section to have a meal and evaluate the server's work. An example of work sampling in restaurants is to ask the chef to prepare a certain dish. The advantage of work sampling is that the analyst sees the work actually being done instead of just seeing the results or hearing recollections of each person doing the work. Disadvantages include the time involved and the cost of hiring an analyst if managers are unable to evaluate the work. To accurately assess current performance, analysts must watch a relatively large number of employees at work. Unless all employees are observed, work sampling is ineffective for identifying individual employee needs.

Job Performance Measurements

Job performance measurements are much like work sampling because both involve analysts. The major difference is that, for job performance measurements, analysts actually perform each job in addition to observing employee performance. This involvement can result in identification of KSAs that other methods do not. However, when assessing jobs that require special skills (e.g., many cooking jobs), it is often difficult to find analysts who can perform all the necessary tasks without training.

Job performance measurements can require a substantial time commitment, especially in cases that involve unusual or infrequent job responsibilities. Many experts view this method as one of the least cost-effective because of the time it takes analysts to observe and participate in each job. In addition, extensive training, which increases costs, is sometimes required to prepare analysts for each position. Although costly, this method is one of the most thorough.

Attitude Surveys

Not all training focuses on improving task completion. Many hospitality companies recognize the importance of employee attitudes and behavior toward guests, coworkers, and managers. **Attitude surveys** can provide an effective means of determining when training is required to improve the behavioral side of service. Attitude surveys are also useful in pinpointing what employees like and dislike about their jobs, fellow employees, and managers. These surveys can be useful in developing training programs that increase employee satisfaction and thereby can help reduce employee turnover. The principal disadvantage of attitude surveys is their relative inability to determine the need for either skills or task-related training.

Performance Appraisals

When used properly, regular performance appraisals help identify individual employees in need of training. Consistent task- or behavior-related problems indicate the need for additional training. However, because many managers do not know how to conduct performance appraisals effectively, this method often identifies training needs incorrectly. Unfortunately, most managers still think of performance appraisals as dreaded meetings with employees to provide negative feedback. Until that atmosphere is changed, performance appraisals won't work well for identifying training needs.

Skills Tests

The use of skills tests is one of the most common methods of assessing training needs. These tests measure an employee's ability to perform a task in a certain way; they test for specific skills or behaviors. For example, a manager might ask an employee to demonstrate the proper method of opening and serving wine to determine whether that employee needs training. Skills tests could also measure a cook's ability to prepare a certain dish, a buser's ability to clear a table efficiently, or a bartender's ability to prepare a wide variety of drinks. Although this method is useful in determining the need for skills-related training, it is not useful for identifying training needs for certain behaviors or more complex tasks.

Performance Documents

Reports pertaining to absenteeism, sales, guest complaints, commendations, and productivity are some of the **performance documents** useful for pinpointing individual training needs. Documents such as turnover or waste reports are useful in determining department training needs. Because such data is often collected during the normal course of business, the use of performance documents represents a low-cost approach to assessing training needs. However, this method is not useful for identifying behavioral training needs because the focus is on data or statistics rather than on behavior.

Guest Feedback

When asked, owners and managers of small hospitality businesses might say they know that their employees need training when guests complain. Unfortunately, many guests tell other people about their poor experience—but do not tell the manager. As a result, guest feedback is not useful for assessing training needs unless the hospitality organization actively collects information from a large number of guests. Active guest feedback collection does have one advantage: it demonstrates a property's commitment to service.

Questionnaires

Questionnaires are useful for gathering information about training needs because of the large amount of data that can be collected easily and cheaply. For example, a company might ask employees and managers throughout a hotel to complete a questionnaire to determine the training needs of housekeeping staff. Questionnaires can also provide an effective means of identifying managerial training needs; experts might collect information from several companies to determine the training needs for managers in a specific hotel.

Exit Interviews

Employees or managers leaving an organization are often willing to share information and experiences that can help managers determine training needs. When properly collected, this information can give managers useful insight into issues that they sometimes cannot see, particularly into those issues that relate to turnover. Some companies even require employees leaving the organization to participate in **exit interviews** before receiving their final paycheck.

However, research indicates that employees rarely give accurate information in exit interviews unless anonymity and confidentiality are ensured. Few employees want to speak negatively of the organization because they may someday need a recommendation from the company they are leaving. Employees are also likely to have friends still on the job who might be hurt by their comments. And, frequently, an employee's reason for leaving may relate to disagreements with the very managers who conduct the interviews.

Exit interviews generally provide a useful method of needs assessment when interviews are conducted either by a third party (someone not associated with the hospitality company) or by computerized surveys that collect data while providing employee anonymity.

Critical Incidents

The **critical incidents** method requires observers (managers or outsiders) to notice and record specific incidents that are examples of either good or poor employee

DID YOU KNOW?

One of the better critical incidents author Bob Woods witnessed occurred at a golf resort and country club in North Carolina. When attempting to leave following lunch at the resort, he discovered the skies had opened with pouring down rain. The cars were all parked in the hotel lot, at least 100 yards away. Without asking for permission, the doorpersons gathered as many umbrellas as they could (even taking the general manager's umbrella from the office). Once they had gathered umbrellas, they handed them out to customers who promised to drop them off on the way out. This is a great example of service and showed how well-suited the employees were for work in hospitality.

performance. This method is particularly useful when the intended training technique involves **case studies** (described below), because the incidents themselves provide the cases to use in training.

When collected over a period of time, critical incident observations identify training needs. There is a drawback, however: such incidents rarely occur when you want them to. As a result, managers can spend considerable time waiting for critical incidents to happen.

5.5 DESIGNING THE TRAINING PROGRAM

Effective training programs do not create themselves. To ensure that employees are well prepared for the jobs they are expected to perform, management must train them properly. First, managers must articulate training objectives. Then, they must establish criteria to meet those objectives. Finding the right trainees is vital to a firm's success. Selecting employees and assessing their skills before training is important so that managers can evaluate the success of the training program upon its completion.

Establishing Training Objectives

Training objectives typically fall into four general categories: reaction-based, learning-acquired, on-the-job behaviors, and results-oriented.

Reaction-Based Training Objectives. Objectives that are based on a trainee's reaction to a training program relate to how trainees view the process. In some cases, a training program objective might simply be to enhance employee regard for the company. Training programs designed to teach employees to read or write, to quit smoking, or to lose weight are examples of programs with reaction-based objectives. In each case, although the achievement of the training objective would benefit the company indirectly, it would benefit the trainee directly. Reaction-based assessment should be a part of every training program, not just those that benefit employees directly.

Learning-Acquired Objectives. In some training programs, knowledge acquisition is the ultimate objective. For example, in the wine service testing example earlier, the program measured employee knowledge of specific skills. This type of training objective is also quite common in management development programs.

On-the-Job-Behavior Objectives. Some training objectives relate to on-the-job behaviors. For example, quality of service is often measured in terms of the degree of sincerity or friendliness displayed by guest-contact personnel. As a result, hospitality companies commonly develop training programs that emphasize positive behavior toward guests as the principal objective.

Results-Oriented Objectives. The most common type of objective is the results-oriented objective. In a results-oriented program, the goal is to improve measurable outcomes of an individual or group. Programs that train employees to use cash registers, check in guests more quickly, reduce waste in kitchens, or increase the number of repeat guests are all examples of training programs with results-oriented objectives.

Although many training programs are based on one type of objective, many use multiple objectives. An example might be a program that trains current employees to perform some task or behavior that qualifies them for merit pay increases. In this case, objectives would be reaction-based, results-oriented, and focused on on-the-job behaviors.

When developing training objectives, it is important that managers identify what they hope to accomplish in clear and measurable terms. Objectives such as "improve employee job satisfaction" fail because they are too vague. However, "reduce turnover" (as a measure of improving job satisfaction) would be a measurable objective. Well-designed objectives can be stated using action verbs such as "describe," "complete," "make," "define," "identify," "participate in," and so on.

Establishing Training Criteria

A training program that correctly assesses needs and clearly identifies objectives is useful only if the criteria for success are clearly outlined. Such criteria establish a benchmark for measuring what will be learned or gained from the training process. For example, in a training program developed for a Virgin Islands resort hotel, the criteria for each session related to subject matter knowledge and to the ability to perform tasks or demonstrate desired behaviors correctly and consistently. During a session devoted to food service training, knowing how to set, bus, and serve a table efficiently was established as a criterion for success. To measure accomplishment, trainers required each participant to perform these tasks independently within a specific time frame. Other criteria could be established to measure behavioral, reaction-based, or learning-acquired objectives.

Selecting Trainees

Employees who participate in training ultimately determine whether a program is successful or not. Selection can be ongoing for training programs that involve several steps or multiple stages.

An example of an ongoing selection process can be drawn from a training program developed for a luxury hotel in the U.S. Virgin Islands. The objective of this program was to train Virgin Islanders for front-line service positions in the hospitality industry. None of the participants had any hospitality training experience. The program was funded partially by the U.S. government through a Partners in Commerce (PIC) program.

The training program was organized in several stages, each related to a different skill or behavior useful to hospitality employees. The eight-week program enlisted specialists to instruct each of the one-week sessions, which ran from 8 a.m. until 4 p.m. Because the number of participants was fairly high (about 100), several classes were offered each week to accommodate participants on a rotating basis.

At the end of each week, instructors from each class met with the local training program director and property managers to evaluate the progress of each participant. After instructors arrived at a consensus, the training director met privately with each participant to discuss individual progress during the week and to establish goals for the following week. Participants who were not progressing were advised—in writing—of their goals for the following weeks. If they did not meet these goals, participants were dropped from the program. As a result, 75 of over 100 original participants eventually graduated from the program.

Pretesting Trainees

Many managers begin training after completing a needs assessment, determining objectives, identifying criteria, and selecting participants. These managers, however, are missing a step: they're failing to establish what their employees already know. Because no baselines of KSAs are identified before implementing training, it is difficult to compare performance before and after training. As a result, it is impossible to evaluate the success of the training program.

Ideally, a hospitality manager should identify two separate groups during pretesting. One group is tested before and after training. The other group is also tested before and after the program but does not receive training. This second group is called the **control group**. This type of testing is called *pretest-posttest design with a control group*.

By measuring both groups—the group that receives training and the group that does not—managers can clearly assess the impact of the training program. Pretesting can be conducted easily after trainees are divided into two groups.

If it is impossible to break the trainees into two groups, managers should test employees both before and after training. Although this method allows managers to assess KSAs both before and after training, it does not yield definite conclusions about the value of the training program because other factors introduced during the training period can affect the KSAs displayed during the posttest.

Unfortunately, some managers simply test their employees' KSAs after training. When no pretest is used, all these managers really know are the employees' KSAs at the time of testing and in that particular setting, time, and place—which provides little useful information about a training program.

Knowledge Checks

1. What are the steps in designing a training program?

2. What are the four categories of training objectives?

3. Why is it important to establish training objectives?

5.6 CHOOSING TRAINING METHODS

Because of rapid advances in technology, new training systems are created almost every year. Just a few years ago, only the most sophisticated training programs used computers. Today, **e-learning** is the primary training method used in many hospitality companies. In some cases, the only training new employees receive is online. Online learning can be more successful than traditional forms of learning because of the wide array of training methods available, including text, videos, audio, graphics, simulations, and interactive games and tutorials. E-learning is flexible, can be accessed on demand, and can be tailored to individual employees and business and industry needs at low cost. **Computer-based training** saves time and money compared to other forms of training. Research also shows that e-learning results in learner retention rates of 25 to 60 percent compared with an average of 8 to 10 percent for in-class learning.[9]

Online learning also offers easier scheduling and deployment and allows organizations to track trainee progress. A survey conducted by CertifyMe.net found that 72 percent of organizations felt that their online learning programs gave them an edge as an organization. CertifyMe also noted that e-learning saves time and money, leads to higher retention of employees, is consistent, and is scalable to larger and smaller sizes.[10]

Although e-learning is used in the hospitality industry, older training methods remain useful. Deciding among methods usually depends on the type of training intended, the trainees selected, the objectives of the training program, and the training environment. Experts say that no single training method is right for every situation. Instead, training is situational; some objectives are more easily achieved with certain methods than with others.

This section discusses popular training methods used today. These methods are grouped into three categories: training for managers, training for nonmanagers, and training for all employee levels.

Training for Managers

The methods appropriate for training managers include:

- Case study training
- In-basket training
- Conference training
- Behavioral modeling
- Training the trainer
- Online training

Case Study Training. Case studies typically detail a series of events—either real or hypothetical—that take place in a business environment. This method challenges participants to sort through provided data to identify problems and then propose solutions to these problems. Researchers have referred to this type of training as "aha learning" because, at some point during case analysis or discussion, participants often suddenly realize—"aha!"—what is and what is not important.

Experts often cite one disadvantage of this approach: cases take place in a vacuum, whereas decisions are made in real time. In other words, in real life, managers don't face just a single issue as they do in case studies. Instead, real-life managers face that issue plus many others at the same time. Participants may tend to approach case studies too analytically. In a real hospitality environment, problems generally come in all shapes and sizes, not in neatly packaged case studies.

In-Basket Training. In-basket training generally presents participants with a wide array of problems similar to those found in their in-basket at work. As a training tool, in-basket training has three objectives:

(1) to train participants to identify which issues require the most immediate response;

(2) to teach participants how to delegate those problems that do not require their personal attention; and

(3) to instruct employees how to work on several problems simultaneously.

In-basket training is sometimes used as a selection process for identifying potential managers. When used as a selection tool, in-basket training may test how applicants prioritize problems and how well they delegate authority. Research has shown that this method effectively predicts future job behavior. In-basket training serves a variety of purposes. Because it takes place in real time and involves everyone in the session, it is useful to start a training session or to provide relief from computer training.

Conference Training. Conference training is essentially a one-on-one discussion between the trainer and trainee. For example, a non-commercial food service manager might use this type of training to explain to a cashier why it is necessary to maintain accurate records of each transaction. The obvious advantage is the reinforcement provided by close contact between trainer and trainee. Disadvantages include the time and cost of individualized training.

Behavioral Modeling. Social learning theory claims that people learn most behavior by observing others, meaning that most people model their behaviors after others' behaviors. Modeling takes advantage of that theory by giving participants the chance to see how a model acts in a certain situation, rather than by simply instructing participants how to act. A sequence of steps must take place to implement modeling:

- A specific interpersonal skill is introduced, usually through lecture.

- A model acts out the skill either on video or in person.

- The trainer highlights key points in the model's portrayal.

- Trainees practice the skill through role-playing.

- The trainer and other participants provide feedback on the role-playing.

The advantage of modeling is its emphasis on doing rather than on telling. Managers can be shown how to delegate, communicate, conduct a meeting, interview an applicant, or discipline an employee. The role of the facilitator in this process is to coach participants to follow the modeled behaviors more closely. Most research shows that this form of training is a good way to teach effective interpersonal skills to supervisors and others.

The disadvantages of this approach are that the training method is limited to behavioral issues and that the training facilitator must be adept at conducting sessions as they can quickly get out of control. However, because hospitality management involves behavioral and interpersonal skill issues, this method can be an excellent form of training, especially for managers and supervisors.

Training the Trainer. Training the trainer entails teaching managers or other employees who have knowledge and expertise how to train other members of an organization. It is important to teach trainers how to teach other people so that they can spread information effectively. Developing an internal training program can be empowering and allow organizations to be more self-sufficient. By training managers and employees to train members of their own organization, knowledge is distributed within the organization so no one person carries all of the organization's expertise. One notable drawback to this method is the cost of training a new trainer when a trainer leaves an organization. Therefore, it is recommended that several members of an organization be trained to train in a given knowledge area.

Online Training. Online training resources for managers have exploded. Although it is important that managers know the source of the online article or training method they choose, many are useful.

Training for Nonmanagers

Training methods suitable for nonmanagement employees include the following:

- On-the-job training
- Job instruction training
- Lectures
- Coaching/mentoring
- Programmed instruction

On-the-Job Training. The most common type of training in the hospitality industry is **on-the-job training (OJT)**. Such training can be an effective method of learning; unfortunately, it is often conducted incorrectly. Typically, one employee is asked to teach another some desired skill. In many cases, trainers are assigned not because they can teach but because they can perform tasks or behaviors well. Being good at a job does not necessarily make someone an effective trainer.

When supervisors or trained trainers are involved, OJT can be very effective and cost-efficient because training can be conducted during business operations in actual work settings. To a degree, OJT resembles modeling, a fairly good method for hospitality training. Typically, a trainer does something and then asks the trainee to replicate it—perhaps over and over until learned.

Like most methods, OJT has its disadvantages. Remember, some training assignments can be inappropriate or ineffective. In addition, training can interfere with normal business. Because the training is fast-paced, trainers generally have little or no time to provide feedback or to reiterate important steps. Imagine a trainee trying to train someone to ring up orders in a restaurant on a busy day when everyone needs to ring up orders! Finally, this type of training perpetuates the status quo, because trainees are very likely to perform exactly the same way as their trainers, right or wrong.

Job Instruction Training. **Job instruction training (JIT)** is a structured approach to training that requires trainees to proceed through a series of steps in a sequential pattern. This type of training is good for task-oriented jobs, such as operating equipment and preparing foods.

Lectures. Perhaps the most common form of **off-the-job training** is an oral presentation of information to an audience. The advantage of a lecture is that large amounts of information can be delivered in a relatively short period of time to a large number of people. As a result, the lecture method is very cost-effective.

One disadvantage of the lecture method, however, is the lack of two-way communication. Lecture attendees listen; they do not ask questions for clarification. In addition, no allowance is made during lectures for the varying levels of understanding among participants. Some participants may find lectures boring and slow while others in the same audience may have trouble keeping up.

Coaching/Mentoring. Both coaching and mentoring have gained favor in recent years because these methods often produce desirable behavioral results. By using a form of conference training and/or modeling, coaches and mentors often concentrate on improving the skills of subordinates. Coaches and mentors are concerned with the overall professional development of their protégés. As a result, they encourage their protégés' skill and leadership development rather than take the narrow-minded approach of just making sure employees know how to do their immediate job tasks. Mentors encourage protégés to work toward greater aspirations or toward their goals.

Programmed Instruction. Working online alone is a form of **programmed instruction** that enables trainees to learn at their own pace. Originally, programmed instruction was accomplished through paper-and-pencil tests that evaluated whether trainees had learned enough to proceed to the next stage. Today, computers have generally replaced papers and pencils, although not always. Self-programmed and self-directed instruction are popular Internet and e-learning programs, partially because students like individualized learning. Research on the effectiveness of such programs has generally been positive. It appears that many employees prefer to learn at their own pace, and when allowed to do so they actually learn and retain more.

Managers using programmed instruction for training should realize that different trainees in the same room may be working at different levels and in different ways. Individuals learn in different ways. E-learning, in any context, requires individuals to apply self-regulated strategies to achieve their training objectives. It has been suggested that self-directed learning leads to more positive outcomes.

Training for All Employee Levels

Methods of training suitable for all employee levels include the following:

- Job rotation
- Role-playing
- Vestibule training
- Business games
- Sensitivity training
- Basic skills training
- Team training
- Diversity training

Job Rotation. According to the Center for Workforce Development, employees learn only about 30 percent of the information and skills needed for their jobs through formal training, and the other 70 percent on the job and from watching coworkers.[11] **Job rotation** involves moving trainees from one job to another. This training method is widely used in training hospitality managers, many of whom spend a certain number of weeks in each job before assuming their managerial duties. An advantage of job rotation is that trainees can see how work is performed in many jobs. Trainees also get to know the employees in each position.

When used to train line-level employees, job rotation actually becomes a method of cross-training that affords employees the knowledge and skills to do different jobs. However, the success of this type of training depends on how information is presented at each step of the process.

Role-Playing. According to Morgan McCall, Robert Eichinberger, and Michael Lombardo, 70 percent of what a person learns is experience-based, 20 percent comes from interacting with other employees and customers, and only 10 percent comes from formal training.[12] **Role-playing** enables participants to experience real or exaggerated work situations. For example, consider the use of role-playing in a training session designed to help participants improve their interpersonal skills. A trainer might ask one participant to role-play a hospitality manager and another to role-play an employee. The purpose is to allow each participant to experience what it feels like to be in that role.

Gaining the opportunity to step into another person's shoes is a principal advantage of role-playing. And because four principles of learning are involved—active participation, modeling, feedback, and practice—role-playing can result in a high level of learning when used properly. Because role-play learning relies on active participation, trainers must encourage trainee involvement. Role-playing has a theoretical basis in behavior modeling that entails observation, practice, and feedback. Emerging simulation-based technologies offer enhancements to behavior modeling that are absent in traditional role-play training.

Vestibule Training. **Vestibule training**—or simulation—involves the virtual duplication of the work environment in an off-site setting. Some hospitality training is well suited for this method. For example, training employees to use electronic equipment such as cash registers or check-in systems can be accomplished through vestibule training by simply setting up the necessary equipment in an empty room. The advantage of using a duplicated environment rather than the actual workplace is that training can take place without interrupting the normal flow of business. Although vestibule training usually results in a fairly high level of learning, it is also regarded as an expensive way to accomplish some training objectives, primarily because of the cost of duplicating the workplace environment.

Vestibule or simulation training is also useful in training managers and employees how to make decisions in specific environments. The theory is that if managers or employees have faced similar situations—even if they were simulated—they will be more likely to make the right decisions. Many business games on the market allow participants to simulate workplace environments. In some of the more complex simulations, participants create and operate simulated organizations for brief periods. Other simulations allow participants to experience what it feels like to be placed in a specific situation.

Business Games. Organizations employ **business games** to make learning more engaging and effective for employees, partic-

DID YOU KNOW?

Intercultural simulations are instructional activities that engage and challenge participants with experiences integral to encounters between people of different cultural groups. These are often used to help employees get to know one another more quickly and to build teams. Two popular simulations are *BaFá BaFá®* and *StarPower®*. In *BaFá BaFá®*, participants learn what it feels like to visit another culture; in *StarPower®*, participants learn how to manage power and how to interact with and without power. These and other simulations have been used since the early 1970s.

ularly for those who were raised on high-action video games. Business games can be an inexpensive and effective way to introduce dry material such as company history or orientation philosophies and can make training more exciting. Commercial forms of this training approach are available from many sources. The advantages of business games are threefold: games are fun, they can provide a setting that simulates reality, and many issues can be introduced using a single game. A disadvantage is that participants sometimes become engrossed in winning and forget that the goal is to learn.

Sensitivity Training. A training method often used to enhance interpersonal skills is **sensitivity training**. Also called *t-group* or *laboratory training*, this method helps participants become more aware of their behaviors toward others. First developed by Kurt Lewin and other scholars, sensitivity training is usually conducted in small groups of four to 10 participants. Typically, each participant is confronted about their behaviors by other group members. Each participant then has the opportunity to express their feelings about the group process. The training facilitator's role is critical because of the deep emotional reaction some participants may experience during the process. The advantage of sensitivity training is that it enables participants, in a constructive way, to see how others see them. The principal disadvantage is that, unless expertly facilitated, the process can become dangerously personal.

Basic Skills Training. Employees' lack of basic skills such as reading, writing, and computing results in an estimated $60 billion loss in productivity for U.S. companies each year.[13] Considering this statistic, investing in employees' basic skills is potentially very worthwhile. Many hospitality employers offer English-language speaking classes and other socially conscious training for new employees. At a major hotel in Las Vegas, for example, more than 85 percent of all housekeepers speak a language other than English as their native language. In an effort to make their jobs and their interactions with guests easier, all new housekeepers go through six weeks of training. During each day of training, they attend English classes in the morning and then learn housekeeping policies and procedures in the afternoon.

Team Training. In the hospitality industry, working together is an everyday occurrence; however, team training is virtually nonexistent. Yet enhancing teamwork through building teams is an important outcome for hospitality organizations. Many off-the-shelf business team-building games are available. Most are both fun and educational. These games assume that the team involved does not know one another and must first become acquainted; they can be used as a fun way to get employees to start working together.

Managers can develop their own successful team training programs if they keep the following points in mind:

- Team-building is a complex and challenging process. Expecting a quick team mentality to develop just because employees are working together is unrealistic. It takes time and effort to build a team.

- The most successful teams are ones that develop over time.

- Team development does not always fit into the "forming, storming, norming,

conforming, and performing" model of team-building stages. Training can help employees work through each stage, but lapses may occur; team members and managers must be aware of this.

- New team members must quickly be brought up to speed. Throwing a new team member in with the group without giving them comprehensive training is detrimental all around.

- Active, hands-on experience yields the best results. Teaching conflict resolution via lecture robs team members of the opportunity to reflect and exchange ideas.

Diversity, equity, and inclusion training. The goal of diversity, equity, and inclusion training is to educate employees to be more sensitive and respectful toward coworkers, guests, and suppliers—essentially to everyone.[14] Diversity training in the hospitality industry is no longer about general diversity understanding. Traditional diversity programs addressed race, gender, disabilities, and perhaps age and sexual orientation. Today, hospitality organizations also address cultural competency with regard to generational diversity, ethnicity, and what it means for people to work together effectively. Good organizations also include training in cultural competence. Cultural competence can be defined as the ability to comprehend, interact, and communicate with someone from a different cultural background appropriately.[15]

Knowledge Check
1. What are the objectives of in-basket training?
2. What is role-playing?
3. What is the purpose of sensitivity training?

5.7 IMPLEMENTING THE TRAINING PROGRAM

Appropriate implementation is just as important to the success of any training program as the appropriate selection of methods, trainers, and trainees. Even if managers plan their training programs thoroughly, they often fail to implement those programs as planned. You know the feeling—you have worked so hard getting it set up that implementation seems obvious—to you (but not to others who will use it). In many cases, managers simply implement the easiest training program possible in some feasible way. This defeats the purpose of planning. Careful follow-through on all planned details is critical in the implementation stage, the stage during which trainees actually undergo training.

Implementation can involve a variety of approaches, and sometimes creativity generates the best solutions. For example, a banking company in New York developed a computer game designed to train its managers and staff about banker strategy and financial rules. Employees were playing solitaire and other games on the company computers anyway; instead of wasting their time, they could learn valuable skills while having fun with the company game. The same approach could work in hospitality. For example, a front desk agent could benefit from playing a hotel management game on a computer terminal during slow times.

One thing to remember when designing and delivering training programs is that you must be aware of people with disabilities and how effective your program will be for them. People with disabilities represent an estimated 10–19 percent of the general population worldwide and are an untapped source of workers for hospitality. Yet the hospitality industry has, so far, been a follower rather than a leader with respect to training and employment practices for people with disabilities compared to other industries.[16]

The stereotype of a "professional hospitality worker" can result in people with learning disabilities being viewed as unprofessional. So, there is a need to give greater attention to disability awareness training, including information about working alongside employees with disabilities. Employers will have challenges about their attitudes toward employing people with disabilities and management of the physical and service environment to make it welcoming for employees with disabilities. This understanding can open opportunities to review and realign hospitality employment and training with ethical and non-discriminatory principles and guidelines, which are

essential if the employment of people with disabilities is to be improved.[17]

Diversity and inclusion should not be a one-time campaign or a one-off initiative. Rather, it is a constant work in progress and should be maintained and promoted to guarantee change.

Knowledge Check

1. At which stage in training does a trainee actually undergo training?

2. Why is careful implementation so important to the success of a training program?

3. What are some factors to consider when designing a training program?

5.8 EVALUATING TRAINING

Simply having a training program is not enough. Considerable evidence suggests that a substantial part of what organizations investment in training is often wasted due to poor learning transfer and trainee relapse. That's because one of the most important steps in training—program evaluation—is conducted poorly. As a result, many companies do not really know what effect a training program has had on employees or on the organization.

There are logical reasons managers fail to evaluate training programs:

1. If managers see some change in one or more employees, they often assume that the training has had an overall effect. (The changes may be outliers, of course).

2. Managers also tend to assume that training works—with or without observed changes—just because it was conducted.

3. Managers often take ownership for training programs because they were the force behind the program. It's their baby they are evaluating!

4. In some cases, managers simply do not want to go through objective evaluations because they might discover that a program was not worthwhile. (And others might notice that they wasted money on determining the program was not worthwhile, too.)

5. Perhaps the most common reason managers fail to evaluate their training programs is that they do not know how.

Measuring Change

The principal goal of any training program is change. Managers should ask two questions during an evaluation: Did change occur? Did this change result from the training? And even if managers can answer both questions positively, they still may want to ask several more: Do the changes benefit the entire organization? Will the same program work again in the future? Should it be altered?

It is important to remember that responses to change can be varied. Therefore, it is preferable to measure training outcomes in terms of change from pretest to posttest, rather than merely through attainment (posttest only) scores. Many colleges and professors give their students a pre-test on the first day of the semester and a post-test at the end. This is because the entire semester is a training program, and it is important to know whether you learned anything.

The following types of objectives form the basis for evaluating training programs:[18]

Reaction. Reaction refers primarily to the views of trainees regarding the training program. Did they like the program? Did they like the methods used? Can they recommend other methods to address the same issues? Can they recommend changes that would improve the program? What did they think of the trainers and the facilities used in the training process? Would the trainees recommend that the program be implemented again? If not, how would they change it? Typically, managers can learn the answers to all these questions through questionnaires, post-training interviews, or a combination of both.

Although reaction is important, sometimes it only provides ratings of the trainer or the course design. More important to the trainee and the organization is whether trainees learned from the process, whether their on-the-job behaviors display this learning, and whether the training produced desirable productivity results.

Learning. Managers must ascertain whether trainees learned anything from the training program. Otherwise, training is useless. A variety of methods are available for evaluating acquired learning. These include tests (oral, written, or performance) and observation of work progress and simulations.

On-the-Job Behaviors. Evaluating on-the-job behaviors in connection with a training program is not the same as evaluating on-the-job behaviors through performance appraisals or employee evaluations. For example, companies that conduct performance appraisals on a regular basis evaluate an employee's behaviors as part of that employee's progress and professional development. Evaluating an employee's behavior immediately after a training program is an effective method of evaluating the program. These appraisals might be conducted by an employee's supervisor, peers, any staff they supervise, guests, or a combination of any of these groups.

Results. The ultimate test of a training program is its effect on an organization. To determine a program's effect, managers should evaluate any measurable criteria. For example, managers can look at turnover rate to measure the effectiveness of training designed to improve employee satisfaction. Productivity would provide a measurable criterion for evaluating training programs designed to reduce the time it takes to perform a given task, such as checking in a guest or preparing a meal. Quality can be measured using guest evaluations of goods and services. For example, directly after room attendants complete a training program on improving guestroom cleaning, guests can be asked to evaluate the cleanliness of their rooms. Cost is also an obvious measurable criterion. Are costs lower than they were before the training program? Has waste been reduced or eliminated? Are employees working fewer hours to complete tasks now than before training? Are profits higher as a result of the training program?

Identifying the Cause

Simply identifying change is not enough; effective evaluations of training programs must also identify whether the changes resulted from training. If this is not determined conclusively, managers cannot assume that the training was the cause; other factors could have influenced the change that managers are observing. The most effective method of determining whether a training program caused the changes is to create a pretest–posttest control group environment (as described earlier in the chapter).

Troubleshooting Program Failures

Not all training programs work. Although managers assume that training will yield the desired results, in some cases the training does not. A variety of factors reduce the effectiveness of training programs, including poor design, poor presentations, and presenting information trainees do not understand. It is also possible that training needs were improperly assessed or that the wrong training method or site was chosen. Finally, training objectives or criteria may have been unsuitable. The point is that training programs themselves are not always to blame when desired change is not achieved. When

this occurs, managers should focus on identifying the cause of the problem.

The Training Payoff

There is ample evidence that training dollars, when properly invested, provide excellent returns. If a company takes the time to conduct needs assessments, establish objectives and criteria, and select the right trainers and methods, training can be one of the best investments a company can make.

An American entertainment company with theme parks and resorts across the globe is a prime example of a hospitality company that takes training seriously. This company has a training program lasting several days in which new employees learn the history of the company, quality standards, traditions, and even a special entertainment-specific language (employees are "cast members," who, when they are working, are "on stage" and wear uniforms called "costumes").[19] During training, new cast members are constantly reminded of the company they have chosen to work for—training takes place at a special institute, classrooms have pictures of famous graduates like beloved cartoon characters, and television clips of the founder are shown throughout as reminders of his vision of the company and its humble beginnings. This company-wide training takes place before new recruits even step foot in their departments. Though it may seem like overkill to the outside observer, this form of training has certainly proven successful for employees and guests alike.

To save on training costs, a food service and facilities management company, held its 2009 diversity and inclusion training and conference in a virtual setting, rather than paying for 450 employees to travel to its headquarters in Paris, as was traditionally done. Attendees logged on to a designated website, heard opening remarks, listened to live presentations, attended training sessions and panel discussions, visited exhibits, and participated in chat room discussions and networking events. Attendees also were involved in an interactive theater, which enabled them to watch actors role-play workplace diversity scenarios. Holding the event virtually saved about $1.8 million in travel-related costs and the equivalent of

900 work days. It was so successful that the 2010 event was also held in a virtual setting, and, in years since, the company has continued that trend with both instructor-led and webinar training. In 2019, more than 5,000 managers participated in diversity and inclusion training. The company was recognized on Fortune's 2019 World's Most Admired list and Bloomberg's 2020 Gender Equality Index as well as a Top 10 Percent Inclusion Index Company on the Diversity Best Practices Inclusion Index from 2016 to 2020.[20]

Knowledge Check

1. How can a manager evaluate an employee's acquired learning?

2. What factors can reduce the effectiveness of training programs?

3. Why is it important to evaluate training?

5.9 CAREER DEVELOPMENT FOR MANAGERS

Training devoted to developing managers is generally called either career development, management development, or career planning. These terms all refer to increasing managerial performance; enhancing job satisfaction; improving knowledge, skills, and abilities; and identifying managerial strengths, weaknesses, and interests.

Managers typically progress through a number of career stages. From an organizational perspective, the most common stages are (1) organizational entry; (2) the reality-shock experienced when a manager realizes that this is their life and career; (3) mid-life or middle-career syndrome; (4) the approach of retirement; and (5) retirement. Helping managers manage with these stages is the focus of most management development programs.

During the organizational entry stage, many companies focus management development training on socialization, learning how to adjust to the hospitality business world, and how to become an effective manager. Training programs that stress managerial role theory, leadership styles, interpersonal skills, assessment centers, role playing, modeling, and management-style training are common during this stage.

During the reality-shock stage, companies generally focus management development on promoting responsibility and growth to reassure managers that there is a place for them in the organization.

Because mid-life or middle-career syndrome is often characterized by boredom with the job, training should emphasize new challenges and objectives. Achievement and motivation are important issues.

When managers approach retirement, training emphasis often shifts to issues associated with mentoring and passing information on to younger generations of managers. Coaching, understudy assignments, and modeling are good training methods to implement at this stage. Because many managers also face a loss of identity with the loss of their jobs, additional training might focus on exploring self-identity and leisure activities.

The problem with career planning and career progression today is that no one knows which jobs are going away and which new ones will be created. The list of jobs going away is long and varied…and getting longer. We have all read about jobs going away, including quick service restaurant cooks and travel agents, to name just two. The problem for managers is that each potential career ladder might suddenly disappear and leave them hanging.

What will happen when people cannot find work is uncertain. In January 2021, McKinsey & Company announced the results of a study that determined that 30 percent of tasks in 60 percent of jobs could simply be eliminated. Most could be taken over by robots. Quick service restaurant cooks face an 81 percent probability of losing their jobs. Think about how that would change a quick service restaurant.[21]

Knowledge Checks

1. What does management development focus on during the reality-shock stage?

2. What is the emphasis of their training when managers approach retirement?

3. Why is it important to have career development for managers?

IN THIS CHAPTER, YOU LEARNED:

- There is a link between training and increased productivity and employees who receive training reach their full productivity levels sooner than employees who don't receive such training.

- Most experts agree that training should be viewed as a continuous cycle instead of a single event. It begins with identification of a problem (also referred to as a needs assessment).

- Needs assessment methods include advisory committees, job descriptions and job specifications, work sampling, job performance measurements, attitude surveys, performance appraisals, skills tests, performance documents, guest feedback, questionnaires, exit interviews, and critical incidents.

- Training methods include job rotation, role-playing, vestibule training, business games, sensitivity training, basic skills training, team training, and diversity training.

- Appropriate implementation is just as important to the success of any training program as the appropriate selection of methods, trainers, and trainees.

- You can evaluate training programs based on reaction, learning, on-the-job behaviors, and results.

KEY TERMS

advisory committee—A committee composed of managers who review the job skills and behavior demands of the organization and compare these skills and behaviors with current levels of employee performance.

attitude survey—A needs assessment method designed to determine when behavioral training is required; also a questionnaire or other information-gathering tool designed to determine how employees feel about work issues.

business game—A training method in which trainees learn how to deal with a variety of issues in a simulated business environment.

case study—A training method in which employees are confronted by a series of events—hypothetical or real—and are asked to solve the problems presented in each scenario.

computer-based training—The use of a personal or networked computer for the delivery and access of training programs.

conference training—A training method that consists of one-on-one discussions between a trainer and a trainee.

control group—The standard to which comparisons are made in an experiment.

critical incident—A job analysis technique based on capturing and recording actual events that occur at work that, when combined, form an accurate picture of a job's actual requirements. Useful in describing how services should be performed. Also used in training and as a measurement in certain performance appraisal systems.

e-learning—Learning that is conducted via electronic media, typically on the Internet.

exit interview—A meeting conducted between an employer and an employee leaving the organization that attempts to identify specific training needs or other work-related problems.

in-basket training—A training method in which employees confront a wide array of problems similar to what they might find in their in-basket (essentially their to do list) when they come to work.

individual analysis—A process that helps managers identify specific training needs for the person performing a particular job.

job instruction training (JIT)—A structured approach to training that requires trainees to proceed through a series of sequential steps.

job performance measurements—A needs assessment method in which a trained analyst performs each job to get a personal feel for the knowledge, skills, and abilities needed.

job rotation—A process of moving employees from one job to another or of changing employee responsibilities to enhance job interest or to cross-train.

KSA—Acronym for knowledge, skills, and abilities.

modeling—A training method designed to encourage employees to behave as role models behave.

needs assessment—The first stage in the training program, in which an organization assesses the need for training.

off-the-job training—Training in which trainees learn job procedures in an environment other than the actual work environment.

on-the-job training—Training in which trainees learn job procedures while watching, talking with, and helping an experienced employee.

organizational analysis—The process in which the entire organization's need for training is assessed; this generally includes an assessment of the effect that training will have on the organization.

performance document—A document relating to absenteeism, sales, guest complaints, or guest compliments that identifies a need for training.

pretesting—A testing process that establishes what employees currently know and what they need to be trained for; conducted before training implementation.

programmed instruction—A training method in which employees learn at their own pace. Originally a paper-and-pencil method; now it is mostly computer-oriented.

role-playing—A training method that allows trainees to assume roles and act out parts in a realistic situation or setting.

sensitivity training—A training method designed to make employees more aware of behavioral or interpersonal training needs.

selection—The action of carefully choosing someone as being the best or most suitable.

sensitivity training—Training intended to sensitive people to their attitudes and behaviors that may unwittingly cause offense to others, especially members of various minorities.

task and behavior analysis—A process that determines which tasks and behaviors are needed for each job.

training criteria—Benchmarks for training success.

training cycle—A continuous series of steps involved in the training process.

training evaluation—A step in the training cycle that determines whether or not the training program is working.

training objective—A measurable end result of a training program. Training objectives are typically classified as reaction-based, learning-acquired, on-the-job behaviors, and results-oriented.

vestibule training—An off-the-job training method that simulates the workplace and asks employees to perform or display knowledge, skills, or abilities similar to those required at work.

work sampling—A needs assessment method of individual analysis in which a trained analyst observes and reviews an employee's work to determine training needs.

REVIEW QUESTIONS

1. Why is training referred to as a cyclical process?

2. What are the stages in the training cycle?

3. What are the 12 methods of needs assessment?

4. When are attitude surveys an effective method of analyzing training needs?

5. What is a training objective?

6. When are case studies an appropriate training method?

7. When is modeling an appropriate training method?

8. What are the three objectives of in-basket training?

9. What are the differences between organizational analysis, task and behavior analysis, and individual analysis?

I Never Wanted to Be a Supervisor Anyway

Johann is a food server at the Lakeside Inn, a 200-room hotel with a coffee shop and a full-service restaurant called Hummingbirds. Two years ago, Johann started out as a buser in the coffee shop, but because of his outstanding performance he was quickly transferred to Hummingbirds and made a food server.

Johann's excellent record continued in his new position. Johann was always on time, was great with the customers, and was a real team player. When the busers fell behind, he helped them catch up without being asked. When another server needed help, Johann was always willing to take on tables in addition to his own. He even got along with the cooks. Within weeks at his new position, he knew everyone's name and was usually the center of attention in the employee breakroom. As time went by, he won employee of the month so many times it became somewhat embarrassing.

Sarita, the dining room supervisor at Hummingbirds, was Johann's boss. Because Johann got along with the staff so well, Sarita asked Johann to fill in for her every Wednesday—Sarita's day off and the slowest day of the week for the restaurant. Johann seemed to do a good job in this role. Serious problems seldom came up on Wednesdays, and if one did, Johann would tell Sarita about it on Thursday morning so Sarita could take care of it.

When Sarita was made restaurant manager of another hotel in the chain, she encouraged Johann to apply for her position. "I think you'd make a great supervisor. The job will be posted internally for three days, and I'm not sure who's going to apply, but you can count on me for a glowing recommendation." Sarita not only thought this would be good for Johann but knew that the company encouraged promotion from within and it would be a feather in Sarita's cap if one of her employees took over her position.

At first, Johann was not enthusiastic about the supervisor job—"I really enjoy what I'm doing," he told Sarita—but, bolstered by Sarita's confidence in him, he finally decided to apply. His interview was with three people: Sarita; Sarita's boss,

Alana, the restaurant manager; and Sanjay, the hotel's human resources director. Johann was outgoing and personable during the interview, and after Johann left the room, Sarita cited Johann's initiative, high energy level, leadership skills, and high quantity and quality of work as reasons Johann should get the nod. Although Alana and Sanjay were concerned about Johann's lack of formal supervisory training, they decided, given Johann's excellent record, to give him a chance.

The next day, Johann went with Sarita to Sarita's new restaurant and spent a week in training. At the beginning of the week, Sarita went over a checklist of supervisory skills Johann needed to acquire and gave him some training materials to study. Throughout the week, Sarita helped Johann fill out the paperwork a dining room supervisor must deal with. At the end of the week, Sarita wished Johann good luck, gave him a pep talk, and told him to call anytime he had a problem.

Johann reported for work at Hummingbirds the next morning, uncomfortable in his new suit and tie but feeling confident and determined to do a good job. It didn't take him long to discover that the biggest adjustment he faced was in relating to his former coworkers. When he was a food server, everyone was his friend and he had enjoyed all the during-work and after-hours socializing the employees did together. But now he was left out. In this and many other ways, his former coworkers made him feel that he wasn't one of the gang anymore.

That was bad enough, but he began to suspect that his friends, now his employees, were taking advantage of him. For one thing, they didn't really treat him as a manager. When Alana walked through the kitchen, all the servers and cooks snapped to attention; when Johann walked through, they just looked around—"Oh, hi Johann"— or didn't acknowledge him at all and continued casually chatting. Because they knew Johann so well, they constantly asked him for favors: "Can I trade nights with Lisa?" "Can I have tomorrow off?" "Can Sam and I switch table assignments?" The requests went on and on. Johann soon learned that, try as he might, he couldn't write a schedule that pleased everybody or didn't have to be changed constantly. The few times he couldn't give employees the day off they wanted, some of them called in sick. Johann wondered if they were lying, of course, but he couldn't prove anything, and he didn't want to think they would treat him so badly. All he knew for certain was that he felt abused and taken advantage of by the very people he used to be so close to.

Despite these feelings, Johann wanted to preserve his relationships with his staff, and he wanted to please his new boss, too. So he didn't let Alana know about the pressures he was feeling, and he granted almost every employee request. This often meant that Johann found himself doing his old job of serving customers, busing tables, even filling in for dishwashers, while his employees either called in with an excuse and didn't show up or didn't put forth the effort Johann thought they should. Too many times Johann found himself waiting tables, fretting about the mountain of paperwork on his desk, and watching other servers working at what he considered half speed.

As the first few weeks went by, he also became disappointed in Martha's performance. Martha was the senior server on the staff, and she had inherited Johann's old role as the head server, the person Johann counted on to be a team leader and fill in for him on his day off. But Martha never did the little things that would have really helped him out, never went the extra mile for anyone. Why couldn't she just volunteer and pitch in like he used to do?

That Monday morning started out like most Monday mornings at Hummingbirds—extremely busy. The normally big breakfast crowd swelled even larger by several busloads of sales executives who had just arrived at the hotel for a four-day meeting. Johann was at his desk, hurrying through some reports he had promised Alana would be finished yesterday. He knew it was only a matter of time before he'd be called into the dining room. His three 6 o'clock servers were trying to take care of the rapidly increasing crowd, and Janice, one of his three 7 o'clock servers, had called him the night before to tell him she wouldn't be in until 11—her basement had flooded, and she had to meet with a cleaning crew and an insurance

adjuster in the morning. So today of all days he would have to serve the breakfast crowd one server short.

When Johann's telephone rang right at 7 o'clock, his heart sank. Sure enough, Rachel, another of his 7 o'clock servers, was calling to say she was sick and wouldn't be coming in. She was a good employee who had never called in sick before, so he fought back his feeling of panic and told her to take care of herself and not worry about a thing. He no sooner thanked her for calling and hung up when the phone rang again. It was Raoul, the third 7 o'clock server, calling in sick, too. This was the fourth time Raoul had called in sick in the two months Johann had been supervisor, and Johann knew that Raoul had a habit of staying up playing videogames until the wee hours then coming in late for work—in fact, Johann used to help Raoul think of excuses to tell Sarita back when Sarita was the supervisor. But he really did sound sick this time, so Johann put aside his suspicions and told Raoul to come in later if he could.

Johann gave up all thoughts of catching up on his reports and grabbed the schedule. The only people he might be able to call in were Ashton and Maria. No answer at Ashton's house. Maria was home, but she couldn't come in because she was a chaperon that morning for her daughter's sixth-grade field trip. She was very sorry. "That's okay," Johann said wearily, and with exaggerated carefulness placed the receiver back in its cradle. It was all he could do to keep from throwing the phone across the room. Instead of six servers for the morning, he was down to three, with a bigger crowd than usual and no one he could turn to for help. Even Alana was unavailable—she was in a staff meeting with the hotel's general manager. Johann grimly straightened his tie and headed for the dining room.

Hurrying through the kitchen, he was assaulted by the sounds of a staff under pressure: cooks yelling orders, dishes clattering violently, oven doors slamming. He charged through the double swinging doors into the dining room just in time to see Steve, one of his busers, heading for the restaurant's entrance, holding a towel tightly wrapped around his right hand. "What happened to him?" Johann asked Martha.

"He was hurrying too much, broke a coffee cup and cut himself. I sent him to the doctor—looks like he'll need stitches."

Great, Johann thought as he surveyed the situation. Every table was packed, and the roar of a hundred conversations made it almost as noisy in the dining room as it had been in the kitchen. Johann couldn't remember the restaurant ever being so crowded, and there was a line of guests extending from the restaurant's entrance into the hotel lobby, waiting for a table.

Taking a deep breath, Johann threw himself into the fray. He tried to be everywhere at once, waiting tables, pouring coffee, seating guests, running the cash register, all the while trying not to notice the frowns from guests angry at the inevitable delays in service. Each guest complaint muttered within earshot—"What kind of a place is this?" "Great service around here!"—hit him like a lash. Johann fought down the waves of helplessness and frustration he felt and threw encouraging words at harried staff members whenever he rushed past one of them. He was in the middle of yet another long apology to an irritated guest when, out of the corner of his eye, he saw Martha at the cash register, standing on tiptoe and waving to him furiously above a long line of guests waiting to pay their bills.

He excused himself with a strained smile and hurried over to Martha. "What's the problem?"

"I don't know," Martha said breathlessly, "the register just stopped working."

Johann stared in frustration at the silent machine; he didn't have a clue about how to get it working again. "What did you do?" he barked at Martha.

"I didn't do anything!" Martha wailed. "It's not *my* fault."

"It's not *my* fault either," Johann snapped. "Damn it, think! Did you do something just before it quit?"

"Hey!" one of the guests back in the middle of the line called up to Johann, "I had to wait for my food, wait for my check, and now I have to wait to give you my money? Come on, do something!"

"I'm trying to do something, sir," Johann said through clenched teeth.

"Well, do it now, 'cause I'm tired of this." There was a murmur of agreement from the other guests in line.

Johann yelled at Martha. "Go to my office and get my calculator."

Martha responded: "I don't know where it is."

Johann slammed his fist down on the counter. "Damn it, do I have to do everything myself?!" he shrieked.

A hush fell over the restaurant. Everyone froze; all eyes turned toward Johann. Martha blinked back tears and was starting to say something when her gaze shifted past Johann's shoulder and her eyes widened. Johann turned around to see his boss, Alana, looking around the restaurant incredulously. "What is going on here?!" she demanded.

Later that morning, Alana looked across her desk at Johann and sighed. What could have gone so wrong? This morning's incident was just the latest in a series of problems she'd had with Johann ever since he took the dining room supervisor's job. Johann didn't seem to understand budgets and was not keeping up with the administrative part of the job—late reports, botched purchase orders, unsigned invoices—the list was rather lengthy. Johann didn't even seem to be handling the people-skills part of his job very well. Several employees had come to Alana with complaints that Johann was playing favorites when it came to scheduling. And yelling at Martha this morning—Alana just hoped she didn't cause the hotel any headaches over that.

It had taken a while, but Alana had gotten Hummingbirds under control again with the help of George, the coffee shop manager. After the crisis was past, Alana had left George in charge of the restaurant and had taken Johann to her office for a long-overdue counseling session. But now she wasn't sure where to begin.

"Johann," she said finally, "what happened? I couldn't believe my eyes when I saw you ranting and raving in front of a room full of guests."

"Look," Johann said defensively, "I had my hands full. You weren't around, we were working short-handed, the register went dead—I didn't know what to do. I was doing the best I could. I was never trained for that kind of situation."

"But Johann, you had training. You spent a week with Sarita; she said you were ready. You worked in the restaurant for two years. I don't know what else we could have done for you."

"You never prepared me for an emergency like that."

"But no one could have foreseen what happened this morning!" Alana exclaimed. "Besides, managers are supposed to be able to cope with all the crazy things that go wrong. That's why we put you in that position; we thought you could handle it."

"Well, maybe you were wrong!" Johann blurted out. "Maybe you shouldn't have promoted me in the first place." Johann looked down at his feet and mumbled, "I never wanted to be a supervisor anyway."

DISCUSSION QUESTIONS

1. Did Sarita and Alana make a mistake in promoting Johann? Why or why not?

2. What should Alana do about Johann?

3. If Johann stays on as supervisor, what are the immediate steps Alana and Johann must take with other people affected by Johann's outburst?

Case number: 3566CA

The following industry experts helped generate and develop this case: Philip J. Bresson, Director of Human Resources, Renaissance New York Hotel, New York, New York; and Jerry Fay, Human Resources Director, ARAMARK Corporation, Atlanta, Georgia.

ENDNOTES

1. Sion Phillpott, "15 Disappearing Jobs that Won't Exist in 2030," last modified July 7, 2020, https://www.careeraddict.com/disappearing-jobs.

2. Ibid.

3. American Hotel and Lodging Association, "State of the Hotel Industry 2021," accessed February 7, 2021, https://www.ahla.com/soti2021.

4. Elise Schoening and Michael J. Shapiro, "The Latest on Hotel Openings and Closings due to Covid-19," last modified April 5, 2021, https://www.northstarmeetingsgroup.com/News/Hotels-and-Resorts/Coronavirus-Update-Hotel-Resort-Casinos-Closed-Economic-Impact.

5. STR, "U.S. Hotel Industry Posts Record Levels in 2019, But Lowest Growth Since Recession," accessed February 28, 2021, https://str.com/press-release/us-hotel-industry-posts-record-levels-2019-lowest-growth-recession.

6. Ana Cvetkovic, "What's the True Cost of Employee Turnover to the Restaurant Industry?," December 27, 2019, https://www.7shifts.com/blog/true-cost-of-employee-turnover/.

7. Linkedin Learning, "2019 Workplace Learning Report," https://learning.linkedin.com/content/dam/me/business/en-us/amp/learning-solutions/images/workplace-learning-report-2019/pdf/workplace-learning-report-2019.pdf.

8. Bonnie J. Knutson, Robert H. Woods, and Carl P. Borchgrevink, "Examining the Characteristics of 'Customers from Hell' and Their Impact on the Service Encounter," *Journal of Hospitality & Tourism Education* 10, no. 4 (1999): 52–56.

9. Inspired eLearning, "Benefits of Computer-Based Corporate Training," last modified August 27, 2019, https://inspiredelearning.com/blog/benefits-of-computer-based-training-for-corporate-education/.

10. Seth Puri, "Five Advantages of E-Learning," last modified November 16, 2018, https://trainingindustry.com/articles/e-learning/5-advantages-of-e-learning/.

11. Cathy Li and Farah Lalani, "The COVID-19 Pandemic Has Changed Education Forever. This Is How," last modified April 29, 2020, https://www.weforum.org/agenda/2020/04/coronavirus-education-global-covid19-online-digital-learning/.

12. Emma Snider, "The 70-20-10 Rule," accessed April 21, 2021, https://searchhrsoftware.techtarget.com/definition/70-20-10-70-20-10-rule.

13. Sandra M. Fowler and Margaret D. Pusch, "Intercultural Simulation Games: A Review (of the United States and Beyond)," *Simulation and Gaming* 41, no. 1 (2010): 94–115.

14. Lin Grensing-Pophal, "Four Steps for Evaluating Your Training Programs," last modified May 22, 2019, https://hrdailyadvisor.blr.com/2019/05/22/4-steps-for-evaluating-your-training-programs/.

15. Dennis Reynolds, Imran Rahman, and Stacey Bradetich, "Hotel Managers' Perceptions of the Value of Diversity Training: An Empirical Investigation," *International Journal of Contemporary Hospitality Management* 26, no. 3 (2014): 426–446.

16. Greg DeShields and Zoe Moore, "The Critical Importance of Diversity, Equity and Inclusion in the Meetings and Hospitality Industries," *Meetings Today*, June 15, 2020, https://meetingstoday.com/articles/142348/critical-importance-diversity-equity-and-inclusion-meetings-and-hospitality.

17. Alison McIntosh and Candice Harris, "Hospitality training as a means of independence for young adults with learning disabilities," *Hospitality Insights for a Sustainable Industry* Vol. 2 No. 2 (2018), https://ojs.aut.ac.nz/hospitality-insights/article/view/38.

18. Rosie, "7 Strategies to Improve Recruitment for Diversity in Hospitality," last modified July 16, 2019, https://harver.com/blog/diversity-in-hospitality/.

19. Bruce Jones, "How Disney Empowers Its Employees to Deliver Exceptional Customer Service," *Harvard Business Review*, February 28, 2018, https://hbr.org/sponsored/2018/02/how-disney-empowers-its-employees-to-deliver-exceptional-customer-service.

20. Sodexo, "Sodexo Named to Highest Level of Diversity Best Practices Inclusion Index," *PR Newswire*, August 19, 2020, https://www.prnewswire.com/news-releases/sodexo-named-to-highest-level-of-diversity-best-practices-inclusion-index-301114978.html.

21. Arwa Mahdawi, "What Jobs Will Still Be Around in 20 Years? Read This to Prepare Your Future," last modified June 26, 2017, https://www.theguardian.com/us-news/2017/jun/26/jobs-future-automation-robots-skills-creative-health.

6

EVALUATING EMPLOYEE PERFORMANCE

Chapter 6 Outline

Learning Objectives

1. Describe general performance appraisal issues and summarize the functions of performance appraisals. (pp. 138–141)

2. Describe potential problems with performance appraisals. (pp. 141–144)

3. Describe the principal types of rating systems used in appraising employee performance and the most commonly used methods of appraising performance. (pp. 144–152)

4. Identify who should evaluate performance, and discuss objectives for programs that train managers and supervisors to conduct performance appraisals. (pp. 152–156)

5. Discuss frequency of performance appraisals, identify potential legal issues, and summarize keys to developing an effective employee appraisal system. (pp. 157–161)

KEY TERMS

Performance appraisal

Performance feedback

Predictive validity

Leniency errors

Severity errors

Central tendency errors

Recency errors

Past anchoring errors

Halo errors

Primacy error

Trait-based ratings

Behavior-based ratings

Results-based rating

Simple (or straight) ranking

Alternative ranking

Paired comparison

Forced distribution

Graphic rating scale

Behaviorally anchored rating scales (BARS)

Critical incidents

Behavioral observation scales (BOS)

Narrative essays

Management by objectives (MBO)

360-degree appraisal

Job relatedness

It is not new for American businesses to use some form of *performance appraisal* to gauge the performance of their employees. One of the earliest forms was applied at the Ford car assembly plant shortly after the company was founded. In this system, when employees were finished with their day's work, they walked past a wall filled with cubby holes, one for each worker, each containing a slip of paper. These slips of paper were their daily performance reviews. If they received a white slip of paper, it meant they were invited back for another day of work. If they received a pink slip of paper, it meant they were fired. This is the origin of the term "pink slip."[1]

Evaluating the performance of an employee or manager is always difficult. One expert even compared performance appraisals to telling someone: "Here's what I think of your baby."[2] No matter what is said during a performance appraisal, employees on the receiving end may see management in a negative light. Performance evaluations often generate anxiety in employees. When these evaluations are improperly managed, an environment of resentment and resistance can develop, leading to organizational problems.

Do performance appraisals help people manage more effectively? Researchers investigated several major U.S.-based corporations (Aetna Inc., IBM, Johnson & Johnson, and Wyeth Pharmaceuticals) and found that time dedicated to conducting and implementing performance appraisals was the most important factor contributing to an ethical and effective evaluation.[3] Yet many managers fail to properly implement performance appraisals. Some failures have been traced to how managers view and understand the appraisal system itself, resulting in evaluations that fail to achieve their intended purpose. All too often, employees are left feeling more confused after their appraisals than before.[4]

Some companies realize that their performance appraisal systems are not working.[5] Does this mean managers should not appraise employees on their performance? The answer is clearly "no." A manager's role is to get the best performance from employees. To do so, managers need some system of evaluating how well employees are doing.

Performance appraisals are subject to human emotions and judgments, and, therefore, human errors. Many managers fail to see that it is impossible to attain an absolutely unbiased and objective evaluation of an employee's performance. Although managers should conduct performance appraisals as effectively as they can, they must also realize that they cannot perfect the process. Managers and employees will always be subject to human conditions that affect performance appraisals.

Sometimes managers use performance appraisals to motivate. Such managers concentrate on finding the good in an employee's performance. At other times, managers may be influenced by political considerations. For example, if a manager considers it advantageous to the organization to keep raises and promotions to a minimum, that manager may give an employee a marginal appraisal.

The goal of this chapter is to describe the ins and outs of performance appraisal so that managers can keep the performance appraisal systems in their organizations flexible, responsive, and, most of all, fair. Appraisals are important. Regardless of the method used, they serve a valuable purpose in hospitality. Exhibit 6.1 illustrates the importance of appraisals in the hospitality industry.

6.1 FUNCTIONS OF PERFORMANCE APPRAISALS

If you were to ask managers why their companies use a certain performance appraisal system, you would probably get many answers. Performance appraisals fill different needs in different organizations. Regardless of the needs they fill, the basic functions of **performance appraisals** are to:

- Provide useful feedback to employees on their performance

- Identify employees who need additional training and establish employee career goals

- Provide a decision-making tool for managers about future promotions, discipline, training, or merit-increase decisions

Exhibit 6.1	Importance of Appraisals in Three Segments of the Hospitality Industry			
Impact on Performance	**Lodging**	**Restaurants**	**Clubs**	**Other Industries**
Very Important to Success	59.4%	38.1%	48.3%	53.7%
Somewhat Important	35.4%	43.7%	38.5%	41.2%
No Opinion	1.2%	10.3%	5.7%	2.2%
Of Little Importance	3.5%	4.8%	6.7%	2.2%
No Importance to Success	0.5%	3.2%	0.8%	0.8%

Source: Robert H. Woods, Michael P. Sciarini, and Jack D. Ninemeier, "The Use of Performance Appraisals in Three Segments of the Hospitality Industry: A Comparative Study," *Journal of Hospitality and Tourism Education* 10, no. 3 (1998): 59–63.

■ Measure the effectiveness of training, policies, and programs

■ Validate selection (and other processes)

Exhibit 6.2 illustrates that different segments of hospitality use performance appraisals for different purposes.[6]

Because performance appraisals can be used for so many purposes, it is probably impossible for one appraisal system to fill all the needs of an organization. Appraisals should be designed with a specific purpose in mind. For example, a hotel company may wish to determine which employees need training. Could a performance appraisal system designed for this use also serve as a tool to determine which employees to promote or terminate? Probably not. A company will likely have several performance appraisal systems in use at the same time, each serving a different purpose. Consider the uses outlined in the following sections.

Performance Feedback

One of the most common uses of a performance appraisal is to provide **performance feedback**. Typically, feedback is intended to

Exhibit 6.2	Uses of Performance Appraisals in Three Segments of the Hospitality Industry		
Use	**Lodging**	**Restaurants**	**Clubs**
Compensation Decisions	86.4%	90.7%	72.2%
Employee Objectives	78.1%	82.6%	77.6%
Establish Training Needs	73.3%	80.2%	60.5%
Promotions	65.0%	77.9%	47.8%

Source: Robert H. Woods, Michael P. Sciarini, and Jack D. Ninemeier, "The Use of Performance Appraisals in Three Segments of the Hospitality Industry: A Comparative Study," *Journal of Hospitality and Tourism Education* 10, no. 3 (1998): 59–63.

reinforce or help improve performance and to motivate employees. Employees normally want to know how well they are doing; if they don't receive regular feedback, they may not have a realistic grasp of their performance. When managers don't speak directly to employees about performance, employees may think their work is fine or worry that their work is poor. Regularly scheduled performance appraisals enable managers to keep employees informed about their performance.

According to one survey, despite the usefulness of performance appraisals, 57 percent of employees reported either never having had a performance review or rated their review as neutral to not useful.[7] One international study, surveying over 10,000 individuals, found that:

- More than 50 percent of respondents felt that their supervisor was "not clear, frank, or complete" in discussing employee work performance;

- 17 percent did not know or were unsure of what the manager thought of their work;

- 22 percent were unsure of or did not know the objectives they were expected to achieve;

- 33 percent reported that their manager supplied little or no assistance in improving their performance, and had failed to initiate any type of formal discussion of their performance; and

- 90 percent claimed to be enthusiastic about an opportunity for "real dialogue" about their performance.[8]

Hospitality professionals suggest that performance feedback sessions should include:

- *No surprises*—Employees should already have a good idea of how they are doing.

- *Employee involvement*—Encourage employees to express ideas and feelings.

- *Primarily objective data*—Measurable factors are more useful and effective than subjective opinions.

Recently, performance reviews have tended to be more frequent, informal check-ins between and among managers. In 2016, *Harvard Business Review*[9] referred to this as "the Performance Management Revolution." Many companies, including Dell, Microsoft, IBM, Adobe, and Juniper, have led the way. One *Washington Post*[10] writer referred to performance reviews as a "rite of corporate kabuki."

Employee Training and Development

Appraisals can help identify employees who need additional training or those who don't and are ready to move on. Appraisals can also be used to determine training needs on a department basis. For example, front desk agents may need additional training after a new computerized folio system has been installed and in place for a while. Managers can determine the need for training by conducting training-oriented performance appraisals with the front desk agents.

In addition, appraisals can be useful aids in establishing career goals or long-term employee development plans. Armed with an employee's record of performance appraisals, managers can provide effective employee guidance and career counseling. One survey reported that only 12 percent of employees had any idea of their own career paths.[11] Effective employee appraisals can help an organization in the career development of individuals, which may lead to greater employee satisfaction.

Decision-Making Tool

When used as a decision-making tool, performance appraisals provide an effective way to link rewards and discipline to performance. Employees who perform well may receive favorable evaluations that can lead to merit pay, promotions, career development assignments, or transfers. Those who consistently receive poor evaluations can be legitimately identified for discipline, demotion, or discharge from the company.

Performance appraisals provide a basis for compensation, promotion, transfer, grievance, or discipline decisions. Merit pay, for example, should relate directly to an employee's performance on the job. Performance appraisals help managers decide who should receive merit pay increases. Some performance appraisals give managers the opportunity to evaluate how employees perform when they are given more authority. Such assessments provide guidelines for promotion decisions. Many of the same performance appraisals used in promotion decisions are useful when making decisions about transfers. In discipline, discharge, and grievance cases, performance appraisals can provide useful background information. Effective employee performance documentation can protect an organization involved in a grievance, lawsuit, or equal employment opportunity discrimination charge.

Evaluation of Training, Policies, and Programs

Performance appraisals can be used to measure the effectiveness of training. Evaluating personnel before and after training measures the effectiveness of a training program. The close contact during an appraisal also provides an opportunity for managers and employees to discuss the goals and problems associated with specific policies or programs. During an appraisal, managers may learn from employees that certain policies or programs do not work as designed. In that sense, appraisals can serve as an evaluation for new policies.

Validation of the Selection Process

The goal of selection is to predict which job candidates will perform best and fit best in the organization. Predictions should be tested to determine whether the selection system works effectively. Performance appraisals provide an excellent opportunity to do just that. For example, when performance appraisals identify recently hired employees who are not performing well, managers may have evidence of a selection system that does not work correctly.

On the other hand, appraisals may indicate that the selection system works by showing that many recently hired employees are meeting the organization's standards. Performance appraisals can also justify selection decisions. When used in conjunction with selection, performance appraisals

may help establish the **predictive validity** of selection methods.

6.2 POTENTIAL PROBLEMS WITH PERFORMANCE APPRAISALS

Performance appraisals are subjective and are influenced by many factors. This section outlines some problems associated with inaccurate performance appraisals. These problems include validity and reliability errors as well as bias or fairness errors. A manager's motives may also adversely affect the performance appraisal process. Understanding the factors that increase the likelihood of error can help managers conduct fair and accurate performance appraisals.

Validity and Reliability Problems

Validity and reliability are important to performance appraisals. Some of the errors that can occur during appraisals and damage their validity and reliability include:

- *Construct validity*—Performance appraisals must measure what they claim to measure. For example, does measuring "service" actually measure the service delivered?

- *Content validity*—Performance appraisals must measure the entire issue, not just a portion or part. For example, a performance appraisal that measures guest service at a front desk can't simply measure the speed in which guests were served, since service involves many other issues.

- *Inter-rater reliability*—When two or more raters agree on the same rating, inter-rater reliability is high. If one rater rates a food server very high whereas another rater rates the same server very low, inter-rater reliability is low.

- *Consistency*—It is important to look for consistency when evaluating employees and not just focus on one point in time. For instance, if sales-per-person is used to measure the productivity of a food server, the appraiser should record several instances over time rather than a single instance, which may be unusually high or low due to factors beyond the server's control.

Bias

Legally, performance appraisals are free from bias if they meet the requirements of Title VII of the Civil Rights Act of 1964 and are fair to all employees. However, according to a 2019 article in *Harvard Business Review*, almost all performance evaluations are biased in some way.[12] Hence, it is difficult for managers to make unbiased decisions at all times.

Managers make a number of errors when conducting performance reviews:

- **Leniency errors**—Some managers give more lenient ratings to employees than they deserve. If a large enough sample were taken, we would expect that employee ratings would approximate the shape of a bell curve; this is not the case with all managers. For example, if all employees were rated on a scale of 1 to 5 (5 = excellent, 1 = very poor), we would expect the majority of employees to land near the midpoint of the scale. Lenient managers rate more employees closer to 5 than to 1, making overall ratings more favorable than normal.

- **Severity errors**—Some managers give more severe ratings than is normal. (This is the opposite of the leniency error.) As a result, more employees are rated near the lowest point on the scale (1) than near the highest point (5).

- **Central tendency errors**—Many managers tend to rate everyone, regardless of their performance, near the midpoint on a scale. In this case, many more employees are rated near the midpoint (or 3) than is normal.

These three errors create problems for two principal reasons. First, because managers in the hospitality industry tend to change jobs a lot, employees are often rated by new managers. If one manager was lenient and the second severe, an employee's performance could appear to be declining. On the other hand, a severe rating the first year followed by a much better rating given by a more lenient manager the second could lead others to conclude—erroneously—that the employee had improved and possibly deserved a raise or promotion.

The second reason that leniency, severity, and central tendency errors create problems is that employees' ratings may depend on who rates them, not on their performance. Employees in one department, for instance, may be passed over for promotions or career development assignments because their manager tends to be more severe. In another department, however, employees may receive promotions or assignments simply because their manager is more lenient.

The following are other common errors managers make in the performance appraisal process:

- **Recency errors**—People tend to remember recent things over those that occurred earlier. For example, a manager is more likely to remember things employees did a few weeks before the performance appraisal than things employees did six months earlier. Unless managers keep a record throughout the year, they are likely to judge employees on recent performance only.

- **Past anchoring errors**—Managers tend to rate employee performance similar to previous ratings. For example, if past ratings were high, managers tend to rate employees high again, even if they deserve lower ratings.

- **Halo error**—This type of error is the result of judging an employee primarily on the basis of a single positive trait, behavior, or action. While people usually perform some tasks well, others poorly, and others about average, the halo effect causes managers to see all performance as good.

- **Primacy error**—Based on first impression errors, primacy can set the tone for a relationship. First impressions are often difficult to eliminate. For example, if a manager's first impression of an employee is negative, this first impression may affect all subsequent interactions. Managers can prevent against this by compiling a list of past performance evaluations for reference, basically a snapshot of past performance.

Other Reasons for Inaccurate Appraisals

Each of the errors just discussed results from the way people think and the way they react to others. Therefore, each error is recognizable and explainable in behavioral terms and is probably unintentional. Other unintentional errors that lead to inaccurate ratings are as follows:

- Attractiveness (especially of female ratees) leads to higher ratings overall by both male and female raters.

- Managers rate employees' personalities rather than their performance.

- Managers allow employee backgrounds to influence ratings.

- Managers see everything about an employee as bad simply because of a single negative trait or behavior (called the "devil's horns" error).

- A performance appraisal lacks clear standards of evaluation.

- Managers don't observe employee performance adequately (either for a specific amount of time or in the appropriate environment).

- Managers compare one employee to another (called the "contrast effect") rather than to a performance standard.

- Fewer middle managers (because of downsizing) means more appraisals must be conducted by each manager who remains. This can lead to manager overload, which can lead to rushed appraisals and errors.

- Increasing task complexity often means that employees have multiple supervisors, each of whom may desire behaviors and outcomes that are in conflict with the wishes of other raters.

- The increase in technology applications in the workplace means less personal interaction. This decreases effective communication of standards and increases the potential for misunderstandings.

- The career mobility of both supervisors and employees means less time is available to gain real and meaningful insights into an individual's true level of performance.[13]

Exhibit 6.3 shows that managers have a variety of motives for rating employees inaccurately or unfairly. Some motives can result in higher ratings than employees deserve; others result in lower ratings. Either way, such actions undermine the performance appraisal system and are regarded as manipulative behavior on the part of the manager. It is precisely because of this type of manipulation that unions have traditionally shown a distrust of management and often attempt to structure pay increases and promotions around seniority rather than performance appraisal results.

Exhibit 6.3 | Rating Errors and Manipulative Rating Behavior

	Inflated Ratings	Deflated Ratings
Positive	■ Keep the employee motivated ■ Maximize the merit pay increase ■ Avoid creating damaging permanent records ■ Reward good recent performance ■ Assist an employee with personal problem ■ Reward effort ■ Like the employee personally	■ Scare better performance out of employee to prevent eventual termination ■ Build a stronger case against the employee who is destined to be terminated
Deviant	■ Avoid hanging out dirty laundry ■ Make themselves look good ■ Avoid conflict or confrontation with employee ■ Promote a problem employee up and out of manager's department	■ Punish an employee ■ Encourage an employee to quit ■ Minimize merit pay increase ■ Comply with organizational edict to keep ratings low

Rater's Motive

Source: Clinton Longnecker and Dean Ludwig, "Ethical Dilemmas in Performance Appraisal Revisited," *Journal of Business Ethics* 9 (December 1990): 966.

One study reported the details of organizations' performance appraisal systems from 33 U.S. companies. Appraiser bias was reported as one of the most common problems with performance evaluations, illustrating the need to identify measurable performance parameters and provide multiple forms of feedback to reduce appraiser bias.[14]

Knowledge Check

1. What are some potential problems with performance appraisals?

2. Explain three common types of errors managers make in the performance appraisal process.

3. Explain how performance appraisals are biased.

6.3 PRINCIPAL APPRAISAL RATING SYSTEMS

When developing a performance appraisal system, managers must first determine the type of behavior they will rate. The three principal types of ratings used are trait-based, behavior-based, and results-based ratings.

Trait-Based Ratings

Trait-based ratings are used primarily to assess the personal characteristics of employees. These ratings rely on factors such as company loyalty, communication skills, attitude toward supervisors, ability to work as part of a team, and decision-making ability. Trait-based performance appraisals seldom stand up in court because they often base ratings on characteristics instead of on job performance.

Behavior-Based Ratings

Behavior-based ratings assess employees on their behaviors rather than on personal characteristics. For example, such appraisals may rate employees on their friendliness toward guests, helpfulness, how often they thank guests for their patronage, and so on. Hospitality operations often emphasize an employee's behavior toward guests and other employees as much as that employee's actual ability to perform specific tasks. As a result, behavior-based ratings are fairly common in hospitality companies.

Behavior-based performance appraisals are more defensible in court than trait-based appraisals because they rate behaviors that directly relate to acceptable job performance. However, these rating systems do have problems. Managers often find that a behavior-based system accepts many behaviors that are each different from one another. Managers may also discover that the system allows for little variation of those behaviors. For example, a company appraisal system may define some behaviors as more acceptable than others—in other words, the system defines behaviors that employees must display to succeed at that company. Consider a manager's dilemma when rating a food server who displays many behaviors that are not consistent with the rating scale, yet is regularly requested by a large number of guests. Although the server's behavior does not meet company standards, guests seem to like the server. If the manager follows the rating system exactly, this employee would receive a low rating even though guests appreciate the server's work.

Results-Based Ratings

The employee we just described would receive a very different performance appraisal in a **results-based rating** system. Even though this server doesn't display desired behaviors, he or she does receive many compliments from guests. Consequently, since the server's results are good, a high ranking would be in order under a results-oriented system. While this seems to makes sense, results-oriented appraisals are not problem-free.

Some managers may focus too much on results at the cost of behaviors or characteristics. Consider how an appraisal system for front desk agents might evaluate the number of guests an agent checks in during a specific time period. If the system evaluates only results, a front desk agent who checks in many guests during this period would be rated higher than one who checks in fewer. However, working under pressure to check in a great number of guests, an agent may fail to make a good impression, alienate guests, and lose future business for the hotel.

Restaurant managers will also find a common problem with results-oriented evaluation. Is a server who serves the most people during a given shift necessarily better than other servers? How do you compare the server to others? If the results-oriented rating is based simply on total sales, the server who serves the most guests will likely be rated the highest.

Deciding which type of rating system to use is a complex decision. In some cases, managers find that the job dictates the type of system. For instance, some properties may determine that cooks should be evaluated with a results-oriented system. In other cases, a combination of trait-based, behavior-based, and results-oriented approaches works best.

Knowledge Check

1. Explain the differences between the three rating systems.

2. Why are behavior-based performance appraisals more defensible in court than trait-based appraisals?

3. Which behavior-based performance appraisal is most effective? Why?

6.4 METHODS OF APPRAISING PERFORMANCE

Several methods of performance appraisal are in use today. Exhibit 6.4 compares the hospitality industry's use of selected

Type	Lodging	Restaurants	Clubs	All Industries
Graphic Rating Scale	28%	35.1%	52.5%	24%
Management by Objectives (MBO)	49%	37%	21.4%	31.8%
Narrative Essay	37%	24.7%	12.1%	33.9%
Behaviorally Anchored Rating Scales (BARS)	41%	19.4%	3.9%	NA
360-Degree Feedback	0	26.4%	8.2%	NA
Other	9%	4.6%	1.9%	10.3%

Source: Robert H. Woods, Michael P. Sciarini, and Jack D. Ninemeier, "The Use of Performance Appraisals in Three Segments of the Hospitality Industry: A Comparative Study," *Journal of Hospitality and Tourism Education* 10, no. 3 (1998): 62.

appraisal systems with the rate of use across all industries. Each method has advantages and disadvantages. This section presents the most commonly used methods and the strengths and weaknesses of each.

Ranking Methods

Three ranking methods are commonly used. Each method results in ranking employees from best to worst, or from first to last. The three methods are (1) simple or straight ranking, (2) alternative ranking, and (3) paired comparisons.

Simple (or straight) ranking requires an appraiser to rank all employees from best to worst. This method has the advantage of providing a simple order for consideration. However, simple ranking has considerable disadvantages, not the least of which is the choice of criteria against which to rank employees. Simple ranking does not distinguish between different aspects of job responsibilities. As a result, appraisers typically consider only one responsibility, or perhaps a few. Appraisers can improve the simple ranking method by identifying job responsibility criteria and ranking each employee on this separate scale. Unfortunately, there is no standard method of measurement, so different raters may have different perceptions of the span between consecutive numbers such as three and four.

Some may think there is a great deal of difference, while others may view consecutive numbers as close together.

Alternative ranking resembles straight ranking in terms of its advantages and disadvantages. The difference between the two methods lies in how the ranking is determined. When using alternative ranking, the appraiser lists each employee on a separate sheet of paper and then chooses the best first, the worst second, the second-best third, the second-worst fourth, and so on until the list is exhausted.

The **paired comparison** method involves directly comparing employees to each other on each job criterion. Exhibit 6.5 shows an example of this method. The simplest way to compute final rankings using the paired comparison method is to count the number of times an employee's name appears on the left side of the ranking chart. The employee whose name appears most often is ranked highest; the one whose name appears the least is ranked lowest.

From an appraiser's point of view, simple ranking, alternative ranking, and paired comparisons clearly identify the most valuable and least valuable employees on staff. However, these methods cannot determine why one employee is more valuable than another or how much more valuable one employee is than another to an organization.

Exhibit 6.5　Example of Paired Comparison Ranking

Employees to be ranked: Alex, Fariq, Taylor, Shona

Alex is better than Fariq

Fariq is better than Taylor   Alex is ranked #1

Shona is better than Fariq   Shona is ranked #2

Alex is better than Taylor   Fariq is ranked #3

Alex is better than Shona   Taylor is ranked #4

Shona is better than Taylor

Forced Distribution

Forced distribution relies on the assumption that, under normal circumstances, the final ratings of all employees would conform statistically to a bell-shaped curve. This method assumes that roughly 5 percent of employees are exceptional, 10 percent are outstanding, 15 percent are above average, 40 percent are average, 15 percent are below average, 10 percent are poor, and 5 percent are very poor. Forced distribution eliminates some leniency and severity problems by creating a central tendency. It can, however, result in dissatisfaction among employees who resent being categorized at the low end of the curve. Exhibit 6.6 shows a sample forced distribution scale.

A famous anecdote pertaining to forced distribution involves Jack Welch's aggressive leadership style as the new CEO of General Electric in 1981. Welch wanted to disrupt the entrenched establishment, so he demanded that his executives identify the top 20 percent of managers and the bottom 10 percent. The top group was positioned for promotion, the other for termination. The subsequent success of GE, eventually becoming the highest market-capitalization firm in the United States, encouraged many executives to embrace a forced distribution concept.[15] A recent study, however, found

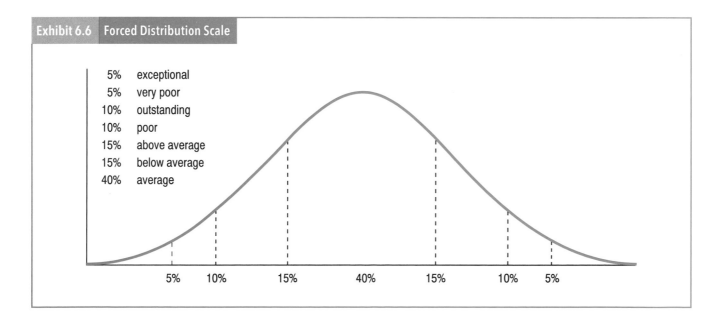

Exhibit 6.6　Forced Distribution Scale

5%	exceptional
5%	very poor
10%	outstanding
10%	poor
15%	above average
15%	below average
40%	average

5%　10%　15%　40%　15%　10%　5%

that many managers employing a forced distribution system thought it was more difficult and less fair than some other systems.[16]

Graphic Rating Scale

The **graphic rating scale** is used most widely for hourly employees. Using the graphic rating scale, appraisers typically rate employees on 10 to 15 criteria using a scale that ranges from 1 to 5. The criteria used generally cover such items as work characteristics, quality of work, quantity of work, dependability, attendance, interaction with people, job knowledge, and attention to detail. Ratings on each criterion are then added together to arrive at a composite score for each employee. A sample section of a performance appraisal using a graphic rating scale is shown in Exhibit 6.7.

This appraisal method is simple to use and provides scores that are readily understandable. However, this method is the most susceptible to rating pattern errors such as leniency, severity, and the halo effect because appraisers may find it difficult to determine the exact meaning of many criteria. For instance, what does "dependability" mean? Does it mean the same thing to all appraisers?

An additional problem with a graphic rating scale is the variability in importance of the different criteria. Appraisers typically apply different levels of importance to different criteria. For example, one appraiser may view attendance as extremely important and rank employees differently on this factor than on a factor considered less important. The level of importance that appraisers assign to each criterion can make a substantial difference in final composite scores. Management can overcome this problem partly by pre-weighting scales based on the importance assigned to each criterion. As a result, final scores can be influenced by multiplying each item by a different weight before the total is calculated.

Behaviorally Anchored Rating Scales (BARS)

Like the graphic rating scale, **behaviorally anchored rating scales (BARS)** require appraisers to rate employees on a scaled continuum. In this case, appraisers rate the specific actions or dimensions of an employee's work based on critical incidents. **Critical incidents** are work-related events that managers observe and record to form an

---

Exhibit 6.7	Example of a Graphic Rating Scale

Quality of skills performance	1	2	3	4	5
	Exceptional	Above average	Average	Below average	Poor

Quality of behavioral performance	1	2	3	4	5
	Exceptional	Above average	Average	Below average	Poor

Attendance	1	2	3	4	5
	Exceptional	Above average	Average	Below average	Poor

Ability to work with others	1	2	3	4	5
	Exceptional	Above average	Average	Below average	Poor

accurate picture of a job's requirements. This method relies less on an appraiser's opinion of what is good and what is bad than other methods do. The critical incidents provided on a BARS appraisal form provide specific examples of what are considered to be good and bad behaviors.

Normally, the critical incidents used on BARS scales are developed by a committee of employees and managers. Since employees participate in determining the criteria for ranking, the BARS method is often more acceptable to employees than other methods of performance appraisal.[17] In addition, the BARS method often provides more accurate ratings of overall performance.

The major weakness of the BARS method is the amount of time and the expense required to develop the system. Each job requires a totally different appraisal system, since critical incidents are different for each. As a result, development can be a very time-consuming and costly process. Exhibit 6.8 provides an example of a behaviorally anchored rating scale.

Behavioral Observation Scales (BOS)

Behavioral observation scales (BOS) were developed in response to criticism about the BARS method. Because the

---

Exhibit 6.8   Example of a Behaviorally Anchored Rating Scale

Rating	Scale	Sample Actions
Communicates effectively with staff members and attends meetings frequently.	7.00	This manager calls a meeting to explain why the hotel will be cutting back on staff. Employees are permitted to ask questions and discuss why certain positions in the hotel are being eliminated.
	6.00	During a busy expansion program, this manager increases the frequency of policy-committee meetings to improve communication about and coordination of the project.
	5.00	About once a week this manager invites several line employees into his or her office for an informal talk about hotel activities.
Communicates satisfactorily with staff members and attends some meetings.	4.00	This manager neglects to discuss with his front-office manager the problem of overstaffing among the bell staff during certain periods of the day, but expresses concern to the resident manager.
	3.00	This manager misses department meetings and fails to visit with subordinates individually, but leaves memos around the hotel with instructions on what should be done.
Experiences difficulty communicating with staff members and attends meetings infrequently.	2.00	During executive-committee meetings this manager dismisses subordinates' comments as stupid.
	1.00	

Source: Robert H. Woods, Michael P. Sciarini, and Deborah Breiter, "Performance Appraisals in Hotels," *Cornell Hotel and Restaurant Administration Quarterly* (April 1998): 25–29.

BARS method allows only one measure of each employee on a specific scale, some researchers thought that it could not provide a fair assessment of employees who sometimes performed well and sometimes performed poorly. Instead of using critical incidents as the measurements, the BOS method establishes critical incidents as the behavior to be observed and asks appraisers to evaluate how often employees behave in this way. For example, a rater could be asked to rate an employee from "always" to "never" based on the number of times he or she "works well with other employees as a team." Exhibit 6.9 provides an example of a behavioral observation scale.

Narrative Essays

Raters using **narrative essays** simply write essays that describe the employees they are rating. Ideally, raters should take the time to write essays that present a good picture of employee performance. When carefully written, these essays are very useful in filling gaps left by more quantitative methods. Also, narrative essays should provide written suggestions on how employees can improve. However, essays rarely turn out this way. Managers typically do not take the time to write careful essays that fully describe the performance of their employees.

Critical Incidents

Managers who conduct appraisals using critical incidents as performance criteria keep individual logs on employees that focus on an employee's behavior in specific situations. This method may be particularly applicable in many hospitality companies, since the behaviors managers usually focus on are exceptionally desirable or undesirable.

For example, consider a parking attendant who lends his umbrella to a guest during a rainstorm. Such a critical incident provides an excellent example of how that company feels employees should behave. The advantage of this method is that it provides information that is readily useful in performance appraisals. For example, a manager could recall a specific incident involving an employee and either commend or reprimand that employee based on what happened. The critical incident method also creates symbolic goals or stories that depict behaviors to emulate. A training video, for instance, might show a bellperson making a special trip to a guestroom to deliver a teddy bear that she saw a guest's child drop in the lobby. This type of critical incident portrays the behavior—attention to guest service—that the property desires.

A disadvantage of this method is that managers must keep careful logs of each critical incident they observe. Even when

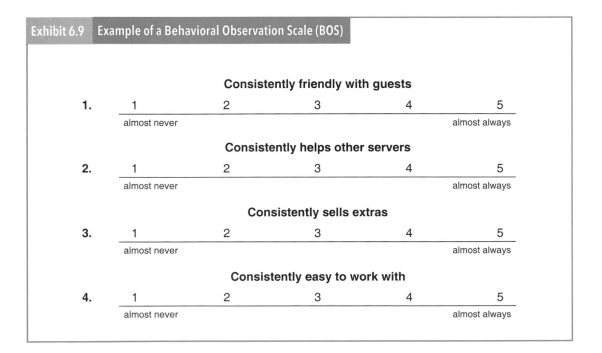

| Exhibit 6.9 | Example of a Behavioral Observation Scale (BOS) |

Consistently friendly with guests

1.   1   2   3   4   5
almost never   almost always

Consistently helps other servers

2.   1   2   3   4   5
almost never   almost always

Consistently sells extras

3.   1   2   3   4   5
almost never   almost always

Consistently easy to work with

4.   1   2   3   4   5
almost never   almost always

accurate logs are kept, it is unlikely that managers will capture enough incidents to fairly assess the unexceptional or normal behaviors of each employee.

Management by Objectives (MBO)

Unlike other methods, **management by objectives (MBO)** involves meetings between employees and managers in which joint goals are established. Specific plans for achieving each goal are also established,

as are the means for measuring progress toward goal achievement. Typically, an MBO system requires regular meetings to assess progress toward established goals; ultimately, employees are rated on their achievement of the goals. Exhibit 6.10 outlines the steps involved in establishing an MBO program; Exhibit 6.11 presents a sample MBO appraisal form.

Some managers and scholars believe very strongly in the MBO approach; they see it as a viable means of performance appraisal as well as a good management

---

Exhibit 6.10	Steps in Establishing an MBO Program

1. The employee proposes goals for the upcoming evaluation period.

2. The employee and manager discuss the goals, modify them as necessary, and agree on specific goals, which are established and agreed to in writing.

3. The employee and manager agree on an action plan to attain the goals.

4. The manager encourages goal attainment informally during the evaluation period.

5. At the end of the period, the employee and manager meet again to discuss accomplishments and to agree on the extent to which goals were attained.

6. The process is repeated.

Exhibit 6.11	Sample MBO Appraisal Form

Hotel _____   Name of Manager _____ _____

Review Period _____   Reviewer _____

Performance goals	Measures of results	Results
(1) Market share	Room-nights	Increase by 3 percent
(2) Guest service guest comments	Ratio of positive to 94 percent	Increase from 90
(3) Room-department profit	Room-department income percentage	Increase by 1 percent
(4) Employee morale	Grievance rate	Decrease by 5 percent
(5) Employee development training completions	Number of completions	Increase by 10 percent
(6) Health and safety conditions	Number of accidents	Decrease by 10 percent
(7) Hotel external relations	Number of leadership positions	No change

Source: Robert H. Woods, Michael P. Sciarini, and Deborah Breiter, "Performance Appraisals in Hotels," *Cornell Hotel and Restaurant Administration Quarterly* (April 1998): 25–29.

philosophy.[18] New software has been developed that allows managers to set and review objectives as well as analyze staff efforts and reward goal achievement to maximize employee performance.[19]

However, others see some shortcomings with the MBO strategy; they see the emphasis that many managers place on setting easy-to-achieve goals to build a good record and, subsequently, positive performance appraisals. This approach creates a culture of "yes-men," which Merriam-Webster Dictionary defines as "people who endorse or support, without criticism, every opinion or proposal of an associate or superior." These people damage organizations because they fail to examine tough-to-achieve alternatives carefully. Critics also suggest that it is difficult to evaluate the accomplishment of different goals by different employees under the MBO system. Some employees set more difficult goals than others. This provides appraisers with yet another challenge when ranking employees.

In the hospitality industry, an MBO system is often tied to the process of customer-based goal setting. For example, if a restaurant wants to improve its speed of service delivery, it might tie the restaurant manager's performance appraisal to a form of timely delivery goal. If the desired service delivery speed is achieved, that manager's performance appraisal would reflect a positive result. Specific goals aside, it is important that MBO standards be challenging but realistic. The supervisor and the employee must work together to establish goals. If that process is given a half effort, the MBO appraisal will have minimal utility.

Peer-reviewed research suggests that the MBO process increases employee performance level and overall firm productivity. When upper management is truly committed to the process and directly participates in key details, productivity gains are even greater.[20]

Knowledge Check
1. What are the three ranking methods used in appraising performance?
2. Why is the graphic rating scale more susceptible to rating pattern errors?
3. When would a manager use narrative essay in performance appraisal?

6.5 WHO SHOULD EVALUATE PERFORMANCE?

Most managers find it simple to determine the line of responsibility for performance appraisals. While immediate supervisors are typically responsible for performance appraisals, they may have little actual contact with the employees they evaluate. In these cases, managers must ask whether the time spent with employees is enough to adequately evaluate their performance. On the other hand, an employee's immediate supervisor may be the person best suited to evaluate that employee's performance in relation to departmental or organizational goals. One issue is fairly certain: immediate supervisors make vastly superior assessments when compared with those of second-level supervisors. The "boss's boss" is normally unaware of a given employee's abilities and/or performance and tends to give ratings that are highly inflated and less accurate.

Raters can be influenced by such factors as mood and stereotypes. It is therefore critical that raters are trained prior to evaluating others to improve their ability to be more accurate and objective and less biased. Research recommends that raters be trained first on the appraisal process, policies, and forms. That should be followed by training that focuses on familiarizing raters with common errors. Finally, it is critical to educate raters on common sets of norms for good and poor performance.[21] What follows is a discussion of the advantages and disadvantages of using different types of raters in the appraisal process.

Peer Evaluations

Peer evaluations can be constructive and contribute positively to employee development.[22] Some researchers contend that peer evaluation is the best appraisal method, due to regular peer contact and the importance of teamwork in the hospitality industry. In fact, research shows that managers often interact with some of their employees only to resolve problems, while employees constantly interact with their peers. Although this makes a strong case for peer evaluation, such appraisals are best used as part of a system that involves appraisals by managers.

Staff Evaluations of Managers

A restaurant company in Seattle has established a policy of allowing employees to evaluate each new manager after the manager's first six months on the job. This idea is often referred to as a 180-degree appraisal, since the traditional direction of evaluation has been reversed.[23] These appraisals are taken so seriously that a poor rating can lead to a manager's dismissal.

While few companies have gone so far as to link employee-driven appraisals directly to manager job retention, there is good reason to use this method of appraisal for management development. Employees typically know the extent of a manager's interpersonal skills. They also know how well that manager delegates authority and leads others. A recent study evaluating 150 managers and more than 500 employees found that when managers receive feedback from their staff, they are more likely to change their management style and subsequently be seen as more effective managers.[24]

Staff appraisals depend on the level of trust among employees, managers, and the organization. Unless the appraisal is strictly quantitative, it may be impossible to do, since managers will know exactly who said what. And in some—if not most—situations, managers hold reward and punishment power over employees.

Self-Appraisal

Research suggests that appraisals can be more productive if workers are given the chance to self-evaluate.[25] When used with other appraisal methods, self-evaluations provide a good basis for establishing goals and objectives, especially for training and development.

The notion that we are always harder on ourselves than on others may not be true when it comes to performance appraisals. In recent studies, gender has been found to play a role in performance ratings. For instance, one survey concluded that males tend to rate themselves higher than their supervisors rate them, leaving them frustrated with their supervisors' evaluations and possibly resulting in undesirable behavior. The same study supported past research suggesting that females tend to rate their own performance lower than males do.[26]

Research indicates that self-appraisals also tend to be less critical than appraisals by others.[27] Self-appraisals can be inflated by self-serving bias. Individuals tend to give themselves extra credit for successes, and they tend to blame others for failures. Another problem with this form of assessment involves inflation due to "blind spots." Individuals have a tendency to guess high when they lack reliable insight or facts about themselves.

Guest/Customer Appraisals

At first, hospitality managers may think that guest appraisals are the best method of employee evaluation, since the ultimate goal of any service organization is guest satisfaction. They can certainly help determine training needs. Unfortunately, collecting accurate information from guests is difficult. Many guests do not fill out items such as guest comment cards unless they are extremely pleased or passionately dissatisfied. As a result, guest appraisals tend to stress the extremes rather than the average. Also, it can be difficult to correlate guest appraisals to exact job responsibilities, which means these evaluations may not stand up in court. When used with another system—such as coworker evaluations—guest appraisals provide a good means of assessing overall performance.

Multiple Rater Evaluation Systems

Using more than one rater can increase the accuracy and perceived fairness of a performance appraisal. An American multinational hotel chain and resort's timeshare club in Las Vegas uses a multiple rater evaluation system, as do all of the club properties. Multiple rater evaluation systems also provide higher-quality management information for selection decisions and better equal employment opportunity documentation, and may reduce overall costs by consuming less management time.

One multiple rater method that has gained popularity is called the **360-degree appraisal**. The 360-degree appraisal approach refers to performance ratings of employee made by multiple individuals with varying relationships to the employee, including supervisors, peers, subordinates, and the employees themselves.[28] A fundamental assumption underlying the collection of ratings from multiple sources is that each rating source has a unique, yet potentially valid, perspective on the employee's performance. This may result in a more accurate evaluation of true performance than any single rating source.[29]

Much research has been done on 360-degree feedback in recent years, particularly related to whether this form of assessment should be used for appraisal or strictly for development.[30] Although it is reported that 90 percent of Fortune 500 companies use 360-degree appraisals, one international study reported a drawback to the system because peer ratings were more lenient, less reliable, and less valid when used for appraisal purposes rather than development.[31] Still, the 360-degree appraisal approach is growing in popularity in part because it is highly valued in team environments. Many industries have moved toward self-managed teams, also known as self-directed workforces. As these teams grow in importance, the 360-degree appraisal is likely to develop even greater popularity in the United States.[32]

In a 360-degree appraisal system, between four and ten raters provide feedback to each ratee. Generally, both objective and narrative/essay comments are included. Often, ratees are required to rate themselves, and then a copy of their self-evaluation is included in a packet other raters use. Unlike other rating systems, 360-degree feedback is anonymous. Although you don't know who your raters are, you may know their positions in the company (i.e., coworker, supervisor, subordinate, etc.). Many who use 360-degree feedback believe the system makes a difference and is useful. Although slanted scores can still occur, the wider range of raters reduces the chance that discrimination or bias will significantly affect the overall appraisal results. Such appraisals may therefore be more defensible in lawsuits.

The following are some recommendations for implementing a 360-degree appraisal system:[33]

- Feedback must be anonymous and confidential, although it is acceptable to identify the appraisers' levels in the company.

- Consider how long the ratee has held the position; some "history" among appraisers and ratee is necessary.

- A feedback expert should interpret the data for accuracy.

- Follow-up is essential; develop a plan of action after providing or receiving feedback.

- Combine narrative ratings with numerical ratings. Numbers alone don't say much.

- To avoid fatigue and overwork, don't evaluate everyone all at once when you implement a new 360-degree appraisal system.

Although it is growing in popularity, the 360-degree appraisal approach has some disadvantages. The use of multiple raters can lead to conflicting opinions, the process is time-consuming and administratively complex, and it requires managers and employees to learn a new system, which raises training costs.

A study by Watson Wyatt Consulting, the Human Capital Index, found that companies using 360-degree appraisals were associated with a 10.6 percent decrease in shareholder value (on average) when contrasted with similarly situated companies using more traditional reviews.[34] Although Watson Wyatt viewed the 360-degree system as a useful tool, it noted flaws that included excessive time and training issues and a tendency for individuals to form "rating alliances" that disrupt the integrity of the system.[35] According to John Sullivan at San Francisco State University, "there is no data showing that [360-degree feedback] actually improves productivity, increases retention, decreases grievances or is superior to forced ranking and standard performance appraisal systems. It sounds good, but there is no proof it works."[36]

Additionally, the end-of-year performance review often becomes a negotiation around compensation and promotion rather than a true development discussion. Still, despite the fact that some researchers question the utility of 360-degree feed-back, many firms believe it to be a superior system that provides incomparable data for determining merit raises, promotions, and terminations. This type of socially based performance system has felt even more urgent since the onset of the COVID-19 crisis because many people are working remotely without the same level of daily interaction with managers.[37]

Using many different types of performance reviews might serve the organization best. However, any new approach is likely to create a "Hawthorne effect"—temporary improvement in productivity that results from the change itself.[38] Therefore, to see how a new performance review system really works, managers must use it for a while.

6.6 PERFORMANCE APPRAISAL TRAINING

When training people to conduct performance appraisals, seven issues are important. Trainees should complete training with:

- An understanding of rating errors, including appraiser bias

- An understanding of how to process observed information

- An understanding of how to establish a frame of reference for what is observed

- A familiarity with the performance appraisal system in use

- The experience of having observed a performance appraisal

- Practice in effective interviewing techniques

- Practice in conducting a performance appraisal

To be effective appraisers, managers must be familiar with the rating errors discussed earlier in the chapter. One way to gain such knowledge is to read materials that describe problems associated with these errors (such as this chapter). Managers and supervisors can be trained to process information through accurate recordkeeping and to more carefully observe employees at work. Recordkeeping training, for instance, can emphasize the importance of noting behaviors and actions throughout the observation period to avoid recency problems.

Appraisers can be trained to become better observers if they're taught how to identify rating criteria and focus on those behaviors and actions. A frame of reference for desired behaviors and actions can be established using examples of critical incidents or films and observations of employees at work. These illustrations help appraisers identify standards of comparison.

Trainees can learn about the performance appraisal system their property uses by listening to a current appraiser or experienced manager discuss appraisal at a training session. Observation of an actual performance appraisal provides the trainee with a real-life example. Interview technique training also provides future raters with the opportunity to hone their interview skills.

Interviewing should emphasize the problem-solving approach to performance appraisals, which generally encourages employee participation. Interviewers should actively listen to and work with employees to set mutually agreeable goals.

While the problem-solving method of interviewing is recommended, managers also sometimes use the "tell and sell" or "tell and listen" approaches. The "tell and sell" approach emphasizes managerial control over the interview and generally recommends that managers tell employees their findings, then attempt to sell employees on the implications of the findings or on goals for improvement. Using the "tell and listen" approach, manager tell employees about their findings, then ask employees to discuss the implications of the appraisal and recommend goals for improvement.

Practice is the final step in training future managers to conduct effective performance appraisals. Role playing with current appraisers is an excellent means of training because it provides trainees with immediate feedback on how to conduct appraisals. This final training step provides appraisers with valuable experience in conducting performance appraisal interviews.

When discussing performance appraisal training, customer service consultant Emily Huling recommends the classic book *The One Minute Manager,* by Kenneth Blanchard and Spencer Johnson. These authors believe that supervisors should continuously practice one-minute praising and one-minute reprimanding. By doing so, the supervisor will not see the formal performance review as an overwhelming task.[39]

Special Training Considerations

Two factors should be taken into consideration when developing a performance appraisal training program: cultural differences among workers in the global marketplace and virtual workers.

Cultural Implications of the Global Marketplace. Any time performance evaluations are executed in an international environment, cultural implications need to be considered. In Western societies, a performance-oriented appraisal is both expected and accepted by the individuals involved. Traditionally collectivist societies or those that have a more Eastern philosophy tend to emphasize harmony, personal relationships, and organizational integration in their employee-evaluation systems.[40]

Certain cultures may also be less likely to embrace two-way appraisal systems. For example, in China, where there is great respect given to authority and age, it may be unreasonable to expect a functional staff-evaluation process; the resistance to the idea of subordinates evaluating managers might be too great.[41] In India, where "fatalistic rationalization" is often referred to when the issue of substandard performance is addressed, the ideas that impact effective rating systems are different than those in the United States. Individuals often demonstrate an external locus of control that does not lend itself to traditional U.S.-style performance evaluations.[42]

The bottom line is that today's diverse work force and global hospitality environment demand sensitivity to the feelings, needs, and values of employees who have different belief systems. Effective hospitality managers need to remain flexible and open-minded if they are to maximize the utility of performance evaluations in an international environment.

Virtual Workers. Many firms allow individuals to work remotely, especially since the onset of COVID-19. In fact, a recent study conducted by Nemertes Research indicates that more than 80 percent of U.S. companies are virtual workplaces, meaning at least some employees work away from their supervisors and work groups.[43] According to the Department of Labor, nearly 20 million U.S. employees work from sites outside their employers' places of business.[44] These off-site workers pose challenges to their supervisors, who have the task of issuing appraisals on individuals they seldom see. Some sales force team members, individuals who are always on the go and rarely check-in with headquarters, also call attention to this problem. The hospitality industry has many workers that fit this description: convention and group sales representatives, various back-of-the-house number crunchers, and even employees who work the graveyard shift (they stay on property, but often find themselves rated by bosses who work the day shift).

One director of human resources for an international firm recommends the following policies for setting up performance appraisals with virtual workers:[45]

- Establish clear goals—make certain everyone is on the same page.

- Evaluate by the bottom line; results and performance are what count. But don't forget, accessibility to team members and clients is part of performance. If the person cannot be reached, you have a problem, and the appraisal should reflect that.

- Set up a monitoring or accountability procedure with periodic face-to-face meetings and required deadlines for results reporting.

- Express trust throughout the process, but be objective in the final analysis of the employee's performance.

6.7 FREQUENCY OF PERFORMANCE APPRAISALS

Research consistently shows that once or twice a year is far too infrequent for performance appraisals. Despite these findings, this is the norm. In fact, believe it or not, a national survey of employers revealed that December 24 is the most popular time for managers to conduct annual performance reviews.[46] The problems with annual or semiannual performance appraisals relate to the appraiser's ability to remember events and behaviors that occurred as long as 12 months ago. Appraisers can minimize—but not eliminate—this problem by keeping thorough notes throughout the year. Although it may be impractical to provide feedback every day, managers should give feedback as frequently as possible.

In the hospitality industry, rapid managerial turnover causes an additional problem regarding annual or semiannual appraisals. Because managerial turnover in many companies is 50 to 100 percent (and sometimes more), employees may actually work under several managers during a single appraisal period. Unless extremely good records are kept, severe distortion in appraisals can result.

If at all possible, hospitality companies should strive for quarterly performance appraisals and should schedule them more often if managerial turnover is a problem. An alternative is to conduct employee appraisals on specific assignments. After an employee completes a training program, for instance, an appraisal should be conducted to establish performance criteria and to set goals. Employees working on special proj-

ects should also have appraisals conducted immediately upon completion or termination of the projects.

If annual reviews are conducted, it is best to conduct all appraisals during the same time period rather than staggering them. With staggering, some employees may get rated in the first quarter and others in the third, for example. The reason for avoiding the staggering approach is fairness. Suppose one employee's appraisal is conducted with the company facing a significant court ruling in two weeks that has every manager on edge. Now imagine that a different employee has the benefit of being evaluated six months later, after a record quarter of earnings that puts every manager in a good mood. As a ratee, which situation would you rather be in?[47]

Exhibit 6.12 reports how frequently appraisals are used in three segments of the hospitality industry. In this exhibit, we see that restaurants probably use performance appraisals most effectively, because they use them most often. Clubs use them least effectively, relying on annual reviews for 80 percent of employees.[48] Most employees want more frequent appraisals, because this approach provides them with more immediate feedback on their performance.

Remote Working and Performance Appraisals

According to Upwork, 41.8 percent of the U.S. workforce was still working remotely in February 2021 as a result of the COVID-19 pandemic. By 2025, 36.2 million, or 22 percent of the workforce, are expected to still be working remotely. Gallup reported that 59 percent of all employees who work from home would like to continue doing so while the remaining 41 percent would prefer to go to work.

Exhibit 6.12	Frequency of Employee Performance Appraisals in Three Segments of the Hospitality Industry			

Frequency	Lodging	Restaurants	Clubs	All Industries
Quarterly	5.6%	11.7%	1.1%	3.6%
Semi-annually	18.2%	27.3%	16.5%	15.6%
Annually	67.1%	41.6%	80.1%	62.9%
Other	9.1%	19.5%	2.3%	18.0%

Source: Robert H. Woods, Michael P. Sciarini, and Jack D. Ninemeier, "The Use of Performance Appraisals in Three Segments of the Hospitality Industry: A Comparative Study," *Journal of Hospitality and Tourism Education* 10, no. 3 (1998): 61.

DID YOU KNOW?

More employees in 2021 would prefer to work at home than at their workplace.

Americans Increasingly Working Remotely

There are some things people may do because of their concerns about the coronavirus. Please indicate if this is something you have done, are considering doing, or have not considered.

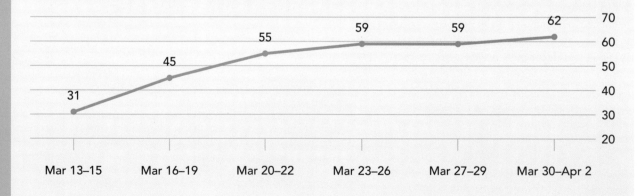

➡ % of U.S. workers who have worked remotely

Megan Brenan, "U.S. Workers Discover an Affinity for Remote Work," *Gallup*, April 3, 2020, https://news.gallup.com/poll/306695/workers-discovering-affinity-remote-work.aspx.

6.8 APPRAISALS AND THE LAW

Because performance appraisals directly influence employment decisions, they come under close scrutiny to ensure that they are not discriminatory. Typically, the key issues in investigations are **job relatedness**—the extent to which a rating system actually relates to the work done—and objectivity. Performance appraisals must relate directly to the responsibilities of the job. Objectivity has been found to be a problem in some companies.

According to noted researchers, a valid performance appraisal system demonstrates a high correlation between the system and the company's established, objective measures of performance and accurately predicts future job success. These authors suggest that managers should submit their performance appraisal system to 10 tests to determine whether it meets the minimum legal requirements for any appraisal system. Five of these tests relate to content (job-related) issues while the other five relate to process requirements (due process issues). The five content issues are:[49]

- Performance standards must be based on an analysis of job requirements.

- Evaluation should be based on specific dimensions of job performance rather than on a single broad measure.

- Performance standards should be objective and observable.

- Ratings should be documented.

- The validity of the appraiser's ratings should be assessed.

The five process issues are:

- Performance standards must be communicated to and understood by employees.

- Specific instructions for appraisals should be put in writing.

- More than one appraiser should be used whenever possible (to create inter-rater reliability).

- Appraisers should carefully review results with employees.

- Each company should establish legitimate, formal appeal procedures and inform employees of such procedures.

Two more items should be added to this list: periodic system evaluation and ample documentation of all issues related to performance appraisals. Documentation should include appraiser findings, interview notes, and employee-signed results. The system should be periodically evaluated and overhauled, if necessary, to meet the job-relatedness requirement. Job responsibilities change, which means performance appraisals must change. Documentation provides the paper trail required to argue a company's case successfully in court, if that becomes necessary. Above all, managers must be sure that appraisals are consistent. Too often, employees are fired in spite of good appraisals. This is called "pretext" (as when a false reason conceals the truth) and can supply grounds for losing wrongful discharge lawsuits.[50]

Performance evaluations are often important evidence in court cases involving the termination of an employee. In one hospitality industry case, the 9th Circuit Appeals Court considered testimony that revolved around low marks on a hotel and casino company employee's evaluations. The plaintiff claimed that these low ratings were an intentional retaliation against her for other non-job-related reasons. But in examining the evidence, the court disagreed with

LEGAL ALERT!

Managers who are tempted to write overly positive or inflated evaluations to avoid conflict or satisfy employees must keep in mind that they are also creating evidence that is both admissible in court and strong evidence of the employee's actual job performance.

this point and found that the appraisals had merit and were a fair analysis of the individual's objective performance.[51] The outcome of the case turned on other issues, but the point is clear: employee performance appraisals will be subject to legal scrutiny if they are disputed by an individual.

In a U.S. Court of Appeals for the 1st Circuit case, a hotel employee's mistakes were tracked by management using a critical incident log. Although the employee sued for various forms of discrimination and for violations of the Family and Medical Leave Act, the court found that the hotel had not acted inappropriately. Evidence of sound procedures for inputs into the critical incident log made an impact on the court's decision.[52]

In one 7th Circuit Appeals Court case, the court looked at the potential wrongful discharge of a former casino coatroom attendant who had been promoted to retail supervisor in the casino's gift shop. Following promotion, the employee proved to be "offensive" to customers and "hard to deal with." The newly minted supervisor "missed an entire shift" and "failed to properly handle a payroll report." The employer documented the employee's behavior and placed the individual on a 30-day corrective action program. Despite the apparent inconsistency of firing an employee soon after a promotion, the case was decided in favor of the casino. Procedures and protocols had been followed in terms of performance evaluations and critical incident reports, and the company was found to be justified in its termination decision.[53]

A district court in Iowa looked at a case involving age discrimination issues at a hospitality supplier. Various supervisors had issued numerous performance evaluations of an older worker over a number of years. These appraisals were deemed to be "somewhat uneven" in their assessment of the employee's performance. Despite this documented inconsistency, the hospitality supplier was able to get the case dismissed. This firm had taken the time to document numerous incidents of sub-caliber work performance by the individual, and it had followed up these warnings with training sessions and coaching. Since the firm appeared to act in good faith to help the worker fix the work-related problems, the firm was ultimately vindicated.[54]

The U.S. case law that involves hospitality companies and performance appraisals is constantly evolving. Although there is no single antidote that will keep a hospitality firm out of court, it is a good idea to keep rigorous documentation on all evaluation activities, and it makes good sense to consistently treat employees fairly and compassionately so that the firm's intentions and actions stand up to significant scrutiny. While litigation over performance appraisal methods and results is not uncommon, concern over it should not deter managers; the advantages of performance appraisals far outweigh their possible disadvantages.

Knowledge Check

1. What is job relatedness?

2. What types of documentation should be kept for performance appraisals?

3. Why is it important that performance appraisals relate directly to the responsibilities of the job?

6.9 FINAL THOUGHTS ON EVALUATING EMPLOYEE PERFORMANCE

Although there is no single performance appraisal system that works best in all circumstances, it is possible to develop a good system that meets an individual company's or manager's needs. The keys to developing a successful employee evaluation system can be derived from the main topic headings in this chapter:

- Identify the functions the performance appraisal will serve (reinforce or improve performance, determine career progress and set goals, validate the selection process, and so on).

- Develop sound criteria for the system (make sure it is valid, reliable, and job-related) to avoid potential problems with inaccuracy.

- Identify the types of performance to measure (traits, behaviors, results).

- Choose the method of appraisal (graphic rating scales, narrative essays, critical incidents, and so on) that will work best for the situation.

- Determine who will conduct appraisals and train those appraisers.

- Determine the frequency of performance appraisals.

- Make sure the system meets all legal requirements.

- Periodically evaluate the appraisal process to ensure that each function still meets the intended purpose.

Although it is difficult to design and implement an appraisal system to evaluate employee performance, it is far better to make the effort than to have no system at all.

The Future of Performance Management

A groundbreaking study in *Harvard Business Review* discusses how one company is rethinking the annual review process and peer feedback. Deloitte realized that its process for evaluating and rewarding its people was not in line with its corporate objectives and set out to reinvent performance management in the U.S. Deloitte thus fundamentally shifted from a focus on past performance to a continual focus on future expectations through weekly check-ins and per-project performance feedback. The theory behind the radically different approach to managing people's performance is based on the need to recognize, see, and fuel performance. The system is meant to be simple, quick, and engaging to use and provides a way for people to share and explore their best attributes and skills.[55]

Meanwhile, DiFiore and Souza (2021) posit in the *Harvard Business Review* that more types of companies are using agile, self-organizing team-based structures for evaluation. In this model, teams and small organizational units have both autonomy and accountability for results. There is no formal boss, so the traditional boss–employee performance management system is no longer applicable.

Knowledge Check

1. What are three keys to developing a successful employee evaluation program?

2. Is there one "best" appraisal system?

3. What does the Deloitte model of review and peer feedback address?

IN THIS CHAPTER, YOU LEARNED:

- The basic functions of performance appraisals are to provide useful feedback to employees on their performance; identify employees who need additional training and establish employee career goals; provide a decision-making tool for managers about future promotions, discipline, training, or merit-increase decisions; measure the effectiveness of training, policies, and programs; and validate selection and other processes.

- The three principal types of ratings used are trait-based, behavior-based, and results-based ratings.

- Methods of performance appraisal include ranking, forced distribution, graphic rating scale, behaviorally anchored rating scales (BARS), behavioral observation scales (BOS), narrative essays, critical incidents, and MBO (management by objectives).

- Ratings can include peer evaluations, staff evaluation of managers, self-appraisals, guest-customer appraisals, and multiple rater evaluations.

- Appraisers can be trained to become better observers if they're taught how to identify rating criteria and focus on those behaviors and actions.

- The cultural implications of the global marketplace and virtual workforces have created special training considerations.

- Research consistently shows that once or twice a year is far too infrequent for performance appraisals; however, this is the norm.

- Because performance appraisals directly influence employment decisions, they come under close scrutiny to ensure that they are not discriminatory. Typically, the key issues in investigations are job relatedness and objectivity.

KEY TERMS

alternative ranking—Rating system in which an appraiser lists all employees and then ranks them from best to worst.

behavior-based rating—Rating system based on the behaviors of employees.

behavioral observation scale (BOS)—Rating system in which appraisers identify how often an employee displays desired behaviors.

behaviorally anchored rating scale (BARS)—Rating system in which appraisers rate employees on specific behaviors displayed.

central tendency error—An error in a performance appraisal or interview that results when managers or interviewers rate all or most employees as average.

critical incident—Job analysis technique based on capturing and recording actual events that occur at work that, when com-

bined, form an accurate picture of a job's actual requirements. Useful in describing how services should be performed. Also used in training and as a measurement in certain performance appraisal systems.

forced distribution—Evaluation method in which a manager ranks employees on an exact bell-shaped curve.

graphic rating scale—Rating system in which appraisers rate employees on specific measurable criteria.

halo error—An error in a performance appraisal or interview that results when managers or interviewers rate employees based on a single positive attribute.

job relatedness—The extent to which a rating system actually relates to the work done.

leniency error—An error in a performance appraisal or interview that results when managers or interviewers rate employees too positively.

management by objectives (MBO)—Performance appraisal system in which a manager meets with each employee and sets specific goals to attain; both the manager and employee meet later to assess the extent to which these specific goals were reached.

narrative essay—Rating system in which appraisers write a narrative essay that describes the strengths and weaknesses of each employee.

paired comparison—A method of evaluating performance that involves comparing the performance, behaviors, skills, or knowledge of each employee with each other employee.

past anchoring error—An error in a performance appraisal that results when managers or interviewers rate employees on the basis of previous ratings.

performance appraisal—A meeting held between a manager and an employee for the purpose of evaluating the performance, behaviors, knowledge, and skills of that employee.

performance feedback—Feedback provided by the manager to an employee during a performance appraisal.

predictive validity—The extent to which a measurement predicts future behavior.

primacy error—An error in a performance appraisal or interview that results when managers or interviewers rate employees based on first impression.

recency error—An error in a performance appraisal or interview that results when managers or interviewers base employee ratings primarily on the most recent events or behaviors.

results-based rating—Rating system based on measuring the extent to which employees accomplish results.

severity error—An error in a performance appraisal or interview that results when managers or interviewers rate employees too severely.

simple (or straight) ranking—Method of ranking all employees in a single list.

trait-based rating—Rating system based on an employee's personal characteristics.

360-degree appraisal—Performance ratings of an employee made by multiple individuals with varying relationships to the employee, including supervisors, peers, subordinates, and the employee themself.

REVIEW QUESTIONS

1. What are the principal differences between graphic rating scales and behaviorally anchored rating scales?

2. How frequently should a property conduct performance appraisals? Why?

3. What is the purpose of a performance appraisal?

4. What are the basic functions of performance appraisals? How might each of these functions be used?

5. How do construct validity and content validity differ? Why is each important to consider when establishing performance appraisal systems?

6. Why is job readiness such an important issue in performance appraisals?

7. What are four types of common rating errors?

8. What are the advantages of using the narrative essay approach to appraisals?

9. What objectives should be included in a training program for appraisers?

Hotel Housekeeping Appraisals

Just 30 days ago, Laverne Wilson was excited when she started her new position as executive housekeeper at the spectacular Melrose Hotel. The Melrose had enticed her away from a competing property with the promise of higher pay, greater prestige, and, of course, more responsibility. With her eye for detail, however, Laverne immediately noticed major housekeeping oversights at the hotel. In fact, on her first day at the Melrose, she was greeted by an overflowing trash can near the main entrance and cigarette butts on the lobby floor.

As Laverne reviewed guest comment cards and the results from guest satisfaction surveys, the problems seemed to multiply. Guest complaints ranged from stained linens to crumpled and soiled stationery in the guestrooms. Worst of all, guest property had been reported missing from rooms on a number of occasions, without resolution. To top it off, guest satisfaction reports over the last six months showed consistently low ratings for the housekeeping department and its services.

The real challenge emerged as Laverne read through the past year's performance appraisals of the housekeeping staff. Performance ratings were based on a scale of 1 to 5 (5 = outstanding, 4 = exceeds expectations, 3 = meets expectations, 2 = needs improvement, and 1 = unsatisfactory). Laverne was surprised to find that virtually every housekeeping employee had received the highest performance rating. "How on earth," she wondered, "could the staff in this department receive such high ratings when the performance of each unit is absolutely substandard?"

Since she was a newcomer to the management team at the Melrose, Laverne decided to tread lightly. She first met with the general manager and asked for advice. He had been aware of the performance problems for some time and was anxious to work with Laverne to correct them. He knew the hotel would suffer financially in the long run if things didn't change, so he gave Laverne the go-ahead to shake things up. While speaking with the GM, Laverne also learned of important incentive changes.

To complicate her task, salary increases and bonuses would now be based on the performance not only of individual employees but of entire units. In fact, each department's share of bonus pool funds would now be based on its overall performance. As the meeting ended, the GM added that guest satisfaction ratings would play a bigger role than ever in determining salary increases.

Laverne felt overwhelmed. How could she convince the various units in her department to improve their performance, particularly when they had been following the same routine for years? She was the new kid on the block, and no one in her department would be very pleased with her for rocking the boat.

Later in the day, Laverne sat down with the human resources director, Rodney Ramirez, to express her concerns.

"Rod," Laverne began, "I have a problem. Certain units in my department are underperforming, yet the employees have been getting stellar ratings on their annual performance evaluations. I need to meet with the unit supervisors, but before I do, I thought I would get your input. How can I encourage supervisors to evaluate their staff more realistically and get them to make the necessary improvements in their units? I don't expect them to be happy with this news, but if things don't change, my department will be in big trouble."

Rod thought about the situation for a moment and then responded. "Yes, you're in a tough spot, especially when you're trying to upset the status quo. It's going to be difficult and you can expect resistance, but we hired you because we knew you could handle the situation. Let's work together on this. I could prepare some refresher training programs for your units, but the bottom line is that different departments in this hotel have been using performance reviews in different ways and for different purposes. To make performance reviews work in the future, you need to recalibrate them. Competencies and evaluation criteria should be consistent throughout your department. To some degree, you're being tougher on your employees, but you're also being fairer.

Keep in mind that all the changes you make will benefit our guests."

Laverne thanked Rod for his time and helpful advice and thought about what to do next. She scheduled a meeting with the supervisors from the three most problematic units in her department: Melika Chinoy, a room inspector; Susan Duvall, the laundry supervisor; and Clarence Patterson, the public space supervisor. After a few days of preparation, she was ready to face the fire.

When they all met the following week, Laverne got right to the point. "Thank you for meeting with me today. I think you all must be aware of some problems facing our department. I called you here today because the problems all seem to point to your units. Let me ask you, What do you think are trademarks of quality housekeeping?" Laverne sat back in her chair with her arms crossed and glared at each supervisor as she waited for their responses.

Melika was the first to speak up, "It's obvious. Clean rooms and linen. Attention to details."

Clarence added, "A nice-looking lobby and clean bathrooms."

"Right," Laverne affirmed. "So tell me why all of these guest comment cards say only bad things about the hotel? Look at this one. A guest says that the room she stayed in was filthy. Here's another complaint about stained sheets. Here's someone else who complained of a foul odor in the lobby. What are you going to do about this?"

Laverne paused. Susan's back straightened in the chair and her face seemed to harden. Melika and Clarence looked at each other. No one offered to speak.

"I want to see improvement in these areas," continued Laverne, "but, oddly enough, when I look at the performance evaluations of your staff, everyone has received a resounding ovation. How can every individual in your units receive a top rating, yet housekeeping underperforms as a department? We are only here to serve the guests of this hotel. If customers aren't satisfied—and judging from the number of complaints we've received, they aren't—then we aren't doing our jobs."

Laverne paused again to observe the threesome's reactions. Melika and Clarence were visibly agitated, while Susan appeared unmoved.

Laverne decided to continue. "Prior to the upcoming annual performance reviews, each of you must reconsider your methods of appraising employees. We need consistent evaluation guidelines that must be closely followed without exception. In other words, it's your responsibility to reevaluate your employees and I want to see concrete improvement in their performance within the next two months. We can no longer gloss over the staff and hope for the best. You should also be aware that next year's bonuses and salary increases will be based on overall departmental performance. We get nothing if this situation doesn't improve. Now I'll listen to your comments."

Susan Duvall, the laundry supervisor, was the first to respond. "With all due respect, Ms. Wilson, you haven't been here very long. I have been here 12 years, and, although I agree with some of the problems you've mentioned, your predecessors never approached us in this way. We have always aimed for a cooperative work environment and I think it is totally unfair that you point the finger at us. This employee reevaluation stuff may be an opportunity for improvement and change, but what about the other units in the department? Aren't they part of the problem too?"

Melika chimed in. "I think re-evaluating our employees is stupid. Like it or not, I need to keep my workers. People aren't lined up trying to get a job here. My unit will suffer if I lose people. It's easier to give them a high rating and then encourage them to do their best. I'm not going to change the way I've always done things. I've got to think about my people."

Clarence, who had never been one to let his opinions go unspoken, was the most outraged. "I've been at this hotel for 10 years and things have been going great, up to now. What the heck do you expect me to do? We've got lousy equipment and this hotel isn't up to the most modern standards, you know. The employees I work with are my friends. Why, I've known old Frank since I started here. Now I'm his supervisor and you want me to tell him his work isn't up to snuff? Forget it. Then you tell us we won't get a raise if we don't work harder? We don't get paid enough as it is!"

DISCUSSION QUESTIONS

1. How could Laverne have approached the supervisors differently?

2. What steps should Laverne now take with each supervisor to ensure that he or she improves employee performance in each respective unit?

Case Number: 3567CA

The following industry experts helped generate and develop this case: Philip J. Bresson, Director of Human Resources, Renaissance New York Hotel, New York, New York; and Jerry Fay, Human Resources Director, ARAMARK Corporation, Atlanta, Georgia.

ENDNOTES

1. Tom Moffit, "Origin of the Pink Slip," *HR Focus* 72, no. 6 (1995): 15.

2. Berkley Rice, "Performance Ratings—Are They Worth the Trouble?" *Psychology Today* (September 1985): 30.

3. George P. Sillup and Ronald Klimberg, "Assessing the Ethics of Implementing performance appraisal systems," *Journal of Management Development* 29, no. 1 (2010): 38–55.

4. Rob Law and Phoebe Tam, "Employees' Perceptions of Performance Appraisals: The Case of an Upscale Hotel in Hong Kong," *Journal of Human Resources in Hospitality and Tourism* 7, no. 1 (2008): 25–43.

5. M. Buckingham and A. Goodall, Reinventing Performance Management, *Harvard Business Review* (2015).

6. Robert H. Woods, Michael P. Sciarini, and Jack D. Ninemeier, "The Use of Performance Appraisals in Three Segments of the Hospitality Industry: A Comparative Study," *Journal of Hospitality and Tourism Education* 10, no. 3 (1998): 59–63.

7. L. Ford, "Boost the Value of Performance Reviews," *HR Focus* 86, no. 12 (2009): 1–15.

8. Les Pickett, "Transforming the Annual Fiasco," *Industrial and Commercial Training* 35, no. 6 (2003): 237–238.

9. Peter Capelli and Anna Tavis, "The Performance Management Revolution," *Harvard Business Review*, February, 2016, https://hbr.org/2016/10/the-performance-management-revolution

10. Jena McGregor, "The corporate kabuki of performance reviews," *The Washington Post* (Washington, DC), February 14, 2013, https://www.washingtonpost.com/national/on-leadership/the-corporate-kabuki-of-performance-reviews/2013/02/14/59b60e86-7624-11e2-aa12-e6cf1d31106b_story.html

11. Robert H. Woods and James F. Macaulay, "Retention Programs that Work," *Cornell Hotel and Restaurant Administration Quarterly* 30, no. 1 (2001): 84.

12. Lori Nishiura Mackenzie, JoAnne Wehner and Sheley J. Correll (2019) "Why Most Performance Appraisals are Biased, and How to Fix Them", *Harvard Business Review*, January, 2019.

13. The last four bullet points in this list were adapted from James E. Neal, Jr., *The #1 Guide to Performance Appraisals: Doing It Right!* 4th ed. (Perrysburg, Ohio: Neal Publications, Inc., 2003), p. 16.

14. Arvind Sudarsan, "Performance Appraisal Systems: A Survey of Organizational Views," *Journal of Organizational Behavior* 8, no. 1 (2009): 54–69.

15. Kim Clark, "Judgment Day," *U.S. News & World Report* 134, no. 1 (2003): 1. Retrieved 11/21/2005 from the Academic Source Primer database.

16. Deidra J. Schleicher, Rebecca A. Bull, and Stephen G. Green, "Rater Reactions to Forced Distribution Rating Systems," *Journal of Management* 35, no. 4 (2009): 899–927.

17. For a description of the development of a BARS scale, see Donald P. Schwab and Herbert G. Heneman III, "Behaviorally Anchored Rating Scales," in Herbert G. Heneman and Donald Schwab, eds., *Perspectives on Personnel/Human Resource Management*, rev. ed. (Homewood, Ill.: Irwin, 1982), 73–74.

18. Gershon Mader and Josh Liebner, "The Four Myths of Strategy," *Chief Learning Officer* 9, no. 4 (2010):32–36.

19. Kathleen M. Iverson, *Managing Human Resources in the Hospitality Industry: An Experiential Approach* (Upper Saddle River, N.J.: Prentice-Hall, 2001), p. 179.

20. D. A. DeCenzo and S. P. Robbins, *Fundamentals of Human Resource Management,* 8th ed. (Hoboken, N.J.: Wiley, 2005), p. 257.

21. Mike Schraeder, J. Bret Becton, and Ron Portis, "A Critical Examination of Performance Appraisals," *The Journal for Quality and Participation* 30, no. 1 (2007): 20–24.

22. Steven H. Applebaum, David Nadeau, and Michael Cyr, "Performance Evaluation in a Matrix Organization: A Case Study (Part 3)," *Industrial and Commercial Training* 41, no. 1 (2009): 9–14.

23. "Callidus Monaco's Objective Management Solution Implemented by Novel," *Telecomworldwire* (March 19, 2010).

24. Nic Paton, "Staff Appraisal of Management Will Curb Stress," *Occupational Health* 62, no. 2 (2010): 1–8.

25. Interview with Harold Johnson, general manager of the Mt. Charleston Hotel, November 8, 2005, Las Vegas, Nevada.

26. Anoop Patiar and Lokman Mia, "The Effect of Subordinates' Gender on the Difference Between Self-Ratings and Superiors' Ratings of Subordinates' Performance in Hotels," *International Journal of Hospitality Management* 27, no. 1 (2009): 53–64.

27. D. A. DeCenzo and S. P. Robbins, *Fundamentals of Human Resource Management,* 8th ed. (Hoboken, N.J.: Wiley, 2005), p. 257.

28. S. Bartholomew Craig and Kelly Hannum, "Research Update: 360-Degree Performance Assessment," *Consulting Psychology Journal: Practice and Research* 58 (2006): 117–122.

29. In-Sue Oh and Christopher M. Berry, "The Five-Factor Model of Personality and Managerial Performance: Validity Gains Through the Use of 360-Degree Performance Ratings," *Journal of Applied Psychology* 24, no. 6 (2009): 1498–1513.

30. Tracy Maylett, "360-Degree Feedback Revisited: The Transition from Development to Appraisal," *Journal of Compensation and Benefits* 22, no. 3 (2006): 12–18.

31. F. Carruthers, "Nothing But the Truth," *Australian Financial Review,* 14 November 2003, 78. Note that this reference is talking about U.S. companies, not Australian; "360-Degree Appraisals 'No Improvement'," *Pulse* 67, no. 11 (2007): 19.

32. Tesone, 155.

33. Mary N. Vinson, "The Pros and Cons of 360-Degree Feedback," *Training & Development* 50 (April 1996): 12.

34. Bruce Pfau, et. al., "Does 360-Degree Feedback Negatively Affect Company Performance?" *HRMagazine: On Human Resource Management* 47, no. 6 (2002): 55.

35. Clark, 1-1.

36. Pfau, et al., 57.

37. DiFiore, A. and Souza, M. (2021) "Are Peer Reviews the Future of Performance Evaluations?" *Harvard Business Review,* January 12, 2021

38. Bohl, 19.

39. Emily Huling, "Bad Management Can Have High Costs," *Rough Notes* 145, no. 10 (2002): 48.

40. Stephan Groeschl, "Cultural Implications for the Appraisal Process," *Cross Cultural Management* 10, no. 1 (2003): 69.

41. Groeschl, 71.

42. Groeschl, 72.

43. "Now They Are 'Virtual' Workers," *Communications News* 44, no. 8 (2007): 8–10.

44. Gus Manoochehri and Theresa Pinkerton, "Managing Telecommuters: Opportunities and Challenges," *American Business Review* 21, no. 1 (2003): 9.

45. "Performance Appraisals for Virtual Workers," *Getting Results for the Hands-on Manager* 42, no. 12 (1997): 3.

46. Timothy D. Schellhardt, "Mr. Cratchit, Let's Have a Word Before You Go Home Tonight," *Wall Street Journal,* 24 December 1996, B1.

47. J. E. Pynes, *Human Resources Management for Public and Nonprofit Organizations,* 2d ed. (San Francisco, Calif.: Jossey-Bass, 2004): pp. 199–200.

48. Woods, Sciarini, and Ninemeier, 61.

49. Umbreit, Eder, and McConnell, pp. 62–63.

50. Jonathan Segal, "Evaluating the Evaluators," *HR Magazine* 40 (October 1995): 46–50.

51. *Barbara L. Steiner, Plaintiff-Appellant v. Showboat Operating Company, d/b/a Showboat Hotel & Casino, Defendant-Appellee.* No. 92-16882 (U.S. Court of Appeals for the Ninth Circuit 1994). Retrieved 11/22/2005, from LexisNexis.

52. *Roy Hillstrom, Plaintiff-Appellant v. Best Western TLC Hotel, Defendant-Appellee.* No. 03-1972 1 (U.S. Court of Appeals for the First Circuit 2003). Retrieved 11/22/2005, from LexisNexis.

53. *Shirley F. Willis Plaintiff-Appellant v. Harrah's Illinois Corp. Defendant-Apellee.* No. 98-2655 1 (U.S. Court of Appeals for the Seventh Circuit 1999). Retrieved 11/22/2005, from LexisNexis.

54. *Judy A. Bauer, Plaintiff v. Metz Baking Co., Defendant.* No. C 98-4058-MWB 1 (U.S. District Court for the Northern District of Iowa, Western Division 1999). Retrieved 11/22/2005, from LexisNexis.

55. Henry Levinson (1976/1977) "Appraisal of What Performance?" *Harvard Business Review,* July 1976, pp. 3–7.

7
TURNOVER, DISCIPLINE, AND EXITS

Chapter 7 Outline

Learning Objectives

1. Describe the hospitality industry's turnover problem, demonstrate how to calculate turnover rates, and identify the costs of turnover. (pp. 172–174)

2. List causes of turnover and summarize methods for reducing turnover. (pp. 174–176)

3. Explain the proper use of discipline in a hospitality organization and describe approaches to employee discipline. (pp. 177–180)

4. Describe common appeals processes in an employee discipline program. (pp. 180–181)

5. Describe the appropriate use of discharge in an employee discipline program and identify several important concerns associated with using discharge. (pp. 181–184)

6. Outline an effective exit interview system. (pp. 184–186)

KEY TERMS

Turnover

Turnover rate

Separation costs

Replacement costs

Training costs

Retention programs

Hot stove approach

Progressive discipline

Preventive (positive) discipline

Hierarchical appeals process

Open-door appeals process

Peer review appeals process

Ombuds appeals process

Mandatory arbitration agreements

Constructive discharge

Discharge interview

Exit interview

Most employees want to work. They want to keep their jobs. Most managers strive to keep their employees. So why is turnover such a problem in the hospitality industry? And why, even when unemployment rates are high, does the hospitality industry continually face labor shortages?

This chapter examines the final stage in the life cycle of a job. Some employment ends when the employee quits, requiring the company to hire or promote a replacement. Other employment ends when the employer decides to discharge the worker. In either event, the result will probably be increased cost and might also be legal liability. Human resources managers can control potential losses by retaining workers they want to keep and by using deliberate methods of managing discipline and discharge.

7.1 THE TURNOVER PROBLEM

Each time a position is vacated, either voluntarily or involuntarily, the employer probably has to hire and train someone new. This exit and replacement cycle is known as **turnover**. Some turnover is based on the employer's decision to discharge and replace a worker. Some turnover is beyond the employer's control, such as workers relocating with their families or retiring. The COVID-19 pandemic may also have long-lasting effects on the hospitality labor market, which suffered 39% of all the job losses due to business shut-downs during this time.[1]

Every workplace experiences turnover, but the hospitality industry has historically experienced turnover rates much higher than other businesses with large numbers of employees. Recognizing and controlling the reasons for turnover are essential to successful human resources management in hospitality.

Determining Turnover Rates

The rate of turnover can be calculated for any time period or any group of workers. Unfortunately, not all hospitality organizations use the same methods for calculating turnover. Some include seasonal and part-time employees in their turnover statistics while others do not. One method of calculating the **turnover rate** is to divide the number of terminations for a time period by the average number of employees for the same period. The easiest way to determine the average number of employees is to add the number of employees at the beginning of the period to the number of employees at the end of the period and divide by two. To express the rate as a percentage, multiply the result by 100. This formula is presented below. The example uses the turnover rate for a mid-size restaurant staffed with 25 servers (average); terminations for the year totaled 75:

$$\text{Annual Turnover Rate} = \frac{\text{Number of terminations}}{\text{Average number of employees}} \times 100$$

$$= \frac{75}{25} \times 100$$

$$= 300\%$$

Companies use this method to determine their total annual (or monthly) turnover rates. This method includes both desired and undesired turnover. (Desired turnover is the loss of employees the company does not wish to keep; undesired turnover is the loss of employees the company wishes to keep.)

A second method adjusts the turnover rate by desired turnover. This method first subtracts the desired turnover, so that the resulting rate represents only undesired turnover during the year or month. To see how this works, we can use the preceding example of 75 terminations for a staff of 25 servers, with the following additional information: 10 of the 75 terminations were desired terminations:

$$\text{Unwanted turnover rate} = \frac{\text{Number of terminations} - \text{Desired terminations}}{\text{Average number of employees}} \times 100$$

$$= \frac{75 - 10}{25} \times 100$$

$$= 260\%$$

Many managers prefer the second method because they can justify desired turnover. In some cases, however, this method provides managers with an opportunity to disguise (or discount the significance of) high turnover rates. These managers might say, "We simply lost employees we didn't want." By including desired turnover, the first method may seem to overstate the degree to which turnover is a problem. Nonetheless, most managers see the first method as a more accurate figure, in part because there are costs associated even with desired turnover.

Turnover varies by region, segment, and company, but the lodging industry turnover rate is about five times the average of all industries in the United States. Hospitality turnover remains high, but it is not because the problem has been ignored. In fact, turnover has been the subject of much study and research, but still there are no clear answers.

Much is already known about turnover. For instance, we know that turnover is costly. Several studies project that the cost of replacing an employee, whether manager, supervisor, or line-level, can be as high as 100% of the annual pay for that employee.[2] The costs include the time and resources necessary to recruit, interview, hire, and train new workers.

Undesired turnover has many significant impacts. For instance, turnover affects those who stay when others leave, in part because the departure affects their working conditions. The loss of talent may also negatively affect company performance and customer service, at least until the replacement is able to perform the job correctly. Unwanted turnover can also contribute to an organization's inability to build an effective team of employees.

The research literature has also provided us with some valuable information on factors that cause turnover. For example, we know the following:

- There is a positive relationship between turnover reduction and employee training.[3]

- Individual and group incentives reduce turnover.

- Encouraging employees to take part in making decisions (even those with negative impacts) reduces employee turnover.[4]

- There is a relationship between organizational size and turnover rates; larger companies tend to experience lower turnover rates.[5]

- Self-directed work teams sometimes reduce turnover.[6]

- Organizations with high levels of effective communication systems have lower levels of dysfunctional turnover.[7]

Unfortunately, all that we have learned so far has not led to curing the turnover problem in the hospitality industry. Whether practitioners have not yet accepted that they need to reduce turnover, or whether scholars have not yet discovered and adequately presented the reasons lodging has high turnover and proposed effective methods to reduce it, research continues to indicate that the lodging industry is still unaware about many issues relating to turnover. Although the hospitality industry is not the only one interested in stemming the turnover tide, the situation has not been nearly so grim in other industries that might seem more volatile. As noted before, turnover rates in the lodging and food service sectors are the highest of all reported U.S. industries, well ahead of construction, retail, and healthcare.[8]

The Costs of Turnover

Turnover costs range from $3,000 to $10,000 per hourly employee and can be even higher. As mentioned previously, in some cases the cost could be as high as 100% of the employee's annual wage. According to the National Restaurant Association, turnover costs for restaurants average about $5,000 per employee. Turnover costs for managers can average $50,000 or more. Many companies equate the cost of losing one trained manager with the amount of that manager's annual salary—it typically takes about a year for a new manager to become fully productive. (It should be noted, however, that some researchers estimate turnover costs at even higher rates. One researcher, for example, suggests that companies can use a metric of 1.25 to 1.7 times annual salary to estimate the cost of each lost employee.[9])

Turnover costs can be classified as tangible or intangible. Tangible costs are incurred directly when replacing employees and range from uniforms to advertisements. Intangible costs (such as lost productivity) do not relate directly to out-of-pocket expenses, but in many cases these losses are significant.

Separation costs are incurred directly with the loss of a current employee. These costs may include separation or severance pay and the costs associated with conducting exit interviews, maintaining files, removing names from the payroll, terminating benefits, and paying unemployment taxes.

Replacement costs are those associated with recruiting new employees: advertising, pre-employment screening, interviews, testing, staff meetings to discuss applicants, travel expenses for applicants, moving expenses for some applicants, medical exams, and other costs.

Training costs are those associated with orienting new employees, preparing and printing new employee information, creating or purchasing training materials, and conducting training. Lower productivity (on the part of those who are conducting the training as well as those who are being trained) is an intangible cost of training.

Trained employees produce more than new employees who are still learning the job. In restaurants, for example, trained employees serve more tables and sell more items than do trainees. The result of training is higher productivity. The time it takes for a new employee to reach a satisfactory level of productivity varies. Studies show that it takes about three months for a new employee to reach the level of productivity of a trained employee.[10]

Managers should also be concerned about curing the turnover problem because of its impact on their own careers. Unwanted turnover curtails company expansion because it eats away at profits. When expansion is curtailed, advancement opportunities for managers diminish. Consequently, those managers who allow the employee turnover problem to persist jeopardize their own chances for growth and promotion.

Causes of Turnover

Most researchers agree that turnover is more related to internal causes (conditions within a company) than to external causes (the economy, new competition, and so on).

Overall, researchers have found three main causes of turnover:

- Low compensation[11]
- Faulty or inadequate hiring practices
- Poor management that weakens morale

Industries or companies with high turnover rates usually exhibit one or more of these conditions.[12] Another study identified culture, hiring practices, and promotion practices as important factors in hospitality turnover.[13]

Other researchers believe that the key to solving turnover problems lies in curing the problem of unmet employee expectations. Employees join an organization with expectations about what the work and the organization will be like. If these expectations are not met, employees often leave. This is the reason realistic job previews are so important.[14]

More than 2,500 studies of turnover have been conducted to date, but not all of the causes of turnover identified pertain to hospitality. Studies of other businesses point to unfavorable work shifts (such as night shifts and irregular hours) as a principal cause of turnover. In contrast, some hospitality employees identify irregular hours as an attractive feature of their employment. Although external influences such as unemployment and new job opportunities seem to have little effect on turnover rates in other industries, the reverse seems to be true for hospitality. As most managers know, new hospitality competitors often attract employees from existing operations.

Both managers and employees cite the quality of supervision as the number one cause of turnover in the hospitality industry. More employees leave because they are unhappy with the quality of supervision than for any other reason. Ineffective communication is the second most often cited cause of turnover. Some communication problems are associated with the quality of supervision—ineffective communication among supervisors and employees is often cited as a major cause of turnover. However, communication among employees is also a major turnover factor.

Turnover is mostly a gradual process. Employees don't usually quit suddenly for a single reason. Rather, they decide to leave over a period of time and because of accumulated reasons. Exhibit 7.1 lists the top causes of turnover in hotel and restaurant companies. Most of them are within a unit-level manager's power to correct. The last cause on the list—unreasonable expectations—is affected not just by the managers and coworkers but also by guests, making it harder to control. Guests expect workers to act the way they are portrayed in advertisements—always smiling, always serving, always at their best. To meet these expectations, hospitality employees must try to display these advertised characteristics. This acting is called *emotional labor*. Over time, this type of labor can take a significant emotional toll on employees, because they are often called upon to act in a manner that is inconsistent with how they really feel in a given moment. Behaviorists call this *cognitive dissonance*.

Retention Programs: Turnover Remedies

Despite the attention turnover commands, many hospitality companies have no specific plans for addressing it. Others, however, have developed complex programs designed to minimize turnover. Such programs are often called employee **retention programs**.

Turnover cannot be eliminated completely. In fact, few operators would want such an outcome. New hires can bring in new ideas and fresh energy, so some turnover is desired. But turnover can be like a disease; if left unattended, it can get worse. The most effective turnover remedies are tailored to a particular company. However, general short- and long-term remedies are often helpful.[15]

Short-Term Remedies. Short-term remedies focus on collecting and using information to address immediate concerns. In some cases, applying the short-term remedies listed in Exhibit 7.2 may be the only action needed.

Long-Term Remedies. Long-term remedies focus on making organizational changes to create a company in which employees want to work. These remedies take time and often cost money. The cost is determined by the degree of current turnover in a company

Exhibit 7.1	Major Causes of Hospitality Turnover

1. Weak or ineffective organizational culture
2. Toxic or uncooperative work environment
3. Poor quality supervision and management
4. Below average compensation and benefits
5. Inadequate career development opportunities
6. Low employee engagement and commitment
7. Incompetent coworkers
8. Poor communications
9. Lack of predictable schedules
10. Work/life imbalance
11. Unreasonable expectations

Adapted from Nombeko Felicity Dwesini, "Causes and Prevention of High Employee Turnover Within the Hospitality Industry: A Literature Review," *African Journal of Hospitality, Tourism and Leisure* 8, no. 3 (2019): 1–15 and Jung Woo Han, "A Review of Antecedents of Employee Turnover in the Hospitality Industry on Individual, Team and Organizational Levels," *International Hospitality Review*, December 8, 2020. https://doi.org/10.1108/IHR-09-2020-0050

Exhibit 7.2	Short-Term Remedies for Turnover

1. Surface the organization's culture.
2. Find out why employees leave.
3. Find out why employees stay.
4. Ask employees what they want.
5. Give employees a voice.
6. Make managers aware of their biases.
7. Develop recruiting programs that meet the company's needs.
8. Develop orientation programs that reflect the organization's culture.
9. Take interviewing seriously.
10. Take managing turnover seriously.

Source: Adapted from Robert H. Woods and James F. Macaulay, "Rx for Turnover: Retention Programs that Work," *Cornell Hotel and Restaurant Administration Quarterly* 30 (May 1989): 80.

and by the need for change. Common long-term remedies for turnover are listed in Exhibit 7.3.

Keys to Successful Retention Programs

Regardless of the turnover remedies that managers choose, three key elements are required for success:

- Executive-level support
- Managerial follow-through on program implementation, maintenance, and support
- Expenditures of time and money

Failure to recognize and provide any one of these key elements can doom a retention program. The place to start when planning a retention program is to compute current turnover costs and then determine the costs and benefits of retention efforts.

A study by the Hay Group of more than 500,000 employees in 300 companies found 50 retention factors.[16] Of these, pay was the least important. Research published in *Training and Development*, based on 2,000 respondents, confirmed this finding, and cited 10 factors that lead to retention:

1. Career growth, learning, and development
2. Exciting and challenging work
3. Meaningful work (making a difference and a contribution)
4. Great people to work with
5. Being part of a team
6. Having a good boss
7. Recognition of work well done
8. Autonomy—a sense of control over one's work
9. Flexible work hours
10. Fair pay and benefits

This report also listed seven steps that managers should take in developing a retention program that works:

1. Collect and analyze all turnover and exit interview information.
2. Conduct a survey to learn company beliefs and attitudes about retention (i.e., what would work).
3. Organize and conduct a "future pull" session. Leap ahead one year and imagine what you are celebrating regarding retention. Set goals this way. For example, one "future pull" might be: "Retained 95 percent of our management team."
4. Gather input and insight from focus groups and interviews of managers and employees.
5. Compile and distribute data. Be sure to use the data you have gathered to plan.
6. Tag a retention champion. You need someone in charge of retention who is empowered to act.
7. Appoint a task force to support the champion.

Exhibit 7.3	Long-Term Remedies for Turnover

1. Develop socialization programs.
2. Develop training programs in additional languages.
3. Establish career paths.
4. Implement partner/profit-sharing programs.
5. Implement incentive programs.
6. Provide childcare and family counseling.
7. Identify alternative sources for employee recruitment.
8. Reconsider pay scales.

Source: Adapted from Robert H. Woods and James F. Macaulay, "Rx for Turnover: Retention Programs that Work," *Cornell Hotel and Restaurant Administration Quarterly* 30 (May 1989): 82.

Knowledge Check

1. How does one compute the turnover rate for a business?
2. Approximately how much does it cost to replace a line-level employee?
3. Identify some factors that influence turnover.

7.2 THE USE OF DISCIPLINE

Discipline is an indispensable management tool, but it is also one of the most difficult for managers to use. Too many managers use discipline inconsistently and unfairly. Some regard discipline strictly as punishment for past behavior rather than as a means of promoting proper conduct in the future. In fact, some managers are unaware that discipline can be used constructively to encourage desired behaviors and to notify employees of problems with their job performance.

Laying the Groundwork

To lay the groundwork effectively for a discipline system that promotes positive behaviors, managers must establish rules of conduct for the workplace and then communicate how those rules should be followed. Employee handbooks, training sessions, orientation, job descriptions, performance standards, and posted notices are some ways rules can be communicated. The following list of major causes of disciplinary problems shows that the importance of clearly communicating rules and expectations cannot be over-emphasized.[17]

- Employees did not know *what* to do.
- Employees did not know *how* to do what they were supposed to do.
- Employees were given unrealistic expectations.
- Employees and the job were a poor match to begin with.
- Employees were not motivated to do a good job.

Reread the list. What it identifies is a lack of communication on the part of management.

Understanding the purpose of discipline should be a prerequisite for every manager with disciplinary responsibilities. It is imperative that managers:

- Establish reasonable rules.
- Make sure employees know the rules and the potential consequences of violating them.

- Enforce the rules fairly, without discrimination.
- Document each employee action or behavior that results in discipline.

Exhibit 7.4 presents an example of posted conduct rules.

Approaches to Administering Discipline

There are at least three basic approaches to discipline: the *hot stove approach*, *progressive discipline*, and *preventive discipline*. In practice, these approaches may overlap; some managers may use elements of any or all three. Two of the three—the hot stove approach and progressive discipline—are traditional approaches that emphasize the administration of discipline after an employee fails to follow organizational norms and standards. The traditional approaches are reactive in nature because the behavior precedes disciplinary action. The third approach, *preventive discipline*, is proactive in that it attempts to establish a means of directing employee behavior before a problem occurs.

The Hot Stove Approach. With the **hot stove approach**, if employees touch a hot stove, they get burned. That is, if they

Exhibit 7.4 | Sample Set of House Rules

Strict enforcement of these policies will help protect our employees and ensure that our hotel runs in an efficient manner. Some of the violations, which may result in immediate suspension or termination at the option of the hotel, include:

- Being discourteous, rude, insubordinate, or using abusive language to a guest or fellow employee.

- Fighting, stealing, unauthorized possession of hotel property, or gambling on the premises.

- Unauthorized use of alcohol; possession, use, or appearance of being under the influence of alcohol, narcotics, intoxicants, or other substances prohibited by law; or the abuse of medication, whether obtained legally or illegally, while on hotel premises.

- Possession of lethal weapons or other items prohibited by law while on hotel premises.

- Indecent, immoral, or disorderly conduct in the hotel, including willful destruction of property and failure to follow safety procedures.

- Falsification of work or time records, reports, or guest checks.

- Being in an unauthorized area of the hotel while working after hours without prior permission from your department head.

- Socializing with guests on hotel premises.

- Removing anything from the hotel without permission.

- Sleeping while on duty.

Source: David Wheelhouse, *Managing Human Resources in the Hospitality Industry* (Lansing, Mich.: American Hotel & Lodging Educational Institute, 1989), p. 353.

break a rule, they are subjected to disciplinary action. This approach has several foundations:

- *Immediacy*: Corrective action must be taken immediately after an infraction occurs. This links discipline with undesirable performance.

- *Warning*: Managers must provide clear and detailed ground rules for behaviors and adequately warn employees of consequences.

- *Consistency*: Corrective action must be consistent (i.e., a hot stove will burn everyone).

- *Impersonality*: Discipline must be linked with the behavior, not the person.

- *Appropriateness*: The degree of discipline must equal the extent of the infraction.

This system seems to make sense because it appears to be fair to all employees and because it correctly establishes which rules result in which disciplinary measures. However, this system has problems. Oddly, the fact that the hot stove does not discriminate is the biggest problem. All employees receive the same punishment for similar infractions. There is no allowance for different situations or individual differences. A new hire who does not fully understand all the rules will be "burned" as badly as the employee who has been with the company for years and has a clear grasp of the rules and consequences. In other words, a toddler would be burned as much as a teenager, but the teenager should know better.

Progressive Discipline. Like the hot stove approach, **progressive discipline** relies on a clear and complete definition of behaviors that will be penalized and the type of disciplinary action that will result for each infraction. A progressive discipline program might dictate that an employee who is tardy for work once will receive an oral warning, an employee who is tardy twice will receive a written warning, and an employee who is tardy three times will be suspended or discharged. This step-by-step punitive approach to discipline is very popular and typical of most collective bargaining agreements because it gives the employee the opportunity and motivation to improve. Most progressive discipline programs include four steps:

■ *Oral warning*: An informal warning with no documentation

■ *Written warning*: A formal warning in which a copy of the documentation is placed in the employee's file

■ *Suspension*: Time off without pay, usually for one to five days

■ *Discharge*: Termination of employment

Managers appear to like the hot stove and progressive discipline approaches because of both clearly establish ground rules and emphasize consistent and non-discriminatory treatment of rule-breakers. Any discrimination under either of these systems more or less ensures that union grievances, discrimination charges, and lawsuits will be filed. As managers know, however, it is a lot easier to describe these systems on paper than it is to carry them out. In addition, even under the best circumstances, these types of discipline result in short-term solutions. Because the system is punitive in nature, some employees won't respond constructively. Also, this system runs the risk of creating unnecessary conflict between employees and managers and the opportunity for favoritism and unfair treatment of workers.

Both traditional approaches focus on the symptoms rather than on the causes of poor performance. Rule-breaking is a symptom of a problem, not a cause.

Preventive (Positive) Discipline. Proponents of **preventive (positive) discipline** point out that the difference between this approach and traditional approaches is that the focus is on the cause rather than on the symptoms of dysfunctional behavior. Communication between supervisor and employee takes place on a "horizontal" level, between adults, with the emphasis on problem-solving rather than on punishment. Employees have the time and opportunity to correct workplace problems once they are brought to their attention but before any negative consequences occur.[18]

Preventive discipline places emphasis on recognizing and reinforcing good performance rather than punishing bad performance. More recently, this process has been known as *coaching* to emphasize the positive approach. Critical stages in this type of disciplinary system include:

■ Extensive orientation and training

■ Oral and written reminders

■ Paid decision-making leave

■ Discharge

At each stage of this process (except discharge), the emphasis is on encouraging good behavior. Oral and written reminders emphasize what should be done, not what was done wrong. Some companies call the paid decision-making leave "Decision Day" because the objective is for employees to use the time to decide whether they want to correct the problem and become a productive worker or look for other employment. Some managers may require an employee to reflect on the problem that led to the day off and write an essay outlining a solution to the problem, to be turned in to management when the employee returns to work. Critics of this type of system contend that paid decision-making leave is counter-productive because it provides employees with an incentive to perform or behave poorly in order to get a day off with pay. However, many employees

Managers in many industries have found that today's younger employees are more likely to respond to positive encouragement than to negative punishment, and that positive discipline also encourages a team approach to problem-solving. Traditional methods often alienate workers and foster adversarial conditions. In hospitality operations, any workplace conflict can lead to inferior customer service.

Another advantage of positive discipline is that it places a great deal of the burden for improvement on the individual. Therefore, it improves accountability within the organization and also sometimes helps prevent lawsuits by making discharge more the result of the employee's personal choice than the employer's punitive action.

view a day off, even with pay, as a punishment, and their behavior often improves as a result of this form of discipline. Some of the largest and most successful companies in the United States use the preventive discipline approach.

Appeals Mechanisms

Any effective discipline program has an appeals system for employees to challenge discipline decisions. A systematized appeals process that is widely understood by employees allows each party to present its side of an issue, giving employees a voice in how an issue is settled. In fact, in some cases that are litigated, the mere existence of appeals mechanisms provides evidence of managerial efforts to ensure due process for employees. Internal appeals provide the employee their "day in court," which may discourage future litigation if the appeal doesn't work. There are five basic types of appeals processes:

- Hierarchical
- Open-door
- Peer review
- Ombuds
- Mandatory arbitration

Hierarchical Appeals Process. The **hierarchical appeals process** is based on an organization's chain of command. In this system, employees who believe that they have been disciplined unfairly appeal first to their immediate supervisor. If unsatisfied with the results at this level, employees appeal at the next level of management in the organization. If still unsatisfied, employees can appeal to each succeeding management level, sometimes all the way to the CEO, until all levels of appeal are exhausted. Appeals generally are made in writing and meetings are arranged within days of the request.

Open-Door Appeals Process. Unlike the hierarchical system, an **open-door appeals process** allows employees to appeal to any manager in the organization, regardless of their position. This allows the employee to go straight to higher levels of management without following the chain of command. Although this program works in many cases, it fails in others because managers are reluctant to overrule fellow managers in other departments. Because of this, appeals are often referred back to the immediate supervisor. Another disadvantage of this system is that treatment is sometimes inconsistent—that is, one manager may work diligently to ensure that the appeals process is fair and that employees have a chance for their voice to be heard, while others may take this responsibility lightly.

Peer Review Appeals Process. The **peer review appeals process** typically requires that committees of employees and managers hear appeals and issue final rulings. Employees usually are elected or volunteer to serve on such committees, whereas managers are appointed. An advantage of this system is that it allows employees to participate directly in the appeals process. As a result, employees often believe that their appeals were conducted fairly, regardless of the outcome.

Ombuds Appeals Process. The **ombuds appeals process** involves the use of an ombudsperson who investigates complaints or a mediator who listens to both sides of a case and attempts to mediate an acceptable solution. Ombudspersons have no authority to issue judgments in the event that the two sides cannot agree, but they typically have the authority of a manager or executive to conduct investigations and make meaningful recommendations. This system is widely used in government and in colleges and universities, but it is not widely accepted in industry.

Mandatory Arbitration. In response to the rising cost and frequency of employment lawsuits, many employers have implemented **mandatory arbitration agreements**. These agreements require employees to forfeit their right to sue the employer for legal violations in exchange for a less formal and less costly internal process. Employers can refuse to hire an applicant who will not sign such an agreement, but the arbitration process cannot be unfairly favorable to the employer.[19] The employees retain all their legal rights, except for a trial by jury. The arbitrator's decision is usually final and binding on both parties, so the employee cannot file a lawsuit, but the employer cannot appeal from or refuse to comply with a decision in favor of the employee. These agreements and their limitations are described in more detail in Chapter 13.

Knowledge Check

1. What are the typical steps in progressive discipline?

2. What is the hierarchical appeals process?

3. What is the role of an ombudsperson?

7.3 DISCHARGE: A LAST RESORT

Managers who use discipline strictly as punishment often view discharge as the ultimate punishment. Most human resources experts are critical of such a view. They question who is really punished the most—the employee who must find a new job or the manager who must find a new employee? For that matter, who is really at fault when a discharge is required—the employee being discharged or the manager who failed to train, motivate, or otherwise help that employee to perform successfully? In some cultures, managers who discharge employees are viewed as failures themselves because they were unable to turn the employees into productive staff members. Many companies in the United States are adopting the same view, largely because it is becoming more difficult and costlier to replace lost employees.

Discharging an employee should be a last resort for managers. It should be approached with great caution and extreme seriousness. The manager deciding on the discharge should meet personally with the employee, and perhaps have another manager or HR professional as a witness. The manager should clearly explain the reason for the decision and the effective date. Although the employee does not have to be allowed to respond, managers find it useful to hear the employee's side of the story to ensure no mistakes or misjudgments are influencing their decision.

When to Discharge

Before managers discharge an employee, they should ask themselves the questions below. If they answer "yes" to each of these questions, proceeding with a discharge may be the right thing to do. If they answer "no," the situation should be investigated or corrected before proceeding with a discharge:

■ Did the employee know what was expected?

■ Were the rules or standards clearly communicated to the employee?

- Did management explain why the rules were important?

- Were the rules that were broken reasonable and important to the organization?

- Did the employer conduct a fair and complete investigation of the facts?

- Is the evidence precipitating the discharge substantial and reliable?

- Is the discipline proportionate to the seriousness of the offense?

- Was the performance appraisal process fair and complete?

- Did management use an appropriate form of discipline to correct the behavior or performance?

- Is punishment for breaking this rule applied consistently to all employees?

- Can I prove the reason for discharge in court if necessary?

- Why is it presumed that the applicant who replaces the discharged employee will be better?

Discharge Lawsuits

Employment lawsuits make up one of the largest categories of all court actions in the U.S., costing businesses over $2 billion in losses per year. Of those cases, the most common are wage and hour violations, discrimination, and sexual harassment.

Discrimination laws protect employees from all sorts of adverse employment actions due to their race, color, religion, national origin, sex, disability, age, and other factors. Although an adverse action can include any action that negatively affects the employee, such as unequal pay or denial of a promotion, most discrimination and retaliation claims arise out of a discharge.[20] In nearly all cases, it is up to the employer to prove a legitimate reason for firing the individual. If the employer can't prove the reason, the jury is free to conclude that the discharge was for an illegal reason. Losses in such a case may include backpay and reinstatement along with emotional distress and punitive damages.

When proving its case in court, an employer cannot always use information it discovers after the discharge to add reasons for the action. So-called after-acquired evidence is usually not permitted to defeat a discrimination lawsuit because it had no bearing on the decision to discharge the worker.[21] This is another reason to investigate potential discharges carefully and completely. If there are multiple reasons for the action, the documents reflecting the action should identify all of them.

Managers sometimes believe they can avoid an employment lawsuit by getting the worker to resign. They might demote them or transfer them or tell them they will be discharged if they don't quit first. But in employment lawsuits, instances of resignation due to an illegal action or intolerable working conditions are treated the same as discharge because the employer's action gave the employee no reasonable option but to quit. This is called **constructive discharge** because it has the same illegal effect on employment. Claims for constructive discharge are most common in retaliation and harassment cases.[22]

Many companies have gone to great lengths to establish sophisticated systems involving complete documentation and progressive discipline to defend wrongful discharge suits. Often, however, the employer can prove the reason an employee was discharged, but then the employee provides evidence that the rules or standards were not enforced equally. Unfortunately, this is the single area in which managers also make the most mistakes. Managers who don't enforce the rules fairly leave the employer vulnerable to claims of unlawful discrimination. If the discharged worker can prove others were treated differently, the employer will have to prove why or face a finding of discrimination even if the different treatment was for a legal reason. To illustrate how difficult this situation can be, consider the following example:

> Employee A is a steady performer who is well-liked by guests, managers, and fellow employees. However, Employee A has a habit of tardiness. Employee B is a poor performer who is not well-liked by either guests, managers, or fellow

employees. Employee B also has a habit of tardiness. If the manager discharges Employee B but not Employee A for tardiness, it will be difficult to prove tardiness was the real reason because Employee A was not fired for the same reason.

Managers must therefore understand the importance of establishing reasonable rules, communicating the rules, fairly enforcing the rules, and maintaining complete files on each employee action or behavior that results in either discipline or discharge. In addition, one of the best defenses in court is consultation with an independent third party (peer group, legal counsel, or management group) prior to dismissal. This step serves to solidify the decision to terminate, if necessary, and protects the company from mistakes that can result in lawsuits.[23]

In addition, many legal and human resources consultants believe the best protection against wrongful discharge litigation is a proactive program in which the employer:

- Effectively communicates the property's employment rules and expectations
- Trains managers in the proper use of progressive discipline
- Enforces all rules, policies, and standards fairly and consistently
- Aggressively manages employee performance to address problems early
- Thoroughly investigates any problem that has the potential to develop into a discharge situation
- Adopts a strict organizational code of ethics
- Adopts confidential procedures for employees to report potential claims
- Purchases employment practices liability insurance

Discharge Interviews

The final step in the discharge process is an interview with the employee to explain the company's decision. The purposes of a **discharge interview** are as follows:

As explained further in Chapter 13, workers in most states are presumed to be employed at will, which means either the employer or the worker can terminate the employment at any time without any reason or advance notice. But firing an employee for no reason is still risky because it leaves the company vulnerable to allegations of unlawful discrimination and retaliation.

LEGAL ALERT!

- Review the history that has led to the interview.
- Explain why the manager must take the action.
- Complete paperwork necessary to finalize the discharge.

There are many risks associated with discharging an employee, but managers who follow a regular procedure should find the task less difficult than they might assume. This does not mean that discharging an employee is an easy or pleasant task, nor should it be. Most discharge interviews are emotionally charged and can result in unwanted confrontations or hostility. By following these guidelines, however, it is more likely that managers will be able to complete them without extreme difficulty or unnecessary risk.

Managers should observe the following guidelines during discharge interviews:

- Respect the dignity of the employee during the interview. The fact that the employee did not work out in this case does not necessarily reflect poorly on them.
- As a general rule, have a witness present during the interview. The witness may

be needed later to substantiate issues discussed during the interview.

- Most states require that discharged employees be paid in full at the time of discharge. Arrange to have the employee's final paycheck ready to give the employee at the meeting.

- Prepare any other required paperwork well in advance of the interview to ease the process.

- Determine whether the worker has any company property to return.

- Use the meeting to find out what went wrong during employment.

- Read all of the supporting evidence for the discharge and make sure it is available during the interview. Documentation should include records of all disciplinary action against the employee and past conditions and terms of the disciplinary action.

- Explain specific reasons for the discharge. Managers cannot get by with simply telling an employee, "It didn't work out" or "We're going in a different direction." If the employee doesn't know why they're being discharged, they may believe the reason was wrong or even illegal.

- Make the employee aware of the appeals process available within the company and encourage them to use it if they think the company is wrong.

- Suggest other avenues for employment, if appropriate. Also advise the employee that, if contacted for a reference, management will be honest regarding the fact that the employee was discharged.

- Ask the employee to participate in a separate exit interview before leaving.

Knowledge Check

1. Define and give an example of constructive discharge.

2. Why is it so important for managers to enforce all the company rules and standards equally and consistently?

3. What options does an employee have if discharged?

7.4 EXIT INTERVIEWS

Exit interviews are conducted with employees who leave an organization for any reason, not just because they've been discharged. Employees who leave voluntarily usually do so for good reasons. Managers should be extremely concerned about learning why employees leave. The purpose of exit interviews is to collect information on why employees leave and learn directly from them what can be changed to ensure that more employees are not lost. From an employee's perspective, the exit interview provides an opportunity to achieve closure about leaving the job.

Exit interviews are valuable only if they are done well. Poorly or improperly conducted exit interviews yield little usable data. Unfortunately, few hospitality companies use exit interviews effectively. Many hospitality managers use exit interviews only to find out if a departing employee is likely to sue the company or to gather information about other employees. Losing an employee can be very disrupting and expensive, but effective turnover management can help to reduce those costs. Even 15 minutes with a departing worker can reveal critical information.

Information is not easy to collect from departing employees. Success depends a lot on who conducts the interviews. Most employers have immediate supervisors conduct exit interviews, but this is the least effective method. Employees often leave because of their supervisor and, as a result, are not likely to be open and honest in an interview with them. In addition, employees often have friends among their coworkers whose jobs they do not want to jeopardize. Many departing employees fear that if they tell the truth during an exit interview, they will not receive a favorable recommendation. Many employees don't think that what they say in exit interviews will be taken seriously by the company, because their managers don't seem to view this as important.

Exit interviews are most effective when conducted by an independent consulting company or data collection contractor. The direct cost of hiring them is likely to be offset by the superior data results. The interviewers are professionals who are skilled at collecting information, and employees will likely speak more freely in an anonymous setting. Professional interviewers also have proven methods and survey types.

Some larger companies employ full-time human resources professionals to conduct exit interviews. Short-term professional training programs can provide the skills necessary to conduct effective exit interviews. Having the same person or persons conduct all exit interviews ensures consistency, which is essential to the value of the data.

Guidelines for Conducting Exit Interviews

Persons conducting exit interviews should try to learn as much as possible from employees who are leaving. The following guidelines are helpful:

- Put the employee at ease by ensuring confidentiality. Explain that the information will be used solely for improvements within the company, not for retribution against the departing employee or friends remaining on the job.

- Ask open-ended questions as much as possible to ensure that the employee has an opportunity to talk about what really caused the turnover.

- Conduct interviews in the final week of employment, but not on the last day if at all possible. Departing employees are too busy with other issues to give exit interviews their full attention on their final day, but they are unlikely to return for an exit interview after leaving.

- Consider providing an online alternative to a live meeting. Many departing employees will participate only if it is convenient for them.

- Make every effort to ensure either anonymity or confidentiality, but do not make promises if you can't keep them. For the purposes of the interview, it's not necessary to include any personal information in the record.

- Probe for the real reasons that employees are leaving. Even when the employee is discharged or laid off, it is useful to hear their perspective if they are willing to speak about it. It's the undesired turnover—the employees who are leaving on their own—who will provide the most useful information about the causes of turnover.

- Schedule a follow-up interview one to three months after the employee leaves. Employees often relate much different (and more accurate) reasons for leaving after they are secure in their new jobs. Having a third party conduct the follow-up works extremely well. Follow-up interviews also represent a good opportunity for employers to find out whether departed employees are interested in returning to work.

What to Ask

Some organizations use a script of standard exit interview questions, and some use strictly true/false and multiple choice questions because the data is easier to collect and analyze. Open-ended discussions prompted by strategic questions ultimately produce the most useful information. Rather than ask a list of specific questions, skilled interviewers ask broad questions and encourage the person to speak freely. Here are some common examples of exit interview questions:

- How would you rate the company's pay and benefits? Why?

- Were the workloads and schedules reasonable? If not, how were they unreasonable?

- How well did your supervisors and managers treat you?

- Did you like working with your coworkers? Why or why not?

- Did you receive the training and information you needed to do your job?

- How would you describe the daily work environment?

- Did you feel you had a good work/life balance? Why or why not?

- Did you have enough opportunities for advancement? Why or why not?

- Is there anything that could have kept you from resigning?[24]

Information obtained in exit interviews is worthless if it not analyzed carefully and used to help correct conditions that cause employees to leave. Monthly reports should summarize the information for review by upper management.

IN THIS CHAPTER, YOU LEARNED:

- High employee turnover is a constant problem in the hospitality industry. It causes direct financial losses and also interrupts business.

- Some employee turnover is necessary, and even productive; but unwanted turnover is usually the outcome of poor management.

- Some companies are much better at controlling turnover. They do it by actively studying the reasons behind it and implementing deliberate permanent strategies to retain their workers. Good managers quickly learn that it is better to help employees improve than it is to lose and replace them.

- The purpose of employee discipline is to improve job performance. Employee discipline may be administered according to the hot stove approach, progressive discipline, or preventive discipline. Many employers use a combination of these methods. In each of them, the final step is discharge from employment, which is taken as a last resort.

- Before discharging an employee, managers must ensure that the action can be defended in court. If the company is sued for discharging a worker, the employer will have to prove a legal and legitimate reason for discharging the worker. Managers can avoid potential legal problems by following specific procedures and examining each case carefully before taking action.

KEY TERMS

constructive discharge—Occurs when an employee resigns due to illegal actions or working conditions that are so hostile that the employee has no reasonable option but to resign.

discharge interview—A meeting between an employee and employer representative in which the purpose is to terminate the employee's employment.

exit interview—A meeting conducted between an employer and an employee leaving the organization that attempts to identify specific reasons for turnover.

hierarchical appeals process—A process that employees who feel they have been treated unfairly can use to take their concerns to succeeding levels of the chain of command.

hot stove approach—An approach to discipline based on immediate punishment for each offense.

mandatory arbitration agreement—A contract in which the employee agrees to submit any legal claims they have against the employer to final and binding private arbitration.

ombuds appeals process—A company representative whose job is to investigate and resolve conflicts and appeals within the company.

open-door appeals process—A process used by employees who feel they have been treated unfairly, in which they are free to take their concerns to any manager.

peer review appeals process—A process used by employees who feel they have been treated unfairly, in which they take their concerns to boards made up of other employees and managers.

preventive (positive) discipline—A type of discipline emphasizing recognition of good behavior and performance.

progressive discipline—A discipline process in which employees are given increasingly stiffer penalties for infractions; usually progressing from an oral warning, to a written warning, to a suspension, and finally to discharge.

replacement costs—Turnover costs associated with replacing lost employees, which include recruiting, advertising, uniforms, manuals, interviewing, and other related costs.

retention program—A program designed to reduce employee turnover.

separation costs—Turnover costs associated with exit interviews, separation pay, closure of employee benefits files, and unemployment taxes.

training costs—Turnover costs associated with preparing new employees to be productive (orientation, training instruction, training materials, and so forth).

turnover—Employees who leave a company or work unit.

turnover rate—The percentage of a workforce who leave the job and are replaced in a given time period.

REVIEW QUESTIONS

1. What are the costs of employee turnover to a business?

2. What are five factors in turnover that front-line managers can influence?

3. What are some immediate actions a manager can take to reduce employee turnover?

4. How is preventative discipline different from progressive discipline?

5. What processes should a manager go through before discharging an employee?

6. From a legal perspective, why is it so important to enforce rules and work standards equally?

7. How should a manager prepare for a discharge interview?

8. Identify and define appeals mechanisms that are used to resolve disputes over employee discharges.

9. How does a company use an exit interview to reduce employee turnover?

Not on Time for the Last Time

Wynette worked as a front desk supervisor for four years at the Grand Hotel before being promoted to rooms manager. During that entire time, she was frequently frustrated by front desk agents being late to work. It seemed like every day at least one of them would be late, sometimes by more than an hour. The previous rooms manager did nothing about the problem and expected Wynette to cover for the agents until they arrived. So, it just continued. When she received the promotion, Wynette decided she would solve the problem and hold the front desk agents responsible for getting to work on time every day.

But first, Wynette had to fill her job as front desk supervisor. Two of the current front desk agents applied for the job, but they were the two who were late more often than any of the others. The agents who applied for the job were Tony and Tina, both of whom were over 50 years old. Wynette decided she could not tolerate a supervisor being late all the time, so she decided to hire Ayla, a much younger applicant from outside the company who had just a few years of experience working in hotels. Both Tony and Tina were upset about Wynette's decision and threatened to sue the hotel for age discrimination.

On Ayla's first day of work, Wynette met with her and told her, "The agents have been getting away with being late for a long time, but it has to stop now. I want you to let them all know the next agent who is more than five minutes late will be fired immediately. I'll back you up no matter who it is. I think that will wake them up."

Ayla sent an email to all front desk agents that said, "I need you all to do a better job of getting to work on time. I'll have to fire someone if it continues, and I really don't want to do that." They all received the email, but they didn't take it seriously because workers in some of the other departments were late just as much and never got fired.

Three days later, Tony was 10 minutes late to work.

DISCUSSION QUESTIONS:

1. If Ayla discharges Tony for being late and Tony sues the hotel, what evidence will he be able to use to prove his case for discrimination? Do you think he'll win?

2. If Ayla just covers for Tony until he arrives and doesn't fire him, what should Wynette do when she finds out?

3. What would be a better way to solve the problem of the front desk agents being late to work?

ENDNOTES

1. U.S. Travel Association, "Leisure and Hospitality Accounts for Whopping 39% of Jobs Lost to Pandemic," February 9, 2021, www.ustravel.org/press.

2. Shane McFeely and Ben Wigert, "This Fixable Problem Costs US Businesses $1 Trillion," *Workplace,* March 13, 2019, www.gallup.com/workplace/247391.

3. George S. Benson, "Employee Development, Commitment, and Intention to Turnover: A Test of 'Employability' Policies in Action," *Human Resource Management Journal* 16 (April 2006): 173.

4. N. Magner, R. Welker, and G. Johnson, "The Interactive Effects of Participation and Outcome Favorability on Turnover Intentions and Evaluations of Supervisors," *Journal of Occupational and Organizational Psychology* 69 (1996): 135–143.

5. William Even and David MacPherson, "Employer Size and Labor Turnover: The Role of Pensions," *Industrial and Labor Relations Review* 49 (July 1996): 707–728.

6. Catherine M. Gustafson, "Employee Turnover: A Study of Private Clubs in the USA," *International Journal of Contemporary Hospitality Management* 14, no. 3 (2002): 106–113.

7. John R. Johnson, M. J. Bernhagen, and Mike Allen, "The Role of Communication in Managing Reductions in Work Force," *Journal of Applied Communication Research* 24, no. 3 (1996): 139–164.

8. U.S. Bureau of Labor Statistics, "Economic News Release," accessed March 11, 2021, www.bls.gov/news.release.

9. Tim R. Hinkin and J. Bruce Tracey, "The Cost of Turnover," *Cornell Hospitality Quarterly* 24, no. 1 (2000): 19; Joe Hadzima, "How Much Does an Employee Cost?" *Boston Business Journal* (2009).

10. Robert H. Woods and James F. Macaulay, "R for Turnover: Retention Programs that Work," *Cornell Hotel and Restaurant Administration Quarterly* 30 (May 1989): 81.

11. Catherine R. Curtis, Randall S. Upchurch, and Denvor E. Severt, "Employee Motivation and Organizational Commitment: A Comparison of Tipped and Non-Tipped Restaurant Employees," *International Journal of Hospitality & Tourism* 10, no. 3 (2009): 253–269.

12. Wim van Breukelen, René van der Vlist, and Herman Steensma, "Voluntary Employee Turnover: Combining Variables from the Traditional Turnover Literature with the Theory of Planned Behavior," *Journal of Organizational Behavior* 25, no. 7 (2004): 893–914.

13. Elisa Moncarz, Jinlin Zhao, and Christine Kay, "An Exploratory Study of U.S. Lodging Properties' Organizational Practices on Employee Turnover and Retention," *Journal of Contemporary Hospitality Management* 21, no. 4 (2009): 457.

14. Cecil A. L. Pearson, "Turnover Process in Organization," *Human Relations* 48 (April 1995): 405–421.

15. Substantial portions of the following two sections are adapted from Woods and Macaulay, 83–89.

16. Nic Paton, "A Turnaround in Turnover," *Personnel Today,* November 15, 2005: 27–29.

17. Paul Falcone, *101 Tough Conversations to Have with Employees: A Manager's Guide to Addressing Performance, Conduct, and Discipline Challenges.* 2nd edition (New York: Harper Collins Leadership, 2019).

18. Marjorie Mader-Clark and Lisa Guerin, *The Employee Performance Handbook: Smart Strategies for Coaching Employees.* (Berkeley, CA: NOLO, 2016); Cynthia J. Guffey and Marilyn M. Helms, "Effective Employee Discipline," *Public Personnel Management* (Spring 2001): 111–127.

19. Sarah Staszak, "Privatizing Employment Law: The Expansion of Mandatory Arbitration in the Workplace," *Studies in American Political Development* July 7, 2020: 1–30.

20. U.S. Equal Employment Opportunity Commission, "Enforcement and Litigation Statistics," accessed March 21, 2021, www.eeoc.gov/statistics.

21. Harold R. Bickham and Mark W. Clark, "After-Acquired Evidence in Employment Discrimination Cases," *The Practical Litigator* 16, no. 1 (2005): 13.

22. Blair A. Copple, "Clarifying Constructive Discharge," *University of San Francisco Law Review* 50, no. 1 (June 2015): 103–118.

23. Helen Rideout, *Employee Risk Management: How to Protect Your Business Reputation and Reduce Your Legal Liability.* (London: Kogan Press, 2014).

24. Marcia Pennington, "Exit Interviews: Learning from Departing Employees," *ABA Law Practice,* January–February 2006, p. 54.

8

COMPENSATION ADMINISTRATION

Chapter 8 Outline

Learning Objectives

1. Identify and describe common types of employment compensation plans. (pp. 194–197)

2. Describe the major content and process theories of motivation and explain their application to compensation plan design. (pp. 197–203)

3. Identify methods of determining job worth and describe the advantages and disadvantages of each. (pp. 203–208)

4. Identify and explain methods of establishing pay structures. (pp. 208–211)

5. Describe current issues and legal risks associated with compensation administration in hospitality. (pp. 211–216)

KEY TERMS

Total reward program

Direct compensation

Indirect compensation

Cost of living

Intrinsic rewards

Extrinsic rewards

Valence

Job worth

External equity

Internal equity

Compensable factors

Pay range

Key jobs

Pay grades

Seniority-based pay

Merit pay

Two-tier wage systems

Skill-based pay

Knowledge-based pay

Team-based pay

Piece rate

Wage compression

Wage expansion

Comparable worth

When most people hear the word *compensation*, they think of the wages or salaries that people earn in return for work. They think of the numbers on the paycheck. However, wages and salaries represent only part of the total compensation most employees receive. An effective compensation program consists of both cash and non-cash rewards—salaries and wages as well as other types of benefits. None of these rewards are randomly chosen, and few are legally required. Instead, they are deliberately selected and combined to support the company's compensation philosophy, attract and retain workers, motivate and reward job performance in line with company objectives, and provide a positive overall rate of return on the company's investments in human resources.

A company's compensation philosophy articulates where the company wants its pay policies to be in relation to the marketplace. It also articulates how the company will attract, reward, retain, and motivate employees.[1] The sum of all of the methods—including cash and other benefits—that an employer uses to compensate employees is called the **total reward program**. The elements of the total reward program are *monetary compensation* and *nonmonetary compensation*. Monetary compensation refers to the pay the employee receives. Nonmonetary compensation includes other benefits, incentives, and intangible social and cultural aspects of the workplace. Nonmonetary compensation is addressed in more detail in Chapter 9. This chapter concentrates mostly on monetary compensation.

Monetary compensation is commonly divided into *direct compensation* and *indirect compensation*. These two kinds of compensation are sometimes further categorized as either *immediate compensation* or *deferred compensation*. Although some elements of compensation are easy to categorize, the complexity of today's compensation options occasionally produces forms of compensation that defy easy or definitive categorization.

Direct compensation involves an employer's payment of money to an employee—either in the present or at some future date—in exchange for that employee's productive work:

- Direct *immediate* compensation includes base wages and salaries, overtime, merit pay, bonuses, piece rates, shift differentials, and so forth.

- Direct *deferred* compensation is money earned in one period that is not paid until a later period. One example is an executive compensation plan that encourages retention by granting bonuses for a given year but paying them only if the executive is still with the company a given number of years later. Some retirement pension plans are also forms of deferred compensation.

Most employees also receive indirect compensation. **Indirect compensation** includes money paid for various protection plans, paid time off, health savings plans, retirement savings plans, and various other services and perquisites (commonly called "perks"). Protection plans include medical insurance, life insurance, disability insurance, Social Security, unemployment insurance, and workers' compensation insurance. Paid time off includes vacation, holidays, sick leave, jury duty, and so forth. Perks might include company cars, travel allowances, and discounts on company products and services. In general, indirect compensation is given as a condition of employment rather than in direct exchange for productive work. For example, if an employee works overtime one week, the employee's direct compensation (wages and overtime pay) will increase to reflect that extra work; however, the employee will not receive "more" health insurance coverage (an indirect form of compensation) for that week.

Exhibit 8.1 shows a basic (but far from exhaustive) diagram of various types of compensation.

8.1 MAJOR INFLUENCES ON COMPENSATION PLANS

While many people think compensation programs relate directly to the amount or type of work done, this is rarely the case. Instead, the rate of compensation is affected by many factors in most hospitality companies.

Exhibit 8.1 Types of Compensation

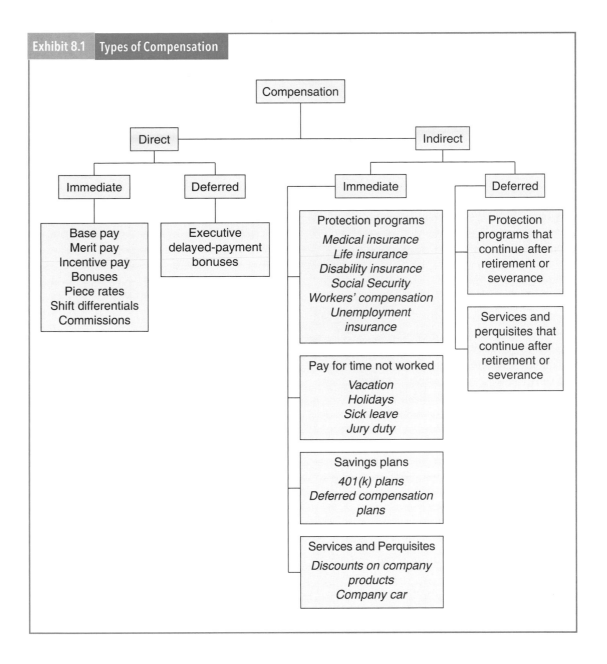

Some influences relate to economic conditions in the company or the community, whereas others relate to internal or external labor market conditions. Other factors that affect compensation include employee perceptions of pay, union contracts, and government influences. Even employee satisfaction and motivation can influence a company's compensation practices.[2] This section discusses some of the external factors employers consider when designing their compensation plans.

Direct compensation in the hospitality industry has historically been significantly lower than in similar jobs and businesses. Some companies are not financially able to pay higher wages, others believe they can attract satisfactory workers with lower wages, and others attempt to balance lower direct compensation with greater indirect compensation.[3] Whatever the reason, a plan that provides overall compensation that is lower than market competitors should naturally be expected to result in overall work productivity that is also lower than market competitors.

Cost of Living

Cost of living refers to the real dollar value of ordinary necessities such as food, housing, transportation, and clothing. The consumer price index (CPI) is generally the best overall indicator of the real value—or purchasing power—of wages or salaries. The CPI is a measurement of changes in the retail prices of necessary goods and services. It is computed by comparing the cost of these goods and services at a fixed point in time with the cost at prior points in time. The U.S. CPI is issued monthly by the Bureau of Labor Statistics, an agency of the U.S. Department of Labor.

The CPI varies according to many environmental and economic factors. As the CPI goes up, the purchasing power of money goes down. For instance, a CPI of 5 percent means that an item that used to cost $1.00 now costs $1.05. An increase in the CPI is often referred to as *inflation*. In times of high inflation, the value of a dollar goes down rapidly. As a result, increases in compensation rates must be large enough to maintain the purchasing power of the compensation. In low inflationary times, the value of a dollar goes down more slowly. As the value or purchasing power of the dollar changes, companies must adjust their compensation rates to remain competitive. Wages in some workplaces adjust automatically to changes in the CPI to guarantee fixed purchasing power, typically called *COLA* for *cost of living adjustment*.

Compensation is also influenced by the cost of living in the location of the employment. For example, a $25,000 salary in Muskogee, Oklahoma, would command much more *real income* (or purchasing power) than the same salary in Minneapolis, Minnesota, because the cost of living is higher in Minneapolis. By the same token, a job that pays $30,000 in New York City would provide much less real income than a job paying the same amount in New Bern, North Carolina.[4]

Labor Market Influences

The amount of compensation required to attract and retain workers depends in part on the number of workers available to do the job. Less compensation is required when many workers are competing for few jobs, but much more is necessary when fewer workers are available. The number of workers available in the labor market varies on national, regional, and local scales. For instance, when the unemployment rate is high on a national level, the number of workers available and willing to work is greater. Conversely, when the unemployment rate is low, the number of available workers declines. The number of available workers also varies by occupation.[5]

During much of the 1980s, for example, the unemployment rate in the oil-producing states of Louisiana, Texas, and Oklahoma was quite high because of low prices for oil and the subsequent lower demand for employees in that industry. As a result, there was an abundant supply of workers in this region. However, during this same period, unemployment in New England was quite low, primarily due to the region's increasing number of technology-related jobs. Because of the increases in high-tech employment, hospitality companies in New England had a very difficult time finding interested workers. In fact, a luxury hotel and resort company had such a difficult time finding room attendants for its Boston location that it imported workers from Texas and converted hotel rooms into employee dormitories. The company found that cost to be less than the cost of wages high enough to attract local workers.

The internal conditions of a company also influence compensation rates. The most obvious example is company profitability. A company making high profits can compensate its employees better than one that is not very profitable. Companies that can respond quickly to changes in the CPI are also able to react to labor market changes. For example, hotel and restaurant companies can react to inflation more quickly than companies in other fields because of their ability to adjust prices on a daily basis. Adjusting compensation rates keeps the company in a competitive position in terms of attracting and retaining employees.

Union Influences

Union contracts typically raise both direct and indirect compensation rates. However, it is unclear whether compensation rates are always higher in union hotels over the long run, because they are subject to periodic negotiation. Compensation in union properties depends as much on the skills of the union negotiation team as it does the performance of the employees themselves or the actual value of the work. A strong negotiation team can provide its union members with compensation rates that exceed their actual worth in the marketplace. In contrast, a weak team can bring about just the opposite. Except in the case of a new union negotiating its first contract, an agreement on wages is also affected by the wage rates in the previous contract. Union contracts are addressed in Chapter 11.

One aspect of union contracts that typically results in higher compensation rates over the long term is the cost of living adjustment (COLA) clause. Some union contracts specify the wages and annual increases for each covered position for the term of the contract, but others rely on COLAs to determine the amount of annual increases. This adjustment became standard in many union properties during the 1970s and 1980s when the cost of living rose dramatically.

Whether unionized or not, hotels in markets in which unions are present generally have higher compensation costs.[6] If a hotel's labor contract establishes wages higher than its non-union competitors, the union position becomes more attractive to workers who might consider leaving their jobs. Depending on the availability of labor, this can force non-union employers to match the area union contract wages and benefits. Compensation of non-union workers that is equal to or greater than that obtained by union-represented workers is also considered an effective method of preventing union organizing. Workers who already enjoy the benefits of the area local labor contract have less reason to desire union representation themselves.

Government Influences

Since the early 1930s, the U.S. and state governments have played a large role in how private enterprises compensate their employees. Laws that mandate minimum wage rates, overtime pay, leaves of absence, retirement benefits, equal employment opportunity, and other aspects all greatly affect both direct and indirect compensation. The major federal laws that regulate employee compensation are described in more detail in Chapter 13.

Not all employees in an organization are protected by all of these laws. For example, employees who work for companies that are not involved in interstate commerce; who work in seasonal industries (20 consecutive weeks or less); or who are salaried executives, administrators, professionals, or commissioned outside salespeople are exempt from most minimum wage and overtime provisions. The absence of government restrictions for those workers means other factors have a greater influence on their compensation.

> ### Knowledge Check
>
> 1. What local economic conditions affect employment compensation?
>
> 2. How do unions affect compensation?
>
> 3. How can the cost of living affect the unemployed?

8.2 MOTIVATING EMPLOYEES

When employers motivate their employees, they stimulate employees to work as the company desires. A compensation plan's purpose is not just to trade money and benefits for work. It must motivate individual employees to work well, consistent with the company's business plan. But not all employees have the same wants and needs. As a result, not all compensation programs work to motivate all employees equally. Although it is easy to assume that money is the principal motivator for employees, this is not always the case. Some employees are motivated only by money, whereas others are motivated by other needs as well. Compensation programs rarely succeed when they are based solely on monetary rewards.

To more fully understand how compensation motivates employees, it is helpful to consider the primary theories that explain what motivates people generally. Motivation theories fall into two principal types: content theories and process theories. Content theories propose that all people are motivated by certain common needs. In contrast, process theories identify the factors in any given situation that determine whether an individual will become motivated or not. No single theory is necessarily correct or equally applicable in every workplace.

Content Theories

The best-known content theories include:

- Maslow's hierarchy of needs theory,
- Alderfer's ERG theory,
- Herzberg's two-factor theory,
- McClelland's N-Achievement theory, and
- Economic man theory.

The theories have a lot in common, but each explains human motivation in a different way.

Maslow's Hierarchy of Needs Theory. Maslow's hierarchy of needs theory contends that individuals have five basic needs. (see Exhibit 8.2):

- *Physiological needs*—This includes basic and essential needs for living, sometimes called biological needs. Examples of these needs include heat, light, food, clothing, and housing. These are the needs measured by the consumer price index, referenced earlier.

- *Safety and security needs*—Once physiological needs are met, Maslow contends that individuals are most influenced by safety and security needs, such as the need to protect oneself from danger, harm, threat, injury, loss, or deprivation. In organizations, this level of need might include an employee's need for job security, seniority, safe working conditions, health insurance, retirement plans, and severance pay. This area can be strongly influenced by unions because many union contracts ensure job security that is greater than what most non-union workers have.

- *Social needs*—After satisfying safety and security needs, individuals seek to fulfill their social needs. These include the need for companionship, love, and belonging. In organizations, such needs may be met through formal and informal work groups, teamwork, company-sponsored activities, and a positive, inclusive work environment.

- *Esteem needs*—After fulfilling their social needs, individuals turn to their personal ego needs: self-esteem, accomplishment, achievement, competence, maturity, independence, and self-respect. In organizations, esteem needs might be satisfied by recognition, titles, praise, status symbols, responsibility, promotions, and appreciation. These needs are met primarily by indirect compensation.

- *Self-actualization needs*—Maslow contends that after the first four levels of needs are satisfied, individuals still have a need for self-fulfillment. Seeking to realize one's full potential, increase knowledge or skills, be creative, or simply "be the best I can be" are manifestations of this need in both personal and professional life. Employee development opportunities and long-term promotion plans can help to satisfy these needs.

Maslow contends that all people experience these five needs, but at different times, depending on individual priorities and circumstances. Maslow therefore assigns an order of priority—or *hierarchy*—to these five needs. Individuals are motivated to fulfill a higher-level need only when a lower-level need is satisfied or nearly satisfied. According to the theory, if managers can identify the stage an employee is at, they can effectively predict what will motivate the employee. The theory also predicts that

Exhibit 8.2 | **Maslow's Hierarchy of Needs**

Self-Actualization

Esteem

Social

Safety and Security

Physiological

employees who are entirely satisfied with their compensation may still seek other employment if their higher-level needs are not met.

Maslow's theory is supported by numerous studies that show that many employees and managers want incentives other than pay.[7] The theory does have application problems, however. Managers may have a difficult time assessing which level an employee is focused on and anticipating changes in their needs. Another problem is that not all employees feel the same needs at the same times. Managers make a grave mistake when they assume that all employees in a restaurant, for instance, are at the esteem needs level. Non-monetary recognition for excellent service does little to motivate a single parent struggling to pay for rent and utilities. Although Maslow's theory does not provide a solution for creating compensation plans, it does help to explain how various forms and combinations of compensation are likely to motivate employees.[8]

Alderfer's ERG Theory. Alderfer agrees with Maslow that individuals have basic needs that can be arranged in order of priority, that there are basic distinctions among those needs, and that those needs need to be prioritized. However, whereas Maslow's theory divides the needs into five categories, Alderfer's ERG theory divides them into only three:

- *Existence*—These needs are satisfied by such factors as food, air, water, pay, and working conditions. These needs are similar to Maslow's physiological and safety needs.

- *Relatedness*—Relatedness needs are satisfied by meaningful social and interpersonal relationships. These needs are similar to Maslow's social needs.

- *Growth*—These needs are satisfied when an individual makes creative or productive contributions. Growth needs are similar to Maslow's esteem and self-actualization needs.

The biggest difference between Maslow's theory and Alderfer's theory is that the ERG theory adds a frustration-regression model. That is, like Maslow's theory, the ERG theory states that an individual will be motivated to fulfill a higher-level need when a lower-level need is satisfied. However, unlike Maslow's theory, the ERG theory also states that an individual will seek further fulfillment of a lower-level need when he or she has continuously failed to satisfy a higher need.[9] An employee who is denied a promotion, for instance, may be motivated to stay by a pay increase.

Herzberg's Two-Factor Theory. According to Herzberg's two-factor theory, employees have just two distinct types of needs, which he calls *hygiene factors* (also called *maintenance factors* or *dissatisfiers*) and *motivators* (also called *satisfiers*).

Hygiene factors include workplace factors like pay, relationships with peers and management, work–life balance, status, and security. They include factors from all five of Maslow's hierarchy. Herzberg's theory contends that hygiene factors alone cannot lead employees to feel satisfied with the work environment because employees expect many of those factors to be present. If hygiene factors are lacking, employees may feel dissatisfied because the compensation does not meet their minimum expectations.

In contrast, unexpected motivators can make employees feel satisfied and motivated to work. Examples include bonuses, recognition, responsibility, and the opportunity to advance. Herzberg's theory states that the presence of motivators can lead to employee satisfaction, whereas their absence leads to either dissatisfaction or to no satisfaction at all. Some authors call motivators that lead to satisfaction **intrinsic rewards**. Hygiene factors can also be called **extrinsic rewards**.[10]

According to the Herzberg theory, money is not a motivator at all. Instead, employees expect fair pay and certain other benefits for the work they do. Although some research has failed to prove the Herzberg theory, many companies have successfully applied it through job enrichment programs. Because they are basically motivators or satisfiers that help employees feel satisfied and motivated to work, job enrichment programs should be considered part of the compensation package.

McClelland's N-Achievement Theory.

McClelland's N-Achievement theory contends that people have three needs: achievement, power, and affiliation. According to this theory, all employees have some combination of these three needs. The theory also contends that companies can predict employee performance by identifying each employee's needs. In addition, the McClelland theory contends that people with a high need for achievement make good managers. These individuals tend to exhibit moderate levels of risk-taking, a desire for concrete performance feedback, problem-solving responsibility, and a tendency to set moderate goals. They may also possess strong organizational and planning skills. To motivate these employees, companies must create opportunities for them to initiate, conduct, and complete jobs.

The McClelland theory portrays the need for power as a desire to assume leadership. For many companies, such a need is perceived as a positive attribute, but of course not every employee can be a leader. The need for affiliation reflects a desire for close, cooperative, and friendly relations with others. According to the theory, people with a high need for affiliation tend to succeed in jobs that require strong social interaction skills, teamwork, and interpersonal skills. It should be no surprise, then, that a study found that front-of-the-house hospitality employees are primarily motivated by a need for achievement and a need for affiliation, but not a need for power.[11]

McClelland identifies three types of managers:

- *Institutional managers* have greater needs for power than for affiliation and tend to exhibit high levels of self-control.

- *Personal-power managers* also have a greater need for power than for affiliation but are more open to social interaction and sharing power.

- *Affiliation managers* tend to have a greater need for affiliation than for power and are more open to interpersonal relationships.

Research by McClelland and others has shown that personal-power managers and institutional managers typically are more productive because of their greater need for power and greater desire to lead and control others.[12]

Economic Man Theory.

The idea that money is the only important goal that people work for is embedded in the economic man theory. This theory states that people simply work in exchange for paychecks to buy food and clothing, the basic necessities of life, and that every employee is motivated primarily by the money they are paid.[13] They have other needs like those discussed in the other theories above, but they seek to satisfy those needs in other social contexts outside the workplace. The economic man theory corresponds to only the first stage of Maslow's hierarchy of needs theory. Critics of the theory say that money as the sole motivator does not explain why some workers are motivated more than others even when they are paid the same.

Process Theories

Process theories of motivation are used to explain other ways employees can be motivated at work. They focus more attention on the employees' perceptions and expectations than on their realities. Process theories do not disprove content theories but rather provide managers additional insight into how to influence employee motivation. The following process motivation theories are widely acknowledged:

- Expectancy theory (Victor Vroom),

- Equity theory (J. Stacey Adams),

- Goal setting theory (Edwin A. Locke), and

- Reinforcement theory (B. F. Skinner).

Expectancy Theory.

According to expectancy theory, motivation is related to an individual's perception of three factors:[14]

- *Expectancy*—The probability that effort will lead to performance.

- *Instrumentality*—The probability that performance will in turn lead to certain desired or undesired outcomes.

- *Valence*—The value the individual attaches to each of those outcomes.

From an employee's perspective, this can be restated as three questions: "If I try my best to perform a certain task or at a specified level, am I likely to succeed? If I succeed, what are the likely results? Do I like or dislike those results?" If an employee believes that working harder will lead to higher performance, the expectancy is strong. If an employee sees no connection between effort and performance, the expectancy is weak. For example, if an employee lacks the knowledge, training, or equipment needed to perform a task, simply working harder is not likely to lead to the desired performance, and therefore the motivation to work harder will be low.

The next element is the individual's perception of whether performance will lead to certain outcomes. An employee might believe that performing at a specified level will lead to praise, higher pay, promotions, and/or job security. If an employee believes that a given outcome or result is likely, the instrumentality is strong. For example, if an employee works in an organization that clearly ties pay to performance, the employee will perceive that higher performance is likely to lead to higher pay. By the same token, an employee who is concerned about being demoted or fired due to poor job performance is also motivated to perform just as well. If there is no clear relationship between performance and certain outcomes, the low instrumentality will weaken motivation.

The third element necessary for motivation is **valence**, which is the individual's opinion of or desire for the likely outcomes. A desired outcome has motivational force, while an undesired outcome weakens or destroys motivation. An employee discount, for example, can decrease motivation if the employees have no intention to purchase the discounted product or service.

The strongest motivation occurs when an employee believes that he or she can perform at a specified level, that doing so will clearly lead to specific outcomes (or rewards), and that those likely outcomes (rewards) are desirable. Motivation will be low if an employee sees no relationship between effort and performance, performance is not likely to be rewarded, or the reward is not considered valuable or desirable.

Managers and organizations can address motivation problems related to each of these three elements. Organizations that select and train employees effectively and give employees the tools and equipment needed to perform their jobs strengthen the employees' perception that effort will lead to successful performance. Next, organizations should clearly tie their reward systems to the desired performance to assure workers that successful job performance will be rewarded in some way. Finally, organizations should ensure that the rewards they offer are in fact valued by employees. Many organizations simply assume that all the rewards they offer are valued. When they are wrong, the effect on motivation can be very harmful.[15]

Equity Theory. The equity theory relates to fairness: whether an employee believes he or she is being treated fairly in comparison to another person perceived as being in a similar position. This theory is based on the assumption that all employees ask two questions about their work:

- "What do I receive in return for what I give?"
- "What do others receive in return for what they give?"

The equity theory contends that employees create mental ratios about their work situations to answer these questions. Note that it is the employee's *perception* of whether equity exists that affects motivation. Thus, perceived inequities in the workplace are just as damaging as real inequities. Employees often do not know how much their coworkers make but often assume or believe that there is inequity, resulting in lower motivation even if they are mistaken.

Equity occurs only when employees believe that the ratio of their outcomes received (pay, benefits, job satisfaction) to their input given (education, knowledge, experience, effort) is equal to the same ratio of a "comparison other" (who may in reality be like or unlike the employee). On the other hand, inequity occurs either when employees believe they are receiving less (under-reward) or more (over-reward) for their efforts than the comparison other. According to this theory, balance is important to people; most workers are uncomfortable with either of these two imbalances.

When inequity is perceived, the theory predicts employees might:

- Work less hard because they believe they are undercompensated compared to others

- Work harder because they believe they are overcompensated compared to others

- Convince others to work harder to restore equity

- Convince others to work less hard to restore equity

- Reassess their perception of equity

- Compare themselves to different others

The sense of equity relates to fellow employees in the company (*internal equity*) and to workers in similar positions in other companies (*external equity*). For example, employees will feel a sense of imbalance if they believe that employees in similar positions in other hotel companies are rewarded more for similar work. As a result, those employees may ask for more money or may go to work for another hotel company. However, they are less likely to leave if they also perceive they will have to work harder at the other company for the increased compensation.[16]

Goal Setting Theory. Goal setting theory, proposed by E. A. Locke, states that setting specific goals motivates better performance. It explains that ambiguous goals like "do our best" cannot motivate individuals to perform better because such goals are too vague. Specific and challenging goals result in higher levels of performance, so long as the individual employees accept the goals.[17] According to this theory, the following goal-oriented factors motivate higher levels of performance:

- *Ability*—Although a difficult or challenging goal could result in better performance, before setting the goal, the manager should consider the ability of the individual employee who will aim for that goal. If a manager sets a difficult goal and an employee lacks the ability

to achieve it, there will be no potential for goal achievement.

- *Goal commitment*—Employees commit to a goal when they accept it. That is, the more accurately a person understands a goal and its purpose, the more likely it is they will attempt to achieve it.

- *Feedback*—To promote performance, managers should provide feedback, which will help employees understand whether they are achieving the goal and how they can improve their likelihood of achieving the goal.

After goals are achieved and employee performance is evaluated, outcomes (rewards) are allocated. In the same manner as in the expectancy theory, employee motivation will be high if rewards are valuable or desirable.[18] Motivation will be low if employees do not believe they can achieve or do not understand the goal, even if the potential reward is highly desired.

Reinforcement Theory. B. F. Skinner's reinforcement theory is based on the assumption that people are *conditioned* to respond to stimuli. In the work world, reinforcement theory suggests that an employee's behavior can be shaped by past experience.

Skinner's reinforcement theory suggests that, if a manager wants to elicit a desired behavior or response from an employee, the manager must reinforce that behavior. The type of reinforcement used can elicit different responses. This theory leads to four possible managerial actions in response to employee behavior:

- *Positive reinforcement*—A manager can encourage repetition of a desired behavior by rewarding that behavior. If a manager fails to reinforce a desired behavior, an employee may not exhibit that behavior again.

- *Negative reinforcement* (also called *avoidance*)—A manager can encourage desired behavior by removing a punishment or unpleasant stimulus (such as criticism of an employee's performance) when the desired behavior finally occurs.

- *Extinction*—A manager can ignore a behavior to discourage it.

- *Punishment*—A manager can punish an employee's undesired behavior to discourage the employee from performing that way again. [19]

Reinforcement theory has been successfully adapted by other behavioral scientists and consultants to align more fully with workplace needs. For example, Ken Blanchard and Spencer Johnson espouse most of this theory in their best-seller, *The One Minute Manager*. In this book, Blanchard and Johnson emphasize positive rewards as the best method of eliciting desired performance in employees. Managers who want to try this method should make it a practice to "catch someone doing something 'good'" and then praise or reward that employee. Blanchard and Johnson encourage public praise to make employees feel good about their behavior and to set examples for others.[20]

Knowledge Check

1. What is the difference between content theories and process theories of motivation?

2. What is the danger of setting performance goals too high?

3. Which content theory explains human motivation the best? Why?

8.3 DETERMINING JOB WORTH

Motivating employees is just one of the goals of a compensation program. Every organization must also develop some method of aligning labor cost to the economic value of the work to the business. Some companies rely on comparisons with other organizations in the same marketplace, whereas others use internally focused methods. This section presents the various methods of evaluating the value of a job, also called **job worth**, as well as the advantages and disadvantages of each method.

External and Internal Equity

Managers can apply the concepts of external equity and internal equity when evaluating and determining job worth. **External equity** (also referred to as *market pay* or *prevailing wage*) relates to pay variations among similar properties in a particular market. **Internal equity** relates to pay variations within a particular company. The advantage of the external equity method is that the market determines pay; hence, the job holder is paid as much as the market is willing to pay for that job. Disadvantages include the fact that (1) different organizational cultures might react to pay needs differently and (2) it is sometimes difficult to find out how much competitors pay. Some scholars contend that paying slightly higher-than-market pay produces the best overall results.[21]

To determine appropriate pay levels, some organizations conduct formal or informal surveys of their competitors. Organizations that do not have personnel with the expertise to conduct or analyze such surveys often hire college professors or outside consultants who specialize in these areas.

Pay surveys are complex. A thorough analysis of external equity conditions must consider many factors, including overall compensation levels in other organizations, union influences, demographic information on the workers employed, local labor market and economic conditions, and financial conditions of the external organizations surveyed.

It is also important to examine the manner in which jobs are designed in surveyed organizations because jobs with similar titles are not the same in every company. In most cases, compensation and salary consultants compare what are known as **compensable factors**, or the common elements of jobs. Exhibit 8.3 shows a sample listing of compensable factors of a job. Doing so eliminates any bias when comparing—across companies—jobs that have dissimilar or unusual tasks and behaviors. Wage and salary surveys must be carefully constructed and pretested to establish their accuracy.

Government agencies can provide some useful information for establishing external equity. For instance, the Bureau of Labor Statistics of the U.S. Department of Labor provides compensation statistics on employment fields and occupations that can be helpful to an external equity analysis.[22]

Exhibit 8.3 Compensable Factor: Use of Equipment

Definition: The factor addresses the types of tools and machines used by employees to perform the essential duties of this position.

Explanation: Responsibilities involving equipment use ranges from working simple machines to managing highly technical computer equipment. The ability to operate particular equipment coincides with assessing a skill level.

Degree	Job Requirements
1	Work requires no previous knowledge or training on specialized equipment. Skills can be acquired through on-the-job training.
2	Work requires use of advanced office equipment, such as a personal computer, but duties are limited to generating documents and files through standardized techniques, such as typing letters or entering data.
3	Work requires use of advanced office equipment to interpret and prepare documents, mainly through word processing capabilities. Training on a PC is required.
4	Work requires significant use of advanced office equipment. Knowledge of additional PC capabilities, such as spreadsheets, software, and statistical manipulation, is necessary to perform job duties and generate information to be used by others.
5	Work requires a regular use of advanced office equipment. In addition, knowledge of software and spreadsheets is critical for analyzing, inputting, and revising data. Also interprets data generated from other sources.
6	Work requires operation of equipment for which extensive training, certification, and licensing are required and that affects the safety of the job holder and others.

Private organizations such as the Society for Human Resource Management can also provide useful information. However, in many cases, this information is either too generic or not industry-specific enough to support an entire compensation program.

For example, most survey results include mean salaries and wages, median salaries and wages, modal (most common) salaries and wages, pay percentiles and pay distributions, or the **pay range** for various jobs. After a properly conducted survey, the information is compared with compensable factors to determine the accuracy of comparisons with external jobs.

Internal equity analysis also depends on establishing meaningful compensable factors and developing and implementing a thorough job evaluation system. The next section discusses different approaches to the development and implementation of job evaluations.

Job Evaluation Methods

The five most widely employed methods of conducting job evaluations are the:

- Ranking method,
- Classification method,
- Point method,
- Factor comparison method, and
- Skill-based pay (which is discussed later in this chapter)

Ranking Method. The ranking method usually uses a team of managers—or an evaluation committee that may include employees—to rank the jobs. This team or committee typically collects examples of all job descriptions used in the organization and ranks these descriptions on a continuum. The scale ranges from hardest to easiest, from most skilled to least skilled, or from most important to least important to the organization.

On the surface, this method seems to provide a simple, fast, and inexpensive means for determining which jobs should be paid the most. However, this approach is much like comparing apples to oranges. Generally, few jobs have the same compensable factors in all workplaces, so comparisons can be inaccurate, and opinions can vary. In addition, it is not possible to establish the distances between jobs on the continuum. For example, although this method might determine that a cook's job is more important and more difficult than a dishwasher's job, it still does not reveal *how much* more important or difficult. Finally, in all but the smallest organizations, it is difficult to assemble a team of managers with the expertise to evaluate *every* job in the company. This method is best used when fewer than 30 jobs are being ranked.

The ranking method can be improved by using the paired comparison method. When this approach is used, each job is compared by job criteria on a one-to-one basis with every other job and then ranked. A comparison of each job with all other jobs provides a more complete picture of job worth than does a simple ranking. However, the distance on the continuum between jobs and the subjectivity of each comparison is still a problem.

Classification Method. Sometimes called *job grading*, the classification method compares each job to a predetermined grade or class. The U.S. government and many state governments use this approach to job evaluation. This system also accounts for the length of service within each grade. The classifications determine compensation and promotion. One advantage of this approach is that new jobs can easily fit into the classification scheme as they are developed. This method also predetermines the starting pay of new workers.

Although this approach seems to solve the problem of how to evaluate each position, it has some drawbacks. Creating an effective scale can be both costly and time-consuming. In addition, each advance in technology that changes a job's importance can render the scale obsolete. The diversity of tasks required by each job can also make classification extremely difficult. Perhaps the greatest disadvantage of the classification method is its emphasis on written job descriptions. Because classification depends on job descriptions, managers, supervisors, and employees may believe that wages can be increased simply by rewriting job descriptions.

Point Method. The point method is probably the most widely used method of job evaluation. The method assigns a point total to each job on the basis of several clearly defined criteria. Jobs are then placed in job grades according to their point totals. Creating a point system is a fairly complex task that often calls for help from outside consultants. Few companies have the expertise to design an accurate point system in-house. Once designed, however, a point system is easy to understand and use.

The point method involves three basic steps:

1. Determining compensable factors,
2. Weighting the relative importance of each compensable factor, and
3. Creating degrees within each compensable factor.

The first step, determining compensable factors, begins with a job analysis of all (or at least representative) jobs in the company. The goal of this analysis is to group similar jobs into "families" that each constitute or fall into a separate job structure. For example, some companies put all administrative employees in one job structure, all clerical employees in another, all service employees in yet another, and so on. To avoid unnecessarily complex compensation structures, however, most companies place all jobs into as few job structures as they sensibly can.

Once these job families have been selected, the compensable factors for each family are identified. Compensable factors are those factors that a company values and for which it chooses to pay. Compensable factors might include education, experience, skills, effort, analysis and problem solving, autonomy, responsibility, interactions with others, working conditions, and any number of other possibilities. They must be demonstrably related to the actual work performed to be credible and acceptable to the people affected by the system. They also need to support the company's culture and values. Overlapping factors should be avoided because they disproportionately reward or penalize certain job elements.

Compensable factors are all valuable to a company, but they are not necessarily *equally* valuable. Once the compensable factors are identified, they must be weighted to reflect their relative importance. For example, the most important may be weighted at 25 percent whereas others are weighted below that.

Although the compensable factors explain the components of work being considered when evaluating a job family, degrees within these factors are needed to provide a mechanism for differentiating between jobs. Compensable factors must be divided into degrees that represent the spectrum of jobs that share that factor. Each degree should be described in narrative form. For example, the ability to operate a restaurant's point-of-sale system is a compensable factor for both a food server and a restaurant manager, but not to the same degree. The server must be able to enter orders and produce customer checks, but the manager must have a higher understanding of the system in order to manage the operation, analyze sales and evaluate the servers. That higher degree of understanding has far less value for a server.

The next step in the point method is a simple calculation to determine the number of points assigned to each degree. To do this, a point total for each job structure must be selected. Once a total is chosen, it is multiplied by each factor weight to determine the maximum points available for each factor.

For example, if a 1000-point plan is chosen and one factor is weighted at 20 percent, that factor qualifies for up to 200 points. This total is divided by the number of degrees to determine the point totals for those degrees. If this factor has 4 degrees, each degree is generally worth 50 points.

After the points are allotted to each factor degree, it is a simple process to apply and total the points for each job. The jobs are then grouped into grades or levels based on their point totals, as shown in Exhibit 8.4.

Factor Comparison Method. The factor comparison method entails identifying **key jobs**. Generally, key jobs are those that the evaluation committee considers extremely important to the success of the organization. For example, cooks and servers are considered key—or benchmark—jobs in a restaurant. When using the factor comparison method, the prevailing hourly wages for key jobs are used as a benchmark for comparing all other jobs.

In this case, assume that the prevailing hourly wage for cooks and servers in the market is $12.50 and $7.50, respectively. Committee members then *work backward* from these totals to assign rates to each of the compensable factors identified as pertinent to the company. The compensable factors used in the example are physical demand, skill, responsibility, working conditions, and interpersonal skills. After pay rates for each of the compensable factors are assigned to key jobs, pay rates for non-benchmark jobs can be established on a factor-by-factor basis. Exhibit 8.5 shows an example of this method.

Among its advantages, the factor comparison method provides a scale that is custom-made for the organization. This scale is also easy to apply. However, the method is ponderous, especially for developing pay rates for supervisory and management-level jobs. The method is also difficult to explain to employees because of its complexity. It is difficult to distribute the total wage for each key job into compensable factors. In addition, choosing key jobs, determining prevailing rates for these jobs, and assigning rates to the compensable factors for non-benchmark jobs are all subjective decisions that can lead to employee dissension and perceptions of inequity.

Exhibit 8.4 Sample Compensable Factors Evaluation Matrix

Compensable Factors	Assigned Weight	Maximum Points/1000	Four Degrees			
			Minimum	Low	Moderate	High
Education	10	100	25	50	75	100
Experience	10	100	25	50	75	100
Skills and abilities	30	300	75	150	225	300
Independent judgment	10	100	25	50	75	100
Responsibility for people	20	200	50	100	150	200
Physical difficulty	20	100	25	50	75	100

Example: Front Desk Supervisor

Education: 75
Experience: 50
Skills and abilities: 225
Independent judgment: 75
Responsibility for people: 200
Physical difficulty: 75

Total points for position: 700 out of 1,000 maximum points.

Exhibit 8.5 Example of Determining Pay Rates

Benchmark Jobs	Physical Factor	Skill	Responsibility	Working Conditions	Interpersonal Skills		Prevailing Wage for Benchmark Job
Cook	2.75	2.75	2.75	2.25	1.00	=	11.50
Server	1.75	1.00	1.50	.75	2.50	=	7.50
Greeter	.50	1.50	1.50	1.00	2.50	=	7.00

Non-Benchmark Jobs	Physical Factor	Skill	Responsibility	Working Conditions	Interpersonal Skills		Prevailing Wage for Non-Benchmark Job
Dishwasher	2.25	1.00	.75	2.00	.25	=	6.25
Prep Cook	1.75	1.75	1.25	1.75	.25	=	6.75
Buser	2.25	1.00	.75	1.25	1.00	=	6.25

8.4 ESTABLISHING PAY STRUCTURES

Determining how to identify the value of different jobs is only part of the pay structure puzzle. Organizations must also determine how the company pay will compare to that of competition in the market, the number of pay grades offered, and how the range of compensation is determined within specific pay grades. The following section summarizes pay structure options.

Competitive Pay Policies

Each hospitality organization must decide how to position its pay policies in comparison to other companies in the market. Collecting information on pay and benefit packages offered by competitors and others in the hotel, restaurant, and tourism industries is critical to successful recruitment and retention. Aggregated national statistics are available for free from the Bureau of Labor Statistics. Some state agencies provide similar information, but the statistics are typically state-wide and categorize businesses and job classifications broadly. Detailed studies of local competitors are also offered by paid consultants.

Most companies position themselves in one of three general categories:

- *Pay leaders*—Pay more than the market average to attract better employees.

- *Pay followers*—Pay below market average to reduce labor cost and increase profits.

- *Meet the competitors*—Pay the prevailing wage in the market to meet competition.

Pay Grades

Each hospitality company must also determine the number of **pay grades** it will use. Typically, a company finds that whatever job evaluation method it uses will create information that can be easily converted to a chart. For example, assume that a company uses the point method to evaluate pay for each job. This evaluation results in assigning a point value to each job on the basis of compensable factors. A completed chart might look like the one depicted in Exhibit 8.6.

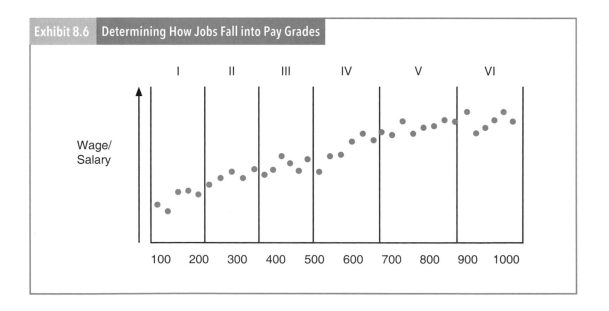

| Exhibit 8.6 | Determining How Jobs Fall into Pay Grades |

Each dot in Exhibit 8.6 represents a job. This clearly shows where each job belongs on the wage continuum. The continuum is then divided into groups, or grades, and each grade is assigned a range of pay rates from the minimum to the maximum. Normally, jobs on the lower end of the pay scale have narrower pay ranges than those at the top of the scale. It is important to establish a range of pay within each grade. This allows employees to receive raises without changing pay grades. For example, a range of pay for dishwashers allows a more experienced or senior employee in this category to make more money than a less experienced or junior employee.

The conventional wisdom is that performance pay must be high enough to effectively reward performance and that there must be observed differences in pay between people who make higher and lower contributions to the organization. As noted previously, pay that reflects the organization's values will likely work best. However, managers should keep in mind that large pay differentials within a single job can create perceptions of inequity, and this can reduce cooperation, quality, and commitment.

Determining Pay Within Grades

In the previous example of two dishwashers, one had more experience and seniority than the other. Seniority provides a good reason for establishing a range of pay within pay grades, particularly in union environments. Most union contracts establish seniority as an important factor in determining employee pay. **Seniority-based pay** is also useful in non-union working environments, especially for employees at the low end of the pay scale.

Many hospitality organizations also link pay directly to performance. **Merit pay** policies are intended to create effective reward systems that motivate employees to try their best at all times. Some experts note that pay-for-performance systems are particularly effective in environments in which a high level of trust exists between management and employees and in which management establishes a fair and ongoing evaluation of performance (such as regular performance appraisals).

Two methods of determining pay scales are broadbanding and careerbanding:

- *Broadbanding* is the elimination of all but a few, say three to 10, comprehensive salary and job classifications. The bands usually have minimum and maximum dollar amounts of pay that overlap and average no more than 130 percent from top to bottom. In broadbanding, for example, all managers might be grouped into one band, all clerical employees into another band, and all part-time employees into still another band. Broadbanding emphasizes titles, grades, and job descriptions.

- *Careerbanding* is similar to broadbanding, but it is more closely tied to career development. Instead of using minimums and maximums to establish pay scales, as in broadbanding, scales are determined by market surveys. For instance, a company might take a market survey to determine how competitors pay and establish its rates based on what it learns.

Two-Tier Wage System

Two-tier wage systems establish two distinct pay structures for employees. Two-tier systems are most common in union environments, in which a union agrees to pay concessions in the form of reduced pay for future employees. These systems provide a higher pay structure for existing employees while a lower one is created for employees hired after the effective date of the contract. For example, a union might agree to wage cutbacks that create a base minimum rate of $10.00 per hour for existing room attendants whereas the minimum rate paid to new hires might be $7.50. This policy must be explained to applicants during the selection process.

A two-tier wage system offers advantages to both current employees and management. The advantage for current employees is that they will be on the higher scale for as long as they work for the company. Management has the advantage of being able to cut back on wage expenses by paying new employees less. Eventually, employees on the old system will retire and the company will be left with only lower-wage employees.

Theoretically, this system offers an effective way for management to reduce labor costs. However, the two-tier system also creates equity problems among employees. When one employee perceives that he or she is working as hard as another employee but is receiving lower pay, a sense of inequity is likely to develop. As a result, motivation and productivity among those earning the lower rate are likely to decline. A two-tier system can also make it more difficult to attract new employees, since the lower tier is likely to fall below the prevailing wage.

Skill-Based Pay

Another method of determining employee pay is to institute a skill-based pay system. **Skill-based pay** systems assume that a company can afford to pay more to people who can do more. Determining pay by the number of skills an employee has is one way to do this. Seniority does not play a role. According to this method, companies base pay on the abilities or skills each employee acquires rather than the job to which the employee is assigned. Hypothetically, all employees start at the same level of pay. As employees acquire new skills, the company increases their rate of pay. The result is a compensation plan that is related directly to the number of different jobs an employee can perform. Research has shown that employees do tend to acquire more and stronger skills under such a system.[23]

Knowledge-based pay is a variation of a skill-based pay system in which pay is tied to knowledge rather than to skills. In such systems, employees can increase their pay by becoming experts at their current jobs.

One of the major attributes of a skill-based pay program is that employees often believe it is fairer than other systems. In a study of 600 organizations, researchers found that employees strongly agreed that skill-based pay programs take much of the subjectivity out of pay evaluations, and they perceive these systems to be more just.[24] Another advantage of a skill-based pay program is that employees typically learn skills that are transferable to other jobs within the company. As a result, these employees

can fill in when temporary labor shortages develop in different areas. In addition, skill-based pay provides extra motivation for employees to learn.

Such pay systems can be particularly useful when technological advancements create the need for new skills or knowledge. Skill- or knowledge-based pay systems also support the use of career ladders for certain jobs. Skill-based pay plans have the advantage of improving staff performance, reducing unwanted turnover, and improving a company's recruitment of new employees.[25] In effect, such systems create additional rungs on the career ladder for employees to climb.

Skill- and knowledge-based pay programs have been effectively employed in several service industries for employees with "short" career ladders. For example, in the late 1980s, such pay programs were introduced to nurses in hospitals. Nurses had only two options before the introduction of such programs: move into management (and out of the hands-on, service-oriented or "caring" side of the profession) or remain in a nursing position. Skill- and knowledge-based pay programs provide a third option for nurses, enabling them to seek title changes or pay raises within the customer-service end of their profession.

Some hospitality companies have had success with skill- or knowledge-based pay programs. Quick service and casual dining businesses, for example, have long used the system to reduce turnover and improve organizational commitment in positions that traditionally require little or no prior education or experience. Employees who learn more about their jobs are less likely to seek other employment—possibly, where their knowledge is not valued. They are also motivated by increased opportunities for advancement.[26]

Of course, there is no guarantee that increased job skills and knowledge will translate to better job performance. If an employee is compensated for acquiring a new skill but doesn't have the opportunity to use that new skill, the additional compensation does not produce any greater job performance. For this sort of system to work, managers must make the best use of the employees' skills and abilities. If a food server, for instance, receives a pay increase after learning to tend the bar but then is never scheduled to work as a bartender, the restaurant has not gained anything by increasing the server's pay.

Like most other systems, skill- and knowledge-based programs have some disadvantages. One problem with skill-based pay systems is that they take some time to establish. If, for example, a company decided to implement a skill-based pay system one year, evaluations related to pay probably could not be used until the following year, after employees have had an opportunity to develop or refine the skills included in the compensation program. Another disadvantage is the increase in labor costs as employees learn additional skills and the cost of providing the education or training needed to acquire new skills. Another is that some employees learn all the skills assigned to their jobs, then "top out" with no place else to go within the organization. Also, such programs can create false expectations for employees who hope to use their new skills in permanent new jobs within the company, only to be disappointed with temporary assignments. Even considering these drawbacks, however, the advantages of such programs can far outweigh the disadvantages.

Team-Based Pay

Hospitality organizations are increasingly depending on teamwork to improve organizational performance. **Team-based pay** rewards employees according to the outcome produced by the team. It has a greater emphasis on goal accomplishment of teams. An example of team-based pay is a commission shared among several members of a sales force that work together to sell a real estate property. Of course, there are potential equity problems when some team members perform more than others for the same pay. A critical part of any team-based compensation system is a method of resolving conflicts concerning the distribution of work within the team and the contributions of each individual to the team's performance. Tip pooling among restaurant servers is a form of team-based pay, although tips are not necessarily considered compensation because they are not paid or provided by the employer.

Piece Rate

Jobs that involve repetitive and quantifiable outcomes, such as cleaning rooms or producing products, are sometimes compensated according to the number of units of work completed. Under a **piece rate** system, housekeepers would be paid a flat rate for each room cleaned, with rate adjustments according to room size or difficulty. The piece rate by its nature motivates employees to work faster but not necessarily better, so the system sometimes requires more attention to quality control. Piece rates are most common in manufacturing jobs and must ensure that each employee's pay meets or exceeds the applicable legal minimum wage.

Knowledge Check

1. How is the amount of pay determined in a skill-based compensation program?

2. How does a two-tiered wage structure reduce labor cost in the long term?

3. Describe the piece rate system and any concerns related to it.

8.5 CURRENT ISSUES IN COMPENSATION ADMINISTRATION

Compensation administration is a changing field. Expectations of employees evolve, and compensation programs have to keep up. This section highlights some current issues in compensation administration: tips, pay secrecy, wage compression and expansion, comparable worth, and wage and hour audits.

Tips

Tips received from customers make up most of the employment compensation for some employees, particularly in food and beverage service. The employer's compensation system may be unimportant or irrelevant to such workers. Some of them can even be paid below the legal minimum wage without any benefits because the tips are sufficient to

Two recent developments concerning tip pools are important to note. In 2020, the U.S. Congress enacted a new provision of the federal wage and hour laws to prohibit the distribution of any money from a tip pool to supervisors, managers, or owners.[27] In some states, however, it is now legal to give a portion of the tip pool to employees who don't ordinarily receive tips, such as cooks, busers, hosts, and dishwashers.[28]

make up the difference. This system of "tip credit" is further explained in Chapter 13.

For those employees, the employer's policies concerning tips are much more important. Some employers simply allow all employees to keep their own tips, which is believed to motivate better individual job performance. Others require employees to pool their tips and split them evenly among themselves, which results in greater pay equity but is subject to the same disadvantages as team-based pay.

Pay Secrecy

One of the most basic problems a hospitality manager must contend with regarding a compensation program is whether to keep pay rates secret. This decision involves at least two issues:

1. Does the company make its pay grades and the pay ranges within those grades known to employees (or, in even greater openness, does it reveal the actual pay of individual employees)?

2. If the company prefers pay secrecy, does it attempt to prevent or forbid employees from discussing their pay with other employees?

Many people assume that full disclosure of salaries and wages creates employee dissatisfaction because they believe employees may see some situations as unfair, especially comparing managers and executives to hourly workers. However, this may not be true. Full pay disclosure is the norm in most government systems at both federal and state levels. Most state universities readily disclose the salaries of professors and staff members. Union labor contracts also specify compensation rates for all workers to see.

Research indicates that when pay is kept secret, employees generally guess the pay of peers and managers incorrectly, resulting in false perceptions of inequity. Interestingly enough, employees generally guess low on the pay of managers rather than high. Most private enterprises still maintain policies of pay secrecy, even though such policies fly against the movement toward more transparency and may encourage discrimination.

An article in *The Academy of Management Review* discussed the advantages and disadvantages of pay secrecy policies. Disadvantages included the following:

- Employees will make judgments about fairness of pay policies without information and anxiety will develop.

- Judgments about pay fairness will be based on a general impression of the organization's fairness. The disadvantage of this is that if someone tends to see the organization as negative, they will be more likely to see many examples of pay inequity.

- Secrecy breeds distrust. Openness signals integrity; secrecy signals that the organization does not trust its employees.

- Pay secrecy could affect the labor market because it might prevent employees from moving. It also makes it harder to recruit others.

There are also advantages to pay secrecy policies:

- Pay secrecy can enhance organizational control and reduce conflict.

- Pay differentials can cause jealousy; hiding them may prevent damage to company morale.

- Secrecy actually increases fairness in the equity sense because people can more easily be rewarded for the full range of their outputs.
- Pay secrecy maximizes the organization's ability to correct historical pay inequities.
- Pay secrecy encourages teamwork and reduces the "superstar" effect.
- Pay secrecy may increase loyalty to the organization.[29]

Pay secrecy policies originated around the time of the passage of the National Labor Relations Act (NLRA) because it was then believed that keeping pay a secret would impede unions. Given that most private U.S. enterprises still embrace policies that forbid or discourage employees from discussing their pay, it is particularly interesting to note that such policies are generally illegal in the United States. The National Labor Relations Board (NLRB) has repeatedly found such policies to be unfair labor practices in violation of employees' rights under the NLRA to discuss the terms and conditions of employment in concert with other employees. The NLRB has repeatedly held that employees fired for discussing salary information with other employees must be reinstated.[30] Many employers *wrongly* believe that NLRA rights and protections do not apply to non-union employees. It appears that enforced pay secrecy policies continue in the United States at least in part because employees are not aware of (or are reluctant to test) their rights under the NLRA.

Given that the assumptions in the absence of full disclosure tend to be incorrect, and that hourly employees have a legally protected right to discuss and compare their pay, it seems a better policy to be transparent about compensation and to openly address perceived inequities.

Wage Compression and Expansion

Wage compression results primarily from competition with other companies for new hires. Faced with a shortage of qualified applicants, many companies increase the starting wages of new employees to com-

pete. However, because competition for current employees is not as great as it is for new hires, current employees may not receive the same salary increases. Employers have several reasons for not increasing the wages of current employees at the same rates as for new hires. Generally, employers reason that current employees are less likely to leave a company once they begin gaining seniority and once their benefit packages start to accumulate.

As a result of wage compression, a company may find that employees with less seniority (sometimes even new employees) often earn as much as those who have been on staff for a significant period of time. The salaries of university professors provide a good example: starting salaries of university professors today are often much higher than were the starting salaries of current faculty members when they were hired. This is due primarily to competition among universities for a smaller pool of qualified personnel. Even though current faculty members receive merit and cost-of-living pay increases, their salaries typically do not catch up to those of new hires. In effect, university faculty can command higher salaries by changing employers than by remaining in long-term positions, resulting in higher turnover and the loss of the most experienced workers.

In the long run, wage compression could lead to dissatisfaction among senior employees who see a shrinking gap between their salaries and those of new hires. Some would argue that current employees are worth more to a company because of their experience and expertise. However, competition for a limited number of new hires can drive up salaries and wages faster than merit pay and cost-of-living increases do for current employees. Companies are caught in a trap of potentially losing senior employees because of the inequity these employees feel when comparing their salaries with those of new hires. Although many employees feel they cannot leave because they are tied to a benefit system, their productivity and motivation may decline as a result of wage compression.

Wage expansion occurs when companies raise the wages of current employees to keep their salaries in line with the higher wages of new hires. Theoretically, such programs can result in substantial increases in the overall wages of all employees, a result that many hospitality companies cannot afford. For instance, a hospitality company may have to increase the pay offered to new room attendants to attract new hires. But if the company increases the wages of *all* room attendants to maintain equity, the next higher group of employees will also want pay increases to maintain what they feel is the appropriate range between salaries. As a result, employers can be forced to successively increase the wages of *all* employees, necessarily increasing labor cost.

The best way to approach the problems created by wage compression and expansion is to analyze the total cost of each employee. It is interesting to note that employees with longer tenure typically cost more in benefits than do new employees. Although replacing current employees with new hires at higher wages may appear to increase the overall compensation program, in reality it may not, primarily because the company pays less in *overall* compensation to new hires. Some companies may justify wage compression by a complete analysis of all compensation programs.

Comparable Worth

Many people confuse **comparable worth** with equal pay. These people typically cite the Equal Pay Act of 1963 as evidence that the U.S. government mandated the abolition of unequal pay on the basis of sex or race. However, comparable worth and equal

pay are substantially different issues. The Equal Pay Act prohibits pay discrimination in the *same* job. Comparable worth deals with the issue of pay in *similar* jobs.

In the United States, some jobs are still considered predominantly "female" jobs and others are considered predominantly "male" jobs. For example, many food servers are female, and many dishwashers are male. Similar types of sex segregation of jobs exist in the hospitality industry. Most room attendants, for example, are female (roughly 88%), whereas many cooks are male (roughly 58%). Although exceptions certainly exist, many jobs are still predominantly single-sex jobs.[31]

Comparable worth advocates cite the fact that pay is based on *job classification* rather than on the work that goes into a job. They may note that, although the work performed in a predominantly "female" occupation is as difficult and important as that performed in a predominantly "male" occupation, traditionally "female" professions are paid only about two-thirds as much as traditionally "male" professions.

Numerous arguments have been made to explain pay differences for comparable jobs. For example, some suggest that the difference between wages for males and females is the result of seniority, not discrimination. According to this view, men typically have been on the job longer and, as a result, earn more than women. Others may say that differences occur because men and women tend to choose different jobs that command different salaries. Others counter these arguments with examples of how women and people of color are paid less even though the compensable factors in jobs may be equal.

Many labor experts believe that the issue of comparable worth is the most important labor issue businesses face. These experts typically cite examples such as the increasing number of women in the work force, the gradual dissolution of boundaries between traditionally "male" and "female" jobs, and court cases that uphold settlements for discrimination on the basis of comparable worth. Yet not everyone agrees. One thing is certain about this issue: if the courts find that businesses are discriminating on the basis of different pay for comparable jobs, the decision will greatly affect the manner in which hospitality companies pay their employees.

In fact, because approximately 60 percent of the employees in the hospitality industry are women[32], such a decision could cause hospitality companies to alter their compensation programs completely.

Wage and Hour Audits

All pay policies and procedures must comply with the provisions of the FLSA. Policies and procedures that are inconsistent with the FLSA can result in fines for a company and backpay for employees.

As some managers know, the U.S. Department of Labor conducts wage and hour audits to determine whether companies are following the provisions of the FLSA. Managers can prepare for such audits by learning and reviewing the issues that such investigations are likely to cover. Exhibit 8.7 presents a 17-point outline that managers can use as a guide. By conducting a self-audit, managers can correct errors in policy or procedure before a visit from federal or state wage and hour investigators. Chapter 13 presents a more detailed examination of the most commonly violated wage laws.

Knowledge Check

1. Is it better to disclose pay rates or keep them secret? Why?

2. What issues arise as a result of wage compression?

3. What is the difference between comparable worth and equal pay?

Exhibit 8.7	Points Focused On by Wage and Hour Investigators

Managers may find it helpful to review the following 17 points in anticipation of any formal review by wage and hour investigators from the U.S. Department of Labor.

1. **Exempt vs. non-exempt employees**
   To meet exempt qualifications, employees must generally be either executive, administrative, or professional employees. Factors considered during an investigation include job descriptions, wage rates, methods of payment, and the functions employees actually perform.

2. **Time period covered**
   Non-exempt employees are entitled to overtime pay. In general, the Fair Labor Standards Act requires that employees be paid overtime for all work over 40 hours per week. A workweek is any consecutive seven-day period designated by the employer. Investigators check this and the "multiplication factor" used to calculate overtime.

3. **Hours worked**
   Investigators check how employees are informed about "signing in" and "signing out" procedures, and whether preliminary work activities such as cleaning up, prep work, and so on are included in work reported. Time sheets or cards are reviewed carefully for accuracy.

4. **Compensable time**
   During an investigation, the investigator will want to examine the hours during which employees are at work, but for which they are not compensated (such as breaks or lunch).

5. **Calculation of overtime rate**
   For some employees, the regular rate of pay and the hourly rate of pay differ. For instance, a bellperson may be paid $7 per hour, but receive an additional $1 per bag delivered. In this case, the regular rate of pay is $7 plus $1 for each bag. Overtime is calculated on the regular rate of pay, not on the hourly rate.

6. **Exemptions from the regular rate**
   Investigators check to see how employees earning commissions or service charges are paid, how such amounts are tracked, and how such compensation for these employees is identified (i.e., flat rate or hourly rate).

(continued)

Exhibit 8.7 Points Focused On by Wage and Hour Investigators *(continued)*

7. **Employees working more than one job**
   Employees working two jobs often receive two rates of pay. Overtime for these employees should be a weighted average of the two rates, not based upon the rate paid while incurring the actual overtime hours.

8. **Gratuity vs. service charge**
   Hospitality companies must keep accurate records of monies paid in service charges to employees for such items as banquet service or room service.

9. **Tip credit**
   Employers should create and maintain a list of employees who qualify for tip credit. This list should be periodically reviewed to determine whether the tip credit is actually being recovered by the employee.

10. **Tip pooling**
    Employers should document and maintain a list of employees included in any tip pooling, the percentages for tip pooling distribution, the employer's method for tracking tip pooling procedures, and management participation in the process.

11. **Discrimination**
    Hospitality managers must be careful not to discriminate with regard to pay. Pay between men and women in similar jobs has been a consistent problem and is a focus of many investigators. Managers should check to ensure either that pay is equal or that there are logical reasons for discrepancies, such as seniority or merit.

12. **Policies and handbooks**
    Many courts hold that handbooks and policy manuals represent implied contracts between employers and employees. Investigators often examine these documents to determine if promises are made to employees that are not kept.

13. **Recordkeeping**
    Hospitality companies must keep employee records for a specified period of time. Managers should review such records and ensure they are kept for appropriate periods.

14. **Independent contractor**
    Some managers attempt to avoid recordkeeping and pay requirements by maintaining that some employees are independent contractors. Investigators examine records for written agreements between employees and employers that substantiate this. They also may investigate the nature of such contractual relationships.

15. **Training time**
    Investigators check to ensure that trainees receive the proper rates of pay while training. Such pay rates vary, of course, depending on the job.

16. **Payment procedures upon termination**
    Terminated employees generally must be paid at the time of termination. Investigators check to see if this pay is accurate and includes time for vacations and other accrued benefits.

17. **I-9 documentation**
    Employers must maintain timely and accurate files on each employee, including completed and accurate I-9 forms when necessary. Employers should check that all forms are completed properly. One potential problem for employers is the type of documentation accepted on the I-9 form as proof of eligibility for work. Employers should read the instructions on the form carefully to make sure they comply with this important documentation.

Source: Adapted from Jay Krupin, "Wage and Hour Policies and Procedures Training Manual for Compliance with U.S. Department of Labor Regulations Affecting Hotels," presented at the Human Resources Executive Forum, Indian Wells, California, 5 February 1992.

IN THIS CHAPTER, YOU LEARNED:

- Employment compensation comes in many forms besides cash payments. Cash payments alone don't always produce the desired job performance.

- Federal and state employment laws regulate some forms of compensation. Every compensation program must ensure compliance with minimum wage and overtime laws.

- Indirect compensation can have a greater effect on employee motivation than direct compensation.

- External factors like local labor markets, economic conditions, and unions can influence compensation rates.

- Employees who are satisfied with their compensation tend to work harder and better.

- Competing theories of human motivation provide some insight into the potential effects of various forms of employment compensation. No single theory explains all employee motivation.

- Employees are not equally motivated by equal compensation. Different forms of compensation are more valuable to some employees than to others.

- There are several effective methods of determining job worth, each with advantages and disadvantages.

- Pay structures establish the foundation of a company's compensation system.

KEY TERMS

comparable worth—The concept of equal pay for men and women performing jobs that require essentially the same skills or contribute the same value to business operations.

compensable factors—Elements common to each job on which compensation is based.

cost of living—A term used to refer to the present real dollar value of essential goods and services.

direct compensation—An employer's payment of money to an employee—either in the present or at some future date—in exchange for that employee's productive work; includes wages, salary, overtime, bonuses, piece rates, and so forth.

external equity—Equity in comparison to employees outside the organization.

extrinsic rewards—job factors that are expected by employees and therefore do not lead to satisfaction or motivation.

indirect compensation—Compensation not directly related to an employee's productive work; includes various insurance protection programs, pay for time not worked, savings plans, and perquisites.

internal equity—Equity in comparison to other employees within the organization.

intrinsic rewards—Unexpected factors in compensation that can lead to job satisfaction and motivation.

job worth—The value of a particular job to desired business outcomes.

key jobs—Fundamentally critical jobs used in the factor comparison method to anchor the scale of each job's value.

knowledge-based pay—A pay system based on the amount of knowledge each employee has.

merit pay—Pay based on the quantity or quality of an employee's job performance over a predetermined period of time.

pay grades—Categories of pay rates for particular jobs in an organization.

pay range—The range between the highest and lowest rates of pay for each job in an organization.

piece rate—Compensation method based on the employee's completion of measurable job units.

seniority-based pay—A pay system based on the length of time the worker has been employed.

skill-based pay—A pay system that assumes a company can afford to pay more to people who can do more.

team-based pay—A pay system based on the outcome produced by a team.

total reward program—The sum of all the methods, including cash, equity, and benefits, that employers use to compensate employees.

two-tier wage system—A pay system that establishes two distinct pay structures for employees—one system for employees with seniority and another for new employees.

valence—In expectancy theory, the strength of an individual's preference for a particular outcome.

wage compression—Pay inequities based on levels of demand that result in higher pay for new employees than for current employees.

wage expansion—A condition that occurs when employers raise the pay rates of current employees to keep salaries in line with the higher wages of new hires caused by wage compression.

REVIEW QUESTIONS

1. What are some of the external and internal factors that may influence compensation programs in your market?

2. What is included in a total reward program?

3. Which theory of motivation places the highest importance on the rewards for desired behavior?

4. How does the equity theory relate to compensation in the hospitality industry? What about the expectancy theory?

5. What are the four methods managers can use to evaluate the worth of jobs?

6. What limitations does the ranking method have?

7. What are the principal differences between pay-for-performance and seniority-based pay systems?

8. What are some legal risks associate with employment compensation?

9. How do wage compression and wage expansion affect an employer's labor cost?

Keeping Housekeeping Staff

Marissa, the Human Resources Manager at Helmsley Hotel, is in her office when Xavier, the Housekeeping Manager, comes in with a problem. He explains, "I've lost three house-keepers in the last month. They all quit to go work for our competitors. And we're not getting enough qualified applicants to apply, so I've had to increase the number of rooms the housekeepers clean every day. More of them are talking about quitting and I don't know what to do. We really need to pay them more."

Marissa decides to investigate. She confirms that the hotel is receiving very few applications for housekeeping positions. The ones who do apply have no experience or training.

Next, Marissa calls some other local hotels and finds out that most of them pay housekeepers from $1 to $3 more per hour than the Helmsley.

Marissa also speaks to some of the current housekeepers and asks them why people are leaving. They tell her they like working at the Helmsley and they all get along, but the pay rates in the company are unfair. Marissa asks what they mean by "unfair."

One of them says, "Some people get paid more than others to do exactly the same job. And the workers who don't work very hard are paid just as much as the ones who do. That's not right." The other adds, "Most of the other hotels around here pay higher wages, so you can't blame them for wanting to leave. I'm thinking about it myself."

So Marissa goes to Danielle, the general manager, and explains the situation. Marissa says, "If you can increase the housekeeping labor budget by 5 percent, I think we can match the local competitors."

But Danielle denies the request, saying, "I really wish we could, but our revenues have been down, and we don't have any room in the next budget for permanent wage increases. You'll have to find another way." She continues, "Speaking of house-keeping, we've been getting guest complaints that some of the rooms are not being cleaned properly. We need house-keepers who are motivated to do a great job for our guests."

Marissa goes back to her office to examine her options and make a plan.

DISCUSSION QUESTIONS:

1. What other information should Marissa get before she decides what to do?

2. What can Marissa do about the housekeepers' perceptions of internal and external inequity?

3. What other methods of compensation might the hotel use to improve the housekeepers' motivation without raising their hourly pay rates?

ENDNOTES

1. Valerie L. Williams and Stephen E. Grimaldi, "A Quick Breakdown of Strategic Pay," *Workforce* 78, no. 12 (1999): 72–76.

2. Edwin Torres and Howard Adler, "Hotel compensation strategies: Perceptions of Top Industry Executives." *Journal of Human Resources in Hospitality & Tourism* 11, no.1 (March 2012): 52–71.

3. Michael C. Sturman, "The Compensation Conundrum: Does the Hospitality Industry Shortchange its Employees – and Itself?" *Cornell Hotel and Restaurant Administration Quarterly* 42, no. 4 (2001): 70–76.

4. "Geographic Information," (n.d.) U.S. Bureau of Labor & Statistics, www.bls.gov/cpi.

5. "Unemployment," (n.d.) U.S. Bureau of Labor & Statistics, https://www.bls.gov/data/#unemployment.

6. Jake Rosenfeld, Patrick Denice, and Jennifer Laird, "Union Decline Lowers Wages of Nonunion Workers," Economic Policy Institute (August 30, 2016) www.epi.org/publication; John Schmitt, Margy Waller, Shawn Fremstad, and Ben Zipperer, "Unions and Upward Mobility for Low-Wage Earners," *Journal of Labor and Society* 11, no. 3 (2008): 337–348.

7. Richard B. Freeman and Joel Rogers, *What Workers Want* (updated edition)(New York: Russel Sage Foundation, 2006).

8. Abraham H. Maslow, *Motivation and Personality* (New York: Harper and Row, 1954); Abraham H. Maslow, "A Theory of Human Needs," *Psychological Review* (1943): 370–396; Peter Heimerl, et al., "Job Satisfaction in the Hospitality Industry: Does the Valuation Make a Difference?" *Anatolia: An International Journal of Tourism & Hospitality Research* 31, no 4 (December 2020): 674–677.

9. Clayton P. Alderfer, *Existence, Relatedness, and Growth: Human Needs in Organizational Settings* (New York: Free Press, 1972); John M. Ivancevich and Michael T. Matteson, *Organizational Behavior and Management*, 6th ed. (Boston: McGraw-Hill, 2002).

10. Frederick Herzberg, "One More Time: How Do You Motivate Employees?" *Harvard Business Review* 46, no. 1 (January/February 1968): 53–62.

11. Catherine R. Curtis and Randall S. Upchurch, "An Application of McClelland's Need Theory to the Casual Dining Industry," *Tourism Analysis* 15, no. 1 (2010): 111–120.

12. David C. McClellan and David H. Burnham, "Power Is the Great Motivator," *Harvard Business Review* 54, no. 2 (March/April 1976): 100–110.

13. Nic Qing-bin, "The Origin of Economic Man Theory," *Journal of Beijing Normal University*, 2007; Justin Fox, "From 'Economic Man' to Behavioral Economics," *Harvard Business Review* 93, no. 5 (May 2015): 78–85.

14. Victor Vroom, *Work and Motivation* (New York: Wiley, 1964).

15. Chun-Fang Chiang and Soo Cheong (Shawn) Jang, "An Expectancy Theory Model for Hotel Employee Motivation," *International Journal of Hospitality Management* 27, no. 2 (2008): 313–322.

16. Stephanie R Thomas, *Compensating Your Employees Fairly: A Guide to Internal Pay Equity*, (New York: Apress), 2013.

17. E. A. Locke and G. P. Latham, *A Theory of Goal Setting and Task Performance* (Englewood Cliffs, N.J.: Prentice-Hall, 1990); Alleah Crawford and Susan Hubbard, "The Impact of Work-Related Goals on Hospitality Employee Variables," *Tourism and Hospitality Research* 8 (2008): 116–124.

18. Ivancevich and Matteson, p. 210; Ayumi Tanaka, et al., "Longitudinal Tests on the Influence of Achievement Goals on Effort and Intrinsic Interest in the Workplace, *Motivation and Emotion* 37, no. 3 (September 2013): 457–464.

19. Adapted from W. C. Hamner, "Reinforcement Theory and Contingency Theory Management in Organizational Settings," in H. L. Tosi and W. C. Hamner, eds., *Organizational Behavior and Management: A Contingency Approach* (New York: Wiley, 1977), pp. 93–112.

20. Kenneth H. Blanchard and Spencer Johnson, *The One Minute Manager* (New York: Morrow, 1982).

21. Michael C. Sturman and David McCabe, "Choosing Whether to Lead, Lag, or Match the Market: Developing a Competitive Pay Strategy for a New Restaurant," *Journal of Human Resources in Hospitality & Tourism* 7, no. 1 (2008): 85–97.

22. "Overview of BLS Statistics on Pay and Benefits," (n.d.) U.S. Bureau of Labor Statistics, https://www.bls.gov/bls/wages.htm.

23. Atul Mitra, Nina Gupta, and Jason D. Shaw, "A Comparative Examination of Traditional and Skill-Based Pay Plans," *Journal of Managerial Psychology* 26, no.4 (May 2001): 278-296; Erich C. Dierdorff and Eric A. Surface, "If You Pay for Skills, Will They Learn?" *Journal of Management* 34, no. 4 (2008): 742.

24. Cynthia Lee, Kenneth Law, and Philip Bobko, "The Importance of Justice Perceptions of Pay Effectiveness: A Two Year Study of a Skill-Based Pay Plan," *Journal of Management* 25, no. 6 (1999): 851–874.

25. Bobette M. Gustafson, "Skill-Based Pay Improves PFS Staff Recruitment, Retention and Performance," *Health Financial Management* 54, no. 1 (2000): 62–64.

26. George Milkovich, Jerry Newman, and Barry Gerhart, *Compensation* 11th ed. 2013. New York: McGraw-Hill Education.

27. Consolidated Appropriations Act, 2018, Pub. L. No. 115-141 (March 23, 2018).

28. "Final Rule: Tip Regulations Under the Fair Labor Standards Act," U.S. Department of Labor, (December 22, 2020). https://www.dol.gov/agencies/whd/flsa/tips.

29. Adrienne Colella, Ramona L. Paetzold, Asghar Zardkoohi, and Michael J. Wesson, "Exposing Pay Secrecy," *Academy of Management Review* 32, no. 1 (2007): 55–71; Jake Rosenfeld, "Don't Ask or Tell: Pay Secrecy Policies in U.S. Workplaces," *Social Science Research,* 65 (July 2017): 1–16.

30. Rafael Gely and Leonard Bierman, "Pay Secrecy/Confidentiality Rules and the National Labor Relations Act," *University of Pennsylvania Journal of Labor and Employment Law* 6, no. 1 (Fall 2003): 121–156.

31. U.S. Bureau of Labor Statistics, Labor Force Statistics from the Current Population Survey (2020). www.bls.gov/cps.

32. Ibid.

9

INCENTIVES AND BENEFITS ADMINISTRATION

Chapter 9 Outline

Learning Objectives

1. Identify the characteristics and advantages of effective incentive programs. (pp. 224–227)

2. Explain how employment benefit and incentive plans can affect employee performance. (pp. 224–226)

3. Describe common individual incentive programs and situations in which such programs might be effective. (pp. 227–229)

4. Describe common group incentive programs and situations in which such programs might be effective. (pp. 229–233)

5. Identify and define the four general categories of employee benefits. (pp. 233–243)

KEY TERMS

Individual incentive program

Group incentive program

Piecework incentive program

Standard hour incentive program

Commission

Bonus plan

Merit pay

Gainsharing program

Cost-saving plan

Employee stock ownership plan (ESOP)

Unemployment compensation insurance

Workers' compensation

COBRA

Preferred provider organization (PPO)

Self-insurance

Contributory retirement plan

Non-contributory retirement plan

Defined contribution plan

Defined benefit plan

ERISA

Employee assistance program (EAP)

Flexible benefits plan

Core spending account plan

Module spending account plan

Flexible spending account plan

Employers frequently combine incentives, benefits, and compensation to form a total reward program for employees. But simply establishing a system of rewards does not necessarily result in optimal job performance. Most employers recognize the direct link between performance and incentives. Pay and performance have been linked by researchers since the early 1990s.[1] Common organizational behavior theories support this approach. For example, both equity theory and expectancy theory suggest that properly managed pay-for-performance systems encourage motivation and productivity. Other researchers note that both individual and group performance are higher when rewards are directly linked to performance. The question most hospitality managers should ask is not whether to offer non-monetary incentives; all companies should have them. The question to ask is, "How should we structure our reward program to create the most effective combination of compensation, benefits, and incentives?"

Chapter 8 discussed the forms of monetary compensation and their potential effects on performance and job satisfaction. But that effect is achieved only when the program is properly managed and administered. This chapter describes work benefits other than compensation and explains how the proper management and administration of a rewards program can maximize productivity and performance.

The reward system must account not just for the employees' performance, but also for the employer's business goals and the customers' expectations. A five-star restaurant, for example, depends heavily on superior service and quality, so a program that incentivizes speed does not support the restaurant's business purposes. A quick service food outlet, on the other hand, depends much more on speed and efficiency. A reward system that motivates creativity and personal interactions may actually work against those goals.

The distinctions among compensation, incentives, and benefits are not always clear. Together, they make up the total reward program; but they don't operate independently. In other words, some forms of compensation serve the same purposes as benefits and incentives. So, although some of the employer's goals in this chapter seem to repeat Chapter 8, it is important to recognize that a distinction does exist.

The amount of compensation is typically determined before the work begins, either as a salary, an hourly rate, or some other predetermined formula. The compensation is the exchange of money for work. Benefits are provided as additional inducement to work for the employer for the agreed compensation—the non-monetary compensation. As seen in Chapter 8, however, compensation and benefits alone can be insufficient to motivate superior performance and long-term organizational commitment because they are not always linked to quality of work. That is where incentives come in. They provide extra motivation to excel.

9.1 EFFECTIVE INCENTIVE PROGRAMS

Some hospitality managers have little faith in incentive programs to improve work performance. The likely reason for this lack of confidence is not the programs themselves, but in how the programs are administered. Nothing is more important for a manager to learn than how to effectively motivate employees to do better work within the system of rewards provided by the company.

One way that managers can better relate to this important task is to consider the role of a coach (or manager) on a sports team and ask themselves whether that person's role is important to team and individual success. In most cases, managers agree that there is a link between a coach's goal-setting and motivation and the team's performance. Research has confirmed this to be the case.[2] Like that favorite coach who seems to get the most out of players, managers must excel in the roles of both leader and motivator. The existence of the incentive program is not enough.

To be effective, incentive programs should have the following critical characteristics. Note how they align with the theories of motivation explained in the previous chapter:

■ The programs must be directed toward attaining clear, specific goals that employees can understand.[3] Employees are not likely to be motivated to perform well when they don't know why it's important.

- Goals must be fair and easy to measure. All too often, managers establish incentives based on subjective measures. By doing so, managers create doubts in employees' minds about how fairly a program is administered. Employees prefer incentives based on objective measures that both managers and employees can understand easily and apply consistently.

- There must be room for improvement in productivity or performance. Insisting that employees improve, when they are already performing at a very high level, is demotivating.

- Goals must be attainable. Employees must have some expectations of success or they will not attempt to achieve the goals.[4] An incentive based on the achievement of an unrealistic goal creates an employee expectation that the incentive will not likely be realized.

- Rewards must be substantial enough to encourage effort. Whether money or merchandise, the rewards must be desirable. Too often, managers set rewards that employees perceive as not worth their effort.[5]

- Increases in productivity and performance should be tied to other non-monetary rewards such as opportunities for advancement. Goals perceived to be linked to both long-term advancement and short-term rewards are more effective than goals linked only to short-term rewards.[6]

- Rewards must be linked to output, not to time invested. The basic principle of any incentive plan is that employees will produce *more* if the reward is linked to their productivity and *better* if the reward is linked to quality.[7]

- Rewards should be administered quickly to reinforce the reason for the reward. For example, incentive pay sometimes lags considerably behind regular wages. If incentive rewards lag too far behind, employees begin to feel that they are either being taken advantage of or that the company is more interested in

increased productivity than in rewarding achievements. Consider a profit-sharing incentive that promises a reward based on the company's annual performance. It may improve the employees' perception of their overall rewards for work, but it's likely to have little impact in the beginning of the year, when the potential reward is far off in the future.

Advantages of Performance-Based Incentive Programs

Linking incentives to performance is likely to improve performance and can also help hospitality managers accomplish four important goals of their own:

- Retain quality employees.

- Increase productivity.

- Reduce labor costs.

- Increase employee focus on organizational objectives.

The first advantage often results from the long-term effect that incentive programs have on personnel. When companies link pay to performance, they often find that the employees who receive the greatest rewards are typically the best performers. These employees also feel the most encouraged to remain with the organization.[8] In contrast, employees who receive the smallest rewards are typically those who produce the least. As a result, low performers are more likely to leave the organization and go elsewhere, where pay is not linked with performance. In this way, over time, companies that use incentive-based pay programs can attain their own goal of having a staff of only high-performing employees.

Similarly, new and probationary employees are motivated to stay and perform to a high level to reach full eligibility for both compensation and incentives, thus reducing turnover.

The second advantage companies gain in linking incentives to performance is improved productivity. When pay is linked to performance, employees have a reason to work harder and produce either more or better goods and services. Researchers have clearly established this link.[9]

The third advantage is the cost savings many companies realize by rewarding performance. By linking rewards to performance, hospitality managers can negate some of the effects of rising salaries and wages by establishing a relationship between organizational success and pay. Some organizations pay employees more when times are good and pay them less when times are bad. Employees tend to understand this good-times/bad-times relationship. Couching goals in those terms will help employees understand why salaries and wages are tied to performance, and how their performance is tied to the company's success.

Finally, pay-for-performance systems increase employee focus on organizational objectives. When incentives are properly linked to organizational objectives, all employees work toward common goals. As a result, organizations may be more successful and more efficient in achieving their defined goals.[10]

Although these four advantages would indicate that linking rewards to performance is always best, not all companies can successfully carry this out. Managers encounter several barriers to implementing reward-for-performance systems. For example, consider what might happen when:

- Rewards that are set too low will not produce an incentive and may be detrimental by creating employee dissatisfaction and resentment, resulting in low performance.

- The link between rewards and performance is not clearly established because the measures for success are not clearly defined or outlined. This can lead to employee mistrust of the company, failure of the company to achieve organizational goals, and employees perceiving inequity between how much they value their contribution to the company and how much the company values this same contribution.

- Supervisors either resist performance appraisals or improperly administer such evaluations—resulting in feelings of unfairness among employees.

- Labor unions typically capitalize on the potential unfairness for performance-based rewards. When rewards are not administered correctly, a union can easily convince workers that such programs undermine the value of seniority, cost-of-living raise programs, and internal equity offered by the union. When this occurs, employees perceive a greater value in restricting the discretion of managers to influence rewards.

- Finally, the design and administration of reward-for-performance systems require careful attention to detail. Some companies are unable or unwilling to devote the attention that such programs require. Employees know when this is the case and have less regard for their managers' abilities. The success of a reward-for-performance system depends heavily on the quality and accuracy of the measurement of performance.

Individual vs. Group Systems

Individual and group incentives can both play significant roles in improving productivity and performance in hospitality organizations. Many organizations want both types of incentive programs in place at the same time. Typically, **individual incentive programs** are most useful when the work involved is not too interdependent or when individual improvement most benefits the organization, such as a sales representative.

Group incentive programs are most useful when cooperation and coordination are the program's goals or when teamwork is an appropriate part of the organizational goal. A hotel housekeeping department is a common example. Group programs have become increasingly popular in recent years as more hospitality companies implement teamwork systems.

Tips may take the form of an individual or a group program. Although the employer hires the worker and provides the opportunity to earn tips, it is the customer who actually provides the reward. The amount is completely in the guest's control. It would seem that restaurant servers, for example, would be highly motivated by their individual opportunity to earn the highest reward one table at a time. However, research has not consistently shown a reliable relationship between the objective quality of the service and the amount of the tip. There are many other factors outside the server's control that also influence the tip amount. Superior service might not result in a superior tip.

Not all servers, however, keep all the tips they earn. Many restaurant servers pool and share their tips, in some cases even with other workers who don't earn tips, like hosts, busers, and cooks. This is similar to a group incentive program—everyone in the group receives a share of the rewards. Many restaurants and servers are happy with this system, but a potential problem exists when employees contribute far less than others to the team effort but receive the same share of tips. Workers who contribute the most tips to the pool would receive more if they could keep their own tips. Although motivating and rewarding teamwork, the effect can be demotivating for the most productive workers.

Knowledge Check
1. When are group-based incentives more effective than individual-based?
2. What are the advantages of performance-based incentives?
3. Why would you prefer either the individual or group system incentives?

9.2 INDIVIDUAL INCENTIVE PROGRAMS

There are six common types of individual incentive programs, each with its own advantages and disadvantages, and each dependent on proper management and administration:

- Piecework incentive programs
- Standard hour incentive programs
- Commission programs
- Bonus plans
- Pay for knowledge (or pay for skills)
- Merit pay

Piecework Incentive Programs

Piecework incentive programs reward employees who exceed established minimums of productivity without regard to the amount of time worked. They are also based on the premise that if jobs involve simple, repetitive tasks, these incentive plans will motivate workers to produce maximum results[11] and the company's performance will prosper as a result. For example, in a catering department where pay is based on piecework, employees might be expected to produce 500 plates for an event. If this were the case, employees should be rewarded if they produce more than 500 plates. Piecework incentives are much more common in manufacturing industries and jobs that require repetitive, small-scale tasks.

Piecework is still used widely in hospitality and other service industries. For example, a food service manager might establish a reward system based on the number of sandwiches a cook produces. Hotel housekeepers are sometimes paid on a piecework basis, too. For example, they might be paid on how many rooms they clean as opposed to how long they work. Some argue that servers also work under a sort of piecework incentive system; that is, servers receive a standard hourly wage for providing service to their stations, plus a reward in the form of a tip, which will increase with the number of sales. Increasingly, however, hospitality operations involve few repetitive units of production, and most performance goals are seen as a combination of individual and team efforts.[12]

Standard Hour Incentive Programs

Standard hour incentive programs are based on the number of units completed per hour (per day would be a *standard day* program). To establish such a program for housekeeping, for example, a manager first determines how many rooms a housekeeper should clean per hour. The manager then divides the hourly wage by the number of rooms per hour to arrive at a benchmark for a standard hour program. If the manager determines that it takes a room attendant an average of 30 minutes to clean one room, then a room attendant should clean two rooms per hour. If the hourly wage for room attendants is $10 per hour, the manager might then decide to pay a fixed rate of $5 per room cleaned ($10 ÷ 2) instead of the hourly wage. Under such a system, room attendants who clean more than two rooms per hour receive

The legal minimum wage is calculated according to hours worked, regardless of the employer's actual method of determining earnings. No matter what system the employer uses, the total pay divided by the number of hours actually worked in any week must exceed the applicable minimum hourly wage. If it doesn't, the employer must pay the employee enough to make up the difference.

more pay, whereas those who clean fewer per hour receive less. In a piecework incentive program, the amount of time it takes attendants to clean rooms is irrelevant.

Many casino dealers are evaluated in this way—by the average number of games they can deal per hour.

Before implementing a standard hour incentive program, managers should establish specific, objective methods for measuring employee success. In the above example, managers need to determine how to measure whether a room is truly clean and how to account for the fact that some rooms take longer to clean than others. For casino dealers, the measurement must consider the number of players at the table because that affects the speed of a game.

Commission Programs

Many hospitality employees are compensated under a **commission** arrangement, in which the employee receives a defined incentive reward determined by the amount of sales. Tipped employees receive a sort of incentive commission that is often influenced more by the amount of the sale than the quality of the service. Hotel sales representatives often receive commission incentives above their base wages. Timeshare sales personnel work on this system—their only compensation comes from sales commissions.

When setting up a commission program, a property should consider how incentives are structured. Typically, incentives should increase as sales increase. This structure provides a series of rewards for each goal attainment. In the case of hotel sales agents, for example, the higher the sales, the more the rewards. Graduated incentive programs provide sales agents with increased incentives for each level of productivity. If there is just one goal and one incentive for reaching that goal, then a salesperson who has met the goal has no incentive to sell more.

To produce the desired effect, a commission system must not sacrifice quality for quantity and must offer each worker an equal opportunity to earn commissions.

Bonus Plans

Bonus plans are based on a combination of compensation and incentive rewards. Two types of bonus plans are common. In the first, all employees share in the achievement of organizational objectives. For example, all employees in a hotel might receive bonuses when certain sales or profit goals are reached. Other bonus plans are linked to individual performance. Group bonuses are becoming more popular as a result of the growing use of teams in the workplace, but they can have a negative effect if one underperforming worker adversely affects the group's compensation.

Typically, bonuses are rewarded when managers and employees attain predetermined goals. It is important that the goals be measurable and understood by both employer and employee. For example, room attendants might receive bonuses for achieving specified goals such as cleaning a certain number of rooms or applying a certain standard of quality to their work. Like piecework, standard hour, and commission incentives, bonuses add to organizational labor costs only when they are rewarded. Bonus plans have additional advantages—they typically require little documentation, can be tailored to almost any goal or situation, and directly link the company's success to employees' rewards.

Pay for Knowledge

Pay for knowledge, a method of determining employee base wages, is also useful in incentive programs. As an incentive, pay for knowledge bases rewards on the goals an employee reaches beyond those specifically required by the current job. Some believe that this represents the wave of the future because many employees are able to attain further education and special skills training outside the regular workplace. Paying for that knowledge can be seen as a form of compensation in lieu of a promotion or base pay increase. Many hotel security workers are paid incentives for learning CPR or emergency first aid—they get paid for gaining the knowledge, not for using it.

Merit Pay

Properties that reward **merit pay** (or merit "raises") typically increase base wages at the end of a specific period. When implemented properly, merit pay systems clearly link rewards to performance. In other words, employees' merit pay is based on their performance of predetermined tasks during a quarterly, semi-annual, or annual evaluation period.

The principal disadvantage to merit pay is the recurring increase in overall wages because rewards increase base pay for future periods. Additional challenges for managers can result when the same employees consistently produce excellent results. For example, a front desk agent may consistently receive excellent evaluations and be in line for higher levels of merit pay at the end of each evaluation period. Over time, the employee's pay can exceed the range approved for employees in that work category—or even exceed that of employees at higher grades. Managers should remember that each job has a theoretical cap (or maximum amount) on what the job is worth. Under a merit pay system, employees who excel during each rating period can become frustrated when they reach their cap and are not able to earn further rewards (sometimes called "topping out"). To make up for it, those employees would likely have to be moved to other types of incentive programs.

Additional problems arise due to subjectivity in the evaluation process. Excellent job performance can be hard to define and even harder to measure. A successful merit pay system must measure merit in a way that is rational, predictable, and fair. Service industry employers must be careful about using customer reviews and ratings. For example, if merit pay is reduced due to customer complaints or poor reviews, the employer must account for the fact that customer reviews are based on multiple factors and that employees have no control over some of those factors. When the evaluation of merit is perceived as unfair, the entire merit pay system will also be perceived as unfair.

Disadvantages of Individual Incentive Programs

All incentive programs require effective and thoughtful administration. Managers must consider whether the cost of administration outweighs the value of productivity improvement. Additionally, many incentives require substantial documentation and computation at the end of each reward period, and rewards that lag too far behind can become disincentivizing to employees, who may start to believe that the organization is taking advantage of their performance. In some cases, employees believe that incentives are not fairly administered or are simply used by management as an excuse to increase expected performance or save labor cost. For example, employees who work particularly hard over a period of time to achieve specific incentives might feel that their increased performance will be used to measure normal performance in the future without an increase in compensation.

Knowledge Check

1. How do employees earn standard hour incentives?

2. How is the amount of a commission determined?

3. Of the six individual incentive programs, which appeals to you the most and why?

9.3 GROUP INCENTIVE PROGRAMS

Group incentives are a good way to motivate employees to perform cooperatively. They can be very effective and useful when cooperation is required to produce the desired outcome. A restaurant, for example, relies on cooperative efforts of hosts, servers, busers, cooks, preps, and dishwashers to produce the product and service. The best server in the world can't make up for poor quality food or dirty dishes.

From a theoretical perspective, group incentives either increase profits or reduce costs by encouraging employees to work efficiently to attain an organization's goals. They also help develop a sense of cooperation and teamwork within a hospitality organization. The most common types of group incentives are generally characterized as **gainsharing programs**, although hospitality managers may never hear of or use this exact term.

Gainsharing programs are typically formula-based incentives that either increase profits, increase productivity, reduce costs, or, in some cases, attain all three objectives. The name "gainsharing" is derived from the practice of sharing a portion of the gains made by the company with employees, but these gains are sometimes calculated according to revenues or profit. Three types of plans are most common:

- Cost-saving plans
- Profit-sharing plans
- Employee stock ownership plans

Exhibit 9.1 illustrates the formulas for calculating profit and gain.

Cost-Saving Plans

Cost-saving plans are also known as *cash-reducing plans* because they increase profit by reducing the amount of cash required to operate a business.[13]

The most common cost-saving plan is the *Scanlon plan*, named after Joseph

Scanlon, a labor union leader in the 1930s. Scanlon's plan was originally designed to promote employment, production, and profits during the Great Depression by motivating managers to control labor costs.[14] The Scanlon plan reward is based on the ratio of labor costs to the *sales value of production (SVOP)*. The SVOP includes both sales revenues and the total value of goods produced. The Scanlon plan is particularly useful in "high-touch labor" companies such as hospitality operations, where labor is typically the largest single operating cost. This is because it directly rewards labor cost savings. It is also used to reward managers who are responsible for controlling labor costs.

A company needs historical data to implement the Scanlon plan. Usually, a company will track historical SVOP data over a period of five to 10 years, then average the costs of production for that period by dividing labor costs by the SVOP. The ratio obtained establishes a benchmark the company can use to evaluate performance of the workforce in the future.

Another cost-saving program calls for dividing labor costs by the *share of production costs (SOP)*. These costs include material, supply, and service expenditures used to produce finished products or services. The result of this division is called the *economic productivity index (EPI)*. When the EPI is lower than historical costs, it means that employees carefully watched the costs of materials used in production and should share in the money saved. In effect, the plan provides incentives for employees based on the difference between net sales (after cost of goods) and costs. Like the Scanlon plan, it requires historical data and usually is monitored by employee committees to ensure transparency.

A third type of cost-saving plan is called *improshare,* for "improved productivity through sharing plans." Through an improshare program, a company computes the standard cost of labor hours per unit of finished goods or services to establish a measure of employee productivity and efficiency. If current costs are below historical costs for the standard, employees get incentive bonuses. This system can work very well in hospitality companies as incentives for employees to reduce high labor costs. The program can run year-round or

Exhibit 9.1	Profit and Gain Formulas

Revenue − Cost = **Profit**

Profit − Loss = **Gain**

on a seasonal or quarterly basis to reinvigo-rate employees to maximize profits without increasing revenue.

Profit-Sharing Plans

The theory behind profit-sharing plans is that if employees can improve profits by reducing costs or streamlining productivity, they should share in that profit. Technically, profit-sharing plans could include any plan that distributes a percentage of profits to employees based on their contribution to the organization's ultimate goals. The primary difference from the plans described above is the focus on the final outcome of the work—the profit—rather than the cost, efficiency, and revenue factors that contribute to it.

Some companies see profit-sharing plans as useful ways to increase productivity and profits. In other companies, such plans have become just another hygiene factor: Employees come to expect a percentage of profits regardless of their individual contri-butions, so the plan no longer provides the intended incentive.

Depending on the type, use, and design of the profit-sharing plan, no incentive costs are incurred unless profits are made or increased. Some see this as an advan-tage because it does not raise labor costs in periods of declining profit. In addition, these plans sometimes make employees more aware of the overall operation costs, competitive market forces, and the fact that management is not always getting rich on the efforts of employees. However, in bad years, all employees go unrewarded regard-less of their individual contributions to the company. Unless employee committees assist in developing and distributing such plans, employees may believe that manag-ers are manipulating profits to reduce the amount of the benefit.

Employee Stock Ownership Plans

An **employee stock ownership plan (ESOP)** establishes a stock account for each employee in the company. Typically, the company distributes either stock or stock options into employee accounts based on employee contributions to the company or its profits. Contributions continue until employees either retire or leave the com-pany. Generally, ESOPs are managed by an *employee stock ownership trust (ESOT)*.

Before the Tax Reduction Act of 1975, ESOPs were primarily for managers and executives. Since that time, such plans have been extended to include employ-ees of all ranks. In 2018, 14 million workers were enrolled in ESOPs, although only about 2 percent of hospitality employers offered them.[15] Even more employers offer stock-purchase plans, where employees purchase shares in the company at a dis-counted price and are free to sell the shares at any time.[16]

ESOPs increase employee commit-ment, company loyalty, and motivation. For example, sales in employee-owned companies are higher than in those not owned by employees.[17] This is due primar-ily to improved employee attitudes and behaviors.[18] Many hospitality operators with ESOPs also have discovered that such plans retain and motivate employees while pro-ducing tax incentives for both the workers and the company.

Although many companies enjoy the benefits of an ESOP, there are nevertheless negatives associated with the plans. Many economists point out the following issues, which can cause failure:[19]

- A "free rider" problem: even if employ-ees as a group have an incentive to work harder and smarter, some individuals will slack off and let others do more of the work and yet gain an equal reward.

- Employees don't necessarily value ownership in the company as much as it costs a company to provide the plan.

- If employee owners are in the majority and actually control the organization, workers may favor higher wages and other short-term benefits at the expense of investment in future growth and profitability.

- The value of a reward of company stock is determined by market forces that are beyond the control of both the work-ers and the employer. If the market value of the stock declines, employees lose money. They may tend to blame that circumstance on the company's management.

When used as part of a pension plan, company stock can cause other problems. For example, when too much company stock is purchased for the pension plan (which many companies tend to do to keep their stock prices up), employees are too heavily tied to the company's performance.[20] This happened in the case of Enron, where thousands of employees lost their entire life's savings because they had invested all of their retirement savings in company stock on the advice of company officers. When the company went bankrupt, these employees were left with nothing.

Companies primarily offer *stock options* to executives and top-level managers. As long as individuals are employed by the company, stock options give holders the right to purchase stock at a price preset in their contract, even when stock prices are higher. The option to buy the stock has intrinsic market value but doesn't require any investment from the employee.

At one time, stock options were a principal method of attracting managers and executives, by providing an incentive for them to help generate profits and thereby increase stock prices. Since the Tax Reform Act of 1986, however, stock options have been viewed less favorably. This is because the gains on stock—when cashed—are treated as ordinary income rather than long-term capital gains. As a result, employee profits gained through stock options may be taxed at higher rates than normal income.

Companies still find stock options an attractive way to recruit new managers, however, by offering them as a basic part of the company's salary and benefits package.[21]

Which Works Best: Money or Merchandise?

Managers often wonder whether incentives should take the form of other rewards such as merchandise, gift cards, or trips in place of cash. Strong arguments can be made for either approach. Merchandise has a longer-lasting effect than money. Merchandise constantly reminds employees of the incentive for the reward. Each time they see the merchandise, employees are likely to think about how they can work harder to receive other rewards. Merchandise can be a source of pride for employees—a tangible symbol of success. In addition, prizes can be purchased below retail rates, at a reasonable cost to a company.

Cash, on the other hand, can be spent easily on whatever employees choose. As a result, employees may be left with no identifiable link between performance and reward. However, cash has an advantage that merchandise does not. Employees can use cash gained through an incentive program to purchase whatever goods or services they need or want. Recall from Chapter 8 that an employee's personal situation affects the motivational value of various types of rewards. Cash awards may be particularly attractive to employees who have difficulty making ends meet on a regular basis. A merchandise award (such as a trip to Hawaii) may not be a motivator if an employee cannot use it. For example, an employee's spouse may not be able to get off work, childcare may not be available or affordable, the added costs of the trip may be too high, and so on.

Some researchers contend that money motivates employees only when tasks are routine.[22] Organizations are creating a variety of ways to motivate employees using non-monetary rewards, spurred on in part by the Great Recession's impact on company bottom lines. For example, one company that could not fund monetary awards found that encouraging workers to brainstorm their own incentives worked well. Among the ideas employees came up with was "Take

Your Dog to Work Day." Of course, that benefit provides no incentive to employees who do not have dogs.

Whether a company chooses money, merchandise, or creative rewards for its staff, its incentive system should reflect the goals of the organization and suit the needs of its employees. Exhibit 9.2 lists creative examples of non-cash rewards.

Disadvantages of Group Incentive Plans

Individual incentive programs can backfire from the employee point of view. As noted earlier, sometimes, employees may work hard to achieve an incentive only to find that their employers come to expect that extra hard work as normal performance.

This disadvantage also applies to group incentive plans. Group incentives, especially the profit-sharing type, have additional problems. Even when employee performance exceeds expectations, employees still suffer when the company has a bad year. Also, unless properly managed, group incentive plans can unfairly reward employees who perform at levels lower than the group as a whole.

Many experts believe that individual incentive plans produce better results than do group incentive plans. Those who have studied the two types often say that group incentive plans result in an indistinct connection between pay and the individual efforts of each group member. They also say that group incentives can cause resentment. For example, some employees may try to get a free ride on the performance of others. Employees who work hard to attain rewards perceive an internal inequity between their own inputs and outcomes and those of other group members.

Resentment and inequities can be overcome in different ways in different environments. In a classroom, resentment and inequities can be minimized if each group member is given an opportunity to evaluate the contribution of other group members. Peer evaluations are also useful in a work environment because they give group members an opportunity to control the disbursement of rewards. When peer evaluations are used, group members typically decide how much of the reward each

---

Exhibit 9.2   Creative Examples of Non-Cash Rewards

Some examples of non-cash rewards might include:

- Bring your pet to work day
- Decorate your cubicle contest
- Jeans Friday
- Employer-paid meals
- Birthday celebrations

---

group member should receive—a way for them to hold each other accountable for their contribution to the group effort. Every method of peer evaluation must carefully monitor the potential influence of personal conflicts among the workers.

Knowledge Check

1. How do employers use company stock as employment incentives?

2. What are the factors that might influence employee incentives in gainsharing programs?

3. What are the advantages and disadvantages of using merchandising as an incentive?

9.4 EMPLOYEE BENEFITS

Benefits are generally thought to be an effective way to attract and retain personnel, motivate performance, and increase job satisfaction. Offering a great benefit package that involves high cost and obligation is an indication of commitment to employees.[23] However, because benefits are not tied directly to performance, their value as a motivator or satisfier is debatable. Because benefits are so common in the United States, employees perceive many benefits as expected compensation rather than as motivators. For example, most industries provide health insurance for all employees, and most employees in the United States receive two or more weeks of paid vacation per year. According to the U.S. Department of Labor, employee benefits accounted for 30 percent of total payroll costs for employers in 2020.[24]

As of 2018, just over half of all private industry employees participated in medical care plans offered by their employers, but fewer than 25 percent in the leisure and hospitality sector participated.[25] One reason for the lower rate in hospitality is the higher than average use of part-time, seasonal, and temporary workers, who rarely qualify for employer-provided healthcare benefits.

The benefits offered by most companies fall into four general categories:

- Mandatory benefits
- Optional (or voluntary) benefits
- Pension and retirement benefits
- Miscellaneous (or "fringe") benefits

Managers should ask themselves several questions when evaluating and establishing benefits programs:

- What benefits am I required to offer?
- What optional benefits can I offer?
- How should I administer the benefits?
- How can I contain the costs of benefits?

The following sections put these questions into context.

Mandatory Benefits

Mandatory benefits are legislated by both federal and state governments. Examples of mandatory benefits include Social Security, unemployment compensation insurance, and workers' compensation.

Social Security. Social Security, which was mandated by the Federal Insurance Contribution Act of 1935 (FICA), was established to protect employees and their dependents by providing retirement income, disability income, healthcare coverage (Medicare), and survivor benefits. As such, Social Security is designed to provide a form of financial security and medical care benefits to employees and their dependents. It is an expensive program for employers. Today,

both employers and employees contribute 7.65 percent of the employees' paychecks per year (up to a total that changes yearly based on inflation) toward Social Security benefits. Employees draw upon these contributions after retirement.

Unlike most insurance programs, Social Security uses current payments to pay benefits to retired employees. For example, employees working today pay for those employees who have retired. Social Security has filled a great need for a long time and has provided financial security to many people at a low cost. Many experts agree, however, that a combination of factors is stressing the program. For example, more employees today are working at lower rates of pay; consequently, fewer dollars are being put into the system. Second, Baby Boomers—people born between 1946 and 1964—are aging, which means that during the next 20 years, more employees than ever before will begin retiring. Retiring Baby Boomers will find themselves depending on the contributions of a smaller demographic group.

Current Social Security provisions permit former employees or their spouses to begin receiving income from this fund at age 65 or 67 with no penalty. They can opt to begin receiving income from Social Security at age 62, but with some substantial and permanent reductions in the amount they receive. These reductions are likely to deepen in the future.

Unemployment Compensation Insurance. Another benefit mandated under FICA is **unemployment compensation insurance**. According to current provisions, former employees who are out of work and actively seeking work can receive up to 80 percent of their normal pay—as long as the employees did not lose their job for reasons of misconduct. Although mandated and partially funded by the federal government, state governments manage unemployment compensation insurance, and some provisions vary from state to state.

Workers' Compensation. **Workers' compensation** provides compensation for employees who become disabled or who die at work, regardless of who is at fault. For that reason, it is known as a "no-fault" program. Although employees are entitled to benefits even when the injury is their own fault, they are prohibited from suing for additional compensation when the employer is at fault.

The program is usually funded by insurance paid for by employers. The rate of contribution is based in part on a company's injury history. Organizations with high injury records have higher costs than those with fewer recorded injuries. Benefits vary from state to state, but typically include:

- Payment of medical and physical therapy bills at no cost to the employee

- Compensation for wages lost due to temporary disability while recovering

- Compensation for permanent disability that will affect the employee's potential future earnings

- Vocational training for workers who are unable to return to their former jobs due to the injury

Exhibit 9.3 shows the most common workplace injuries.

On average, the hospitality industry's workplace injury rate is consistently well above the average of all industries. Housekeepers have the highest incidence rate in the industry, typically exceeding all other jobs in strain/sprain injuries, slip and falls, and harmful chemical exposures.

Exhibit 9.3	Most Common Workplace Injuries
Overexertion, strains, and sprains	31%
Slip/trip and fall injuries	27.5%
Equipment and machinery injuries	25.8%
Transportation accidents	5.6%
Workplace violence	5%

Source: National Safety Council, "Top Work-Related Injury Causes" (2019). Injuryfacts.nsc.org

Hospitality companies can reduce workers' compensation claims by addressing the problems that cause injuries. For example, slip-and-fall accidents can be reduced by up to 90 percent if companies either provide or teach employees how to pick proper slip-resistant footwear.[26] Other hotels have found success providing inexpensive back braces and training employees in proper lifting techniques.

Voluntary Benefits

Organizations offer a wide range of voluntary benefits. Life insurance and health insurance benefits are among the voluntary benefits that employees often expect. Many hospitality companies excel at providing these benefits and offer innovative insurance programs to attract personnel; others lag far behind and fail to address these important needs.

Group Life Insurance. Group life insurance coverage is usually based on the annual earnings of the employee, although most plans provide employees the opportunity to purchase additional coverage. The typical rule of thumb for calculating life insurance coverage is to multiply the employee's annual earnings by two. Thus, an employee who earns $40,000 per year would be offered $80,000 in life insurance. Long-term disability insurance generally is offered in conjunction with life insurance.

Group Health Insurance. Group health insurance (see Exhibit 9.4) is a benefit especially valued by employees. The rapidly rising costs of medical services have rendered group health insurance the costliest benefit that companies offer to workers[27] (see Exhibit 9.5). Employers have met rising costs with strategies such as raising premiums, reducing maximum benefits, and increasing employee copayments.[28] Employees on average pay 17 percent of the cost for their individual coverage and 27 percent of the cost for family coverage.

One reason for the rapid increase in healthcare insurance costs in recent decades was the passage of the Consolidated Omnibus Budget Reconciliation Act of 1986, otherwise known as **COBRA**. Under this act, following certain "qualifying events" such

Exhibit 9.4   Group Health Insurance Terms

The following is a list of common health insurance terms that employees should be familiar with:

- *Premium:* the cost of the insurance policy. The employer may simply provide access to a group a healthcare plan or may pay up to 100 percent for the employee and for all/part of the employee's family.

- *Deductible:* the amount the employee must pay for medical services before the healthcare plan starts covering the cost.

- *Co-pay:* a flat fee charged each time the employee (or family member, if covered) has an office visit (or sometimes other medical services), regardless of the cost of the procedure.

- *Co-insurance:* the employee is responsible for paying a certain percentage of the total cost of care.

- *Out-of-pocket maximum:* the maximum amount the employee must pay toward healthcare annually.

- *Open enrollment period:* time period each year during which the employee can change the type or amount of coverage or number of dependents.

- *Flexible spending accounts:* accounts that permit an employee to set aside pretax earnings to pay for healthcare costs, including certain medications, and other services such as childcare and health insurance. If the amount set aside in the account is not entirely used by the end of the year, the employee loses the unused amount and it is turned over to the employer.

Source: U.S. Department of Commerce, Bureau of Economic Analysis, National Income and Product Accounts, 1960–2008.

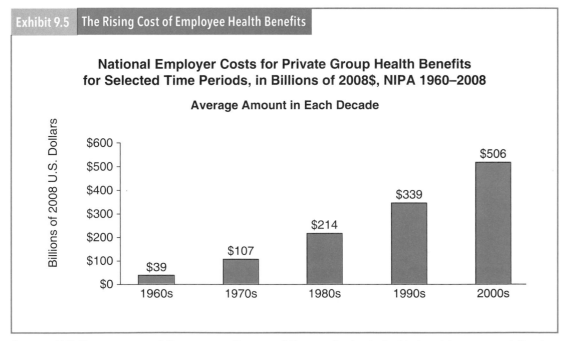

Exhibit 9.5   The Rising Cost of Employee Health Benefits

National Employer Costs for Private Group Health Benefits for Selected Time Periods, in Billions of 2008$, NIPA 1960–2008

Average Amount in Each Decade

Source: U.S. Department of Commerce, Bureau of Economic Analysis, National Income and Product Accounts, 1960–2008.

as termination, death, or divorce, employers must allow terminating employees and/or their dependents to continue purchasing group health insurance under the company plan for up to 18 months (for employees) or 36 months (for dependents). The ex-employee or the dependent must pay the full cost of the premiums for the coverage, and the employer is allowed by law to charge the ex-employee or dependent a 2 percent surcharge to cover administrative expenses. The surcharge, however, does not begin to cover all the employer's costs, which include notifying, tracking, and documenting all facets of compliance with this highly complex law[29] (see Exhibit 9.6).

Health Insurance Alternatives. In response to the high costs of medical insurance, several alternative programs have become popular. Health maintenance organizations, preferred provider organizations, and self-insurance illustrate what experts describe as efforts to reduce costs of health insurance in any way possible.

Health maintenance organizations (HMOs) offer medical coverage for a fixed annual fee. These organizations emphasize preventive care based on the theory that people who see their doctors regularly develop fewer long-term illnesses and disabilities. Since the Health Maintenance Act of 1973, employers with 25 or more employees have been required to offer HMOs as an alternative type of health insurance coverage if such coverage is available in the local area. Under this act, employers must pay the same amount to HMOs that they would for employee insurance. If costs are greater than those for regular health insurance,

---

Exhibit 9.6	COBRA Costs to Employers

COBRA costs to employers include the following:

- Proof of COBRA training

- Written COBRA procedures (manual with instructions)

- Documentation of program design (1986 or 1987) and program updates (to present)

- Documentation of program monitoring

- Initial notification

- Stacked event notification

- Disability extension notification

- Conversion notification (required if employer's group health plan has a conversion option)

- Documentation of events reported to employer/plan administrator for divorce-dependent events and disabilities

- Open enrollment notice

- Expiration notice (recommended—not a specific requirement)

- Insignificant premium underpayment procedure (possible notice)

- Premium billing procedures (optional—not a requirement)

- Complete and accurate disclosure to healthcare providers

- Cancellation procedures (voluntary and involuntary)

- Verification of correct election

employees pay the rest. Health maintenance organizations purport to lower the cost of care by regulating who patients can see for healthcare and what treatments they receive. For example, HMO patients must be referred to a specialist by their primary HMO care physician for coverage to be in force.

Health insurance offered through a **preferred provider organization (PPO)** is based on agreements made between employers and healthcare providers. Generally, PPO providers agree to provide health services at reduced costs to participants. Patients pay a higher portion of the cost for treatment by providers who do not belong to the PPO network. The guarantee benefits both employers and medical providers. Employers can provide medical care coverage at a reduced cost while medical providers receive a guaranteed base of customers.

Some employers use **self-insurance** to reduce healthcare costs. With self-insurance, employers simply pay directly for their employees' healthcare costs rather than indirectly through insurance company plans. Companies with self-insurance plans take the risk that the costs they incur will be less than the costs they would incur by buying health insurance. In many cases, employers with self-insurance also negotiate with certain providers in the market to provide lower-cost medical coverage for their employees. Some hospitality companies—particularly larger ones—use self-insurance plans to contain their healthcare costs. However, hospitality employers should carefully weigh this option, as research has shown the cost of self-insurance to be higher in most cases. Obviously, the largest companies generally realize the greatest savings. Hospitality managers should check all options and do a good deal of research, including contacting their state and national associations for advice, before adopting a self-insurance program. Savings may or may not be possible, but higher than anticipated medical costs can cost a company millions of dollars more than traditional HMO or PPO plans.

Other insurance programs include *indemnity plans*, such as Blue Cross/Blue Shield, that allow patients to visit the doctor and specialist of their choice. Indemnity plans tend to be more costly to companies. Another choice is the *medical savings account (MSA)*. This offers an option funded by employees' pretax contributions, which are used to pay for routine medical care. These plans are paired with catastrophic medical insurance to cover the costs of serious illnesses.

Self-insurance, HMOs, and PPOs are not the only methods employers can use to contain healthcare costs. Some companies emphasize outpatient care rather than in-hospital care. These companies pay the full bill on outpatient care and establish copay plans for in-hospital care. Other companies have increased deductibles (the amount that each employee and family member must pay annually before health insurance payments begin) so that employees pay the small costs associated with health coverage.

Another way companies contain costs is to develop copay programs in which employers and employees share the burden of health costs. In typical copay programs, employers pay from 80 to 90 percent of the costs of services while employees pay the remaining 10 to 20 percent. Some companies also require employees to get second opinions for some services and procedures such as elective surgery.

Employers are also trying to reduce healthcare costs by encouraging employees to think more about their health. Many medical professionals support the idea that people can avoid or minimize certain health problems that require costly care by making and maintaining certain lifestyle changes. This concept is referred to as *preventive healthcare*. Some companies hold "health fairs" that are specifically designed to encourage employees to think about and practice preventive healthcare.

Cafeteria plans, established by the Revenue Act of 1978, come in two basic forms:

■ Premium-only plans (POPs): The most popular type of plan, POPs allow employees to deduct their share of the premiums from pre-tax wages. The advantages of this type of plan is that it allows employees to spend pre-tax dollars, and therefore take home more money, and it allows the company to eliminate the 7.65 percent FICA and Medicare taxes on the wages used to pay for these plans.

- Flexible spending accounts (FSAs): FSAs provide employees with a pre-tax method to pay for medical expenses and/or dependent care that is not covered by insurance. Employees choosing this method set aside a specific amount each year to be used for these purposes.

Large companies may also be able to afford a full cafeteria plan, which allows companies to allot a set amount of money for employees to pick and choose from a variety of benefit plans, each plan with its own established cost to the employee. Cafeteria plans are discussed in greater detail later in the chapter.

One way to cut benefit costs that is becoming more popular with many companies is to offer "voluntary" benefits. These programs are called voluntary because employees have access to a variety of types of benefits and choose the ones they want. Typically, these benefits are placed in a cafeteria plan and employees choose the ones they want.

Pension and Retirement Benefits

Pension and retirement benefits are additional optional benefits that many employees expect. These benefit programs vary substantially from company to company. In some cases, employers pay the entire cost, whereas in others, employees and employers share the costs. In all cases, the cost to employers can be quite high.

The principal reason many companies offer pension and retirement benefits is to develop a stable and reliable work force. On the surface, such plans seem ideally suited to help cure some of the problems faced by hospitality, including high turnover and the poor perception employees have of hospitality work. However, the industry has not adopted pension and retirement plans to the extent other industries have.

In 1997, Congress passed a law that allowed small businesses, especially family-owned businesses, to take advantage of more pension plans. This provision was part of the Small Business Jobs Protection Act. Under this plan, family-owned businesses can offer retirement benefits to all family members who work for the company. Previously, small businesses could offer only what were known as "aggregate plans" that prohibited family members from making full contributions to 401(k) plans. Under the previous plan, if family members wanted to make contributions to a 401(k) plan, their contributions were limited to an aggregate total, not individual totals. This substantially reduced the amount they could contribute.[30]

One objective of most pension and retirement plans is to defer income tax costs from the present to the future or, basically, to the time when a person's income will be lower because of retirement. Each of the pension and retirement benefits programs discussed in this section meet the "qualification" requirements of the Internal Revenue Code for tax deferral. Interest and dividends earned by the pension fund are also tax deferred. Taxes are payable after retirement, when monies from the plan are withdrawn.

Employers use two principal types of pension and retirement plans. In **contributory retirement plans**, both the employer and employee contribute to retirement accounts (most popularly on the basis of 50 cents contributed by the company for every dollar contributed by the employee). In **non-contributory retirement plans**, only the employer contributes to employee retirement programs.

Defined Contribution Plans. In **defined contribution plans**, fixed-rate contributions are made into an account for each employee. Both employers and employees may contribute money to such plans. *Money purchase* and *profit-sharing plans* are examples of defined contribution plans.

An employee stock ownership plan (ESOP) is a type of defined contribution plan. Benefits payable to employees on retirement include interest and accumulation of capital and dividends. This type of plan is popular because it emphasizes organizational growth and success. However, it provides less security than do plans that deposit funds into accounts serviced by outside companies.

Defined Benefit Plans. Under **defined benefit plans**, the amount of retirement benefits are fixed, depending on the length of service and average earnings of employees during their employment. Employers generally service such plans by setting monies aside in escrow for the retirement benefits of their employees. With a defined benefit plan, employees have the advantage of knowing their exact retirement income in advance. These are sometimes called *pensions*.

Employee Retirement Income Security Act of 1974. The Employee Retirement Income Security Act of 1974 (**ERISA**) established reporting requirements, fiduciary responsibilities, and guidelines for participation, vesting, and funding for retirement and pension plans. It also established a federal insurance agency—the Pension Benefit Guaranty Corporation—to insure defined benefit retirement and pension plans so that employee pensions are protected if sponsoring companies go bankrupt. To qualify for coverage, employers must meet specific provisions and pay premiums of more than $15 per employee.

According to ERISA, any employee 21 years old or older who has worked for a company for at least one year is eligible to enroll in retirement or pension plans provided by the company. The act also includes provisions to prevent employers from firing long-term employees just to avoid paying pensions.

At the time ERISA was enacted, Congress had three objectives:

(1) to encourage employers to establish and maintain retirement income for their employees,

(2) to encourage employees to utilize the plans and save for retirement, and

(3) to create legal protection for those employees to ensure that the retirement benefits being promised were actually there when they retired.

ERISA has accomplished those goals very substantially. The growth in pension plans, both in terms of the number of participants and money contributed, has been phenomenal, totaling over $5 trillion nationwide.

While ERISA has been in place, the greatest changes have come from two areas:

- the shift from defined benefit plans to defined contribution plans, and

- the growing emphasis and impact of ERISA protections for employees.

The change from defined benefit plans to defined contribution plans has also resulted in shifting the risk for poor investment performance from the sponsor (or the Pension Benefit Guaranty Corporation) to the individual employee. Now employees are more responsible for the performance of their own investments, thus shifting decision-making from sponsor to employee and reducing the employer's financial risk.

Union Plans. Many large labor organizations have established their own medical and retirement benefit plans for the employees they represent. Rather than providing the insurance themselves, employers agree to pay the union to provide the benefits. The amount of the employer's contribution is determined by the collective bargaining contract. This can be a big benefit for employers because it shifts the risk of rising health and retirement costs to the unions, but the amount of contributions required can exceed the employer's cost of providing the same benefits directly. Union plans are so popular among some employees that prolonged labor strikes have resulted from employers insisting on covering employees on their own plans.

Salary Reduction Plans/401(k) Plans. *Salary reduction plans* allow employees to make tax-deferred contributions to retirement accounts in company profit-sharing plans. These plans are also known as *401(k) plans* and *capital accumulation plans*. Until 2001, the annual limit on contributions to an individual's 401(k) plan was $10,500. Since then, the limit has been raised to $19,500. Under these programs, taxes are deferred until the money is withdrawn after retirement.

Many companies encourage employees to participate in these plans through matching contributions. Many companies pay $0.50 to $0.60 on every dollar an employee puts into the plan, up to 6 to 8 percent of their total salary.

Other Benefits

Employees can enjoy a wide variety of benefits offered through other company-sponsored plans. Among the most common are educational benefits, employee assistance programs, child and dependent care programs, cafeteria and flexible benefits plans, long-term care policies, and pay for time not worked. Other benefits include paid leave banks, flexible work schedules, and a cap on work hours.

Educational Benefits. Educational benefits have become very commonplace. Usually, companies reimburse employees for tuition when the employer approves of the course work. In some cases, tuition for spouses and children is also included. Whereas some employers pay only tuition, some pay all the costs associated with education, including books and supplies. Some employers pay full tuition, whereas other employers cover only part. Passing grades are generally a requirement for receiving educational benefits.

Employee Assistance Programs. The number of U.S. employers providing **employee assistance programs (EAPs)** has rapidly increased, due, in part, to drug abuse prevention awareness. EAPs were introduced in the 1940s to combat alcohol-related work problems. Today, EAPs typically focus on drug- and alcohol-related problems but can also provide counseling to employees for marital problems, personal finance issues, career concerns, and problems on the job. EAPs have become so widespread that more than 80 percent of the Fortune 500 companies today provide some sort of EAP program. Some companies establish in-house EAP programs, while others contract with referral systems to provide employees with professional EAP services.

Child and Dependent Care Programs. In 1981, Congress passed provisions that permit employers to exclude up to $5,000 from employees' taxable income to pay for child and dependent care expenses. As a result, employees can now pay for this type of care with pretax dollars, thus stretching their income. Before 1981, employees had

According to a 2018 study presented in the *Journal of Global Business Insights*, many hospitality companies that were listed in the Great Places to Work For survey applied innovative employee benefits, such as:

- Healthcare/medical benefits
- Stress management
- Family-friendly benefits
- Healthy lifestyle incentives
- Flexible schedule
- Working environment

to pay for child and dependent care out of after-tax earnings.

Research reveals that three out of four employees in the service industries need childcare services. On the average, employees miss about eight days of work per year because of childcare-related problems.[31] Given these figures, it clearly benefits hospitality companies to offer childcare programs to their employees.

Cafeteria Plans and Flexible Benefits Plans. In the past, employers merely decided which benefits plans to offer and then offered them to *all* employees. This situation has changed substantially in most companies. A traditional uniform benefit program is unlikely to fully satisfy more than half of any given employee population. Recent employee surveys have found that most employees are satisfied with their benefits and that benefit flexibility was an important factor. Clearly, employees who have some control over the selection of their benefits are more often satisfied with the entire benefit package.[32] Many employees today have a great deal of control over which company-sponsored plans they enroll in because of cafeteria plans and **flexible benefits plans**.

Although generally regarded as the same, cafeteria and flexible benefit plans are different. Technically, cafeteria plans offer either benefits or cash in lieu of benefits to employees; flexible benefits plans offer only benefits. Both offer the employees choices.

Cafeteria and flexible benefits plans offer substantial advantages to employees, especially those in households with two wage earners. For example, if a married couple works for companies that provide cafeteria or flexible benefit plans, one wage earner can choose one set of benefits while another can choose a different set. Three types of benefit plans come under the general heading of cafeteria and flexible benefit:

- **Core spending account plans** provide a series of "core" benefits to every employee, plus a list of other benefits from which employees can choose.

- **Module spending account plans** offer a choice of preestablished "packages" of benefits to every employee. Employers determine the benefits included in each package.

- **Flexible spending account plans** provide a given amount of money that the company will spend on benefits for employees and allow each employee to decide which benefits are best for his or her personal needs. This program is similar to the core spending account plan, except that there are no designated "core" benefits.

The advantages of cafeteria and flexible benefits are obvious: Employees have more freedom to choose benefits. However, such programs also have disadvantages. The most common disadvantage is the increased costs of administration.

Pay for Time Not Worked. Pay for time not worked includes vacation pay, holiday pay, sick leave, dependent care leave, religious holiday leave, personal leave, bereavement leave, military duty, jury duty, and other time off during which the employer continues to pay employees. In many companies, full-time employees receive vacation pay after completing one year of service. Company policies vary substantially regarding pay for time not worked. State and federal laws mandate some employment leave, such as for medical, military, and religious reasons, but none of those laws require the employer to pay the employees for their time off.

Some companies even offer their employees sabbaticals, or extended time off. A quick service restaurant company established a sabbatical program in 1977. Full-time corporate employees with 10 years of service are eligible for an eight-week paid leave. It is still in operation, and many other companies have established similar programs.[33] Sabbatical time must be taken all at once; in that way, it offers a long enough period to accomplish personal or professional goals.

Paid Leave Bank. Employee absenteeism and its associated costs are on the rise. One way for companies to curb absenteeism costs is to include all "time off" plans together and let the employee decide how to use the time. *Paid leave banks* have two major advantages over other leave programs: Employees bear the responsibility for managing their time off and they have the flexibility they desire. Paid leave banks—combined with accrued leave time plans—can help prevent the high incidence of vacations and sick days taken at the end of the year. The average employee takes four to seven sick days per year. Research has shown that by lumping vacation, personal, and sick days together in one paid-time-off category, the average number of employee days off is actually going down, not up.[34]

Flexible Work Schedules. A current trend is for companies to offer flexibility in employee work schedules. Employers are recognizing that people have responsibilities away from work and are trying to be more accommodating to individual needs. Workplace flexibility has become a great benefit for employees seeking balance in their personal lives. Employees are given flexibility for accommodating health issues, for childcare, or for schooling. Workplace flexibility is wide in its range, from sick and FMLA leave to telecommuting, job sharing, compressed workweeks, and phased retirement. As more employees expect some flexibility with work schedules, hospitality employers will have to find innovative ways to balance the needs of workers and the needs of business.[35]

Knowledge Check

1. What is the difference between a defined benefit plan and a defined contribution plan?

2. What alternative programs do employers use to provide health insurance benefits for employees?

3. What are some of the non-cash benefits that employers offer?

IN THIS CHAPTER, YOU LEARNED:

■ Many employment incentives may be used to motivate excellent job performance, including both individual and group incentives.

■ To be effective, incentive programs must be administered in a way that is fair, objective, and predictable. Employees will be demotivated by a reward system they believe is unfair.

■ Individual incentives are useful when the business success depends on the performance of individual employees.

■ Individual incentives include performance bonuses, piecework incentive programs, standard hour incentive programs, commission programs, pay for knowledge, and merit increases.

■ Group incentives are most effective when the business relies on the outcomes of group efforts.

■ Common group incentives include cost-saving plans, profit-sharing plans, and employee stock ownership plans.

■ Employment benefits that are required by law include Social Security, unemployment compensation insurance, and workers' compensation coverage.

■ Healthcare and retirement income are the most common non-mandatory employment benefits in the hospitality industry.

■ Benefits motivate employees to remain employed, reducing the costs of employee turnover, while incentives motivate employees to excel in their job performance.

KEY TERMS

bonus plan—A variable one-time payment in addition to the regular rate of pay.

cafeteria plan—A benefit program that offers either a variety of benefits or cash in lieu of benefits from which the employees can choose.

COBRA—The Consolidated Omnibus Budget Reconciliation Act, passed in 1985. It requires employers to offer continuing health insurance coverage to eligible former workers and their dependents.

commission—An incentive determined by a percentage of the employee's sales.

contributory retirement plan—A pension or retirement program in which both the employer and the employee contribute.

core spending account plan—A benefit plan that provides a series of benefits to every employee plus a list of additional benefits from which employees may choose.

cost-saving plan—A group incentive benefit based on the amount of production and labor costs.

defined benefit plan—A pension and retirement program in which employers set aside amounts of monies at regular intervals to meet specific retirement benefits.

defined contribution plan— A pension or retirement program in which contributions are made at a fixed rate by the employee, the employer, or both.

employee assistance program (EAP)—An employer-sponsored counseling program designed to help employees deal with personal problems related to drug or alcohol abuse, stress, family tension, finances, career goals, or other situations that affect their health or work.

employee stock ownership plan (ESOP)—A compensation plan that establishes an account in the employee's name to which the company makes contributions based on either employee contributions or on company profits.

ERISA—The Employee Retirement Income Security Act of 1974, Federal legislation that established reporting requirements, fiduciary responsibilities, and guidelines for participation, investing, and funding for retirement and pension plans.

flexible benefits plan—A benefit program that offers a variety of benefits for employees to choose from.

flexible spending account plan—A benefit program that provides employees with a specific amount of "money" to spend on benefits. Typically, employers provide a wide variety of benefits at specific costs and allow employees to decide how to spend the monies allotted to them for these benefits.

gainsharing program—A formula-based group incentive program in which employees receive a percentage of the company's revenue, profits, or net gains.

group incentive program—A goal-based reward system that links incentive benefits to group performance.

health maintenance organization (HMO)—A voluntary health benefit program that offers medical coverage to employees within an established provider network.

individual incentive program—A goal-based reward system that links incentive benefits to individual job performance.

merit pay—An incentive reward based on an evaluation of employee's performance over a predetermined period of time. Also known as an annual "raise."

module spending account plan—A benefit program that provides employees a choice of preestablished "packages" of benefits.

non-contributory retirement plan—A pension or retirement program in which only the employer contributes.

piecework incentive program—An incentive program based on rewards for an established number of work tasks completed.

preferred provider organization (PPO)—A medical insurance benefit program in which employees can choose their own healthcare providers.

self-insurance—A benefit program in which employers pay directly for the cost of employee healthcare rather than pay indirectly through an insurance provider.

standard hour incentive program—An incentive program based on the number of units completed per hour (per day would be a standard day program).

unemployment compensation insurance—A mandated benefit that requires employers to purchase insurance for benefits paid by the state government to individuals who are out of work.

workers' compensation—A mandated benefit insurance plan that provides medical and disability benefits for employees who are injured at work, regardless of fault.

REVIEW QUESTIONS

1. How are incentives different from compensation and benefits?
2. What are the characteristics of an effective incentive program?

3. What are some disadvantages of group incentives?

4. How do piecework and standard hour incentives motivate employees to work faster? What are some jobs in the hospitality industry that might benefit from these types of rewards?

5. What rights are created by COBRA?

6. What are the mandatory benefits that employers must provide their employees?

7. What are the most common types of healthcare benefits offered by employers?

8. Which retirement benefit plan do you think is better for workers: defined contribution plans or defined benefit plans? Why?

9. Which types of employment incentives do you think would be most effective to motivate excellent job performance in typical hospitality operations?

10. How do managers ensure that merit pay programs are fair?

11. What are some reasons an employee might not want to participate in a gainsharing incentive program?

When Time Is Money

Rani is the executive housekeeper at Mill House Hotel. The property has 200 guest rooms, which range from single king rooms to executive suites. The housekeepers are full-time employees and are paid by the hour.

For three quarters in a row, Rani has exceeded the department's labor cost budget, mostly because of overtime pay. The time records show that the hotel is paying a lot of overtime to housekeepers because they are not completing all of their rooms within the eight hours they are scheduled to work each day.

Rani has counseled the housekeepers before about completing all of their work on time, but she cannot fire them for working too slow. The local unemployment rate is very low, and there have been very few qualified applicants for housekeeping positions.

Charley, the general manager, calls Rani to her office to discuss the labor costs. "I know your labor budget is pretty tight in housekeeping," she begins, "but we can't afford to go over again. You've been over for three straight quarters and it's going to hurt our profits if we can't control it."

Rani explains, "I've done what I can; but if I can't replace them, it's hard to get them to work hard. They're just not getting the job done."

Charley offers, "You've been over by at least 10 percent the last three quarters. For the next quarter, I'm going to increase your labor cost budget by 8 percent, but you absolutely cannot go over it. You can spend the additional amount however you want, but you have to find a way to motivate the workers to get it done."

DISCUSSION QUESTIONS

1. What are some incentives Rani could use to motivate the housekeepers to finish their work on time without sacrificing quality? Which ones do you think would be most effective?

2. What are some potential disadvantages of those incentives?

3. How might Rani use the budget increase to attract more qualified applicants to replace the slowest workers?

ENDNOTES

1. Lynn Summers, "Integrated Pay for Performance: The High-Tech Marriage of Compensation Management and Performance Management," *Compensation & Benefits Review* 37, no. 1 (2005): 18–25.

2. Christopher M. Spray, C. K. Wang, Stuart J. Biddle, and Nicos Chatzisarantis, "Understanding Motivation in Sport: An Experimental Test of Achievement Goal and Self Determination Theories," *European Journal of Sport Science* 6, no. 1 (2006): 43–51.

3. John P. Meyer, Thomas E. Becker, and Christian Vandenberghe, "Employee Commitment and Motivation: A Conceptual Analysis and Integrative Model," *Journal of Applied Psychology* 89, no. 6 (2004): 991–1007.

4. Gary Latham, "Goal Setting and Goal Orientation: An Integration of Two Different yet Related Literatures," *Academy of Management Journal* 47, no. 2 (2004): 227–239.

5. Larry Howard and Thomas W. Dougherty, "Alternative Reward Strategies and Employee Reactions," *Compensation & Benefits Review* 36, no. 1 (2004): 41–51.

6. Melissa S. Baucus and Caryn L. Beck-Dudley, "Designing Ethical Organizations: Avoiding the Long Term Negative Effects of Rewards and Punishments," *Journal of Business Ethics* 56, no. 4 (2005): 355–370.

7. Ken Bates, Hilary Bates, and Robert Johnston, "Linking Service to Profit: The Business Case for Service Excellence," *International Journal of Service Industry Management* 14, no. 2 (2003): 173–183.

8. Sara Rynes, Barry Gerhart, and Laura Parks, "Personnel Psychology: Performance Evaluation and Pay for Performance," *Annual Review of Psychology* 56 (2005): 571–600.

9. Angela G. Morgana and Annette B. Poulsen, "Linking Pay to Performance: Compensation Proposals in the S&P 500," *Journal of Financial Economics* 62 (2001): 489–523.

10. Steven Currall, Annette Towler, Timothy Judge, and Laura Kohn, "Pay Satisfaction and Organizational Outcomes," *Personnel Psychology* 58, no. 3 (2005): 613.

11. Thomas B. Wilson, "Is It Time to Eliminate the Piece Rate Incentive System?" *Compensation & Benefits Review* 24 (March/April 1992): 43–49.

12. Mary Jo Ducharfme and Mark Podolsky, "Variable Pay: Its Impact on Motivation and Organizational Performance," *International Journal of Human Resources Development and Management* 6, no. 1 (2006): 68–76.

13. Chris Lee, "Best Idea That Got Lost in the Shuffle," *Training* 36, no. 2 (1999): 35–36.

14. National Center for Employee Ownership, "Employee Ownership by the Numbers," last modified September 2020, www.nceo.org/articles.

15. Arindrajit Dube and Richard B. Freeman, "Complimentarity of Shared Compensation and Decision-Making Systems: Evidence from the U.S. Labor Market," *NBER Working Papers Series*, W14272 (2008): 222.

16. Brent Kramer, "Employee Ownership and Participation Effects on Outcomes in Firms Majority Employee-Owned through Stock Ownership Plans in the U.S.," *Economic & Industrial Democracy*, last modified April 20, 2010. https://journals.sagepub.com/doi/10.1177/0143831X10365574.

17. Dermot McCarthy, Eoin Reeves, and Tom Turner, "Can Employee Share-Ownership Improve Employee Attitudes and Behaviour?" *Employee Relations* 32, no. 4 (2010): 382–395.

18. Joseph Blasi, Dan Weltmann, and Douglas Kruse, "The State of ESOPs: What's Past Is Prologue," *Journal of Participation and Employee Ownership* 2, no. 3 (2019): 177–182; Raymond S. Schmidgall and Christian Bechtel, "ESOPs: Putting Ownership in the Employee's Hands," *Cornell Hotel and Restaurant Administration Quarterly* 30 (February 1990): 81.

19. Cory Rosen, John Case, and Martin Staubus, "Every Employee an Owner. [Really.]," *Harvard Business Review* 83 (June 2005): 122–130.

20. Lisa Meulbroek, "Company Stock in Pension Plans: How Costly Is It?" *The Journal of Law and Economics* 48 (2005): 443–474.

21. Phillip C. Hunt, "Tax Reform: Its Impact on Compensation and Benefits," *Employment Relations Today* (Spring 1987): 39–52.

22. Kuvaas, Robert Buch, Antoinette Weibel, Anders Dysvik, and Christina G.L Nerstad, "Do intrinsic and extrinsic motivation relate differently to employee outcomes?" *Journal of Economic Psychology* vol. 61 August 2017: 251.

23. Angela Maas, "Small Companies, Big Rewards," *Employee Benefit News* 19, no. 2 (February 2005): 27–45.

24. U.S. Bureau of Labor Statistics, "Employer Costs for Employee Compensation," accessed December 17, 2020, https://www.bls.gov/news.release/ecec.toc.htm.

25. U.S. Bureau of Labor Statistics, "Healthcare Benefits: Access, Participation, and Take-Up Rates in Private Industry," accessed March 2019, www.bls.gov/ncs/ebs.

26. "Survey of Occupational Injuries and Illnesses Data," U.S. Bureau of Labor Statistics, (2019). https://www.bls.gov/iif/soii-data.htm.

27. Chris Montross and Bill Gonser, "Controlling Costs and Liabilities Related to Housekeeper Injuries," *Lodging Hospitality* (January 31, 2012).

28. Stephen Miller, "15 Ways Employers Can Reduce Healthcare Spending That Aren't Cost-Sharing," last modified February 27, 2019, https://www.shrm.org/ResourcesAndTools/hr-topics/benefits/Pages/top-ways-employers-hold-down-healthcare-spending.aspx.

29. U.S. Department of Labor Employee Benefits Security Administration, "An Employer's Guide to Group Health Continuation Coverage Under COBRA," last modified September 2018, https://www.dol.gov/sites/dolgov/files/ebsa/about-ebsa/our-activities/resource-center/publications/an-employers-guide-to-group-health-continuation-coverage-under-cobra.pdf.

30. U.S. Department of Labor Employee Benefits Security Administration, "401(k) Plans for Small Business" accessed November, 2020, https://www.dol.gov/agencies/ebsa/about-ebsa/our-activities/resource-center/publications/401kplansforsmallbusinesses.

31. Sherwin Kaplan, "The Next 25 Years of ERISA—and How to Prepare for Them," *Employee Benefits News* 14 (April 1, 2000): 41–44.

32. Stephen LaJacono, "Mildly Ill/Backup Child Care: A Benefit for Employees and Employers," *Employee Benefits Journal* 25 (December 2000): 48–51.

33. Jose M. de la Torre-Ruiz, M. Dolores Vidal-Salazar, and Eulogio Cordon-Pozo, "Employees Are Satisfied With Their Benefits, But So What? The Consequences of Benefit Satisfaction on Employees' Organizational Commitment and Turnover," *International Journal of Human Resource Management* 30, no. 13 (July, 2019): 2097–2120; Lisa Greenwald and Paul Fronstin, "The State of Employee Benefits: Findings From the 2018 Health and Workplace Benefits Survey," *EBRI Issue Brief* No. 470. (January 10, 2019): 1-16.

34. Dana Sitar, "These 7 Unexpected Companies Will Actually Let You Take Sabbatical Leave," last modified December 18, 2019, https://www.thepennyhoarder.com/make-money/career/sabbatical-leave/.

35. Mark C. Bolino, Thomas K. Kelemen, and Samuel H. Matthews, "Working 9-to-5? A Review of Research on Nonstandard Work Schedules," *Journal of Organizational Behavior* 42, no. 2 (2021): 188-211; Kishor S. Chandran and Alaa Nimer Abukhalifeh, "Systematic Literature Review of Research on Work-Life Balance in Hospitality Industry Since Millennium," *Review of Integrative Business and Economics Research* 10, no. 1 (2021): 14–33.

10
EMPLOYEE SAFETY AND HEALTH

Chapter 10 Outline

Learning Objectives

1. Summarize the OSHA standards and regulations applicable to the hospitality industry and describe how the law is enforced. (pp. 252–254)

2. Describe the legal rights of employees under applicable safety and health laws and the consequences of violating them. (pp. 254–259)

3. Identify the sources, consequences, and methods of reducing workplace stress. (pp. 259–262)

4. Describe the components and potential benefits of an employee assistance program. (pp. 262–264)

5. Explain the potential benefits of programs to promote employee health and wellness. (pp. 264–265)

6. Identify current evolving issues in hospitality workplace safety and health. (pp. 265–268)

KEY TERMS

Occupational Safety and Health Administration (OSHA)

Occupational Safety and Health Review Commission (OSHRC)

National Institute for Occupational Safety and Health (NIOSH)

Compliance officer

Material safety data sheet (MSDS)

Repetitive strain injury (RSI)

Stressor

Burnout

Employee assistance program (EAP)

Wellness program

Safety and health are critical issues in any workplace because they cause disruption in operations, increased administrative costs, and medical and lost-time costs. Workplace injuries and illnesses cost U.S. companies nearly $100 billion in workers' compensation and administrative costs annually.[1] That equates to an average of $1.21 per $100 of total wages. The leisure and hospitality sector accounts for about 3.5 percent of those losses, with over $2 million due to serious injuries involving at least five days of missed work.[2] Falls, lifting injuries, repetitive muscular strains, and chemical exposures combine to cause over half of all losses due to employee injuries in the hospitality industry.

Meanwhile, the injury incidence rate in accommodations and foodservice businesses was 3.1 per 100 full time equivalent workers in 2019, meaning that on average about three out of every 100 full time workers suffered a work-related injury or illness in that year. Although declining substantially in recent years, the hospitality industry incidence rate continues to exceed the national average by about 10 percent.[3]

Employers have both a legal duty to furnish a safe workplace and a financial incentive to control the costs of workplace injuries and illnesses. To do so, employers must invest considerable time and money to promote health and safety in the workplace and to prevent accidents. Unfortunately, many managers wait until accidents happen or until fines for safety violations are incurred before addressing these issues. Proactive managers find they can prevent many accidents if they implement programs to anticipate, recognize, and respond to employee health and safety needs. Although these programs cost money, the returns reliably outweigh the costs, which may include workers' compensation payments, inefficiencies, and administrative costs. Workplace safety and health are also key factors in employee satisfaction and motivation, especially in more dangerous workplaces.

This chapter begins by outlining the employer's legal duties and government enforcement of workplace safety and health standards. The chapter then introduces approaches managers can use to reduce or prevent workplace injuries and to promote good employee physical and mental health.

10.1 OCCUPATIONAL SAFETY AND HEALTH ACT OF 1970

The U.S. Congress enacted the Occupational Safety and Health Act of 1970 to enhance the regulation of workplace safety, to expand workplace safety protections to all workers, to standardize national safety requirements, and to establish reliable methods of enforcing workplace safety laws. Before the act became law, workplace safety was regulated, if at all, by state agencies and courts with different rules and standards from one state to the next. Many workplaces were extremely unsafe, and worker injuries were much more frequent and severe than they are today. For most employers, the penalties for creating dangerous working conditions were minimal, so significant investments in employee safety and health were considered unnecessary. The Occupational Safety and Health Act was designed to remedy that situation.[4]

The Act created three new government agencies:

- the **Occupational Safety and Health Administration (OSHA)**,

- the **Occupational Safety and Health Review Commission (OSHRC)**, and

- the **National Institute for Occupational Safety and Health (NIOSH)**.

OSHA is a branch of the U.S. Department of Labor. This agency is responsible for formulating and enforcing regulations for on-the-job safety, inspecting workplaces, investigating serious injuries and illnesses, and issuing citations and penalties. Of the three agencies created by the Occupational Safety and Health Act, OSHA is the largest and most powerful.

The OSHRC is an appeal board composed of three members appointed by the President of the United States. The main purpose of this body is to adjudicate disputes between OSHA and organizations cited by OSHA.

The NIOSH is part of the Centers for Disease Control and Prevention within the U.S. Department of Health and Human Services. Unlike OSHA, NIOSH is not a regulatory agency. NIOSH is responsible for conducting research that evaluates workplace health and safety and making recommendations for the prevention of work-related injuries and illnesses. Typically, NIOSH develops the regulations and enforcement procedures carried out by OSHA and informational publications for employers.

The Occupational Safety and Health Act authorizes states to adopt and enforce their own workplace safety standards and enforcement mechanisms. About half of the states have done so. State plans require advance approval and continuing oversight from OSHA and cannot set standards or penalties below those established by the federal law. If a state's plan is approved, all employers in the state are responsible for complying with that state's regulations. The state must also create a state agency to enforce the laws in place of OSHA. Exhibit 10.1 lists the states that have their own workplace safety and health plans.

OSHA Coverage and Scope

OSHA's first task was to develop national safety standards and regulations. Initially, OSHA tried to establish a policy for developing guidelines to make all workplaces free of risk of injury. In the late 1970s, however, the U.S. Supreme Court issued a series of decisions against OSHA, forcing a major change in policy. These decisions stated that the "no-risk" policy was too strict and too difficult for employers to follow. As a result, OSHA replaced its "no-risk" policy with the "sufficiently risk-free workplace" policy, which emphasizes the protection of workers from health and safety hazards that are known or reasonably foreseeable. Thus, OSHA strives to eliminate workplace safety and health hazards that employers know about and those they should know about.

Every U.S. business in every industry, no matter how small, is responsible for complying with the applicable OSHA or state law regulations and standards. Even if no employees are actually injured, the employer may be found guilty of violating the legal requirements for protecting employees from workplace hazards.

The federal regulations establish four basic requirements:

1. Employers in certain industries are required to comply with specific safety rules and standards. These include special rules for particularly dangerous types of work such as construction, long-haul driving, and heavy machinery operation. There are no such specific standards applicable to typical hospitality organizations.

2. Every employer in every industry must ensure the workplace is free of "recognized hazards," meaning dangers the employer knows or should know about that could cause death or physical injury. This is known as the "general duty" clause. Recognized hazards in the hospitality industry include slippery floors, risk of fire, handling heavy objects, chemical

Exhibit 10.1	States that Have Their Own Workplace Safety and Health Plans

Approved state plans applicable to private businesses:

■ Alaska	■ Maine	■ New Mexico	■ Utah
■ Arizona	■ Maryland	■ New York	■ Vermont
■ California	■ Michigan	■ North Carolina	■ Washington
■ Hawaii	■ Minnesota	■ Oregon	■ Wyoming
■ Iowa	■ Nevada	■ South Carolina	
■ Kentucky	■ New Jersey	■ Tennessee	

exposures, blood-borne pathogens, and workplace violence.

3. Employers must report any workplace fatalities to OSHA within eight hours and any incident involving hospitalization of multiple employees within 24 hours. Employers must maintain records of all other injuries and illnesses that require medical treatment beyond basic first aid. Employers must make those records available to both workers and OSHA inspectors and report them annually. Exhibit 10.2 is a sample injury log published by OSHA.

4. Employers are prohibited from requiring or allowing underage workers to perform certain dangerous job tasks. For employees 16 or 17 years of age, those tasks include operating meat slicers, grinders, compactors, and power-driven bakery machines like industrial mixers. Delivery driving is also prohibited even if the worker has a valid driver's license. Employees under 16 years of age are also prohibited from cooking over open flames, baking, and cleaning heavy machinery; but they are permitted to operate dishwashers, blenders, coffee/espresso machines, toasters, and microwave ovens.

Foodservice and especially quick service food outlets typically employ minors and are frequently cited for violating these age-related standards. OSHA maintains a detailed self-assessment tool specifically for restaurants employing minors to ensure their compliance.[5]

LEGAL ALERT!

Although the employer is liable for monetary fines, individual managers who are responsible for deliberate safety violations causing serious harm or death are subject to prosecution for aggravated assault and, in extreme cases, manslaughter.

Enforcement of OSHA Standards

OSHA inspectors have the authority to inspect most businesses in the United States. These **compliance officers** inspect workplaces and issue citations for violations of standards. By law, compliance officers must arrive at a workplace unannounced, present their credentials, and hold an opening conference with management. The U.S. Supreme Court has ruled that employers can require OSHA inspectors to obtain a search warrant before conducting any inspection.[6]

Generally, compliance officers begin an inspection by determining whether a business has OSHA-required posters displayed in conspicuous places. (Exhibit 10.3 shows a sample OSHA poster.) These posters explain various aspects of the Occupational Safety and Health Act and requirements for job safety and health protection. Compliance officers also check to see whether an employer has established a hazard communication program that includes provisions for container labeling, informational documents, and employee training.

OSHA inspectors have the right to observe and interview employees, inspect for hazards, examine health and safety records, check for first aid and required medical devices, and examine emergency procedures. The most common violations in the hospitality industry relate to machinery operation, slippery floor surfaces, and hazardous cleaning chemicals.

At the end of an inspection, compliance officers meet a second time with management to discuss their findings, issue citations, suggest improvements, and establish timetables for remedies. If citations are issued, employers have 15 days to appeal to OSHRC. If no appeal is filed within 15 days, citations are final. Penalties of up to $136,532 per willful or repeated violation can be issued by OSHA inspectors. The maximum penalty for other violations is $13,653.

Employee Rights Under OSHA

Under OSHA regulations, employees cannot be punished for refusing to work in unsafe environments or for reporting violations to OSHA. In addition, employees have the right to know if hazardous or toxic materials are being used in the workplace and to receive proper training for handling them.

Exhibit 10.2   OSHA Log and Summary

OSHA's *Form 300* (Rev. 01/2004)

Log of Work-Related Injuries and Illnesses

Attention: This form contains information relating to employee health and must be used in a manner that protects the confidentiality of employees to the extent possible while the information is being used for occupational safety and health purposes.

U.S. Department of Labor
Occupational Safety and Health Administration

Form approved OMB no. 1218-0176

Year 20 ____

You must record information about every work-related death and about every work-related injury or illness that involves loss of consciousness, restricted work activity or job transfer, days away from work, or medical treatment beyond first aid. You must also record significant work-related injuries and illnesses that are diagnosed by a physician or licensed health care professional. You must also record work-related injuries and illnesses that meet any of the specific recording criteria listed in 29 CFR Part 1904.8 through 1904.12. Feel free to use two lines for a single case if you need to. You must complete an Injury and Illness Incident Report (OSHA Form 301) or equivalent form for each injury or illness recorded on this form. If you're not sure whether a case is recordable, call your local OSHA office for help.

Establishment name _____

City _____   State _____

Identify the person

(A) Case no.

(B) Employee's name

(C) Job title (e.g., Welder)

Describe the case

(D) Date of injury or onset of illness   ___ month/day

(E) Where the event occurred (e.g., Loading dock north end)

(F) Describe injury or illness, parts of body affected, and object/substance that directly injured or made person ill (e.g., Second degree burns on right forearm from acetylene torch)

Classify the case

CHECK ONLY ONE box for each case based on the most serious outcome for that case:

(G) Death
(H) Days away from work
(I) Remained at Work — Job transfer or restriction
(J) Remained at Work — Other recordable cases

Enter the number of days the injured or ill worker was:

(K) Away from work ____ days
(L) On job transfer or restriction ____ days

Check the "Injury" column or choose one type of illness:

(M)
(1) Injury
(2) Skin disorder
(3) Respiratory condition
(4) Poisoning
(5) Hearing loss
(6) All other illnesses

Page totals ►

Be sure to transfer these totals to the Summary page (Form 300A) before you post it.

Page ____ of ____

Public reporting burden for this collection of information is estimated to average 14 minutes per response, including time to review the instructions, search and gather the data needed, and complete and review the collection of information. Persons are not required to respond to the collection of information unless it displays a currently valid OMB control number. If you have any comments about these estimates or any other aspects of this data collection, contact: US Department of Labor, OSHA Office of Statistical Analysis, Room N-3644, 200 Constitution Avenue, NW, Washington, DC 20210. Do not send the completed forms to this office.

Source: U.S. Department of Labor, Occupational Safety and Health Administration, Washington, D.C.

Exhibit 10.3   OSHA Job Safety and Health Protection Poster

OSHA
Occupational Safety
and Health Administration

U.S. Department of Labor

Job Safety and Health
IT'S THE LAW!

All workers have the right to:

- A safe workplace.

- Raise a safety or health concern with your employer or OSHA, or report a work-related injury or illness, without being retaliated against.

- Receive information and training on job hazards, including all hazardous substances in your workplace.

- Request a confidential OSHA inspection of your workplace if you believe there are unsafe or unhealthy conditions. You have the right to have a representative contact OSHA on your behalf.

- Participate (or have your representative participate) in an OSHA inspection and speak in private to the inspector.

- File a complaint with OSHA within 30 days (by phone, online or by mail) if you have been retaliated against for using your rights.

- See any OSHA citations issued to your employer.

- Request copies of your medical records, tests that measure hazards in the workplace, and the workplace injury and illness log.

This poster is available free from OSHA.

Contact OSHA. We can help.

Employers must:

- Provide employees a workplace free from recognized hazards. It is illegal to retaliate against an employee for using any of their rights under the law, including raising a health and safety concern with you or with OSHA, or reporting a work-related injury or illness.

- Comply with all applicable OSHA standards.

- Notify OSHA within 8 hours of a workplace fatality or within 24 hours of any work-related inpatient hospitalization, amputation, or loss of an eye.

- Provide required training to all workers in a language and vocabulary they can understand.

- Prominently display this poster in the workplace.

- Post OSHA citations at or near the place of the alleged violations.

On-Site Consultation services are available to small and medium-sized employers, without citation or penalty, through OSHA-supported consultation programs in every state.

1-800-321-OSHA (6742) • TTY **1-877-889-5627** • **www.osha.gov**

The OSHA Hazard Communication Standard requires employers throughout the United States to tell their employees about hazardous materials they may be required to handle on the job. This communication is accomplished by providing a **material safety data sheet (MSDS)** for each hazardous chemical or material. MSDS forms provide information on chemicals or cleaners used at a property, including hazardous ingredients, health hazard data, spill or leak procedures, and any special precautions or protective gear required when using the product. These sheets can be obtained from the chemical supplier.

All employees who handle hazardous materials must receive and have continual access to the MSDS forms. Exhibit 10.4 is an OSHA form listing the required content of an MSDS.

Exhibit 10.4 MSDS Quick Card

Hazard Communication Safety Data Sheets

The Hazard Communication Standard (HCS) requires chemical manufacturers, distributors, or importers to provide Safety Data Sheets (SDSs) (formerly known as Material Safety Data Sheets or MSDSs) to communicate the hazards of hazardous chemical products. The HCS requires new SDSs to be in a uniform format, and include the section numbers, the headings, and associated information under the headings below:

Section 1, Identification includes product identifier; manufacturer or distributor name, address, phone number; emergency phone number; recommended use; restrictions on use.

Section 2, Hazard(s) identification includes all hazards regarding the chemical; required label elements.

Section 3, Composition/information on ingredients includes information on chemical ingredients; trade secret claims.

Section 4, First aid measures includes important symptoms/effects, acute, delayed; required treatment.

Section 5, Fire-fighting measures lists suitable extinguishing techniques, equipment; chemical hazards from fire.

Section 6, Accidental release measures lists emergency procedures; protective equipment; proper methods of containment and cleanup.

Section 7, Handling and storage lists precautions for safe handling and storage, including incompatibilities.

(Continued on other side)

For more information:

OSHA Occupational Safety and Health Administration
U.S. Department of Labor   www.osha.gov (800) 321-OSHA (6742)

OSHA 3493-01R 2016

Hazard Communication Safety Data Sheets

Section 8, Exposure controls/personal protection lists OSHA's Permissible Exposure Limits (PELs); ACGIH Threshold Limit Values (TLVs); and any other exposure limit used or recommended by the chemical manufacturer, importer, or employer preparing the SDS where available as well as appropriate engineering controls; personal protective equipment (PPE).

Section 9, Physical and chemical properties lists the chemical's characteristics.

Section 10, Stability and reactivity lists chemical stability and possibility of hazardous reactions.

Section 11, Toxicological information includes routes of exposure; related symptoms, acute and chronic effects; numerical measures of toxicity.

Section 12, Ecological information*
Section 13, Disposal considerations*
Section 14, Transport information*
Section 15, Regulatory information*

Section 16, Other information, includes the date of preparation or last revision.

*Note: Since other Agencies regulate this information, OSHA will not be enforcing Sections 12 through 15 (29 CFR 1910.1200(g)(2)).

Employers must ensure that SDSs are readily accessible to employees.
See Appendix D of 29 CFR 1910.1200 for a detailed description of SDS contents.

For more information:

OSHA Occupational Safety and Health Administration
U.S. Department of Labor   www.osha.gov (800) 321-OSHA (6742)

OSHA recommends, but does not require, the establishment of company-sponsored safety and health programs. Many companies have some such programs, frequently in the form of a safety committee or other permanent working group. To be effective, a safety program should:

- Involve both top management leadership and frontline workers

- Clearly establish responsibilities for safety and health

- Identify all potential workplace hazards

- Include extensive employee training in safety and health precautions and first aid

- Review accident records and immediately correct causes of accidents

- Encourage awareness of workplace safety and health issues

Hospitality and OSHA

Kitchen areas can present very costly safety problems for hospitality operators. Grease buildup is the primary cause of many kitchen fires. Wet, greasy, and cluttered floors account for a large portion of injuries, and not just in kitchens. Housekeepers are also vulnerable to fall injuries, chemical exposures, and muscle strains from repetitive and strenuous work. Effective safety committees continually monitor and address these common risks.

Managers can reduce the likelihood of accidents by focusing on three elements: signage, training, and preventive maintenance. Posting signs near areas where serious accidents can occur can remind employees to be careful. For example, signs near fryers remind employees of the potential hazards of burns or grease fires and outline proper equipment use. Training is an effective way to communicate proper use of equipment and property safety standards. Well-structured training is usually effective in minimizing the number and frequency of accidents. A regular program of preventive training and maintenance—especially for the most problem-prone areas—can substantially decrease the financial losses associated with a hospitality workplace.

Repetitive strain injury (RSI), sometimes known as repetitive stress injury,

commands more attention all the time. Employees incur such injuries by repeating manual tasks over and over. Casino dealers, food preparers, assembly workers, cashiers, and many other types of workers are vulnerable to this type of injury. Carpal tunnel syndrome is a common example. Repeated motions of the hands over a long period of time can severely damage ligaments in the wrists, sometimes requiring surgery. Keyboard design has been cited as a contributing factor in several musculoskeletal problems in the hands, arms, and neck.[7] Employees who spend long hours on a computer may also experience fatigue, psychological distress, and eye strain. Exhibit 10.5 lists guidelines for workstation ergonomics.

Managers can reduce the frequency of some repetitive strain injuries by purchasing desks designed specifically for keyboards and computers, wrist rests, ergonomic keyboards, and glare-reducing computer screens. Other strategies—such as rotating workers, increasing the variety of tasks done by one worker, and making sure workers take regular rest breaks—have proven effective in promoting safety.[8] Employees who frequently bend over or lift heavy objects are frequently provided back braces.

Measuring Health and Safety

OSHA is primarily concerned with creating safe and healthy work environments. Managers can measure their overall safety and health records by using a simple formula. The result of this formula—called the *incidence rate*—reflects the number of injuries for every 100 full-time employees per year:

$$\frac{N}{TH} \times 200,000$$

N = number of injuries and illnesses or lost workdays

TH = total hours worked by all employees during calendar year

200,000 = 100 full-time employees × 40 hour week × 50 weeks

Although there is no "acceptable" incidence rate, this formula allows an employer to track and predict the occurrence of injuries over time. This number can be

Exhibit 10.5 | Workstation Ergonomics

- The keyboard and monitor should be directly in front of the person to avoid twisting the body.

- The height of the table and chair should allow wrists to be positioned at the same level as the elbow.

- The monitor should be at or just below eye level.

- The monitor should be a distance of 18 to 30 inches (45.72 to 76.2 centimeters) from the eyes. Prescription glasses must be for this distance.

- The keyboard should be at a level where wrists are straight and in a neutral position rather than bent forward or flexed for long periods of time.

- The wrists should be able to rest lightly on a pad for support.

- The head and neck should be upright, not tilting forward or to the side.

- The chair should provide lower- and middle-back support.

- The feet should be flat on the floor or on a footrest so the knees are parallel at a 90-degree to 110-degree angle.

- There should be three to six inches (7.62 to 15.24 centimeters) of leg room between the person's lap and the keyboard.

compared to national and industry averages published annually by OSHA. The most recent national rate was 2.8, while the rate within leisure and hospitality was 3.1.[9]

Knowledge Check

1. What are the most common workplace hazards in the hospitality industry?

2. What is the purpose of a material safety data sheet?

3. Why is workstation ergonomics important in the workplace?

10.2 EMPLOYEE STRESS AND EMOTIONAL HEALTH

A study by the Families and Work Institute found that 41 percent of U.S. employees who were surveyed experienced three or more indicators of stress "sometimes," "often," or "very often." The same study reported that U.S. workers felt stressed more often than they did 10 years before.[10] A similar study found that the levels of stress among hotel managers had increased substantially within a 10-year period—to the point that most hotel managers surveyed experienced dangerous levels of stress, more than managers in many other fields. More recent research has found this trend to be continuing in the industry.[11]

Sources of Stress

Some stress on the job is good. Just the right amount of stress can contribute to good job performance and corresponding satisfaction—much like when a guitar is tuned, just the right amount of string tension results in the desired pitch and tone. Not enough stress produces the wrong sound, but too much stress can cause guitar strings to stretch or break.

Some people are more prone to stress than others.[12] "Type A" people are typically impatient, hard-driving, competitive individuals who work under strict self-induced

| Exhibit 10.6 | Standardized Social Readjustment Rating Scores (SRRS) |

Rank	Life Event	Mean Value
1.	Death of spouse	119
2.	Divorce	98
3.	Death of a close family member	92
4.	Marital separation	79
5.	Fired at work	79
6.	Personal injury or illness	77
7.	Jail term	75
8.	Death of a close friend	70
9.	Pregnancy	66
10.	Business adjustment	62
11.	Foreclosure on mortgage or loan	61
12.	Gain of a new family member	57
13.	Marital reconciliation	57
14.	Change in health of family member	56
15.	Change in financial state	56
16.	Retirement	54
17.	Change to a different line of work	51
18.	Change in number of arguments with spouse	51
19.	Marriage	51
20.	Spouse begins or ends work	46
21.	Sexual difficulties	45
22.	Mortgage loan	44
23.	Son or daughter leaving home	44
24.	Change in responsibilities at work	43
25.	Change in living conditions	42
26.	Change in residence	41
27.	Trouble with in-laws	38
28.	Begin or end school	37
29.	Outstanding personal achievement	36
30.	Change in work hours or conditions	35
31.	Change in schools	30
32.	Holidays	29
33.	Trouble with boss	29
34.	Change in recreation	29
35.	Low mortgage loan	28
36.	Change in personal habits	27
37.	Change in social activities	27
38.	Change in eating habits	27
39.	Change in sleeping habits	26
40.	Change in the number of family get-togethers	26
41.	Vacation	25
42.	Change in church activities	22
43.	Minor violation of the law	22
	Grand mean for all events	49

Source: M. A. Miller and R. H. Rahe, "Life Changes Scaling for the 1990s," *Journal of Psychosomatic Research* 43, no. 3 (1998): 279–292.

time constraints. "Type A" people tend to have higher levels of stress than "Type B" people, who characteristically lead unhurried lives. Not all stress relates to personality type, however. Many stress experts identify four different sources of stress, or **stressors**:

- Extra-organizational sources: personal problems with family, marriage, finances, and children

- Individual sources: overwork, failure to manage time effectively, health problems, and procrastination

- Group sources: poor teamwork, interpersonal conflict, and inequitable demands or rewards

- Organizational sources: unreasonable rules and regulations, unclear or excessive expectations, poor management styles, and abuse of power

Other stressors in the hospitality industry include chronic labor shortages, high staff turnover, long and inconsistent hours, continual interaction with guests, and long periods of high-pressure conditions.[13] Casino managers have been found to experience more workplace stress than other hospitality managers, in part due to the added high degree of regulatory control and fast-paced work environments.[14]

Many life events that trigger stress are related to major personal and family crises rather than work. According to the Social Readjustment Rating Scale (SRRS) presented in Exhibit 10.6, the top five most stressful events are the death of a spouse, divorce, the death of a close family member, marital separation, and being fired at work. Other common conditions that cause stress are loneliness (research has found that social isolation is as dangerous as smoking), high blood pressure, obesity, and high cholesterol. One study found that 40 percent of workers cited workload as their main cause of stress, 34 percent cited people issues, and 21 percent cited balancing work and life.[15]

Some of the items on the SRRS—for example, outstanding personal achievements, vacations, and holidays—would seem to be positive events in the lives of managers. However, handling the circumstances before and after these events also requires a substantial amount of energy and preparation. Even a vacation, perhaps the most positive event on the SRRS list, is stressful, because it is necessary to help plan the vacation and arrange for others to cover the manager's responsibilities during the vacation. Although holidays would normally be considered positive for individuals, this might not be the case for hotel managers, many of whom are busier and have less time off during the holiday season.

Consequences of Stress

Too much stress is bad for employees and organizations alike. For individuals, too much stress can lead to a variety of health problems, from headaches to depression. Stress has also been linked to serious health problems, including heart disease and weakened immune systems.[16]

For organizations, stress can lead to **burnout**. Symptoms of burnout include emotional exhaustion, a tendency to depersonalize and become unresponsive to other people, and a low sense of personal commitment. These symptoms are very likely to negatively affect both customer service and employee relations. Hotel managers experience much higher levels of burnout than managers in other lines of business.

Burnout also leads to employee turnover, absenteeism, and decreased productivity. The turnover rate among employees in service fields is twice as high as in non-service fields (25 to 30 percent versus 8 to 15 percent). The hospitality middle-manager turnover rate is significantly higher than in other service areas. Seventy-six percent of employees said that the most damaging effect of burnout was increased absenteeism, and 70 percent of employees worried about decreased productivity.[17]

Too much stress can also lead to workers' compensation claims. Approximately 11 to 15 percent of all workers' compensation claims are related to stress. Hospitality employees may cope with stress in unhealthy ways that ultimately affect their job performance, such as heavy drinking and harmful eating habits.[18]

Stress Reduction

Stress reduction programs have two goals: to reduce individual-induced stress and to reduce organization-induced stress. Individuals learn to control stress through exercise and diet and by modifying or eliminating their consumption of alcohol, tobacco, or drugs. Stress reduction programs may also include financial and family counseling programs. A simple stress reduction plan might recommend the following guidelines for reducing workplace stress:

- Rank individual tasks by importance and address the most important task first.

- Delegate authority and responsibility appropriately.

- Set and follow realistic deadlines and schedules.

- Plan ahead to avoid surprises.

- Take frequent breaks, even if for a minute or two.

- Avoid procrastination.

- Learn and use simple quick stress reduction techniques such as deep breathing, envisioning yourself in a favorite spot, or meditating.

- Get enough sleep, and ensure work schedules allow for regular sleep cycles.

An organizational stress reduction plan might recommend the following guidelines for reducing workplace stress:

- Design jobs to eliminate or reduce unnecessary or particularly stressful aspects.

- Schedule workflow to minimize bottlenecks and delays.

- Clarify individual roles and responsibilities.

- Develop a system to efficiently resolve interpersonal conflicts.

- Promote job security and opportunities for advancement.

- Establish job enrichment programs to promote job satisfaction.

- Establish wellness programs to promote good health.

10.3 EMPLOYEE ASSISTANCE PROGRAMS

Employees who abuse alcohol and drugs cost U.S. employers astronomical amounts of money. The National Institute on Drug Abuse states that substance abuse, including drug abuse and addiction, costs the U.S. economy over half a trillion dollars annually.[19] These losses are sustained through inefficiency and lost productivity, theft, absenteeism, turnover, reduced employee morale, on-the-job injury, and skyrocketing healthcare costs. Eighty percent of alcohol abusers in the United States are employed or are dependents of an employee.

According to the Centers for Disease Control, as much as $250 billion is wasted each year because of excessive alcohol consumption by employees.[20] Employers have recognized these losses and found typical medical benefit plans insufficient to address the problem effectively.[21]

An **employee assistance program (EAP)** is designed to help employees cope with personal problems like drug and alcohol abuse as well as emotional disorders and stressful events. The first EAPs were created in the early 1970s to help employees with alcohol problems. Since then, EAPs have expanded their offerings to assist employees with a wide range of problems that can negatively affect their work performance.[22]

EAPs are as varied as U.S. businesses. In some cases, programs help employees with specific problems like alcohol or drug abuse. In other cases, EAPs include such services as family counseling, personal health management, financial counseling, and educational or career counseling.

Setting Up an EAP

Establishing an EAP is a four-stage process. The first stage involves identifying workplace problems and employee needs. The second stage is devoted to program development. The third stage is implementing the plan, and the fourth is evaluation and revision.

Most EAPs include programs that focus on preventing or reducing drug and alcohol abuse. Many people assume that such programs are typical of EAPs in the hospitality industry because its traditional work force is in the age group most likely to abuse drugs and alcohol. However, employers should assess their individual work environments to determine what other programs their employees may also need. Assessment—usually conducted by third parties to ensure anonymity—may include observations, interviews, employee surveys, and personality testing. Examination of health benefit plan expenses may also reveal persistent employee health problems.

Once the needs for an EAP have been determined, managers can concentrate on program development. Many EAPs use both internal and external services and programs. Employees generally have an easier time participating in in-house programs conducted on company premises. In-house programs reduce anonymity, however, and create a risk of unauthorized sharing of confidential employee information. Exhibit 10.7 lists appropriate ways to refer an employee to an EAP.

Hiring and training personnel for in-house programs may cost more than using external services, which offer advantages over internal programs such as increased anonymity and, sometimes, more professional expertise. When implementing EAPs, the most critical elements are gaining management support, ensuring employee anonymity or confidentiality, and thoroughly communicating information about the services and how employees can access them.

After a program is put in place, an evaluation can examine productivity increases, reductions in turnover and costs, and the number of employees who use the EAP.

Costs Saved by EAPs

EAPs cost money to establish and operate, and they may not result in the anticipated return in the form of lower overall employee

Exhibit 10.7   Referring an Employee to an Employee Assistance Program

When Referring an Employee to an EAP:

Don't say	Do say
You seem to have a drinking problem.	You have been late to work three times in two weeks, your performance is slipping, and I've smelled alcohol on your breath.
You are all stressed out. I think you better get help.	We have received six complaints from coworkers about you yelling at them. This cannot continue.
The EAP will provide the help you need.	The EAP can help you address your performance.
We would like you to get therapy for your problems.	We would like you to try the EAP for assistance with these concerns.

Source: Jane Easter Bahls, "Handle With Care," *HR Magazine* 44 (1999) 3: 60–65

expenses, particularly for small employers. According to one study, companies realize between $5.17 and $6.47 in returns for every dollar they spend on an EAP.[23] Other studies, however, suggest that EAPs do not save money in the long run. In fact, research has shown that some aspects of wellness programs, such as short-term corporate weight loss, usually fail or even backfire by incentivizing people to binge before the first weigh-in and crash diet before the followups.[24]

A study by the RAND Corporation suggests that some portions of health programs are good investments whereas others are not. RAND found that 87 percent of the savings in wellness programs come from disease management as opposed to lifestyle programs.[25] Disease management consists of efforts to ensure that employees who are sick continue to take medications that help such issues as existing heart disease, diabetes, and emphysema. According to that study, disease management programs return $3.80 for every dollar invested whereas lifestyle programs return only about $0.50 per dollar invested.

LEGAL ALERT!

Employees with drug and alcohol use disorders may be considered disabled for purposes of state and federal disability protection laws. Although EAPs are not required by law, employees using the program may be entitled to reasonable accommodations for their conditions, such as time off for treatment and minor alterations in their job duties or workplace. Some employees who are not considered disabled may still be eligible for medical leaves of absence due to drug or alcohol addiction.

Although some companies have not established EAPs, others are forging ahead to address broader issues with their EAPs. One trend is to combine EAPs with other healthcare programs to realize even further reductions in employer costs. For example, one company announced a new program in 2019 to include both physical and mental health components and a new meditation app for all its workers.[26]

Knowledge Check

1. What are the potential benefits of an EAP?

2. What are the steps in creating an EAP?

3. Why would an employee need an EAP?

10.4 OTHER ISSUES IN SAFETY AND HEALTH

Substance use and stress are not the only health-related issues managers and employees face in the hospitality industry. This section addresses several other important health concerns that exist in today's business environment.

Choosing the Right Medical Care

A recent study found that preventable medical error is the third leading cause of death in the U.S.[27] Another study concluded that the number of deaths attributable to medical error may be more than 440,000 per year.[28] The most common types of medical errors causing deaths or prolonging treatment fall into three major categories:

- *Diagnostic problems* include errors or delays in diagnosis, failure to employ indicated tests, use of outmoded tests or therapies, and failure to act on results of monitoring or testing.

- *Treatment errors* occur in the performance of operations, procedures and tests, errors in administering treatments, errors in dosage or usage of drugs, avoidable delays in treatment, and inappropriate care.

- *Preventive errors* include failure to provide treatment and inadequate monitoring or follow-up of treatment.

Tom Emerick, a well-known healthcare consultant, is among many voices that advise that businesses can reduce their costs of insurance, work time lost, and other losses by simply identifying the few doctors and medical facilities where such errors occur too regularly. Emerick and others believe that a company can substantially cut costs by establishing a list of what they call "centers of excellence"—hospitals and providers with low error rates that do not overtest, overprescribe or overtreat workers.[29]

Many People Hate Their Jobs

Unfortunately, as many as 70 percent of people in the U.S. report that they hate their jobs, resulting in a number of problems, including disengagement with work.[30] Hospitality managers recognize that job satisfaction directly affects customer service. Employees who are unhappy with their jobs can do permanent damage to customer relations, even when their unhappiness is temporary. Job misery is also responsible for weight gain, weakened immune systems, ruined relationships (with coworkers and families), loss of sleep, risk of serious injury, and rapid aging.[31]

How employers react to people who are unhappy in their jobs is important. It may not be possible to make certain jobs more fun, interesting, or entertaining. It is therefore important to take recruiting, hiring, training, and evaluating employees seriously.

Depression

Depression is now the most common health problem around the globe. It affects one in five people at some point in their life.

Although depression affects all genders and ages, it is most common in those 24 to 44 years of age, and twice as common in women as in men. Depression can have a huge effect on the workplace; it is estimated that over six million workdays are lost annually due to the illness. In addition, depression can cost many working days of reduced productivity per year because those who are depressed work at a diminished capacity. One employee in 40 is likely suffering from untreated depression.[32] Many EAPs address mental health conditions.

Wellness Programs

Healthy living has become an obsession to many people in the United States. Many U.S. companies have responded to this trend by establishing **wellness programs** designed to help employees live healthier lives. The theory behind wellness programs is that healthier employees are more likely to be productive, satisfied, and reliable and should save the company on health-care costs. In a recent study, 90 percent of hospitality industry executives agreed that employee wellness programs improve not just employee health but also job satisfaction and customer relations.[33]

Most wellness programs have three components:

1. *Health screening and assessment.* Most wellness programs screen and assess employees before enrolling them, primarily to determine health and exercise needs. At a minimum, this process includes physical exams and tests to determine cholesterol, blood sugar, stress, and blood pressure levels.

2. *Physical fitness programs.* A component of wellness programs may be classes or facilities for aerobic exercise and weight training, with exercise equipment such as stationary bicycles, rowing machines, and treadmills.

3. *Education and training.* Many wellness programs offer clinics on smoking cessation, cholesterol reduction, stress reduction, diet management, and mental wellness.

The success of wellness programs in improving employee performance is up for debate. Some say that only those employees who do not need wellness programs enroll. Others believe that such programs can help all employees. Each organization should assess the need and cost of such programs and keep records of who participates and who does not to resolve these issues for themselves.[34] Exhibit 10.8 lists the six pillars of the most successful employee wellness programs.

Exhibit 10.8 | **The Six Pillars of the Most Successful Employee Wellness Programs**

The pillars of effective employee wellness plans:

- Multi-level leadership from executives to middle managers to dedicated wellness program managers

- Alignment with business goals and strategies, demonstrating the connection between wellness and job performance

- Scope, relevance, and quality of programs to address the full range of wellness issues facing employees, as opposed to a focus on just a few health issues

- Convenience and either free or affordable access to programs

- Strong partnerships with quality external providers

- Communications with workers about available programs, personal benefits, and participation opportunities

Adapted from: Leonard L. Berry, Ann M. Mirabito and William B. Baun, "What's the Hard Return on Employee Wellness Programs?" *Harvard Business Review* 89, no.3 (2010): 1–9.

Sixteen million Americans are living with smoking-related illnesses, costing more than $300 billion each year in medical care costs and lost productivity. That's nearly $9,000 in direct and indirect annual losses for the average working smoker.[35]

Smoking in the Workplace

Education about and emphasis on the hazards of smoking have helped to greatly reduce the number of people in the United States who smoke tobacco products. Employer-sponsored smoking cessation plans have played a large role. The percentage of U.S. adults who smoke tobacco has declined from a high of over 40 percent in the 1960s to 14 percent in 2019. Today, there are about 34.1 million smokers in the United States—still a significant portion of the U.S. workforce.

Most U.S. workplaces have banned smoking entirely, and many states and cities continue to pass indoor and outdoor smoking bans, but bars and restaurants are the most common businesses exempted from smoking ban laws. Hospitality workers in more than half the states are still exposed to tobacco smoke at work every day. Tobacco remains a lawful product and the Occupational Safety and Health Act does not require smoke-free workplaces.

Although hospitality companies can regulate workplace smoking or prohibit it altogether, in many states they cannot discharge, refuse to hire, or otherwise discriminate against people who smoke outside of work.[36]

Work/Life Balance

Work/life issues have become much more prominent in recent years. Employees have come to expect an acceptable balance between their work and personal lives, and many employers have recognized the importance of maintaining an appropriate balance between the two. Employer expectations that do not account for this balance can have profound effects on job satisfaction, turnover, job performance, and employee health. But work/life balance is not accomplished just by having enough time off from work to pursue personal interests. It means different things to different people. Employers must recognize the competing demands on the lives of workers and explore ways to avoid the conflicts that may cause harm if not addressed.

Quality of life programs originally arose from increases in two-income and dual-career families in the United States. Child and elder care are two of the greatest challenges employees encounter while attempting to balance work and family life. In previous generations, it was traditional in two-parent households—when economically feasible—for men to work outside the home and for women to stay at home to care for children and aging parents and manage the household. As a result of socioeconomic and other changes in the United States, today both parents in two-parent households are often members of the workforce.

Although dual-career families sometimes enjoy an increase in disposable income, they can also experience unique problems and stress. Many working men and women, for example, care for both their young children and parents. This "sandwich generation" represents the largest percentage of employed persons in the United States. To them, work/life balance may mean keeping up with the many demands on their time and energy. Many households require one or more paid daycare providers. This problem can be much worse in hospitality operations, where employees also have to deal with irregular work hours.

One way people can reduce this conflict is to reduce the demands of their personal lives. Young people are delaying marriage and having children. An analysis of U.S. census data reveals that 35 percent of U.S. adults between 25 and 50 years old have never married—an all-time high.[37] The percentage of women who have never had children has risen to nearly 50 percent. Many attribute work requirements to this significant increase.[38] And it's not just family demands—

employees need time off to exercise, sleep, and participate in social and recreational activities to maintain their health.

Companies that understand and address the competing demands on their employees are frequently rewarded with lower turnover and absenteeism, increased productivity, improved job satisfaction, and an advantage in recruiting. About 75 percent of U.S. adults listed a family friendly work schedule as a top priority when choosing a job.[39]

The desire and demand for work/life balance is unique to each employee's circumstances, but employers have found some innovative ways to improve the situation and reduce the conflicts that work can cause in employees' personal lives. Most of causes of work/life conflict are caused by time constraints and scheduling conflicts, so many of them focus on that aspect of the job. Some common examples are:

- Flexible work patterns and schedules

- Predictable working hours

- Remote telecommuting

- Job sharing and part time work opportunities

- Reducing "homework" and relieving workers from all duties when they are not at work

- Dependent care spending accounts that allot employees designated funds to spend on childcare

- Company-sponsored or subsidized childcare programs

- Adult day care and long-term care insurance

- Expanded family and medical leave beyond what is required by law

- Paid maternity leave

- Employee assistance programs that address emotional and mental health[40]

Workplace Violence

The U.S. Department of Labor identifies workplace violence as any act or threat of physical violence, harassment, intimidation, or other threatening disruptive behavior that occurs at the work site. It ranges from threats and verbal abuse to physical assaults and homicide. About 15 percent of all workplace fatalities in the U.S. are caused by violence.[41]

The organizational consequences of any form of violence in a workplace can be disastrous; companies should prepare in advance to reduce their risks and to respond when necessary. The fallout for organizations affected by workplace violence includes:

- Changes in employee work performance, commitment, and motivation

- Changes in relationships between employees

- Changes in employee perceptions of management and the workplace

Proper preparation for dealing with workplace violence starts with developing training about workplace violence and planning an effective response. In addition, organizations should develop a crisis management team to step in immediately, identify outside assistance resources, conduct an audit to identify vulnerabilities, develop policies and procedures, and even practice what to do when violence occurs. The most dedicated training and prevention programs cannot stop all workplace violence, so it is critical to be prepared and to respond immediately when it occurs. This includes keeping communication lines open with employees and necessary outside sources while working through a problem.

Infectious Disease

The COVID-19 pandemic has devastated the entire hospitality industry, but as businesses re-open, there are new issues with employee health and safety. As of this writing, OSHA has not created any formal regulations about keeping workers safe from being infected, but it has issued recommendations to address employee exposure to the disease.[42] They include the following:

- Conduct an assessment of the health risks for each job classification.

- Identify control measures to limit the spread of the virus, including requiring employees and customers to wear approved face coverings and sanitizing surfaces frequently.

- Communicate new safety policies and procedures to all workers.

- Implement protections from retaliation for workers who raise related concerns.

Currently, there are no employer penalties for failing to protect workers from COVID-19. Nonetheless, many hospitality employers are requiring vaccination or frequent testing for employees. Some are offering additional paid sick leave to encourage employees to stay home when they are ill. The industry has no experience with an outbreak of this magnitude but must respond in a manner that best protects both employees and guests.

Knowledge Check

1. What are the three components of a typical employee wellness program?

2. What are some negative workplace effects of work/life imbalance?

3. What are some examples of real-life workplace violence?

IN THIS CHAPTER, YOU LEARNED:

- Federal and state laws protect the health and safety of all workers throughout the hospitality industry by regulating known workplace hazards, hazardous materials and chemicals, and job duties of minors. These laws are enforced by both state and federal government agencies that have the authority to inspect workplaces, investigate injuries, and impose penalties for violations.

- Employees have the legal right to a workplace that is free of known or foreseeable health and safety hazards. Federal and state laws also guarantee their right to refuse to perform very hazardous work and to report safety violations to the proper authorities. Retaliation against employees who exercise those rights can result in substantial penalties.

- Workplace stress affects many employees and can cause many problems in the workplace. Personal stress may be reduced by prioritizing tasks, delegating responsibility, setting realistic goals and deadlines, taking short breaks, and avoiding procrastination. Organizational stress may be reduced by designing clear and realistic job duties, scheduling efficiently, resolving conflict among coworkers, promoting safety and security, and creating opportunities for growth and advancement.

- Employee assistance programs provide support and resources for employees with drug or alcohol addictions. The potential benefits of providing the programs include reduced turnover, improved job satisfaction and performance, and healthcare cost savings. To be effective, however, EAPs must be structured to be affordable, convenient, accessible, and effective.

- Employee wellness programs provide support and resources to improve health, such as exercise and diet programs. Because they are available to all workers, they can be an attractive benefit for recruiting and retention purposes.

- Work/life balance is increasingly important to workers and can have both negative and positive consequences in the workplace.

- Hospitality managers must be mindful of emerging issues in employee health and safety because they directly affect job performance, efficiency, and costs.

KEY TERMS

burnout—Emotional or physical exhaustion due to stress, often resulting in disengagement from work.

compliance officer—Workplace inspector employed by the Occupational Safety and Health Administration.

employee assistance program (EAP)—An employer-sponsored program designed to help employees deal with drug or alcohol use, stress, family conflict, finances, and other personal issues.

material safety data sheet (MSDS)—A document informing employees of the safety hazards and protection procedures associated with a hazardous chemical and material used at work.

National Institute for Occupational Safety and Health (NIOSH)—A federal agency whose primary purposes are to carry out research and to recommend occupational safety and health standards.

Occupational Safety and Health Administration (OSHA)—An agency within the U.S. Department of Labor created to establish occupational safety and health standards and regulations, conduct inspections, issue citations, and propose penalties for non-compliance.

Occupational Safety and Health Review Commission (OSHRC)—An independent federal agency that decides employer appeals from citations and penalties issued by OSHA.

repetitive strain injury (RSI)—An injury that results from a frequently repeated stress on a particular part of the body; also known as repetitive stress injury.

stressor—An item, situation, or condition that causes stress.

wellness program—A voluntary program offered to improve employee health and welfare.

REVIEW QUESTIONS

1. What injuries and illnesses are most common in the hospitality industry?

2. What rights are guaranteed to employees under OSHA regulations?

3. How are federal and state workplace safety laws enforced?

4. What are the elements of an effective workplace safety program?

5. What are some sources of employee stress?

6. What are the principal methods of reducing organizational workplace stress?

7. What are the potential benefits of instituting an employee assistance program?

8. What are some important factors in successful employee wellness program?

9. What are the primary causes of work/life imbalance? How can employers address this?

Managing Risk

Sergio was recently hired to be the director of risk management at Helmsley Hotel. The day he arrived, he met briefly with Martina, the general manager, who told him, "Your first priority is to address some problems we've been having in housekeeping. Seven of the guest room attendants filed workers compensation claims in the last year. Plus, a lot of the attendants and porters are calling in sick, and a few have quit. All this is driving up our labor costs, and we have to get this under control. See what you can come up with and send me some ideas next week."

Sergio's first step was to discuss the problems with Chen, the director of housekeeping. He told him the workers compensation claims were mostly back injuries, and one attendant said she gets skin rashes from the new cleaning chemicals. He continued, "We get call-outs every day for all kinds of reasons. Usually, it's because they're sick or they can't find daycare for their kids. We're paying a lot of overtime to cover for them, but just last week two more quit because they just got tired of all the extra hours."

DISCUSSION QUESTIONS

1. What other information should Sergio collect before deciding what he will recommend?

2. Other than labor costs, what are some potential negative consequences that may result if these problems are not addressed?

3. What are some options Sergio might recommend?

ENDNOTES

1. National Academy of Social Insurance, "Workers' Compensation: Benefits, Coverage, and Costs," last modified November, 2020, https://www.nasi.org/sites/default/files/research/November%202020%20-%20Benefits,%20Coverage,%20and%20Costs.pdf.

2. Liberty Mutual Insurance, "Workplace Safety Index 2020: Leisure and Hospitality," last modified May, 2020, https://viewpoint.libertymutualgroup.com/wp-content/uploads/2020/04/WSI_1004.pdf.

3. U.S. Bureau of Labor Statistics, "Employer-Reported Workplace Injuries and Illnesses – 2019," last modified November 4, 2020, https://www.bls.gov/news.release/archives/osh_11042020.htm.

4. Occupational Safety and Health Act, Public Law 91-596, 84 Statutes at Large 1590 (December 29, 1970).

5. U.S. Occupational Safety and Health Administration, "Young Workers Safety in Restaurants," accessed April 28, 2021, www.osha.gov/SLTC/youth/restaurant.

6. U.S. Occupational Safety and Health Administration, "OSHA Inspections," accessed April 28, 2021, www.osha.gov/sites/default/files/publications/factsheet-inspections.pdf.

7. David Rempel, Alan Barr, David Brafman, and Ed Young, "The Effect of Six Keyboard Designs on Wrist and Forearm Postures," *Applied Ergonomics* 38, no. 3 (2007): 293–298.

8. National Institute for Occupational Safety and Health, "A Primer Based on Workplace Evaluations of Musculoskeletal Disorders," March 1997, *DHHS (NIOSH) Publication* No. 97-117. https://www.cdc.gov/niosh/docs/97-117.

9. U.S. Occupational Safety and Health Administration, "Industry Injury and Illness Data," 2019, https://www.bls.gov/iif.

10. Kerstin Aumann and Ellen Galinsky, *The State of Health in the American Workforce: Does Having an Effective Workplace Matter?* (New York: Families and Work Institute, 2009).

11. Misty M. Johanson, Hyewon Youn, and Robert H. Woods, "A Study of Stress Levels Among Hotel General Managers–A Comparison Between 1998 and 2008," *Journal of Human Resources in Hospitality & Tourism* 10, no. 1 (2010): 32–44.

12. George Fink, *Stress Consequences: Mental, Neuropsychological and Socioeconomic* (San Diego, Calif.: Academic Press, 2010).

13. Ian Buick and Mahesh Thomas, "Why Do Middle Managers in Hotels Burn Out?" *International Journal of Contemporary Hospitality Management* 13, no. 6 (2001): 304–309.

14. Margaret Tiyce, Nerilee Hing, Grant Cairncross, and Helen Breen, "Employee Stress and Stressors in Gambling and Hospitality Workplaces," *Journal of Human Resources in Hospitality & Tourism* 12 (2013): 126–154.

15. American Psychological Association, "2021 Stress in America," (2015). www.apa.org/news/press/releases/stress.

16. George Fink, *Stress Consequences: Mental, Neuropsychological and Socioeconomic* (San Diego, Calif.: Academic Press, 2010).

17. Ian Buick and Mahesh Thomas, "Why Do Middle Managers in Hotels Burn Out?" *International Journal of Contemporary Hospitality Management* 13, no. 6 (2001): 304–309; Joan M. Lang, "Foodservice Industry: Career Burnout," *Restaurant Business* 90, no. 4 (1991): 131–148.

18. Okumus Bendegul, Suja Chaulagain, and Ibrahim Giritioglu, "Examining the Impacts of Job Stress and Job Satisfaction on Hotel Employees' Eating Behavior," *Journal of Hospitality Marketing & Management* 28, no. 5 (2019): 558–575.

19. National Institute on Drug Abuse, "Costs of Substance Abuse," archives.drugabuse.gov/trends-statistics/costs-substance-abuse.

20. Centers for Disease Control and Prevention, "Excessive Drinking Is Draining the U.S. Economy," last modified December 2019, www.cdc.gov/features/costsofdrinking.

21. Roberto Ceniceros, "Most Health Plans Poor at Addressing Alcohol Problems, Researcher Claims," *Business Insurance* 39, no. 33 (2005): 4–6.

22. Tom Anderson, "Employers Should Promote EAPs to Maximize ROI," *Employee Benefit News*, 1 June 2005.

23. George E. Hargrave, Deirdre Hiatt, Rachael Alexander, and Ian A. Shaffer, "EAP Treatment Impact on Preabsenteeism and Absenteeism: Implications for Return on Investment," *Journal of Workplace Behavioral Health* 23, no. 3 (2008): 283–293.

24. Al Lewis and Vik Khanna, "Corporate Wellness Programs Lose Money." *Harvard Business Review*, October 15, 2015, https://hbr.org/2015/10/corporate-wellness-programs-lose-money.

25. RAND Corporation, "Do Workplace Wellness Programs Save Employers Money?" RB-9744-DOL (2014). http://www.rand.org.

26. Amanda Schiavo, "Mental Health: Starbucks' Employee Assistance Program Gets a Double Shot with Enhanced Mental Health Benefits," *Employee Benefit News* 33, no. 6 (November 1, 2019): 11.

27. "Medical Error: The Third Leading Cause of Death in the U.S." *BMJ* 353, no. 2139 (May 3, 2016), https://doi.org/10.1136/bmj.i2139.

28. John T. James, "A New, Evidence-Based Estimate of Patient Harms Associated with Hospital Care," *Journal of Patient Safety* 9, no. 3 (September 2013): 122–128.

29. Tom Emerick and Al Lewis, *Cracking Health Costs: How to Cut Your Company's Costs and Provide Employees Better Care* (Hoboken, New Jersey: John Wiley & Sons, 2013).

30. Steve Slebold, "New Gallup Poll Shows 70 Percent of Americans Are Disengaged From Their Jobs," *Huffington Post* (June 19, 2013). www.huffpost.com/entry.

31. Alexander Kjerulf, "5 Ways Hating Your Job Can Ruin Your Health (According to Science)," March 26, 2014, www.huffpost.com/entry/happiness-tips_b_5001073.

32. Amir Shani and Abraham Pizam, "Work-Related Depression among Hotel Employees," *Cornell Hospitality Quarterly* 50, no. 4 (2009): 446–459.

33. Tingting Christina Zhang, Edwin Torres, and Melissa Farboudi Jahromi, "Well on the Way: An Exploratory Study on Occupational Health in Hospitality," *International Journal of Hospitality Management* 87 (May 2020): Article 102382.

34. Laura Petrecca, "Cost-Conscious Companies Re-Evaluate Wellness Programs," *USA Today*, June 19, 2009.

35. Centers of Disease Control and Prevention, "Current Cigarette Smoking Among Adults in the United States," last modified 2020. www.cdc.gov/tobacco.

36. Workplace Fairness, "Smoking and the Workplace," last modified 2019, www.workplacefairness.org.

37. Wendy Wang, "The Share of Never-Married Americans Has Reached a New High," September 9, 2020, www.ifstudies.org.

38. Emma Gray, "A Record Percentage Of Women Don't Have Kids. Here's Why That Makes Sense." *Huffington Post*, April 9, 2015, www.huffpost.com/entry/childless-more-women-are-not-having-kids-says-census_n_7032258.

39. Marija Kovachevska, "30 Home-Invading Work-Life Balance Statistics for 2020," *Health Careers*, March 30, 2020, https://healthcareers.co/work-life-balance-statistics.

40. M. Deery and L. Jago, "Revisiting Talent Management, Work-Life Balance and Retention Strategies," *International Journal of Contemporary Hospitality Management* 27, no. 3 (2015): 453–472.

41. U.S. Bureau of Labor Statistics, "Census of Fatal Occupational Injuries Summary," last modified December 16, 2020, www.bls.gov/news.release/cfoi.nr0.htm.

42. U.S. Occupational Safety and Health Administration, "Protecting Workers: Guidance on Mitigating and Preventing the Spread of COVID-19 in the Workplace," last modified January 29, 2021, https://www.osha.gov/coronavirus/safework.

11

LABOR UNIONS

Chapter 11 Outline

Learning Objectives

1. Describe the role of labor unions in the hospitality industry and their effects on hospitality operations. (pp. 276–278)

2. Explain why employees join unions and why union membership has declined in the United States for over 50 years. (pp. 276–277)

3. Describe the rights of employees under U.S. labor laws. (pp. 278–283)

4. Identify employer actions that violate U.S. labor laws. (pp. 278–287)

5. Outline the sequence of events in organizing and certifying a union. (pp. 283–287)

6. Describe how unions are adapting to industry and economic changes. (pp. 287–288)

KEY TERMS

Wagner Act of 1935

National Labor Relations Board (NLRB)

Unfair labor practice

Taft-Hartley Act

Security agreement

Right-to-work law

Landrum-Griffin Act of 1959

Craft union

Industrial union

Union steward

Bargaining unit

Authorization card

Voluntary recognition

Organizing drive

Card check

Bargaining order

Decertification

A labor union represents workers in all aspects of their relationship with their employer. The union's agents bargain directly with the employer not just about compensation and benefits, but about subjects like job duties, work rules, and job security. Usually, the negotiations produce a legally enforceable contract lasting two to five years. During that period, the contract, not the management, dictates the terms and conditions of the workplace. Managers are required to comply with it. In other cases, negotiations break down, resulting in a strike.

This chapter addresses the rights of employees to support and join unions, the reasons they may choose to do so, and the potential outcomes in the workplace if they do. Chapter 12 examines labor contracts, labor strikes, and best practices for successfully managing in a union workplace.

Currently, labor unions represent less than 5 percent of all workers in the U.S. hospitality industry. Yet, they continue to play a significant role in the work of many hospitality managers. In a few major cities, such as New York, Chicago, San Francisco, and Las Vegas, unions represent a much higher portion of the hospitality workforce and have significant economic and political influence.[1] And, even where union membership has declined sharply, many hospitality businesses have at least some employees who are represented by unions. These unions can affect the business in many ways beyond just representing workers. Even companies that presently have no unions may experience new organizing efforts and are required to respect workers' legal rights. Most hospitality workers never join unions, but most hospitality managers, at some time in their careers, will need to understand them.

11.1 UNIONS IN HOSPITALITY

Union membership in the United States peaked in 1954, about 20 years after the right to unionize was first protected by the Wagner Act (described below).[2] At that time, 35.8 percent of non-agricultural workers belonged to unions. Since then, the percentage of the total workforce belonging to unions has steadily declined. By 2020,

the percentage of unionized workers in all U.S. industries was just 10.8 percent.[3] Hawaii and New York have the highest percentages (also called *union density*), while South Carolina and North Carolina have the lowest. These numbers, however, are somewhat deceiving because they include government employees, who are represented by unions at a far higher rate (34.8 percent) than in private businesses (6.3 percent). The United States ranks among the lowest countries in terms of union density. Table 11.1 displays the most current numbers for countries with the highest union membership rates. Most of them, however, have declined recently as well.

Exhibit 11.1 shows union membership in the United States from 1950 to 2020.

Table 11.1	Union Density in the Top 20 Countries
1. Denmark	66.5
2. Sweden	64.9
3. Finland	60.3
4. Belgium	50.3
5. Norway	49.2
6. China	44.9
7. Egypt	43.2
8. Italy	34.4
9. Russian Federation	39.5
10. Austria	26.3
11. Canada	25.9
12. Israel	25.0
13. Ireland	24.1
14. United Kingdom	23.4
15. Greece	20.2
16. Germany	16.5
17. Netherlands	16.4
18. Switzerland	14.9
19. Australia	13.7
20. Spain	13.6

Source: Organization for Economic Co-operation and Development, "Trade union density," 2018. www.stats.oecd.org.

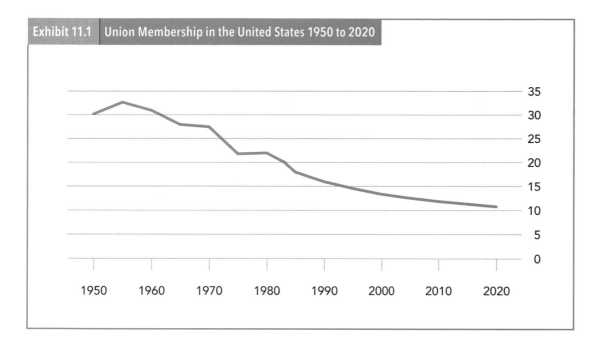

Exhibit 11.1 | Union Membership in the United States 1950 to 2020

1950	1960	1970	1980	1990	2000	2010	2020

The percentage of workers who belong to unions has declined in the United States for several reasons. One is the decline in manufacturing jobs, which are more commonly unionized than service jobs. Another significant factor has been the enactment of numerous state and federal laws that protect employee rights (see Chapter 13). Laws regulating workplace health and safety, wages, equal employment opportunity, and employee benefits have diminished the need for union protection because they mandate the very workplace practices that were once achieved only through collective bargaining and strikes.

White collar workers have offset some of the losses associated with manufacturing-based union membership. Government employees have gained the right to organize and to bargain collectively more recently, and the percentage of government employees belonging to unions has grown greatly. Increased unionization among teachers has also made a significant contribution to the growth of some unions.

The experience of hotel and restaurant unions has mirrored that of other service industries. The labor union representing the most hospitality workers is the Hotel Employees and Restaurant Employees (HERE) International Union, which merged with a textiles union in 2004 to create UNITE HERE. The HERE began in the 1860s as local affiliations of bartenders, cooks, and waiters in Chicago, New York, and San Francisco.[5] It peaked in membership around 1970, with just over half a million members, but by 2004 had dropped to half that. UNITE HERE currently represents about 300,000 workers throughout North America.[4] Table 11.2 lists the primary unions representing hospitality workers in the United States.

A principal obstacle to effectively unionizing large segments of the hospitality industry is that hotel and restaurant workers are just not easy to organize. They tend to move frequently from job to job, so they are not as interested in job security issues and long-term benefits compared to employees who plan to remain with the same employer for many years.[5] Smaller workplaces, including most foodservice operations, do not have enough workers to make organizing a priority for an established union. Unions thrive in markets where large numbers of hospitality workers are concentrated in a small area, like New York City and Las Vegas. Another reason that unions historically have been unsuccessful at organizing hotel and restaurant workers is that most workers have been women and people of color, who were less likely to join unions. Reversing that trend has been the key to UNITE HERE's recent growth. The largest local union affiliated with UNITE HERE, the Culinary Workers Union Local 226 in Las Vegas, reports that 55 percent of its members are women and over 80 percent are immigrants and people of color.[6]

Table 11.2 Unions Representing Hospitality Workers

Hospitality Industry Unions	Typical Jobs Represented
UNITE HERE	Food servers, cooks, bartenders, housekeepers
International Brotherhood of Teamsters	Valet drivers, warehouse workers
International Union of Operating Engineers	Facilities and maintenance workers
United Auto Workers	Casino dealers
International Alliance of Theatrical Stage Employees	Stagehands, entertainment technicians

Labor unions have found other creative ways to grow. Using members' pension funds, unions in Philadelphia and elsewhere began to invest in the 1990s in new hotels and renovations. For example, at least $40 million was invested in an American multinational hospitality company's business "resort" location in Philadelphia. Such investments have a direct correlation to union members' jobs because as investors, unions increase their say in how the properties are managed.[7] The AFL-CIO also finances hotels. With about $1 billion in union pension fund assets, the AFL-CIO allocates a portion of its annual investments to hotel properties. The money comes with a hitch: The hotels must use union construction workers during construction and must allow unions easy access to organize the hotel's new employees. Some also commit to recognize the union if a majority of employees sign union cards, so no election would be necessary. Projects have included hotels from several popular hospitality companies in Philadelphia, San Francisco, Jacksonville, Florida, and Champaign, Illinois.[8] In 2018, a council of unions partnered with an American multinational hotel, resort, and timeshare company to launch a new stylish and sociable hotel brand.[9]

Knowledge Check

1. How has the percentage of workers represented by unions changed over time?

2. Which unions represent the most hospitality workers?

3. What are three advantages of being in a union in the hospitality industry?

11.2 LEGISLATION AFFECTING LABOR RELATIONS

Much of the U.S. legislation regulating unions resulted from the Great Depression. Before then, Congress had passed the Railway Labor Act in 1926 in response to several disruptive and violent railroad worker strikes. This act minimized the impact of railway labor disputes on the economy by providing workers the right to unionize and creating a mediation and arbitration system to help settle labor disputes.

The success of the Railway Labor Act in reducing railroad strikes led Congress to address ongoing labor disputes in other industries, primarily steel and coal mining. The Norris-LaGuardia Act (1932), a part of President Franklin D. Roosevelt's New Deal, limited the use of court injunctions to break strikes. Before this act, employers regularly used federal court orders to prevent workers from striking and used the U.S. National Guard to enforce them. Under the Norris-LaGuardia Act, employers can secure injunctions only when they can prove that a strike will cause irreparable damage, violence, or harm to innocent parties. Even then, injunctions are allowed for only five days.

Although the Railway Labor Act and the Norris-LaGuardia Act showed that the government could establish effective legislation regulating labor relations, they did not prevent employers from using tactics designed to break unions or punish employees who joined unions. Tactics included threatening union supporters, firing employees who tried to organize, and refusing to meet with union representatives. The scarcity of good jobs during the economic recovery left workers with little legal protection from employer abuse.[10]

Wagner Act of 1935

The first real effort to protect workers who unionize came with the passage of the **Wagner Act of 1935**, referred to now as the National Labor Relations Act (NLRA). The Wagner Act gave employees the legally protected rights to organize, strike, and bargain together through an elected representative. It likewise protects an employee's right to refrain from union activity. The major provisions of the Wagner Act continue to play a very significant role in union–management relations. It is the law that requires employers to bargain in good faith with union agents and to abide by the contracts they reach.

It is important to note that the term "employee" under this law excludes supervisors and managers. Workers with supervisory authority over other workers do not have rights to organize and join unions.

The Wagner Act also created the **National Labor Relations Board (NLRB)** and empowered it to enforce the law and regulate the process of union organizing. The NLRB has exclusive jurisdiction over these activities, meaning the states have no authority to pass their own laws regulating unions. Members of the NLRB are appointed by the President and confirmed by the Senate for six-year terms.

A violation of the NLRA is called an **unfair labor practice**. Examples include:

- Interfering with or coercing employees to discourage them from forming or joining unions. Employers may not threaten employees or promise them additional benefits for the purpose of influencing their decision to unionize.

- Attempting to dominate, support, or influence the operation of unions. Before the Wagner Act, employers sometimes entered into so-called "sweetheart" arrangements with union leaders by bribing them to force their membership to accept terms the company wanted in contracts.

- Discriminating against employees for exercising their rights under the law. Violations include not just discharge but also unfavorable job assignments and disciplinary warnings.

- Retaliating against employees who file unfair labor practice charges with the NLRB or participate in NLRB proceedings.

- Refusing to bargain in good faith with the union selected by the employees.

Exhibit 11.2 outlines the National Labor Relations Board Administrative process.

Taft-Hartley Act of 1947

In 1947, the Wagner Act was amended by the **Taft-Hartley Act**. The Wagner Act addressed only employee rights and employer unfair practices. The Taft-Hartley Act attempted to balance the relative power of unions and employers by placing similar requirements on unions. Provisions of this act:

- Prohibit closed shops, which meant that unions and employers could not require union membership as a precondition of employment. However, unions and employers *can* agree to require employees to join the union within 30 days after being hired. Such a contract provision is known as a **security agreement** and such workplaces are known as *union shops*.

- Establish the rights of states to enact **right-to-work laws**. These laws ban union shops. This does not mean unions are forbidden in these states or that employees have the right to opt out of union representation by an elected union. The laws simply provide employees the right to decide for themselves whether to join a union (i.e., they are not required to do so to keep their jobs).

- Prohibit unions from conducting *secondary boycotts*, which are directed by a union against an employer with whom the union has no dispute. The objective of a secondary boycott is to pressure the neutral employer to discontinue business with another employer with whom the union has a dispute.

- Establish unfair labor practices of unions, which include threatening or coercing

Exhibit 11.2 The National Labor Relations Board Administrative Process

Please Review the Following Important Information Before Filling Out a Charge Form!

- Please call an information officer in the regional office nearest you for assistance in filing a charge. The information officer will be happy to answer your questions about the charge form or to draft the charge on your behalf. Seeking assistance from an information officer may help you to avoid having the processing of your charge delayed or your charge dismissed because of mistakes made in completing the form.

- Please be advised that not every workplace action that you may view as unfair constitutes an unfair labor practice within the jurisdiction of the National Labor Relations Act (NLRA). Please select the "Help Desk" button for more information on matters covered by the NLRA.

- The section of the charge form called, "Basis of Charge," seeks only a brief description of the alleged unfair labor practice. You should **NOT** include a detailed recounting of the evidence in support of the charge or a list of the names and telephone numbers of witnesses.

- After completing the charge form, be sure to sign and date the charge and mail or deliver the completed form to the appropriate regional office.

- A charge should be filed with the regional office that has jurisdiction over the geographic area of the United States where the unfair labor practice occurred. For example, an unfair labor practice charge alleging that an employer unlawfully discharged an employee would usually be filed with the regional office having jurisdiction over the worksite where the employee was employed prior to his/her discharge. An information officer will be pleased to assist you in locating the appropriate regional office in which to file your charge.

- The NLRB's Rules and Regulations state that it is the responsibility of the individual, employer, or union filing a charge to timely and properly serve a copy of the charge on the person, employer, or union against whom such charge is made.

- By statute, only charges filed and served within *six (6) months* of the date of the event or conduct, which is the subject of that charge, will be processed by the NLRB.

---

employees to join a union, discriminating against non-members, and refusing to bargain in good faith with the employer.

- Prohibit so-called *hot cargo agreements*, in which an employer agrees to purchase supplies only from unionized employers.

- Protect the rights of employees to cross picket lines and continue working during a strike.

- Establish the Federal Mediation and Conciliation Service (FMCS), a government agency to help unions and management reach agreements and resolve labor disputes before they result in strikes.

- Protect the right of management to oppose union organization and discuss advantages and disadvantages of unions with employees (as long as management does not commit an unfair labor practice).

Exhibit 11.3 is the form for filing a complaint, called a *charge*, of an unfair labor practice against an employer. When the NLRB receives a charge, a regional officer investigates and issues a recommendation to dismiss the charge or to proceed with a formal complaint. A formal complaint is forwarded to the office of the General Counsel, who acts as the prosecutor in the proceedings. The case is heard and decided by an administrative law judge in a formal trial. There is no jury. The judge issues a decision, which can be appealed by either party to the five-member NLRB. Further appeals to the U.S. Court of Appeals and U.S. Supreme Court are possible but very rare.

As of April 2021, 27 states have enacted right-to-work laws:

Alabama	Kentucky	South Carolina
Arizona	Louisiana	South Dakota
Arkansas	Michigan	Tennessee
Florida	Mississippi	Texas
Georgia	Nebraska	Utah
Idaho	Nevada	Virginia
Indiana	North Carolina	West Virginia
Iowa	North Dakota	Wisconsin
Kansas	Oklahoma	Wyoming

Source: National Conference of State Legislatures, "Right-to-Work Resources," www.ncsl.org.

The penalties for committing an unfair labor practice are not severe. The employer may be required to post an official notice to employees in the workplace, but there are no financial penalties. However, when the employer has discharged an employee in violation of the law, the employer may be required to reinstate the worker and reimburse them for the wages they would have earned in the meantime.

Landrum-Griffin Act of 1959

Congressional investigations in the 1950s uncovered abuses of power, unethical conduct, and corrupt practices in some unions. As a result of these findings, Congress enacted the **Landrum-Griffin Act of 1959**, which was designed to regulate internal union operations and to require them to report some of their activities. This act is also referred to as the Labor-Management Reporting and Disclosure Act. The provisions also regulate the activities of outside consultants hired by management to defeat unions in elections or to decertify existing unions. Under this act, such consultants are required to register and to submit reports of their activities to the U.S. Department of Labor.

The Landrum-Griffin Act was also designed to eliminate the influence of corrupt union leaders. Provisions of this act:

- Provide a "Bill of Rights" for union members that gives members the right to nominate candidates, vote, attend meetings, participate in union business, sue unions in civil court if employee rights are abridged, and obtain written copies of the collective bargaining agreements that apply to them.

- Require secret ballot union elections once every five years for national and international officers.

- Require unions to submit their bylaws and constitutions to the U.S. Department of Labor, where they are available to the public.

- Regulate financial transactions involving union funds and require unions to file annual financial reports.

Although the Landrum-Griffin Act eliminated much of the racketeering that was prevalent in unions at the time, some argue that it did not curtail the influence of organized crime. For instance, in 1985, the President's

Exhibit 11.3   Sample NLRB Form: Charge Against Employer

FORM EXEMPT UNDER 44 U.S.C 3512

INTERNET
FORM NLRB-501
(2-08)

UNITED STATES OF AMERICA
NATIONAL LABOR RELATIONS BOARD
CHARGE AGAINST EMPLOYER

DO NOT WRITE IN THIS SPACE

Case	Date Filed

INSTRUCTIONS:
File an original with NLRB Regional Director for the region in which the alleged unfair labor practice occurred or is occurring.

1. EMPLOYER AGAINST WHOM CHARGE IS BROUGHT

a. Name of Employer

b. Tel. No.

c. Cell No.

f. Fax No.

d. Address (Street, city, state, and ZIP code)

e. Employer Representative

g. e-Mail

h. Number of workers employed

i. Type of Establishment (factory, mine, wholesaler, etc.)

j. Identify principal product or service

k. The above-named employer has engaged in and is engaging in unfair labor practices within the meaning of section 8(a), subsections (1) and (list

   subsections)   of the National Labor Relations Act, and these unfair labor

   practices are practices affecting commerce within the meaning of the Act, or these unfair labor practices are unfair practices affecting commerce
   within the meaning of the Act and the Postal Reorganization Act.

2. Basis of the Charge (set forth a clear and concise statement of the facts constituting the alleged unfair labor practices)

3. Full name of party filing charge (if labor organization, give full name, including local name and number)

4a. Address (Street and number, city, state, and ZIP code)

4b. Tel. No.

4c. Cell No.

4d. Fax No.

4e. e-Mail

5. Full name of national or international labor organization of which it is an affiliate or constituent unit (to be filled in when charge is filed by a labor
organization)

6. DECLARATION
I declare that I have read the above charge and that the statements are true to the best of my knowledge and belief.

By _____

(signature of representative or person making charge)   (Print/type name and title or office, if any)

Tel. No.

Office, if any, Cell No.

Fax No.

e-Mail

Address _____   (date)

WILLFUL FALSE STATEMENTS ON THIS CHARGE CAN BE PUNISHED BY FINE AND IMPRISONMENT (U.S. CODE, TITLE 18, SECTION 1001)

PRIVACY ACT STATEMENT
Solicitation of the information on this form is authorized by the National Labor Relations Act (NLRA), 29 U.S.C. § 151 et seq. The principal use of the information is to assist the National Labor Relations Board (NLRB) in processing unfair labor practice and related proceedings or litigation. The routine uses for the information are fully set forth in the Federal Register, 71 Fed. Reg. 74942-43 (Dec. 13, 2006). The NLRB will further explain these uses upon request. Disclosure of this information to the NLRB is voluntary; however, failure to supply the information will cause the NLRB to decline to invoke its processes.

Source: National Labor Relations Board, Washington, D.C.

Commission on Organized Crime noted the substantial influence of organized crime in the Teamsters, Laborer's International, International Longshoremen's, and Hotel Employees and Restaurant Employees unions.[11] Criminal practices this commission found included the extraction of "insurance" payments against strikes from some companies and improper handling of union membership benefit funds.

The Landrum-Griffin Act also allowed for what has become known as the "financial core" membership in unions.

Knowledge Check

1. What are an employee's rights under U.S. labor laws?

2. Why did Congress pass laws to regulate unions?

3. What are some examples of illegal union practices?

11.3 UNION STRUCTURES AND ORGANIZATION

There are two principal types of unions: craft unions and industrial unions. **Craft unions** represent workers who essentially have the same skills or perform the same tasks. A union consisting solely of plumbers or electricians is a craft union. **Industrial unions** represent various workers in given industries. A union consisting of auto workers, steelworkers, or hotel and restaurant employees is an industrial union.

Typically, unions are organized much like management. Responsibilities of the **union stewards** closely resemble those of front-line supervisors on the management side: They monitor the workplace and are the first to address conflicts and disputes. Responsibilities of union business agents or chief stewards resemble those of department managers. Local union presidents are comparable to general managers in stature, while officers of national or international unions are comparable to CEOs.

Unions differ from management by organizational structure and authority. Distinct relationships exist between local union chapters and national or international unions. Local unions are chartered either by national or international unions, which retain the authority to monitor activities of the local unions to ensure that national rules are followed. According to the Landrum-Griffin Act, national unions also have the right to impose trusteeships or replace management in local unions if national guidelines are not met. In return, the national or international unions provide grievance, arbitration, strike support, and political representation services to local unions.

Management sometimes mistakenly believes that employees join unions just

LEGAL ALERT!

Provisions of U.S. labor relations laws allow unions and employers to agree that employees will be required to join the union and pay dues and initiation fees within a reasonable period after joining the workforce. However, unions cannot require employees to participate in union activities or to pay for union activities other than representing them at the workplace. The 3rd U.S. Circuit Court of Appeals upheld this provision by ruling that union members can change their membership to "financial core" and return to work during a strike after notifying the union. Members who choose to cross picket lines are immune from union discipline.[12]

because they want more pay, but money is only one reason. In some cases, it is not a major reason at all. Employees join unions primarily because they believe unions will help them accomplish their goals. Economic security is one goal. Other goals are the assurance of safe and comfortable working conditions, respect, job security, fringe benefits, and control over their own work. Employees are also driven toward unions by poor dispute resolution and communications systems, layoffs, inconsistent policy enforcement, and unfair treatment by management. The theories of motivation explored in Chapter 8 apply equally well to union organizing.

Employees are more likely to want to join a union because they are dissatisfied with management—not because they are dissatisfied with pay. Employees expect fair treatment, communication of policies and procedures, and job security. When managers don't meet these expectations, employees often turn to unions. They often believe, or at least hope, that union representation will increase their control over the workplace and protect them from unfair and abusive managers. In a sense, employees who vote for a union in their workplace are voting against management as much as for the union.[13]

Organizing Drive

To represent employees in a workplace, a union must be certified as their legal representative, which can occur in three ways:

1. The NLRB can hold a secret ballot election to determine whether a majority of employees want the union.

2. The employer can voluntarily acknowledge that a majority of employees want the union and bypass the election.

3. The NLRB can, in rare cases, certify a union without an election.

Any of these will give rise to the employer's duty to bargain with the union.

Union organizers can obtain an NLRB election when they can prove that a minimum of 30 percent of employees in the bargaining unit want the union to represent them. The **bargaining unit** is the specific group of employees seeking union representation. It might be the workers in one or more departments or the entire business. Union organizers prove this percentage by gathering employee signatures on **authori-**

zation cards. Exhibit 11.4 is a sample union authorization card.

Although unions are required to obtain signatures for only 30 percent of employees to begin the election process, unions typically gather signatures from at least 65 percent of employees to make sure they have the support of more than half before the election takes place. Unions can stimulate employee interest in signing authorization cards by placing leaflets on cars, distributing leaflets outside work, making telephone calls, posting on social media, and organizing meetings. In some cases, unions mount media campaigns to win the public over to their cause and to persuade employees to sign authorization cards.

Union agents don't have a legal right to enter the workplace to communicate with workers. Current employees, however, do have the legal right to discuss the union among themselves when they are off duty. In many cases, the union recruits current employees to assist with communications and to collect authorization cards. Some unions use a practice called *salting*—sending union agents to seek jobs at non-union companies—specifically to gain the legal protection to organize workers inside the workplace.[14]

More recently, unions have turned to an alternative approach to organizing. If a union obtains signed authorization cards from a majority of employees, the company

---

Exhibit 11.4   Sample Union Authorization Card

I hereby authorize _____ *Union to bargain on my behalf in regard to the wages, hours, terms, and conditions of my employment, or to petition the NLRB for a secret ballot election to determine union representation.*

Name: _____

Department: _____   Job Title: _____

Address: _____

_____

Signature: _____

can voluntarily recognize the union without an election and begin to bargain with union agents. **Voluntary recognition** is never required by law no matter how many employees sign authorization cards, but the union and employees can legally strike, picket, boycott, or mount media campaigns to persuade the employer to bypass an election and begin bargaining.

Employers are also permitted—but never required—to agree in advance to allow the union access to workers and to recognize the union if a majority of employees sign cards within a given time. In some cases, the employer further agrees to remain silent or neutral during the **organizing drive**, which essentially guarantees its success.

UNITE HERE has successfully used this **card check**/neutrality procedure to organize hundreds of hospitality workplaces around the country.[15] The practice, however, has faced legal challenges, including a recent case by employees of an upscale, all-suite hotel in Seattle, who objected to the agreement and the hotel's subsequent voluntary recognition of UNITE HERE. The employees claim the practice violates the Wagner Act's prohibition of employers assisting or supporting unions.[16]

In rare cases, when evidence indicates that an employer's unfair labor practices dramatically changed the outcome of a union organizing election, the NLRB can install the union without a ballot. Under these circumstances, the NLRB issues a **bargaining order** that certifies the union as the legal representative of the employees. However, this can be done only when the union can prove that at some time before the unfair labor practices, it enjoyed the support of a majority of employees. This can be proven with authorization cards or union memberships.

Elections

When a union files a petition for an election, the NLRB conducts a secret ballot election at the workplace during regular work hours, usually within 45 days. The ballot simply asks whether the employee desires to be represented by the union. NLRB agents count the ballots immediately after the poll closes. If the union receives a majority of the votes cast, it is certified the winner, subject to some possible objections. Exhibit 11.5 shows a sample NLRB secret ballot.

When more than one union is on the ballot, employees must identify which union they prefer. A majority is required for one union to become the workers' legal representative. If no single union receives a majority of the votes, a runoff election is held between the two unions that received the most votes.

If a majority of the employees favor a specific union, the NLRB *certifies* the union as the legal representative of all the employees in the **bargaining unit**, not just the ones who voted for the union. In such a case, the employer is bound by law to bargain in good faith with the union to attempt to reach a contract that details the relationship between employer and employees. The collective bargaining process is described in more detail in Chapter 12.

Decertification

Employees can also decide to *decertify* a union. **Decertification** is just the opposite of certification; it occurs when the employees do *not* want to be represented by their union any longer. Between 1977 and 1989, 120 decertification elections occurred in hotels and 275 in restaurants. Most of these elections occurred at properties organized by HERE. Overall, unions lost the decertification votes in 70 percent of the hotel elections and 83 percent of the restaurant elections.[17] Decertifications occurred in other industries during this same time as well. However, in recent years, the decertification trend has stabilized. From 2010 to 2019, the number of petitions filed declined by nearly 50 percent, but unions continued to lose more than half of the decertification elections.[18]

Decertification elections are called in the same way as certification elections. At least 30 percent of represented employees must express an interest in decertifying the union. However, a decertification vote cannot be called for 12 months after the original certification or during the term of a labor contract. To call for a decertification vote, a petition must be filed with the NLRB by the workers—the employer is not permitted to initiate or influence the process. Exhibit 11.6 is a sample petition used to request a decertification election.

Exhibit 11.5 | Sample Secret Ballot

Source: National Labor Relations Board, Washington, D.C.

Employer Strategies

The Wagner Act prevents employers from interfering with union organizing campaigns by coercing or restraining employees; employees have the right to join unions free of the employer's interference. Any action by management to take away this right can be considered an unfair labor practice. Discharging union sympathizers, threatening to close operations, and offering extra benefits to employees who vote against unionization are all unfair practices, as is discriminating against employees in hiring or promotion decisions. Asking job applicants whether they would join or vote for a union is also an unfair labor practice.

The law, however, does not prevent employers from strongly opposing union organization both before and during an organizing drive. In fact, the employer's opposition has been found to significantly reduce the union's chance of winning an election.[19] Some have found that proactive and reactive measures are useful tools in avoiding unionization. Proactive measures are designed to eliminate the need and desire for unions. When employers establish fair pay policies, good working conditions, two-way communication, fair grievance procedures, and reliable job security, unions may have little more to offer employees. This is how union contracts can influence the wages and other conditions at area employers who do not have unions.[20]

However, not all companies implement such policies; some companies take reactive measures. They might hire labor attorneys who specialize in organization and election campaigning or consultants who specialize in training managers in effective resistance methods and persuading employees to vote against the union. Campaigns generated by outside consultants and attorneys typically emphasize the cost of union dues and the hardships that occur during strikes. They emphasize the rewards of current benefits and how employee–management relationships can change when a union takes over. Both proactive and reactive measures can accomplish desired results.

Exhibit 11.6 | **Sample NLRB Petition**

INTERNET
FORM NLRB-502
(2-08)

UNITED STATES GOVERNMENT
NATIONAL LABOR RELATIONS BOARD
PETITION

DO NOT WRITE IN THIS SPACE	
Case No.	Date Filed

INSTRUCTIONS: Submit an original of this Petition to the NLRB Regional Office in the Region in which the employer concerned is located.

The Petitioner alleges that the following circumstances exist and requests that the NLRB proceed under its proper authority pursuant to Section 9 of the NLRA.

1. PURPOSE OF THIS PETITION (if box RC, RM, or RD is checked and a charge under Section 8(b)(7) of the Act has been filed involving the Employer named herein, the statement following the description of the type of petition shall not be deemed made.) (Check One)

☐ RC-CERTIFICATION OF REPRESENTATIVE - A substantial number of employees wish to be represented for purposes of collective bargaining by Petitioner and Petitioner desires to be certified as representative of the employees.

☐ RM-REPRESENTATION (EMPLOYER PETITION) - One or more individuals or labor organizations have presented a claim to Petitioner to be recognized as the representative of employees of Petitioner.

☐ RD-DECERTIFICATION (REMOVAL OF REPRESENTATIVE) - A substantial number of employees assert that the certified or currently recognized bargaining representative is no longer their representative.

☐ UD-WITHDRAWAL OF UNION SHOP AUTHORITY (REMOVAL OF OBLIGATION TO PAY DUES) - Thirty percent (30%) or more of employees in a bargaining unit covered by an agreement between their employer and a labor organization desire that such authority be rescinded.

☐ UC-UNIT CLARIFICATION- A labor organization is currently recognized by Employer, but Petitioner seeks clarification of placement of certain employees: (Check one) ☐ In unit not previously certified. ☐ In unit previously certified in Case No. _____

☐ AC-AMENDMENT OF CERTIFICATION- Petitioner seeks amendment of certification issued in Case No. _____
Attach statement describing the specific amendment sought.

2. Name of Employer	Employer Representative to contact	Tel. No.
3. Address(es) of Establishment(s) involved (Street and number, city, State, ZIP code)		Fax No.
4a. Type of Establishment (Factory, mine, wholesaler, etc.)	4b. Identify principal product or service	Cell No. / e-Mail

5. Unit Involved (In UC petition, describe **present** bargaining unit and attach description of proposed clarification.)	6a. Number of Employees in Unit:
Included	Present
Excluded	Proposed (By UC/AC)
	6b. Is this petition supported by 30% or more of the employees in the unit?* ☐ Yes ☐ No *Not applicable in RM, UC, and AC

(If you have checked box RC in 1 above, check and complete EITHER item 7a or 7b, whichever is applicable)

7a. ☐ Request for recognition as Bargaining Representative was made on (Date) _____ and Employer declined recognition on or about (Date) _____ (If no reply received, so state).

7b. ☐ Petitioner is currently recognized as Bargaining Representative and desires certification under the Act.

8. Name of Recognized or Certified Bargaining Agent (If none, so state.)		Affiliation	
Address	Tel. No.	Date of Recognition or Certification	
	Cell No.	Fax No.	e-Mail

9. Expiration Date of Current Contract. If any (Month, Day, Year)	10. If you have checked box UD in 1 above, show here the date of execution of agreement granting union shop (Month, Day and Year)

11a. Is there now a strike or picketing at the Employer's establishment(s) Involved? Yes ☐ No ☐	11b. If so, approximately how many employees are participating?

11c. The Employer has been picketed by or on behalf of (Insert Name) _____ , a labor organization, of (Insert Address) _____ Since (Month, Day, Year) _____

12. Organizations or individuals other than Petitioner (and other than those named in items 8 and 11c), which have claimed recognition as representatives and other organizations and individuals known to have a representative interest in any employees in unit described in item 5 above. (If none, so state)

Name	Address	Tel. No.	Fax No.
		Cell No.	e-Mail

13. Full name of party filing petition (If labor organization, give full name, including local name and number)		
14a. Address (street and number, city, state, and ZIP code)	14b. Tel. No. EXT	14c. Fax No.
	14d. Cell No.	14e. e-Mail

15. Full name of national or international labor organization of which Petitioner is an affiliate or constituent (to be filled in when petition is filed by a labor organization)

I declare that I have read the above petition and that the statements are true to the best of my knowledge and belief.

Name (Print)	Signature	Title (if any)
Address (street and number, city, state, and ZIP code)	Tel. No.	Fax No.
	Cell No.	eMail

WILLFUL FALSE STATEMENTS ON THIS PETITION CAN BE PUNISHED BY FINE AND IMPRISONMENT (U.S. CODE, TITLE 18, SECTION 1001)
PRIVACY ACT STATEMENT

Solicitation of the information on this form is authorized by the National Labor Relations Act (NLRA), 29 U.S.C. § 151 et seq. The principal use of the information is to assist the National Labor Relations Board (NLRB) in processing unfair labor practice and related proceedings or litigation. The routine uses for the information are fully set forth in the Federal Register, 71 Fed. Reg. 74942-43 (Dec. 13, 2006). The NLRB will further explain these uses upon request. Disclosure of this information to the NLRB is voluntary; however, failure to supply the information will cause the NLRB to decline to invoke its processes.

Source: National Labor Relations Board, Washington, D.C.

Knowledge Check

1. What are authorization cards used for?

2. How do employees obtain a secret ballot to elect a union representative?

3. Why would employees decertify their union?

11.4 THE FUTURE OF UNIONS

It is difficult to say whether unions will remain viable or whether the decades-long downward trend will continue until it approaches zero. Evidence supports both alternatives. In 2020, 65 percent of Americans approved of labor unions, although a majority said that unions are harmful to the economy.[21] In contrast, over 70 percent of Americans favored unions when the Wagner Act was enacted. The percentage peaked at 75 percent in the 1950s.[22] Public support for unions dropped below 50 percent for the first time in the years following the Great Recession of 2008, but it has rebounded in tandem with national economic conditions.

It is not easy to reconcile the low rate of actual unionization with the much higher rates of public support. If more than half of Americans support union representation, why have so few of them actually achieved it? Some believe it is due to more aggressive employer opposition, while others point to the minimal penalties for unfair labor practices and to proactive employer measures to reduce the reasons for employees to desire a union.[23]

Unions, however, have succeeded in organizing more than eight million government employees in the United States since they were first permitted to do so in 1962. Union density among government workers is more than three times that of workers in private businesses. Unions today also focus on service industries and teachers to gain new members. The AFL-CIO has reported organizing victories in the fields of home health aides, tech industry workers, graduate student employees, and government workers.[24]

Union organizing efforts within the hospitality industry have also increased in recent years. In July 2010, for example, UNITE HERE held large protests against an American multinational hospitality company in 15 cities in the United States and Canada, among them Chicago, Los Angeles, Boston, and San Francisco. Also in July 2010, 400 workers rallied in downtown Pittsburgh to protest the lack of unions in the hospitality industry. In February 2010, UNITE HERE Local 11 held a hunger strike outside a famed entertainment, theme park, and hospitality company's hotel and spa resort in California to call attention to the fact that workers had been operating without a contract for more than two years. In 2019, UNITE HERE vowed to organize an additional 100,000 hospitality industry workers in the next five years.[25]

More recently, many unions have adopted a new strategy: to organize and mobilize workers without formally seeking certification to bargain collectively on their behalf or requiring them to join. This sort of "open source" unionism may lead to dramatic changes to both their organizing and their influence, but perhaps at the cost of formal membership.[26] Large national unions, for example, have provided much of the support for recent protests and efforts to increase wages in the quick service food industry. Unions are also making much greater use of social media to communicate with and recruit potential new members. In response to the COVID-19 pandemic, hospitality unions have taken a leading role in promoting job protection, paid leave during shut-downs, and worker safety as workplaces reopen.[27]

One cannot safely assume that unions will not grow in strength and numbers within the hospitality industry. For example, many of today's hospitality workers moved here legally from other countries in which unions were larger and more common, making them a prime target for union organizing efforts. The representation of women and people of color in UNITE HERE, for example, has grown more than the union's overall membership has declined.

There are some ongoing political efforts to revise the National Labor Relations Board activities in some significant ways, including financial penalties for unfair labor practices, mandatory recognition without an election based solely on petitions or authorization cards, and the nationwide abolishment of state right-to-work laws. The Protecting the Right to Organize Act passed the U.S. House in 2020 and was pending the Senate at publication.[28] The NLRB has issued procedures for mail-in voting during the COVID-19 pandemic, which may also improve unions' performance in elections.[29]

Unions are likely to remain a significant part of the hospitality industry, especially in highly concentrated markets. Their long-term survival, however, seems to depend on their ability to adapt to new workplace realities, new forms of communication and organization, and new ways to influence employment standards.

Knowledge Check

1. How does current public support for unions compare to previous times?

2. How would the Protecting the Right to Organize Act change U.S. labor laws?

3. What will determine the role of unions in the future?

IN THIS CHAPTER, YOU LEARNED:

- A labor union represents workers in all aspects of their relationship with their employer. The union's agents bargain directly with the employer not just about compensation and benefits, but about subjects like job duties, work rules, and job security.

- The labor union representing the most hospitality workers is the Hotel Employees and Restaurant Employees (HERE) International Union, which merged with a textiles union in 2004 to create UNITE HERE.

- The percentage of workers who belong to unions has declined in the United States for several reasons. One is the decline in manufacturing jobs, which are more commonly unionized than service jobs. Another significant factor has been the enactment of numerous state and federal laws that protect employee rights.

- Employees are allowed to elect a union and to decertify it.

- To represent employees in a workplace, a union must be certified as their legal representative, which can occur in three ways: (1) the NLRB can hold a secret ballot election to determine whether a majority of employees want the union; (2) the employer can voluntarily acknowledge that a majority of employees want the union and bypass the election; or (3) the NLRB can, in rare cases, certify a union without an election.

- The Wagner Act prevents employers from interfering with union organizing campaigns by coercing or restraining employees; employees have the right to join unions free of the employer's interference. Any action by management to take away this right can be considered an unfair labor practice.

- Union organizing efforts within the hospitality industry have increased in recent years. More recently, many unions have adopted a new strategy: to organize and mobilize workers without formally seeking certification to bargain collectively on their behalf or requiring them to join. This sort of "open source" unionism may lead to dramatic changes to both their organizing and their influence, but perhaps at the cost of formal membership.

KEY TERMS

authorization card—A document signed by an employee authorizing a union to seek an election and bargain collectively with the employer on their behalf.

bargaining order—An order issued by the National Labor Relations Board that certifies a union to represent employees without an election.

bargaining unit—The specific group of employees represented by or seeking representation by a union.

card check—An employer's agreement to recognize a union without an election if a majority of employees sign authorization cards.

craft union—A union that represents workers of multiple employers who have essentially the same skills or who perform the same tasks.

decertification—The process that employees can use when they no longer want to be represented by a specific union.

industrial union—A union that represents workers in a specific industry.

Landrum-Griffin Act of 1959—Legislation that outlined legal responsibilities of unions and forced unions to follow specific election procedures and ethical standards, sometimes called the "Bill of Rights" for union members.

National Labor Relations Board (NLRB)—The independent federal agency created by the Wagner Act of 1935 to administer and enforce federal labor laws.

organizing drive—A period in which union organizers collect signatures of employees on authorization cards in an attempt to obtain a union election or voluntary recognition.

right-to-work law—Legislation passed by some states that allows each employee of a unionized company to choose to join the union or not and prohibits security agreements.

security agreement—A policy in a union contract with management that requires employees to join the union.

Taft-Hartley Act—Legislation that banned closed shops, outlined unfair labor practices for unions, and empowered states to choose to enact right-to-work laws. This amended the Wagner Act of 1935.

unfair labor practice—An action specifically prohibited by the National Labor Relations Act.

union steward—A company employee who also acts on behalf of a union.

voluntary recognition—An agreement by an employer to recognize and bargain with a union without an election.

Wagner Act of 1935—Legislation that outlined the responsibilities of the management to bargain collectively with unions, and that defined unfair labor practices for management—also called the National Labor Relations Act.

REVIEW QUESTIONS

1. What are the main rights of employees under U.S. labor laws?

2. What are unfair labor practices by employers?

3. Why has the percentage of employees represented by unions declined in the past 60 years?

4. What percentage of the employees in a company must sign authorization cards before a union certification election can be called?

5. What are the steps in the process of organizing a union in a workplace?

6. What are the steps in the NLRB's processing of an unfair labor practice charge?

7. How do employers without unions guard against union organizing?

Unionization Confrontation

You heard that some employees in your hotel have been trying to persuade others to join them in promoting a union. You confirm this when you overhear three employees trying to talk others into signing authorization cards for a union election during a company-sponsored softball game.

The next morning at work, you call the three employees you heard talking about the union into your office. You ask them about the union directly. Two of the employees admit that they were trying to talk others into joining a union; the third denies involvement. To eliminate this union "threat," you reduce all three employees to part-time jobs and start scheduling them for weekends only. You also call an all-employee meeting in which you openly discuss what you have heard. You tell employees that if they refrain from signing authorization cards, you will grant them an extra holiday per year. You also promise to increase their health insurance coverage. Two weeks later, you receive a notice from the National Labor Relations Board that an unfair labor practice charge has been filed against you.

DISCUSSION QUESTIONS

1. Did you commit any unfair labor practices?
2. What might be the consequences if you did?
3. What can you legally do proactively to convince the employees not to unionize?

ENDNOTES

1. Influence Watch, "Labor Unions: Unite Here," https://www.influencewatch.org/labor-union/unite-here/.

2. Drew Desilver, "10 Facts About American Workers," August 29, 2019, https://www.pewresearch.org/fact-tank/2019/08/29/facts-about-american-workers/.

3. U.S. Bureau of Labor Statistics, "Union Members Summary," January 22, 2021, https://www.bls.gov/news.release/union2.nr0.htm.

4. "Who We Are," *UNITE HERE*, accessed April 12, 2021, https://unitehere.org/who-we-are/.

5. David Jordhus-Lier and Anders Underthun, *A Hospitable World? Organizing Work and Workers in Hotels and Tourist Resorts* (London: Routledge, 2015); Suzanne K. Murrmann and Kent F. Murrmann, "Union Membership Trends and Organizing Activities in the Hotel and Restaurant Industries," *Hospitality Research Journal* 14 (1991): 491–504.

6. Culinary Workers Union Local 226, "Our Union," accessed April 12, 2021, https://www.culinaryunion226.org/union.

7. "Unions Smart to Invest in Hotel Projects," *Philadelphia Business Journal,* 3 (1999): 50.

8. Kathy Seal, "Union Pension Funds Fill Financing Void for Hotel Projects," *Hotel & Motel Management,* 6 March (2000): 15-16.

9. Northwest Labor Press, "Introducing the Moxy: Union pension funds will finance a new downtown Portland hotel." September 5, 2018, accessed April 12, 2021. https://nwlaborpress.org/2018/09/introducing-the-moxy-union-pension-funds-will-finance-a-new-downtown-portland-hotel/.

10. Nelson Lichtenstein, *State of the Union: A Century of American Labor* (Princeton: Princeton University Press, 2013).

11. "Trade Unions: The Usual Suspects," *The Economist,* 4 May (1985): 29.

12. Ann C. Hodges, "Imagining US labor relations without union security," *Employee Responsibilities and Rights Journal* 28, no. 2 (June 2016): 135-145; William E. Lissy, "Election of 'Financial Core' Union Membership," *Supervision* 51 (September 1990): 22–23.

13. Steven Greenhouse, *Beaten Down, Worked Up: The Past, Present, and Future of American Labor* (New York: Anchor Books, 2019).

14. Constance B. DiCesare, "Salting," *Monthly Labor Review* 119 (April 1996): 29–30.

15. Rafael Gely and Timothy D. Chandler, "Card Check Recognition: New House Rules for Union Organizing?" *Fordham Urban Law Journal* 35, no. 2 (2008): 247–276.

16. National Right to Work Legal Defense Foundation, "NLRB moves to prosecute Embassy Suites and UNITE HERE union for violating worker rights with coercive 'card check' unionization." July 2, 2020, https://www.nrtw.org/news/nlrb-prosecutes-unite-here-seattle-07022020/.

17. Murrmann and Murrmann: 500.

18. National Labor Relations Board, "NLRB Case Activity Reports: Decertification Petitions." 2019. https://www.nlrb.gov/reports/nlrb-case-activity-reports/representation-cases/intake/decertification-petitions-rd.

19. Christopher M. Lowery, N. A. Beadles II, and William J. Miller, "Antecedents of union support in the United States Hospitality industry," *Journal of Human Resources in Hospitality & Tourism*, 18(3, Jul–Sep2019): 275–298.

20. Lynn Rhinehart and Celine McNicholas, "Collective bargaining beyond the worksite: How workers and their unions build power and set standards for their industries," *Economic

Policy Institute, May 4, 2020. https://www.epi.org/publication/collective-bargaining-beyond-the-worksite-how-workers-and-their-unions-build-power-and-set-standards-for-their-industries/.

21. Megan Brenan, "At 65%, approval of labor unions in U.S. remains high," September 3, 2020. https://news.gallup.com/poll/318980/approval-labor-unions-remains-high.aspx; Hannah Fingerhut, "More Americans view long-term decline in union membership negatively than positively," June 5, 2018, https://www.pewresearch.org/fact-tank/2018/06/05/more-americans-view-long-term-decline-in-union-membership-negatively-than-positively/.

22. Lydia Saad, "Labor Unions See Sharp Slide in U.S. Public Support," September 3, 2009, https://news.gallup.com/poll/122744/labor-unions-sharp-slide-public-support.aspx.

23. Steven Greenhouse, supra.

24. AFL-CIO, "Recent organizing wins," accessed March 25, 2021, www.aflcio.org/formaunion.

25. Daily Labor Report, "Organize 100,000 new workers in 5 years? UNITE HERE says it will," July 1, 2019, https://news.bloomberglaw.com/daily-labor-report/organize-100-000-new-workers-in-5-years-unite-here-says-it-will.

26. Alex Bryson, Richard Freeman, Rafael Gomez, and Paul Willman, "The twin track model of employee voice: An Anglo-American perspective on union decline and the rise of alternative forms of voice." In: Peter Holland, Julian Teicher, and Jimmy Donaghey (Eds.) *Employee Voice at Work: Work, Organization, and Employment.* (Singapore: Springer, 2019).

27. Paul Solmon, "Is this Las Vegas hospitality workers union the future of American labor?," *PBS NewsHour*, (January 9, 2020). https://www.pbs.org/newshour/show/is-this-las-vegas-hospitality-workers-union-the-future-of-american-labor.

28. Protecting the Right to Organize Act of 2019, HR 2474 (116th Congress), www.congress.gov/bill.

29. National Labor Relations Board, "NLRB establishes standards for mail-and manual-ballot representation elections during the COVID-19 pandemic," November 9, 2020, https://www.nlrb.gov/news-outreach/news-story/nlrb-establishes-standards-for-mail-and-manual-ballot-representation.

12

NEGOTIATION AND COLLECTIVE BARGAINING

Chapter 12 Outline

Learning Objectives

1.   Explain what it means to bargain in good faith. (pp. 296–297)

2.   Describe how managers should prepare for collective bargaining. (pp. 298–300)

3.   Explain the roles of mediation and arbitration in collective bargaining. (pp. 300–301)

4.   Identify the types of labor strikes. (pp. 301–303)

5.   Describe how to prepare for a strike. (p. 303)

6.   Describe common provisions in collective bargaining agreements. (pp. 304–306)

7.   Explain how grievances are resolved under a collective bargaining agreement. (pp. 306–308)

KEY TERMS

Collective bargaining agreement

Good faith

Impasse

Ratification

Attitudinal structuring

Mediation

Arbitration

Lockout

Picket line

Economic strike

Unfair labor practice strike

Wildcat strike

Sit-down strike

Slowdown

Secondary strike

Boycott

Just cause

Progressive discipline systems

Grievance

Final and binding

The National Labor Relations Act (NLRA) of 1935 (also known as the Wagner Act) requires employers and unions to bargain in good faith over the wages, hours, terms, and conditions of employment. The resulting agreement is usually called a **collective bargaining agreement** or *labor contract*. Refusal to bargain in good faith is an unfair labor practice. But good faith bargaining does not always lead to an agreement. The law does not require either party to agree to any proposal or to make any concessions in the negotiations, so an employer can fulfill its duty to bargain in good faith without ever agreeing to any of the union's demands. Employees, however, have the legally protected right to pressure the employer by picketing and going on strike.

Unions can affect a workplace in many ways. They may increase or decrease employee satisfaction with the job or work environment, which in turn can affect service quality and customer satisfaction. Unions can increase the overall cost of labor, which may reduce profits. They can protect workers from being fired and limit the authority of supervisors. However, these effects don't occur just because employees are represented by a union. They are the result of the contract that the company and the union reach through collective bargaining.

Managing human resources in a union environment poses unique challenges. Managers must understand the provisions of the labor contract and manage effectively without violating that contract. Although each collective bargaining agreement is unique, nearly all contain some similar provisions. This chapter elaborates on common labor contract provisions and strategies for successfully managing union workers.

12.1 THE DUTY TO BARGAIN IN GOOD FAITH

One of the NLRA's purposes was to encourage management and unions to resolve their differences at the bargaining table, thereby reducing the number and duration of debilitating and sometimes violent strikes in the nation. As noted above, although the law requires unions and employers to bargain in good faith, it does not require them to agree on anything. It also doesn't mandate any way of resolving labor negotiations that do not lead to an agreement.

Good faith in labor negotiations is defined as an honest attempt to reach an agreement. Employers whose representatives try to reach a favorable agreement with the union are not acting in bad faith just because they don't agree or just because they use extreme bargaining tactics to persuade the union. However, some negotiating tactics are considered unfair labor practices:

- Refusing to meet with the union's selected negotiators

- Refusing to give the union relevant information about the workers, such as their current wages and benefits

- Changing the terms or conditions of employment during negotiations without the union's agreement

- Communicating a contract offer directly to the employees and asking them to vote on it

- Offering a single "take it or leave it" proposal

- Refusing to discuss any mandatory subject of bargaining[1]

Negotiating a labor contract can take months or even years, but most of the time, the employer and union eventually reach an agreement and sign a contract lasting from one to five years. There are also times when the negotiations, even in good faith, just don't lead to an agreement.[2] An **impasse** occurs when the parties reach a stalemate—they are at the point where neither side is willing to concede anything further. When negotiations are at an impasse, the parties may agree to participate in some method of mediation or arbitration to resolve the remaining issues, but no formal efforts are required by law. The company is then free to unilaterally change the wages, hours, terms, and conditions of the employment, but only to the extent of its last offer to the union before the impasse. The union, of course, can attempt to continue bargaining, file an unfair labor practice charge, or take some action like picketing or a strike.

In some cases, multiple employers negotiate together with the union and reach a single agreement that applies to all of them. This approach reduces the time and expense of negotiating individual contracts and also establishes standard wages and benefits for all workers in that segment of the industry. Multi-employer groups are common in the hotel industry, particularly in large cities like New York, Los Angeles, San Francisco, Chicago, Boston, and Honolulu.

More recently, UNITE HERE has adopted a different strategy, demanding to bargain with multiple properties within the same corporation. In 2018, employees of an American hotel chain at locations nationwide went on strike simultaneously and obtained a single contract covering 7,700 workers—nearly 40 percent of all the employees the union represents.[3] The union is expected to continue this approach as more single-property contracts expire.

Subjects of Bargaining

The employer's duty to bargain in good faith is limited to the wages, hours, terms, and conditions of the employment. These are the *mandatory subjects of bargaining*. Refusal to discuss a mandatory subject constitutes an unfair labor practice. The law does not itemize the mandatory subjects, but they generally include everything directly related to the employment relationship. Exhibit 12.1 is a partial list of those subjects.

The employer and union are legally free to negotiate over other matters, but neither is required to do so. Some examples are agreements concerning the amount of union dues, compensation of managers, and the authority of supervisors. These issues are known as *permissive* or *voluntary subjects* of bargaining. Agreements concerning mandatory and voluntary subjects are equally enforceable in the contract, but neither party can declare an impasse in the negotiations over a disagreement about a voluntary subject. To do so would amount to refusing

Exhibit 12.1	Mandatory Subjects of Bargaining Examples	
Dues check-off	Strikes and lockouts
Grievance procedures	Termination of employment
Healthcare benefits	Training
Holidays, vacations, and time off	Wages and overtime
Job duties	Work quality standards
Parking	Work rules
Retirement benefits	Work schedules
Seniority	Workplace safety

to bargain in good faith about the remaining mandatory subjects.

The NLRA prohibits some subjects of bargaining altogether, so the parties cannot include them in a collective bargaining agreement even if they agree to do so. Illegal subjects of bargaining include agreements to give preferences to union members and any employment practice that would violate other laws.

Preparing for Negotiations

Most of the progress in collective bargaining occurs during the primary bargaining stage of negotiations. At this point, both sides are more likely to make concessions, to debate issues openly, and to focus on the issues that are easiest to resolve. It is critical to make progress during the primary bargaining stage because both sides are likely to become more entrenched in their positions as negotiations continue, making a final resolution less likely. If the parties begin with a difficult subject, it may prevent them from making progress on other issues.

Successful negotiations depend on extensive preparation. In preparing for negotiations, management must establish and prioritize its objectives for bargaining, and anticipate the union's priorities and objectives as well. Management should also prepare several alternate proposals and set limits that allow for some concessions. Preparations for bargaining usually begin months or even years before the opening of negotiations. Some experts believe management should begin preparing for the next collective bargaining session immediately after a contract is approved.[4]

Management should thoroughly analyze grievances filed during the previous contract period. Disputes over interpretation of contract terms should be resolved in the next negotiations. When negotiating wages and benefits, it is helpful to know in detail what is offered by competitors and what is provided under similar contracts with the same union.

It is also important to involve managers and supervisors in preparations. They have the most knowledge of daily operations and are aware of disagreements and problems that have arisen from the expiring contract. They will also be the ones to implement much of the new contract, so their input can help to predict the operational consequences of new contract proposals. Exhibit 12.2 is a more detailed sample of a negotiation checklist.

Choosing a Negotiating Team

The union negotiating team usually consists of a lead negotiator or attorney, a local union officer or business agent, and sometimes a few employees or stewards. The management negotiation team typically consists of an attorney, the head of the human resources department, sometimes a consultant trained in collective bargaining negotiations, and sometimes a general manager or corporate financial officer. The management team should always include an expert or consultant skilled in labor and benefit cost analysis to help evaluate the long-term costs of wage proposals. Because labor law is a unique specialty in legal practice, employers frequently hire lawyers with significant expertise and experience negotiating labor contracts.

It is not necessary for either bargaining team to include the person or persons who actually have the final authority to agree to the contract, but negotiations are much less efficient if the people negotiating can't actually agree to anything without securing approval of someone who is not there. Sometimes this is aided by having an executive with final authority standing by or available for short conferences during negotiations.

According to most union bylaws, contracts cannot be approved by union officials without a vote of employees, called a **ratification**. Employee representatives in negotiations do not have the final authority to sign a contract, although they will recommend ratification of the agreement they reach before the vote. In nearly all cases, members vote overwhelmingly to accept the contract.

Negotiation Strategies

The NLRA does not dictate how negotiations are conducted; it only requires the parties to meet and confer at reasonable times and places. What happens at the meetings is up to the parties. As long as they don't commit unfair labor practices, the company and union are free to use

Exhibit 12.2 Preparing for Negotiation

Negotiation Checklist

A systematic way to ensure you are well prepared before your next negotiation.

☑ *Item accomplished*

A. About You

❑ 1. What is your overall goal?

❑ 2. What are the issues?

❑ 3. How important is each issue to you?

   Develop a scoring system for evaluating offers:

   ❑ (a) List all of the issues of importance from step 2.

   ❑ (b) Rank order of all the issues.

   ❑ (c) Assign points to all the issues (assign weighted values based on a total of 100 points).

   ❑ (d) List the range of possible settlements for each issue. Your assessments of realistic, low, and high expectations should be grounded in industry norms and your best-case expectation.

   ❑ (e) Assign points to the possible outcomes that you identified for each issue.

   ❑ (f) Double-check the accuracy of your scoring system.

   ❑ (g) Use the scoring system to evaluate any offer that is on the table.

❑ 4. What is your "best alternative to negotiated agreement" (BATNA)?

❑ 5. What is your resistance point (i.e., the worst agreement you are willing to accept before ending negotiations)? If your BATNA is vague, consider identifying the minimum terms you can possibly accept and beyond which you must recess to gather more information.

B. About the Other Side

❑ 1. How important is each issue to them (plus any new issues they added)?

❑ 2. What is their best alternative to negotiated agreement?

❑ 3. What is their resistance point?

❑ 4. Based on questions B.1, B.2, and B.3, what is your target?

C. The Situation

❑ 1. What deadlines exist? Who is more impatient?

❑ 2. What fairness norms or reference points apply?

❑ 3. What topics or questions do you want to avoid? How will you respond if they ask anyway?

D. The Relationship Between the Parties

❑ 1. Will negotiations be repetitive? If so, what are the future consequences of each strategy, tactic, or action you are considering?

❑ 2. ❑ (a) Can you trust the other party? What do you know about them?

   ❑ (b) Does the other party trust you?

❑ 3. What do you know of the other party's styles and tactics?

❑ 4. What are the limits to the other party's authority?

❑ 5. Consult in advance with the other party about the agenda.

Source: Tony Simons and Thomas M. Tripp, "The Negotiation Checklist: How to Win the Battle Before It Begins," *Cornell Hotel and Restaurant Administration Quarterly* 38 (1997): 14-23.

whatever bargaining strategies and tactics they choose to obtain the best deal possible. Moments of conflict and anxiety inevitably occur, but typical labor negotiations are professional, thoughtful, and mostly cooperative.

They are also time consuming. The parties must discuss dozens of mandatory subjects. Some of them, like pay scales and scheduling rules, can be complex. Some collective bargaining agreements are over 200 pages long. When a union is first elected in a workplace, the initial collective bargaining is especially cumbersome because every detail requires an agreement. Subsequent negotiations have the benefit of the expiring contract as the foundation, so they just need to address proposed changes and updates.

The bargaining teams usually meet in a conference room at the employer's property, the union office, or an attorney's office. Sessions can go on all day, and the entire process may require 10 or more meetings,

but most of the work is done outside the conference room. Many negotiations begin with an exchange of written contract proposals before teams ever meet. Both sides submit a complete contract and then work through the differences one at a time. Then, based on the discussions, they exchange revised proposals and repeat the process. Reading, analyzing, and preparing the proposals often require much more time and effort than the meetings themselves.

During negotiations, both sides may try to establish impressions of friendliness, trust, respect, and cooperation to influence or manipulate one another. This type of bargaining is known as **attitudinal structuring**. Attitudinal structuring also occurs when one side attempts to create a negative impression of the other side. Such tactics can sometimes be advantageous,[7] but management must bear in mind the long-term effects of establishing harmful relationships with union representatives and by extension the workforce.

Voluntary Dispute Resolution

When parties are unable to agree on important terms of the contract, they may attempt some methods of breaking the stalemate and finalizing the contract. None of these are required by law, and they all depend on the voluntary participation of both sides. The two most common methods in labor negotiations are **mediation** and **arbitration**.

Mediation

A *mediator* is a third party who attempts to help both sides reach an agreement. Mediators can make recommendations, but they do not make final decisions or establish terms of the contract. They can help parties see their positions from a neutral perspective and suggest alternatives to conflicting proposals. Reliable mediators can be contacted through the Federal Mediation and Conciliation Service, an agency of the U.S. government designed to help prevent and resolve labor disputes. Several private organizations also provide professional mediators on short notice. A successful mediation results in an agreement, but in some cases the parties end up no closer to a contract than they were before mediation began.

Some negotiators believe a more aggressive approach results in a better deal. They are more prone to hostility and harsh tactics. But in the hospitality and service industries, employers often find that antagonism and hostility in negotiations spill over into the workplace even after the contract is finalized. This hurts their relationships with both their employees and customers.[5] Workers in a negative or combative work environment are far less likely to provide excellent customer service. So, many hospitality employers choose to use more cooperative and peaceful methods to reach a contract that supports superior job performance and customer service.[6]

Successful mediation requires cooperation, compromise, and flexibility.

Arbitration

Unlike mediators, *arbitrators* have the power to decide the dispute and dictate terms of the contract. The arbitrator's authority is only what the company and the union both agree to, so finding a neutral and trusted arbitrator is critical to both parties committing to the process.[8] Arbitrators can be contacted through the same sources as mediators or through the American Arbitration Association or the National Academy of Arbitrators.

In some cases, the arbitrator hears both sides and then decides what the contract will be, incorporating proposals from both sides and terms that constitute a compromise between the two. In *final offer arbitration*, an arbitrator chooses one side's entire proposal without modification. This is often called *baseball arbitration* because of its common use in deciding Major League Baseball player salary disputes. Both methods are designed to motivate parties to propose agreements as close to the middle ground as possible. This method is most effective when parties agree on most issues and are close to an agreement on the others but are unwilling to concede anything more.

Knowledge Check

1. What is "good faith" in labor negotiations?

2. What are mandatory subjects of bargaining?

3. What is the difference between mediation and arbitration?

12.2 STRIKES

Strikes are used as last resorts in negotiations because of their severe economic effect on both sides; but when a company simply refuses to agree, employees may feel they have little other choice. Before agreeing to strike, union members must decide whether they can sustain the economic losses incurred during a strike period, especially loss of wages and depletion of the union's assets. Management also must carefully consider the effect of strikes. The loss of business, alienation of clientele, and disruption of normal business can add up to significant economic losses. Management also should consider other hardships, such as slowdown and start-up costs, shareholder losses, reduced profits, reduced employee morale, and the development of harsh feelings on both sides. Strikes can break down lines of communication and teamwork that sometimes take years to develop. Strikes often last longer than either side anticipates, which means the costs are usually greater than predicted.

Strikes rarely result in one side winning and one side losing. In that sense, strikes are comparable to hockey fights: both participants sustain some injuries, but there is rarely a clear "winner." Most strikes end with a compromise that neither side was willing to accept before sustaining the damage caused by the labor stoppage. Even the threat of a strike may be a powerful motivator. Unions often hold strike votes when negotiations are near an impasse to demonstrate their solidarity and the will of the workers to strike if necessary.

Types of Strikes

The object of any strike is to cause economic damage to the company, but not all strikes are the same. The differences relate to the legality of the strike and the amount

State and local law enforcement officers do not have the legal authority to interfere in strikes because the right to strike is guaranteed by federal law. They do, however, retain the right to enforce ordinary state laws during a strike. Employees who commit crimes like trespassing and assault during a strike are still subject to being arrested by local law enforcement.

LEGAL ALERT!

of protection afforded union members during the strike. The type of strike is usually determined by the reason behind it.

A **lockout** is essentially a strike that is called by the employer. Rather than the employees refusing to work, the employer refuses to let them work. The purpose is to pressure employees and the union to make concessions in bargaining.

Although the NLRA affords all employees the legal right to strike and the right to return to work after a strike, the law does not protect any activity that is illegal under any other law. Strikers do not have the right to damage property, to trespass on private property, to threaten anyone doing business with the employer, or to physically block access to the employer's business. A **picket line** can be particularly contentious in the hospitality industry because the business depends on many customers and suppliers entering and exiting the property throughout the day. Strikers can legally form a line around the property and attempt to dissuade people from doing business with the employer, but they cannot threaten anyone or physically prevent them from entering.

Economic Strike. **Economic strikes** most commonly occur when the sides reach an impasse during the negotiation of mandatory subjects such as wages, benefits, or working conditions. The objective is to pressure the employer to agree to the union's demands by causing it to lose business. During an economic strike, management has the right to hire replacement employees, to assign other supervisors or other employees to work in the bargaining unit positions, and to encourage striking employees to cross picket lines. After an economic strike, workers do not necessarily go right back to work. The employer cannot discriminate against an employee for exercising their right to strike, but an individual striker does not have the right to return until their replacement leaves the job. Many strike settlement agreements, however, include the employer's agreement to discharge the replacements and return all strikers to work immediately.

Unfair Labor Practice Strike. Union members can strike to protest management's unfair labor practices, such as refusal to bargain, interference with organizing activities, or discrimination against union members. The objective is to persuade the employer to stop the unfair labor practice. Similar to an economic strike, the employer has the right to hire replacement workers, but after an **unfair labor practice strike**, the employer must reinstate all striking workers immediately.

Wildcat Strike. Most labor strikes are organized and sanctioned by the union, but employees retain the right to strike even without the union's approval and when a majority of the workers do not join the strike. A **wildcat strike** can occur when one group of employees believes that it is being treated unfairly by both the employer and the union. Striking employees can be legally replaced during a wildcat strike and can be legally fined by the union for striking without the union's approval.

Sit-Down Strike. In a **sit-down strike**, employees stop working but remain inside the workplace to disrupt the business or prevent continuing operations. This type of strike is illegal. Although employees have the right to strike, they do not have the right to occupy company property without the company's permission. The company has the right to continue business operations during a labor strike. Picket lines must remain on public property, usually the adjoining public sidewalk. Management can order sit-down strikers off company property, and if they refuse, they are likely to be arrested for trespassing. Unions continue to use the tactic, knowing they'll be arrested, because it usually generates a great deal of publicity.

Slowdown. Workers sometimes attempt to cause economic harm to the employer without going on strike. Rather, they just work more slowly to reduce production or degrade service. **Slowdowns** are also unprotected by the law, and employees who participate may be legally discharged. So long as the employees remain on the job, and continue to be paid, the employer is entitled to expect their full devotion and efforts to completing the work as expected.

Secondary Strike. A **secondary strike** is waged against an employer who does business with the company that has the dispute with the union. The objective of a secondary strike is to pressure the supplier to stop doing business with the company, such as a hotel, during the strike. Such strikes are not protected by the law.[9] For example, union workers on strike at a hotel cannot establish a picket line against a supplier company's business.

Managing Strikes

A company has the protected right to continue business operations during a strike, but without committing unfair labor practices. An additional consequence of an unfair labor practice during an economic strike may be to convert the strike into an unfair labor practice strike. This would strengthen the union's position by giving employees a greater right to return to work when the strike is over.

Typical unfair labor practices committed by employers during labor strikes include:

- Offering extra benefits to strikers who resign from the union and return to work

- Refusing to allow employees to resign from the union and return to work

- Threatening strikers with loss of jobs or other discipline or loss of benefits for striking

- Discharging employees who take part in legal strikes or picketing

- Refusing to continue bargaining with the union during the strike

An essential part of preparation for bargaining includes planning for the possibility of a strike. The employer's ability to maintain operations and minimize the damage caused by the strike depends almost entirely on the employer's advance preparation. At a minimum, any strike contingency plan should include:

- Evaluating the ability to continue full or partial operations with reduced staff

- Planning to recruit, hire, and train replacement workers who will be available on short notice and who will accept the job knowing it is probably temporary

- Identifying parts of the business that can be temporarily closed during a strike if sufficient replacement labor is not available

- Identifying alternative suppliers in case some delivery drivers refuse to cross the picket line

- Designating a single company spokesperson to manage publicity and respond to media inquiries

- Planning extra security precautions to protect the company from illegal strike activity[10]

In 2018, the hotel industry experienced record numbers of labor strikes nationwide, mostly by workers represented by UNITE HERE. Some of the strikes were held simultaneously at multiple properties of the same parent company. Other strikes were organized at multiple companies in one location, in some cases shutting down 20–30 properties in the same city all at once. The union's success in winning favorable settlements has raised concerns that similar actions will continue to disrupt large segments of the industry.[11]

Actions Beyond Strikes

A strike is not the only way a union can pressure an employer to compromise. Union workers can picket and protest outside the employer's property on their own time without going on strike. A tactic used by unions today is to publicize their dispute on YouTube and other social media in an attempt to organize a public **boycott** against the company. This can be much more harmful to businesses because of the reach of the messages the unions send. UNITE HERE, for example, maintains a website advising tourists of pending labor disputes with hotel properties and promoting properties that have agreed to labor contracts.[12]

Knowledge Check

1. Do workers who go on strike have the right to return to work when the strike is over?

2. What is the difference between a strike and a lockout?

3. What is a secondary strike?

12.3 COLLECTIVE BARGAINING AGREEMENTS

In most cases, there is no strike or lockout and the union and employer eventually reach an agreement. No two labor contracts are exactly the same, but many standard provisions are common to most of them. Some examples are:

■ **No Strike/No Lockout:** This hallmark labor contract provision simply prohibits any strikes or lockouts during the term of the contract. The parties sometimes agree to severe penalties for violations.

■ **Seniority:** Under a seniority system, preferences for shifts and overtime, days off, transfers, and so on are made strictly according to how long the employees have worked there. Decisions such as promotions and scheduling that would otherwise be made by management are made according to the relative seniority of the employees in question.

■ **Union Security:** The employer typically agrees to withhold union dues from the employees' paychecks and pay them directly to the union. This pro-

cess is known as *dues check-off*. This relieves the union of the need to collect dues from its members. Union security may also include an agreement that all employees be required to join the union, but only in states where such an agreement is legal. State right-to-work laws are discussed in Chapter 11.

■ **Just Cause:** Union employees often have greater job security because the contract requires the employer to have a fair and legitimate reason for discipline and discharge decisions. Absent a union contract, most employees are *at will*, meaning the employer needs no reason at all for taking action against an employee. The concept of **just cause** is complex and dependent on the unique circumstances of each case; but in essence it requires a good reason for the action, a fair decision process, and equal application of the rules or expectations to all employees. Unless the contract defines just cause with more detail, most arbitrators follow some variation of the seven-question guideline in Exhibit 12.3 to evaluate cases for just cause.

■ **Layoff and Recall:** Very few labor contracts prevent the employer from laying

---

Exhibit 12.3	Elements of Just Cause

1. Did the company notify the employee of the possible consequences of the employee's conduct?

2. Was the company's rule or standard reasonably related to business operations?

3. Did the company investigate the facts before taking action against the employee?

4. Was the investigation fair and objective?

5. Was there real evidence of the employee's misconduct?

6. Were the rules and standards enforced equally?

7. Was the disciplinary action taken proportionate to the seriousness of the misconduct?

Adapted from *Enterprise Wire Company and Enterprise Independent Union*, Volume 46 Labor Arbitration Reports p. 359 (1966).

off workers due to interruptions in business, but most require the employer to select the employees to be laid off and recalled according to their seniority.

- **Work Jurisdiction:** The employer commits to assign certain work only to members of the bargaining unit. This protects employees from having their job duties taken over by employees who are not represented by the union, but it also creates the basis for some "not my job" conflicts.

- **Pay Scale:** The contract establishes the workers' hourly wage rates for the entire term of contract, including schedule guaranteed raises.

- **Benefits:** Many unions, including UNITE HERE, maintain their own health and retirement plans. Rather than providing those benefits themselves, employers agree to pay a set rate per employee, and the union directly provides or arranges for the employee benefits.

- **Guaranteed Schedules:** Many labor contracts do not allow managers to send employees home early or to cancel previously scheduled shifts.

- **Progressive Discipline:** Employees who violate work rules or standards must be given at least one formal warning before being discharged from the job. Exceptions are made for extreme cases like fighting, theft, and working under the influence of drugs or alcohol. Most **progressive discipline systems** have three or four steps, beginning with informal and formal warnings, then escalating to suspensions and finally discharge.

- **Management Rights:** Nearly every collective bargaining agreement expressly reserves to the employer the right to run the business as the management sees fit. The contracts specify those rights to make it clear that the company will not bargain over such decisions as management promotions, staffing levels, methods of operations, work quality expectations, and sources of supplies.

- **Grievance and Arbitration:** A **grievance** is a claim by the union or the employer that the other has violated the contract. U.S. courts do not have

the power to decide labor contract grievance cases, so the parties establish their own internal process. The contract usually specifies a multi-step procedure for resolving disputes that arise during the term of the contract. Most of them begin with informal meetings and conclude with **final and binding** arbitration. The parties commit in the contract to comply with the decisions that result from the process. We discuss grievance procedures in more detail next.

Grievance Procedures

No matter how complex and detailed it is, any contract leaves room for disagreement. Some grievances result from disagreement between union and management over the interpretation of contract terminology. If a union has committed that it will not "strike or picket" during the contract, is it a violation if it uses social media to promote a consumer boycott against the company? Does a "graveyard shift" refer to a work schedule from 2 a.m. to 10 a.m. or some other time frame? This is why it's important to review prior grievances before negotiating a new contract—it gives the parties the opportunity to prevent future disputes by clarifying any ambiguities or misunderstandings that have already arisen.

Most grievances, however, are claims that the employer took some action that directly violated the terms of the contract. This might be awarding a shift preference to a less senior employee, paying an employee improperly, or assigning a union member's work to a supervisor. By far the most common grievance claim is that an employee was disciplined or discharged without just cause.

There is not one standard grievance procedure for union contracts. The parties to each agreement are free to establish whatever process they desire. Grievance processes are designed to resolve disagreements efficiently, so they include very short timelines and preferences for informality. A typical union grievance procedure includes the following steps:

1. The employee, a union representative, and the immediate supervisor or manager meet to discuss the employee's

complaint. The union representative explains the reason for the grievance and the supervisor or manager has a short time to either reverse the decision or deny the grievance. Most grievances are minor disagreements or misunderstandings that are easily resolved at this level. Cases involving discharge of a worker or a significant contract interpretation, however, are rarely concluded at this stage.

2. If the first step does not result in a resolution, the case becomes a formal grievance and escalates to higher officials on both sides. The union presents evidence of the alleged violation and the company formally responds. If the case is not resolved, the union notifies the company if the employee desires to proceed to the next step.

3. Under many labor contracts, cases at this stage are heard by panels of both employees and managers, or even by managers from other departments or properties. Under some contracts, a mediator is designated to intervene. Decisions and recommendations at this stage are typically not final and binding but can be persuasive if the process is fair and balanced. Even though they are not required to comply with the outcome, the parties are required to partic-ipate in the process before proceeding to formal arbitration.

4. If all attempts to resolve the grievance fail, the case is submitted to a neutral arbitrator for a final and binding decision.

Grievance Arbitration

Nearly every labor contract grievance procedure ends with a formal hearing before a neutral professional arbitrator, who is paid for the service. In most cases, the contract stipulates that the cost for arbitration be split equally between the union and management. This cost can be substantial. Arbitration can cost the parties between $5,000 and $100,000 in fees and costs, lost work time, and legal fees.

Arbitrators are selected by whatever means to which the parties agree. One method is to contact the American Arbitration Association, the National Academy of Arbitrators, or Federal Mediation and Conciliation Service[13] and an arbitrator will be appointed. In some cases, the service provides a list of potential arbitrators. Each side then alternately strikes one name from the list until only one name is left. That person is chosen as the arbitrator for that particular grievance. In other contracts, the parties identify a panel of named arbitrators during the contract negotiations and select one from the list in a similar way.

An arbitration hearing closely resembles a trial in court. Each side can present documents or video evidence, call and cross-examine witnesses, and argue its position. The parties are very often represented by attorneys skilled in litigation. The rules of procedure and evidence are established by the arbitrator, who acts as both judge and jury and issues a formal written opinion.

Unions and employers avoid taking cases to arbitration due to the time and expense involved. Even though arbitration is less expensive and faster than litigation in court, it can still take up to a year for an arbitration case to be prepared, heard, and decided. Grievance procedures are designed to limit formal arbitration to cases of important contract interpretation and discharge of employees. When the arbitration concerns a termination of employment, the employer bears the burden of proving that it had just cause to fire the worker.

Preventing Grievances

Nearly every dispute that occurs during the term of the collective bargaining agreement arises between a front-line supervisor or manager and an employee. For that reason, front-line supervisors and managers are in the best position to protect the employer from union grievances. Their decisions will form the basis of potential grievances and their knowledge of the process will likely affect the outcome for the employer. So successful managers of represented employees are skilled in both avoiding grievances and in winning them when they do occur.

All managers in union properties can expect to face grievance situations from time to time. No manager can avoid every possible grievance without just agreeing to whatever the union or employees demand, but some basic actions can reduce the time and effort necessary to resolve disputes and protect the company in the event of a formal grievance:

- Post in a conspicuous location the "house rules" that employees are expected to follow. Some such rules are mandatory subjects of bargaining, but establishing detailed conduct and performance guidelines in advance avoids disputes during the term of the contract.

- Document everything possible, including informal warnings or inadequate job performance. Any time an action occurs that requires discipline or corrective action, a manager should first document the facts in their entirety, including a thorough description of what happened. The description should also include dates and times of the event, names of the people involved, names of any witnesses, and any other pertinent facts.

- Investigate all cases of misconduct thoroughly to ensure the company is complying with the contract.

- Use progressive discipline fairly and consistently, not just as a way to win grievances, but as a way to correct and improve job performance.

Union Rights in Investigatory Interviews

Under most union contracts, the workers have the right to have a union representative present during investigatory interviews. Although managers are not bound to advise employees of this right, they must honor it when requested. If an employee requests that a union representative be present during an investigatory interview, managers should accommodate the request or delay the interview until a union representative can be present. Managers should never refuse the request and proceed with the interview; unions view such conduct as another reason to file a grievance over the disciplinary action. Managers are not required to negotiate with union representatives during investigatory interviews. The role of union representatives in this process is limited—they may not interfere with the interview or instruct the employee not to answer, but they are allowed some involvement in the process. The applicable labor contract may also set guidelines for union participation in interviews.

Establishing Non-Union Property Grievance Procedures

Many employers establish grievance procedures even in the absence of any union or threat of union organization.[14] One reason for such procedures is to eliminate the need that employees may feel for union protection. Grievance procedures in non-union settings differ from those in union settings because no union representatives are involved and so the entire process is controlled by the company.

The success of non-union grievance procedures depends on fairness and management support. For such a system to work, managers must inform employees of their opportunities to dispute work-related issues, provide the avenue for such complaints, and support the system. Managers who undermine or disregard grievance committee decisions send the wrong message to their employees. Such behavior demonstrates that managers do not believe in the system and may not abide by its findings. If that happens, the system can cause more harm than good, because it shows employees that managers do not follow the rules. This sets a poor example for employees and damages (or corrupts) the system; it may also lead employees to look to unions for more reliable protection. A typical non-union property grievance procedure is outlined in Exhibit 12.4.

Knowledge Check

1. What is the meaning of "just cause" in a collective bargaining agreement?

2. What is the first step in most labor contract grievance procedures?

3. Why do some employers establish grievance procedures even in the absence of any union or threat of union organization?

12.4 MANAGING UNION WORKERS

The relationship between the employer and the union can directly affect the quality of service in any hospitality operation. One of the motivating factors at work is the environment itself—the quality of relationships among workers and managers. The employer's relationship with the union is part of that. Research has shown that adversarial, antagonistic relationships between managers and union agents are likely to

result in lower employee satisfaction, lower employee motivation, and lower quality guest service. Hospitality employers have found that cooperative partnership-like relationships with unions promote both productive work and quality customer service. UNITE HERE is directly involved in some of the efforts to make that type of relationship the industry norm.[15]

Successful managers in union settings follow a few basic guidelines:

1. Every manager must know and abide by the contract. New managers should be trained extensively in their responsibilities under the labor contract.

2. Maintain a professional and respectful relationship with union stewards and others who act on behalf of the union and workers. The labor relations environment has a powerful effect on job performance and the quality of customer service.

3. Commit to resolve disputes promptly. The grievance system is intended to encourage honest discussions and efficient resolution of any problems or disagreements over the implementation of the contract. Issues that are not resolved early typically become bigger problems, causing unnecessary arguments and cost.

4. Document disciplinary actions carefully. In grievance and arbitration procedures, it is usually up to the employer to prove

---

Exhibit 12.4	Sample Grievance Procedure: Non-Union Property

1. The employee makes a complaint to the supervisor.

2. The employee makes a complaint to any manager in any department.

3. The employee takes the complaint to a grievance committee composed of employees and management representatives.

4. The grievance committee formally posts the grievance and results in a conspicuous place for all employees to see.

that it had just cause to discipline or discharge a worker. Clear documentation of progressive discipline is essential for that purpose.

5. Keep in mind the importance of equality to workers and the union. Fair and equitable management supports a positive work environment and prevents grievances.

Managing union workers can be challenging, but managers who follow the contract and respect the rights of workers are most likely to maintain a cooperative relationship with the union, and least likely to incur unnecessary costs and hardships.

Knowledge Check

1. How can a cooperative relationship with a union benefit a hospitality business?

2. Why should managers commit to promptly resolve disputes?

3. Why is it important to document employee misconduct and poor performance?

IN THIS CHAPTER, YOU LEARNED:

- What it means to bargain in good faith and negotiating tactics that are considered unfair labor practices.
- That managers prepare for collective bargaining by establishing objectives, preparing alternate proposals, and setting limits that allow for some concessions.
- The role of mediation and arbitration in collective bargaining.
- That the types of labor strikes include a lockout, a picket line, economic strike, unfair labor practice strike, wildcat strike, sit-down strike, slowdown, and secondary strike.
- How to prepare for a strike.
- The common provisions in collective bargaining agreements include no strike/no lockout, seniority, union security, just cause, layoff and recall, work jurisdiction, pay scale, benefits, guaranteed schedules, progressive discipline, management rights, grievance, and arbitration.
- How grievances are resolved under a collective bargaining agreement.

KEY TERMS

arbitration—A voluntary process used to settle a labor dispute through the use of a third party (known as an *arbitrator*), whose decision is usually final and binding.

attitudinal structuring—A negotiation strategy in which one or both sides attempt to establish an impression of friendliness, trust, respect, and cooperation to manipulate or influence the other.

boycott—A refusal to buy products or services offered by a company with which employees have some dispute, which may include public actions to persuade others to join.

collective bargaining agreement—A contract resulting from collective bargaining between a company and the union that represents its employees; also known as a *labor contract*.

economic strike—A strike over mandatory subjects of bargaining such as wages or working conditions.

final and binding—A characteristic of many grievance and arbitration procedures in which the parties agree in advance to accept

and abide by the outcome of the process without any right to appeal.

good faith—The honest intention to reach an agreement through collective bargaining.

grievance—A claim by one party that the other has violated the terms of a collective bargaining agreement.

impasse—A point at which neither the union nor management will give up on any point or issue and at which agreement is yet to be reached.

just cause—A typical clause in a collective bargaining contract that requires a fair and legitimate reason for employee discipline or termination.

lockout—A management action to refuse to allow represented employees to work.

mediation—A process used to resolve a stalemate in negotiations in which a third party (known as a *mediator*) helps the parties arrive at a voluntary compromise.

picket line—A line formed by workers around an employer's property, usually carrying signs to publicize a labor dispute and to dissuade customers and other employees from entering the business.

progressive discipline systems—Discipline processes under many labor contracts in which employees are given increasingly stiffer penalties for infractions; usually from an oral warning, to a written warning, to a suspension, and finally to discharge.

ratification—A vote of the members of a bargaining unit to approve or reject a proposed contract.

secondary strike—An illegal strike against an employer with whom the union has no dispute.

sit-down strike—A strike that occurs when union members stop working but remain on the premises.

slowdown—A deliberate reduction in productivity designed to pressure the employer in negotiations.

unfair labor practice strike—A strike to protest management's refusal to bargain or other unfair labor practice.

wildcat strike—A strike not recognized or authorized by union leadership.

REVIEW QUESTIONS

1. What does the duty to bargain in good faith require an employer to do?

2. Give three examples of mandatory subjects of bargaining other than wages and benefits.

3. Why is it an unfair labor practice to insist on the union's agreement to a voluntary subject of bargaining?

4. What is an impasse and what can happen after an impasse in collective bargaining?

5. How do just cause and progressive discipline provisions protect the job security of employees covered by a labor contract?

6. Why is it important to include front-line supervisors and managers in preparations for collective bargaining?

7. Which types of strikes provide the most legal protection for employees? Which types provide the least?

8. What are the differences between arbitration and mediation? How are they used in collective bargaining?

9. How do grievance procedures facilitate the efficient resolution of disputes that arise under a collective bargaining agreement?

Addressing Staff Problems

One night during a large convention at the Torrence Hotel, the hotel bar suddenly became very busy. Kaleena was the only bartender scheduled to work that night, and she could not keep up. Shona, the food and beverage manager, stepped in to help for a short while. Although it was still busy, Shona had to leave due to a problem at the restaurant.

When Shona returned to the bar 10 minutes later, business had slowed down, but Kaleena was arguing with a guest at the bar. Shona told Kaleena to take a short break. Then, when Kaleena had left, Shona asked the guest what happened.

He said, "I waited 10 minutes for a beer and when I reminded her I was still waiting, she was very rude and slammed a beer bottle on the bar in front of me. It was not what I ordered anyway, so I got up to leave. Then she accused me of walking out on my tab and threatened to call the police."

"I'm very sorry about that," Shona said. "It's not the first time with her. If you want to stay, I'll give you a beer on the house." The guest declined and went back to his room.

When Kaleena returned to the bar, Shona told her, "I'll cover the rest of your shift. Go home and call me before you come to work tomorrow."

Kaleena is represented by the Bartenders Union. Their current contract with the Torrence Hotel contains just cause and grievance procedure provisions similar to those described in this chapter.

DISCUSSION QUESTIONS

1. What must Shona do before deciding what action to take against Kaleena?

2. If the guest's story is true, does Shona have just cause to fire Kaleena?

3. If Shona fires Kaleena and the Bartenders Union files a grievance, what process will be used to decide the case? What do you think would be the outcome?

ENDNOTES

1. National Labor Relations Board, "Employer/Union Rights and Obligations," accessed April 21, 2021, www.nlrb.gov/about-nlrb.

2. James R. Pickworth, "An Experiential Approach to Collective Bargaining," *Cornell Hotel and Restaurant Administration Quarterly* 28, no. 2 (August 1987): 60–66.

3. Lynn Rhinehart and Celine McNicholas, "Collective Bargaining Beyond the Worksite: How Workers and Their Unions Build Power and Set Standards for Their Industries," last modified May 4, 2020, https://www.epi.org/publication/collective-bargaining-beyond-the-worksite-how-workers-and-their-unions-build-power-and-set-standards-for-their-industries/.

4. Harry C. Katz, Thomas A. Kochan, and Alexander J.S. Colvin, *An Introduction to U.S. Collective Bargaining and Labor Relations,* 5th edition (Ithaca, NY: ILR Press, 2017); Kathryn Tyler, "Good-Faith Bargaining," *HR Magazine* 50, no.1 (January 2005): 48–53.

5. Lina Hipp and Rebecca Kolins Givan, "What Do Unions Do? A Cross-National Reexamination of the Relationship Between Unionization and Job Satisfaction," *Social Forces,* 94, no. 1 (2015): 349–377.

6. Kathryn Tyler, "Good-Faith Bargaining," *HR Magazine* 50, no.1 (January 2005): 48–53.

7. Roger Fisher, William L. Ury, and Bruce Patton, *Getting to Yes: Negotiating Agreement Without Giving In,* 3rd revised edition (New York: Penguin Books, 2011).

8. Kenneth May, ed., *How Arbitration Works,* 8th edition (New York: Bloomberg BNA, 2006).

9. National Labor Relations Board, "NLRA and the Right to Strike" accessed April 21, 2021, https://www.nlrb.gov/strikes.

10. Alfred T. DeMaria, "The Corporate Campaign: The Challenge Continues," *Management Report* 39, no. 1 (January 2016): 3–4.

11. Paul B. Hertneky, "How to Deal with a Walk-Out," *Restaurant Hospitality* (February 1995): 65–66.

12. UNITE HERE, www.fairhotel.org.

13. American Arbitration Association, www.adr.org; National Academy of Arbitrators, www.naarb.org; Federal Mediation and Conciliation Service, www.fmcs.gov.

14. Lawrence Nurse and Dwayne Devonish, "Grievance Management and Its Links to Workplace Justice," *Employee Relations* 29, no. 1 (2006): 89–109.

15. Stuart R. Korshak, "A Labor-Management Partnership: San Francisco's Hotels and the Employees' Union Try a New Approach," *Cornell Hotel and Restaurant Administration Quarterly* 41, no. 2 (April, 2000): 14–29.

13

EMPLOYMENT LAWS

Chapter 13 Outline

Learning Objectives

1. Describe the basic legal rights of all employees and job applicants. (pp. 316–333)

2. Identify the government agencies responsible for enforcing employment laws. (p. 318)

3. Describe the potential consequences of violating employment laws. (pp. 316–319)

4. Describe the circumstances in which employment discrimination is legal. (pp. 320–321)

5. Identify interview questions that violate various employment laws. (pp. 319–326)

6. Explain the limits on an employer's duty to accommodate disabled workers. (pp. 322–324)

7. Describe best management practices to avoid claims for violating employment laws. (p. 334)

KEY TERMS

At will

Respondeat superior

Wrongful discharge

Whistleblower

Class action

Right-to-sue letter

Back pay

Business necessity

Bona fide occupational qualifications (BFOQs)

Essential functions

I-9 form

Constructive discharge

13.1 THE LAW OF EMPLOYMENT

Employment is a voluntary relationship: The company chooses to hire the worker, and the worker chooses to work for the company. In that sense, it's like many other contracts. The specific terms, conditions, and benefits of the relationship—the pay, hours, benefits, and type of work—are left to whatever the company and the worker agree to. But there are limits. Employment laws regulate aspects of every workplace, and workers have many legal rights. Every manager is responsible for knowing and following employment laws. Ignorance is no defense, and the company will be liable for violations committed by any of its managers. The best managers don't just know the laws, they know how to work within the laws and avoid common legal problems in HR management.

Employment at Will

All employment is a contract of sorts, but few hospitality employees have a written employment contract that defines and guarantees the terms and conditions. Those with written employment contracts are mostly executives, highly paid individuals, and workers with rare skills or knowledge. Some workers are covered by union contracts, which are addressed in Chapter 12.

In the absence of any such contract, employees in all U.S. states are employed **at will**.[1] This means there is no definite period of employment; rather, it's until one or the other decides to end it. Employees can quit any time without any reason and without giving advance notice. The employer retains the same right—to end the relationship any time for any reason without notice. The same is true for all of the terms and conditions of the job. The employer is free to change the pay, hours, duties, and benefits at any time. The employee's only recourse is to quit or, possibly, sue.

The law of employment at will distinguishes U.S. employment law from that of many other countries. In Canada, for instance, the concept of "at will" employment does not exist. An employee in Canada is entitled to advance notice of termination without cause. If the employer does not give the required notice, it must pay the employee for the notice period. Any agreement to the contrary is voidable, meaning the employee is still entitled to the notice or pay even after agreeing otherwise. No advance notice is required, however, for termination of employment with cause.[2]

Hundreds of U.S. state and federal laws affect all aspects of the employment relationship. Minimum wage laws, for example, place a lower limit on the pay the company and the employee can agree to; it can't be below a certain amount. And even though the employer does not need specific grounds to fire an "at-will" employee, there are a number of reasons that are illegal—race, religion, sex, age, and many more.[3] The legal rights created by these laws cannot be taken away by any employer, even if the employee consents. In other words, employers and employees are not permitted to agree that the laws won't be followed. The legal boundaries are the same for everyone.

The consequences of violating employment laws can be severe. Employment law cases are the most common type of lawsuit filed in U.S. federal courts and cost companies hundreds of millions of dollars every year. In many cases, companies lose because of a manager's misunderstanding, or ignorance, of the law. Employers don't usually lose lawsuits because they *intend* to violate anyone's legal rights. They lose lawsuits because their managers didn't anticipate the potential legal consequences of their actions and decisions. Employers who intentionally violate employment laws are subject to higher losses, but even an honest mistake can result in an expensive legal claim.

Under the laws of every state, companies are legally responsible for the acts of their employees while they are working. This is commonly referred to as the rule of ***respondeat superior***, Latin (roughly) for "the employer is responsible." This means a company cannot avoid legal liability for a manager's violation of a law, even if the manager violated established policies and was immediately fired for doing it. The company is still responsible for the manager's violation. That's why it is so important not just to educate managers about their legal responsibilities, but also to monitor their compliance.

Wrongful Discharge

Most employment lawsuits arise from an employee being fired ("discharged," "terminated," or "dismissed" are also used interchangeably). **Wrongful discharge** is not the same as a discharge that violates an employment law, but it's more than just discharge for a bad, illogical, or unfair reason. Wrongful discharge refers only to a few relatively rare exceptions to the "at-will" employment rule.

There are two basic categories of wrongful discharge: *contract theory* and *public policy theory*. In contract theory, employees may prove that an employee handbook or some other company document created an implied contract and that they were dismissed in violation of this contract. These claims occasionally succeed against employers who make promises of job security that are inconsistent with "at will" employment, like "the company does not fire workers without a good reason." Most employers protect themselves from claims of an implied contract by stating in the handbook and other documents that they are not intended as contractual promises, and clearly notifying workers that their employment is "at will." Exhibit 13.1 is a sample of such a handbook disclaimer.

In public policy theory, employees might claim they were dismissed for refusing to do something illegal or for exercising some legal right at work, such as filing a workers' compensation claim. This exception also protects a **whistleblower** from retaliation for reporting illegal activities to authorities.

Federal Employment Laws

Many employment laws are federal laws, made and enforced by the U.S. government. They apply to workplaces in every state. Some are statutes passed by Congress and

others are regulations made by government agencies such as the U.S. Department of Labor (DOL). Some federal employment laws date back 100 years or more, but the law of employment is always changing, so managers must keep up with those modifications. Some recent federal employment law changes have outlawed discrimination on the basis of gender identity, sexual orientation, and genetic information. Others have established workplace safety standards for protecting employees from COVID-19.

State Employment Laws

In addition, nearly every state has its own employment laws, and they are not all the same. Federal laws apply to everyone, so a state cannot make a law that takes away rights created by federal laws. A state cannot, for example, establish a legal minimum wage that is lower than the federal minimum

Exhibit 13.1	Example of Contract Theory Handbook Disclaimer

Nothing in this handbook is intended to create a legally binding contract or imply a promise of continued employment. The company's employees are employed "at will," meaning either the employer or the employee can end the employment with or without cause or notice. This handbook does not change that relationship. The company reserves the right to revise its policies without notice.

wage. However, state laws can add to the legal rights created by federal law, such as establishing a minimum wage higher than that established by federal law. Many states have done this. Some federal laws do not apply to small employers, but many similar state laws cover smaller companies. So, in addition to the federal laws described in this chapter, managers must be aware of state laws wherever they are located. This is particularly important to keep in mind when moving from one state to another, because the applicable laws will not be the same.

Enforcement of Employment Laws

The employment laws covered in this chapter are enforced in different ways. The most common form of enforcement is via a private lawsuit brought by an individual in federal or state court. But when the same violation happens to many employees (at least 20), they can band together into a **class action** and sue the company with a few people acting as representatives of the group. This makes the case easier and less expensive for them, but it has the opposite effect on the company. Cases involving hiring discrimination can include thousands of affected applicants.

Federal and state governments also have agencies that enforce employment laws. They can investigate complaints, impose penalties for violations, and, in some cases, sue the company on behalf of employees (one or more). Table 13.1 describes the responsibilities of government agencies.

In cases of employment discrimination, an employee must contact the Equal Employment Opportunity Commission (EEOC) before filing a private lawsuit. The EEOC, or its state government equivalent, has the opportunity to investigate and attempt to resolve the complaint before the employee can go to court. The agency can either arrange a settlement of the case, take the case to court itself, or give the employee the right to sue the employer in a private lawsuit. This document is called a **right-to-sue letter**, and it merely states that the employee has given the agency a chance to investigate and resolve the case. It does not mean the agency finds the complaint to be true, but it allows the employee to proceed with a lawsuit.

Remedies in Employment Lawsuits

The money the company is required to pay after losing a case is called the remedy. Because most cases are by former employees who were dismissed, a common remedy is paying former employees the money they would have been paid for continuing to work if they had not been illegally fired. This is known as a **back pay** award.

In some cases, plaintiffs can also win compensation for the pain, suffering, and anxiety caused by the legal violation. Such payments are common in harassment and discrimination cases. A company found in violation of an employment law may also be required to reinstate illegally dismissed

Table 13.1	Government Agencies and Their Enforcement Responsibilities

Government Agency	Enforcement Responsibilities
Department of Labor (DOL)	Wage and hour laws, pay discrimination, family and medical leave
Equal Employment Opportunity Commission (EEOC)	Employment discrimination laws
Occupational Safety and Health Administration (OSHA)	Workplace safety and worker protection laws
U.S. Department of Homeland Security (DHS)	Immigration employment authorization laws
State Agencies	Workers' compensation laws, unemployment benefits, other state laws

persons and to reimburse them for their attorney's fees and costs. Under some laws, such as the federal minimum wage laws, the court can double the amount of the remedy as an additional penalty. This additional amount, called *liquidated damages*, is also paid to the worker.

Knowledge Check

1. How are employment laws enforced?

2. What are some illegal reasons for firing an "at will" employee?

3. List three reasons why employees might file a class action lawsuit.

13.2 LAWS AFFECTING RECRUITING, INTERVIEWING, AND HIRING

Employment Discrimination Laws

Human resources management is the practice of *legal* discrimination. Selecting an applicant to hire or promote, for example, is a form of discrimination: It involves choosing one individual over another based on some identifiable difference between them. There are many legal reasons for discriminating, such as previous experience, education, and special skills. There are also many illegal reasons for discrimination, such as race, sex, disability, and age.

Illegal discrimination can occur at any stage of the employment process. Although most employment discrimination claims involve employees being either refused a job or fired from a job, anti-discrimination laws apply equally to other forms of employment action, including promotions, discipline, benefits, and scheduling. Job advertising that seeks "young," "recently graduated," or "female" applicants are common forms of employment discrimination in the recruiting process. Terms like "hostess" and "doorman" can indirectly indicate an illegal preference based on gender. Interview questions can also violate discrimination laws, such as asking a female

applicant if she plans to have children soon or rating an applicant's communication skills lower due to a foreign accent. Managers who participate in any part of the employment process must be aware of the constant potential for a claim of unlawful discrimination.

Illegally discriminating against an applicant or employee can have severe legal consequences. Exhibit 13.2 shows the employment discrimination complaints reported between 1997 and 2018.[4]

The annual total of discrimination complaints received by the EEOC has declined significantly in the past 10 years. The 2020 total of 67,448 was the lowest in over 20 years. All of the forms of discrimination depicted in Exhibit 13.2, however, have been exceeded in each year by complaints of unlawful retaliation, which now make up more than half of all claims filed with the agency.

Most employment discrimination complaints are dismissed or withdrawn with no payment to the employee, but in 2020 alone, the EEOC secured $439.2 million for victims of employment discrimination, mostly by private settlements outside of court.[5]

The average award in an employment discrimination lawsuit is about $200,000, and in most cases, there is a cap of $300,000. In some cases, the company is able to settle the case for less before trial. In a class action lawsuit, the cap is per person, so the potential losses can be millions. In 2018, for example, a Miami hotel paid $2.5 million to settle an EEOC lawsuit alleging racial discrimination against 17 dishwashers.[6] In the same month, two restaurants paid nearly $1 million to settle sexual harassment claims by 16 female workers.[7]

Equal Employment Opportunity Legislation: Title VII of the Civil Rights Act of 1964

Title VII of the Civil Rights Act of 1964 prohibits employment discrimination based on race, color, sex, religion, and national origin. Until recently, it was unclear whether "sex" was meant to include sexual orientation and gender identity. The U.S. Supreme Court settled the question in 2020 and held that both are illegal reasons for discrimination.[8] Employers with fewer than 15 employees

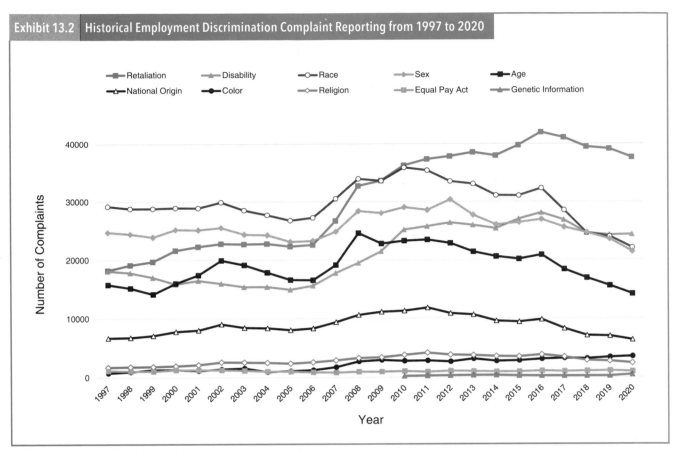

Source: U.S. Equal Employment Opportunity Commission.

are not covered by Title VII but may still be subject to state antidiscrimination laws that are similar to the federal Civil Rights Act.

A violation of Title VII is proven by showing that an applicant or employee was treated differently than a similar applicant or employee who is not in the plaintiff's protected category. The plaintiff does not have to directly prove that the reason for the action was purposeful or even illegal. For example, if a Hispanic man is promoted instead of an Asian man who has the same or greater qualifications, that decision may or may not have been influenced by race or ethnicity, but it will be impossible to prove directly unless the person who made the decision admits it. The decision might have been because of legal reasons for discrimination, like punctuality, attitude toward the work, or career goals. But if the employee was treated differently, the employer must prove the legal reason. If it cannot, the judge or jury can conclude that the real reason was illegal.

Two possible defenses to discrimination exist under Title VII: business necessity and bona fide occupational qualifications

(BFOQs). The **business necessity** defense applies to cases when a legal reason for discrimination has a disproportionate impact on a certain protected category of workers. An example is a physical strength requirement, such as the ability to lift 50 pounds repetitively. That qualification can exclude more women than men, or more older workers than younger workers, from the job. That is, the impact on women and older workers is disproportionate to their numbers in the applicant pool. To defend against a claim of this type of illegal discrimination, the employer would have to prove that the lifting requirement is a business necessity—that the job truly requires lifting that much weight that frequently. Even though the requirement itself is neutral—it applies equally to everyone—the discriminatory impact it has will be illegal if it can't be justified. These types of cases can be particularly severe because a discriminatory hiring policy can affect hundreds or even thousands of people over a period of years.

Testing of ability is allowed if it can be shown that the test is truly required—and if it is not used to discriminate unfairly. For example, it is allowable to require applicants for a cook's position to perform a cooking test and to require applicants for an accounting job to demonstrate proficiency in accounting software. To be considered a business necessity, the test must be for a skill that is truly required for the job.

Bona fide occupational qualifications (BFOQs) permit deliberate discrimination based on the need to hire certain types of people for specific jobs. The employer must prove that intentional discrimination based on sex, religion, or national origin (never color or race) is truly required—that the job cannot be performed by another. Jobs that require a person to be a certain sex, religion, or national origin are rare and only include positions such as female locker room attendants, male models for male clothing, and religious affiliation for ministers. It is the employer's burden to prove that the qualification is *bona fide*, or truly necessary.

Policies intended to perpetuate an image or satisfy a customer preference are generally seen as overtly discriminatory, even though a company deems them necessary. For instance, a restaurant that hires only young people because it wants to create a youthful image is guilty of age discrimination; no bona fide occupational qualification prevents older employees from performing jobs in the restaurant. Similarly, it is neither a business necessity nor a BFOQ for all employees of an ethnic restaurant to be the same ethnicity. Exhibit 13.3 lists discriminatory interview questions.

Religious Discrimination

Title VII of the Civil Rights Act makes it illegal to refuse to hire someone simply because of their religious beliefs. It is illegal to refuse to hire individuals whose religious beliefs might prevent them from working at certain times. However, a company can refuse to hire someone because of their religious beliefs if it can prove that the company will incur undue hardship when the employee takes time off for religious reasons; the company must also show that the job cannot be performed by anyone else during such times. Hospitality companies may face other issues involving religious beliefs, such as appearance, dress codes, and work schedules. In addition, employers must keep the workplace free from religious bias and harassment by employees or guests. The EEOC has issued religious discrimination guidelines to help employers comply with regulations regarding religious beliefs.[9]

Pregnancy Discrimination Act

Before the enactment of the *Pregnancy Discrimination Act of 1978*, an employer could require an employee to take pregnancy leave for a stipulated period or at a specific time in her pregnancy. This is no longer the case. Under this act, an employer cannot dictate the beginning and ending dates of a pregnant employee's maternity leave. In addition, this act prohibits employers from refusing to hire pregnant applicants as long as they can perform the major functions of the job. It also prohibits employers from providing health insurance that does not cover pregnancy or that imposes higher costs for this type of coverage. The law does not require an

Exhibit 13.3	Discriminatory Interview Questions

- Where is your family originally from? What is your native language?

- Do you have any religious practices or beliefs that might interfere with your job?

- What gender is your spouse/partner?

The Family and Medical Leave Act, described more thoroughly later in this chapter, provides additional rights for pregnant employees, including the right to some unpaid leave even if it is not provided to other employees.

LEGAL ALERT!

employer to make special accommodations for pregnant workers or for medical conditions directly related to pregnancy.

Pregnancy and complications, however, may require workers to be off work for a longer time than they would be eligible for under the company's usual employee benefits or policies. The law does not require the employer to allow pregnant employees time off beyond what is provided to other employees, but the law does require the same benefits and policies be available to pregnant employees as are provided to other employees for other types of temporary disability. For example, if an employer routinely assigns injured workers to temporary "light duty" positions until they recover, it must offer the same opportunity to pregnant workers.

The act prohibits employers from discriminating against pregnant women on the basis that these women may not fit the image the company wants to project. As a result, a hospitality employer cannot require an employee to take a leave of absence simply because her appearance doesn't reflect the company image or because there is no uniform that fits pregnant women. In a typical case in 2018, the EEOC sued a California restaurant and nightclub for reducing a server's hours after learning she was pregnant and eventually removing her from the schedule. The restaurant settled the case for $82,500.[10]

Exhibit 13.4 lists interview questions prohibited by the Pregnancy Discrimination Act.

Age Discrimination in Employment Act

The *Age Discrimination in Employment Act (ADEA)* prohibits employment discrimination on the basis of age against people 40 years of age or older. People under 40 years of age are not protected, so it would not be a violation to give a hiring preference to a 25-year-old over a 35-year-old because of their age. It would be a violation to hire a 45-year-old over a 65-year-old for that reason. All employment actions—hiring, recruiting, appraisals, promotions, firing, and so on—affecting employees who are 40 or older are subject to the ADEA.

This is not to say an employer has to give preferential treatment or consideration to older workers. It is not a violation to hire a younger worker even when the two are equally qualified, so long as age is not a factor in the decision to hire the younger worker. But if age is a factor in the decision, the consequences can be expensive.

In a noteworthy recent case, a restaurant chain paid $2.85 million to settle a lawsuit by job applicants age 40 and over who were passed over for front of the house jobs and told during interviews that the company hired younger workers for those jobs.[11] In 2017, another restaurant chain paid $12 million to settle a similar case covering discriminatory hiring at multiple locations over a span of seven years.[12] Both companies claimed unsuccessfully that a younger age was a BFOQ for hosts, servers, and bartenders. Exhibit 13.5 lists age discriminatory questions.

Americans with Disabilities Act

The Americans with Disabilities Act of 1990 is one of the most significant employment laws enacted since the Civil Rights Act of 1964. It is estimated that more than 60 million people in the United States have disabilities—or about one out of every four adults. Before the law's effective date in 1992, only employees of the government

Exhibit 13.4	Interview Questions Prohibited by the Pregnancy Discrimination Act

- Are you pregnant now?
- Do you plan to be pregnant any time soon?
- Are you going to have children?

Exhibit 13.5	Age Discriminatory Questions

- How old are you?
- When did you graduate from college?
- How old are your children?
- When do you plan to retire?

and government contractors were protected. The ADA extended that protection to all workers with disabilities.

The ADA's purpose is not just to prevent employment discrimination against people with disabilities. The law goes further, to require employers to make workplaces accessible to people with disabilities who are otherwise qualified and able to work, so long as the cost is not excessive. Employers are required by the law not just to treat people equally, but also to make "reasonable" changes to the job and workplace to remove the barriers that exclude qualified workers with disabilities from employment. It is a violation of the law to discriminate against a job applicant with disabilities because of the added cost of making the accommodation, so long as the cost is not unreasonable. It is up to the employer to prove that a requested accommodation is too difficult or too costly.

Companies that fail to comply with the ADA are subject to stringent penalties. In some cases, the U.S. Department of Justice files the lawsuit on behalf of an individual or group of workers. A court can assess penalties against any employer to a maximum of $75,000 for a first violation and up to $150,000 for subsequent violations of the rights of individuals with disabilities. The ADA also provides for equitable remedies in job discrimination lawsuits, which are court orders to reinstate the worker and provide the necessary accommodation.

Defining Disability

Under the ADA, individuals are considered to have a disability when they: (1) have a physical or mental impairment that substantially limits one or more major life activities, (2) have a record of such an impairment, or (3) are regarded as having such an impairment. Major life activities include seeing, hearing, communicating, walking, breathing, eating, sleeping, lifting, reading, performing manual tasks, learning, thinking, concentrating, caring for oneself, and working. Note that number (3) includes people who are not actually disabled but are believed to be.

In addition, people with diseases such as cancer, heart disease, cerebral palsy, epilepsy, multiple sclerosis, arthritis, asthma, and diabetes are protected, as are people with HIV and AIDS. Drug and alcohol addiction is considered a disability if a person participates in a supervised rehabilitation program or has undergone rehabilitation and is not currently using drugs or alcohol. Other conditions covered under the ADA include autism, Alzheimer's disease, head injury, and brain injury. The act also encompasses general categories of impairment such as orthopedic, neurological, psychological, and respiratory disorders and diseases.

Qualifying for Work

Under the ADA, people with disabilities are qualified if they can perform the **essential functions** of the job with or without reasonable accommodation. Essential functions are job tasks required for the job. For instance, lifting dishes is essential for a restaurant buser. However, the ability to hear orders is not necessarily essential for a cook, since other means exist for communicating orders. As a result, an operation might be required to make reasonable accommodation so that cooking positions are open to people who are deaf or who have hearing loss. Exhibit 13.6 lists examples of reasonable accommodations.

"Reasonable accommodation" refers to what employers must do to make the workplace accessible to people with disabilities.

The EEOC has found that more than half of all accommodations provided for employees who are disabled cost nothing. The employer is not required to make an accommodation that would be unreasonable, or an "undue burden," considering the difficulty and the expense involved.[13] Exhibit 13.7 lists illegal disability-related questions.

Exhibit 13.6	Reasonable Accommodations

- Lowering a blackjack table for a dealer who uses a wheelchair

- Eliminating non-essential functions from job duties

- Transferring injured workers to available jobs consistent with work restrictions

- Making office spaces accessible to employees who are disabled

- Do you have any serious medical conditions?

- Do you have any medical restrictions on your ability to work?

- Have you ever needed an accommodation for a disability at work?

- Have you ever been treated for drug or alcohol addiction?

Uniformed Services Employment and Reemployment Rights Act

The Uniformed Services Employment and Reemployment Rights Act (USERRA) was enacted in 1994 to protect the jobs of employees departing for active military service. The law does not require any preferential hiring for active duty or retired military, but it does prohibit discrimination against them and provides re-employment rights upon their return from duty. An employee's rights may include exceptions to a company's ordinary leave of absence policies. For example, a company that automatically terminates a worker who is on leave of absence for a long period of time must make exceptions for employees serving military duty. Also included are veterans recovering from service-related injuries or disabilities. Exhibit 13.8 lists unlawful questions to ask uniformed services members.

Returning members of the military who gave advance notice of their deployment are entitled, for a maximum of five years, to:

- Reemployment into the same or similar position as they held when they left

| Exhibit 13.8 | Unlawful Questions |

- Do you have plans to join the military?

- Will you need a lot of time off for military service?

- Any promotion, pay increase, or seniority credit they would have received had they not been on leave

- Continuation of healthcare plan coverage for a maximum of 24 months

Immigration Reform and Control Act of 1986

The Immigration Reform and Control Act (IRCA) of 1986 mandates that employers verify each employee's legal eligibility to work in the United States. This places the burden on employers for ensuring that all new hires are legally authorized to work. This verification must take place within three days after hire by completing the Employment Eligibility Verification Form—commonly called the **I-9 form**. The I-9 must be completed on paper or printed from a form available online.[14] Many private organizations offer software that enables new hires to fill out I-9s, additional federal and state documents, direct deposit forms, and other necessary documentation.

Employers are not required to submit the form to the federal government. They are required to keep the forms for three years after a worker is hired or one year after they leave the employment, whichever is longer, and to provide them for inspection when requested by government enforcement officials, which can occur at any time.

To complete the I-9, an employer is required to verify both the applicant's identity and legal authorization to work. Several documents can be used to establish an employee's identity and authorization to work. A U.S. passport is evidence of both, as is a permanent residency card. A driver's license or similar government-issued identification card may be used to verify identity, but they do not prove authorization to work. Applicants can verify their lawful work status by showing a U.S. birth certificate, Social Security card, employment authorization card, or alien registration form.

Even with advanced document security controls, fake immigration documents are still possible. It is not an employer's job to question or verify the authenticity of a document that appears on its face to be valid.

Employers who fail to verify an employee's authorization to work in the United States are subject to both civil and criminal penalties. The penalty for knowingly hiring someone who is not authorized to work can be as high as $20,130 per violation. An employer can be fined as much as $2,292 for failing to complete and keep an I-9, even when the person is legally eligible to work.

It is important to note that the law does not create any legal basis for discrimination based on citizenship. All applicants who are legally authorized to work in the United States are equally protected from national origin discrimination.

Fair Credit Reporting Act

The Fair Credit Reporting Act (FCRA) protects U.S. consumers from false and fraudulent credit reporting and gives them rights to see and dispute credit reports provided to banks, merchants, and employers. Exhibit 13.9 identifies three major credit reporting agencies.

Some employers find it useful to review job applicants' consumer credit history before hiring them, especially in cases where employees will be responsible for large amounts of money. Some employers believe a poor credit rating might be evidence of an increased risk of theft or financial mismanagement. Other employers don't believe there is a reliable correlation and don't check credit histories at all.

A company can legally obtain an applicant's credit history from one of the major credit reporting agencies or from other services that combine information from two or three of them. A credit report can be obtained only if the applicant or employee consents in writing, but an employer can legally refuse to hire an applicant who refuses to consent.

The FCRA provides job applicants some protection, but it does not restrict an employer's ability to make employment decisions based on a person's credit rating or history. Most of the law's provisions protect consumers from inaccurate credit reports and unfair credit rating methods. It does not protect job applicants from being refused work because of their credit rating or history. An employer can lawfully obtain and rely on a credit report if it follows these steps:

- The applicant's consent must be in writing and signed, and a separate document must advise the applicant that the company might make the employment decision on the basis of the report.

- If the employer decides not to hire the applicant because of the information in the credit report, the applicant must be informed of that fact and must be provided with a copy of the credit report the company obtained and a copy of a document explaining the person's rights under the law.

- The employer should keep the credit report and the information in it strictly confidential and protected from data breach. A credit report contains a great deal of personal information and should be protected with the utmost care. Providing any such information to anyone else is a separate violation of the law.

The employer is not required by law to justify its decision and is not required to consider any other related information, such as a pending dispute over something in the report. If applicants dispute the accuracy of the report, they have the right under the law to have that dispute considered and resolved by the credit reporting agency, but the employer is not required to wait for that process to conclude.

Employee Polygraph Protection Act of 1988

In the past, it was fairly common for employers to require employees and applicants to submit to polygraph or "lie detector" tests in a number of situations, including job interviews. The test itself, however, has proven unreliable. The Employee Polygraph Protection Act of 1988 prohibits the use of the tests in most employment situations in which they were previously used. Under this law, employees are protected from discrimination on the basis of results of a polygraph

Exhibit 13.9	Major Credit Reporting Agencies
	■ Equifax
	■ Experian
	■ TransUnion

exam or their refusal to submit to a polygraph exam.

Employers can require polygraph tests under a very narrow exception. This exception permits an employer to use the tests to investigate an economic loss or injury when there is good reason to believe a particular employee was involved. Even then, the test is legal only if the employee voluntarily consents. No action can be taken against an employee for refusing to consent. In effect, this law has eliminated the polygraph test from the private workplace. Many other types of tests are permitted, so long as they don't have a discriminatory effect. Exhibit 13.10 is an example of an illegal polygraph interview question.

Knowledge Check

1. What are the employment rights of active members of the U.S. military?

2. What are some examples of reasonable accommodations for workers who are disabled?

3. What is an example of a bona fide occupational qualification?

13.3 LAWS AFFECTING COMPENSATION AND BENEFITS

Fair Labor Standards Act

In 1935, the U.S. Fair Labor Standards Act (FLSA) established the first legal minimum wage: 25 cents per hour. As of early 2021, the minimum hourly wage of $7.25 set in 2009 remains in place. Some workers are exempt from the minimum wage, but few employees in the hospitality industry meet the strict criteria for being paid less than the legal minimum.

Exhibit 13.10	Illegal Interview Question

Are you willing to take a lie detector test before being hired?

One exception applies broadly throughout the hospitality industry: Employees who earn tips on a regular basis are not exempt but may be paid as little as $2.13 per hour, so long as their tips are enough in every workweek to make up the difference between the wages paid and the legal minimum. This is called a "tip credit" because the employer is taking the credit for the tips toward its obligation to pay the minimum wage. If the employee's tips are not enough to result in the payment of at least the minimum wage in any workweek, the employer must make up the shortfall. Some states, however, establish a higher "tipped" minimum wage, while others do not allow the tip credit at all.

When the employer is permitted to take a tip credit and pays a worker below the minimum wage, strict regulations exist about the ownership and pooling of tips. When the employer pays the full minimum wage, it can require that servers pool their tips and give some of the tips to employees who don't earn tips, such as cooks and dishwashers. However, following a 2018 amendment, the employer and managers are never allowed to take a share of the tips.[15]

The other main provision of the FLSA requires overtime pay of at least 1.5 times the regular hourly rate for hours worked in excess of 40 hours in any workweek. Minimum wage and overtime obligations are always calculated on a weekly basis, so there is no "carrying over" hours from one week into another. Many state laws also require overtime pay for hours worked over eight in one day.

Some types of workers are exempt from the overtime requirement, the most common of which are salaried employees. But just because workers are paid a salary does not mean they are not entitled to overtime pay. It is legal to pay any worker a regular weekly rate, so long as they are additionally compensated for overtime when they work over 40 hours in a week. A salaried worker is exempt, meaning not legally entitled to overtime pay, only if three requirements are met:

1. They are paid a weekly salary of at least $684.

2. The salary does not change depending on the hours of work.

3. The worker is employed in a bona fide executive, administrative, or professional capacity.

Table 13.2 outlines the requirements necessary to meet each exemption.

The FLSA is enforced by the U.S. Department of Labor (DOL), state labor agencies, and private lawsuits. Employees claiming a violation of minimum wage and/or overtime laws can file a complaint with the DOL, but they are not required to do so before proceeding with litigation. To complicate the risk, many of these cases involve company policies or practices that affect many employees, sometimes thousands. Class action lawsuits are particularly appropriate in those cases and may result in enormous losses. Employees have two years to file a claim for unpaid wages, and three years in cases of intentional violations.

Like the EEOC in discrimination cases, the DOL can prosecute the case on behalf of the employees, saving them attorney's fees and court costs. The agency recovers over $200 million per year on behalf of underpaid workers. Several recent class action lawsuits for unpaid overtime have cost restaurant companies more than $20 million.

Child Labor

The FLSA also includes federal restrictions on employing minors. Quick service restaurants are frequently targeted for such violations.

Minors are also particularly vulnerable to sexual and other forms of harassment.

Most U.S. states have added to these limitations on workers under 18 years of age. It is important to note that there are strict limits on both the hours and type of work. Table 13.3 shows the minimum standards under the federal law on workers under 18 years of age.

Equal Pay Act

The Equal Pay Act requires employers to pay men and women equally for performing equal work. Two jobs are considered "equal" if they require equal skill, effort, responsibility, and conditions. The jobs don't

Table 13.2	Requirements to Meet Each Exemption	

Executive	Administrative	Professional
Supervisors	Department heads	Attorneys
Managers	Administrators	CPAs
Officers		Architects
Executives		Doctors
Supervises two or more employees Has input in hiring and firing decisions Primary job is management	Performs non-manual labor Works in an administrative capacity Exercises independent discretion	Holds a professional degrees or license Exercises independent discretion

Table 13.3 Federal Minimum Standards on Workers Under 18 Years of Age

Age	Maximum Hours	Examples of Prohibited Work
18 and over	Unlimited	Regulated by OSHA
16–17	Unlimited	Meat slicers and grinders Commercial mixers Trash compactors Quick service food delivery Driving at night
14–15	Must be outside school hours: Three hours on school day Eight hours on a non-school day 18 hours per week between 7 a.m. and 7 p.m. during school year 40 hours per week between 7 a.m. and 9 p.m. outside school year	In addition to all of the above: Cooking over an open flame Broilers, rotisseries, pressure cookers Baking

have to be identical, just "substantially similar." Job titles and job descriptions are evidence, but the courts look at the actual tasks the workers perform when judging their similarity. The law requires that men and women receive an equal rate of pay, not necessarily an equal amount of pay due to differences in hours worked or sales commissions.

The Equal Pay Act doesn't just apply to wages: it requires gender equality in all forms of compensation and benefits, including health insurance, vacation, profit-sharing, and commissions. There are four exceptions. It is legal to pay men and women differently for performing equal work for one of the following four reasons:

1. Seniority: Wage differences can result from fair and equal seniority systems.

2. Merit: Employers can pay workers more based on better job performance.

3. Productivity: Employers can pay a higher rate for higher quality or quantity or work, so long as both men and women have equal opportunity to earn the higher rate.

4. Factors other than sex: Paying a premium for a graveyard shift, for example, might result in some men earning more than some women, but sex is not the reason for the difference.

Employee Health Insurance and Retirement Benefits

Health and retirement benefits are highly regulated and subject to too many laws to summarize here. The three most noteworthy are:

- The Employee Retirement Income Security Act (ERISA) protects pension and retirement benefits and requires strict employer reporting, non-discriminatory benefits, and detailed financial disclosures.

- The Older Worker Benefit Protection Act (OWBPA) prohibits age discrimination in employment benefits and sets strict guidelines for retirement agreements that include a promise not to sue for age discrimination.

- The Consolidated Omnibus Budget Reconciliation Act (COBRA) provides employees and their dependents the right to continue health insurance coverage (at their own cost) for 18 to 29 months following separation of employment.

Workers' Compensation

Nearly every state requires employers to contribute to a system of insurance for workplace injuries and illnesses. Although state laws vary widely in many respects, commonalities exist.

Workers' compensation for the most part is "no-fault" insurance. This means all workplace injuries are covered regardless of whether the injury was the employer's fault, the employee's fault, a coworker's fault, or nobody's fault.

Employers can obtain workers' compensation insurance in several ways. Some are permitted by state laws; some are mandatory. Some employers can "self-insure," so they pay the benefits directly to employees. In many states, employers purchase insurance from private insurance companies, which take responsibility for any claims. Other states have established state-run workers' compensation, in which the employers pay a premium to the state agency, which pays benefits to injured workers.

Employers who do not have the required workers' compensation insurance are subject to high fines and to being directly responsible for any workplace injuries or deaths. Except in rare circumstances, the benefits established by state law are the employee's "exclusive remedy" for the injury, which means they cannot sue the employer in court even when the injury is the employer's fault.

An injured worker may be entitled to some or all of the following benefits, depending on the type and severity of the injury:

- Payment of all related medical and rehabilitation costs

- Temporary disability pay to replace wages lost due to temporary inability to work

- Permanent disability pay to replace lost future wages due to permanent inability to work

- Vocational rehabilitation to retrain the injured worker for employment in another job

Family and Medical Leave Act of 1993

The Family and Medical Leave Act (FMLA) requires employers with 50 or more employees to offer up to 12 weeks of unpaid leave per year for specified reasons:

- To care for a newborn or adopted child

- To care for an ill parent, spouse, or child

- To recover from the employee's own medical condition

To be eligible, a worker must have been employed for at least 12 months and have worked at least 1,250 hours for the company.

The right to take leave for a new child applies to males and females equally. Intermittent leave, taken in increments of hours or days at a time, cannot be taken for birth or adoption but is available for treatment of employee or family illnesses. Employers are not required to compensate employees on leave but must continue their healthcare coverage. Employees may be required to use any paid time off benefits before taking unpaid leave.

Upon returning from leave, employees are entitled to return to the position they were in, with no loss of status or benefits. Exceptions may apply in cases where the job has been eliminated, but the employer cannot refuse to reinstate workers from leave just because someone else has been hired to fill their position in their absence.

The FMLA is enforced by the DOL. Penalties for violation are severe for employers: up to 100 percent of lost wages and benefits, plus attorney's fees and court-related costs. The DOL publishes extensive employer guidance for complying with the FMLA and determining employee eligibility for leave.[16]

Knowledge Check

1. What factors determine whether an employee is exempt from overtime pay?

2. What benefits are typically paid to injured workers?

3. Why are there federal laws for workers younger than 18 years of age?

13.4 LAWS AFFECTING MANAGING PERFORMANCE AND OPERATIONS

Occupational Safety and Health Act

The Occupational Safety and Health Act was enacted in 1970 to protect the health and safety of U.S. workers. The law applies to all workplaces and workers in the hospitality industry.

Like many employment laws, the act allows states to adopt their own higher standards, and nearly half have done so.[17] In states that establish their own occupational safety and health laws and agencies, the employer is required to comply with those standards, and violations are investigated and resolved by the state agency.

The Occupational Safety and Health Act, and most state safety laws, establish six primary requirements. Employers must:

- Comply with standards of safety published by federal and state regulations

- Train and educate workers on workplace safety standards and practices

- Keep the workplace free of recognized hazards that could cause serious injury or death

- Allow inspections by federal or state regulators at any time

- Respect employees' rights to ask about job dangers, report safety issues, and refuse to work in hazardous environments

- Maintain records of all workplace injuries and deaths, and report them to state or federal agencies

Employees have the right to report unsafe working conditions to the Occupational Safety and Health Administration (OSHA) or to their state agency, but they do not have the right to sue the employer for violating the act. An employee injured at work would be entitled to workers' compensation benefits, but since the insurance is paid regardless of fault, it doesn't matter in a workers' compensation case whether the employer violated the law.

Common workplace hazards in hospitality include using commercial cleaning chemicals, working in kitchens, and lifting heavy objects.

Harassment

Beginning in the late 1970s, the EEOC and the U.S. courts recognized that harassment on the basis of sex is a form of illegal discrimination. Since then, the courts have also recognized cases for harassment based on every illegal reason for employment discrimination. Harassment is considered discrimination due to the different effect it has on people of a particular race, religion, and so on. For example, if Muslim employees are subjected to repeated harassment because of their religion, that creates a workplace that is different for them, and it is due to an illegal reason.

The rules of sexual harassment liability are complex, and the potential losses are extreme. It is always advisable to contact an HR manager or legal counsel upon receipt of any harassment complaint. Prevention of harassment occurs at the front line of management because the employer is responsible for harassment as soon as a manager sees it, knows about it, or should have known about it.

To best protect the company from claims of harassment, managers must follow certain basic procedures:

- Take harassment training seriously and repeat it frequently. A company can lose a case for the sole reason that its prevention measures were inadequate.

- Report and take immediate action to stop any harassment you see or hear about from anyone. This includes harassment by customers. The company is liable for allowing harassment even if the victim never actually complained to management about it.

- Make sure employees know they have a safe and confidential way to report harassment.

- Keep the victim informed about what's happening next. An employee who quits because of harassment can still make a legal claim based on the employer's inaction after receiving the information.

Americans with Disabilities Act

The requirements for reasonable accommodations for employees with disabilities was addressed earlier, but there may also be cases where the need for accommodation arises after the employment has begun. In either case, the same rules and limitations apply.

Workers returning from a workplace injury with permanent restrictions on their ability to work may be considered disabled and entitled to a reasonable accommodation. This might require rearranging the workplace or job duties and accommodating medical needs.

National Labor Relations Act

The National Labor Relations Act guarantees U.S. workers the right to form, assist, and join labor unions; to go on strike; and to bargain collectively with the employer through their union representative. The act and related union laws are covered in detail in Chapters 11 and 12.

Knowledge Check

1. What steps can a company take to protect itself from cases of sexual harassment?

2. What does the Occupational Safety and Health Act require an employer to do?

3. List two examples of harassment in the workplace.

13.5 LAWS AFFECTING EMPLOYMENT TERMINATION

Discrimination Laws

As noted above, any type of adverse job action can be the basis for a discrimination claim. By far, the employment action that most frequently results in a violation of discrimination laws is termination of employment. The legal standards for discrimination claims are described in more detail above, but in cases of employment termination, it is important to be mindful of the way in which they may be proven in court. Discharged employees who file a complaint for discrimination do not have to prove that the action was taken for an

LEGAL ALERT!

Employees who quit because of illegal activity at work or because of a discriminatory work environment can still sue as if they were terminated. This is called **constructive discharge**. It occurs when the employer's inaction leaves employees with no reasonable option but to resign.

illegal reason. They have to prove that a similar person outside their protected category was treated differently—that is, not fired in similar circumstances. This is not always difficult to prove, especially in a large workplace with thousands of employees and inconsistent management.

At that point in the lawsuit, the employer can escape liability for discrimination in only three ways:

1. Refute the employee's claim that the employee being compared was in "similar circumstances"

2. Prove a legitimate non-discriminatory reason why the two employees were treated differently

3. Prove the business necessity or BFOQ defense

This way of proving discrimination highlights the importance of thoughtful, fair, and consistent applications of workplace rules and standards. An employer can lose a discrimination lawsuit when there was no intention whatsoever to discriminate. That happens because the employer is unable to adequately prove a legitimate non-discriminatory reason for the action.

Here's an example: A 55-year-old is fired for being late to work and sues for age discrimination. A younger worker was also late to work and was not fired. That is all the older employee has to prove. The employer might disprove the case by showing that the two cases were not similar, for example if the younger worker was only five minutes late and the older worker was five hours late. It's a legitimate reason and applies to all ages—that is, if it has been enforced consistently up to then.

But even if it has, the fired worker still gets a chance to challenge the employer's reason and prove it is not true. For example, if other older workers have been fired for being five minutes late and other younger workers were not fired for being five hours late, then it calls into question whether the employer's reason for discriminating is true. If the judge or jury disbelieves the employer's stated reason, they can conclude that the real reason was illegal—even if the real reason was inconsistent enforcement, or ignorance, of the company policy.

Worker Adjustment and Retraining Notification Act

The Worker Adjustment and Retraining Notification (WARN) Act (29 U.S.C 2101 et seq.) requires larger employers to notify employees 60 days in advance of closing the business or laying off a large portion of the workforce. Exceptions exist for natural disasters, unforeseeable business circumstances, or financial necessity.

The act applies only to employers with 100 or more workers and in cases of a layoff of at least 33 percent of the full-time workforce, or 500 full-time workers, whichever is less. If the employer fails to deliver the proper notice, employees are entitled to be paid for the last 60 days. No federal agency has authority to investigate or process claims for violation of the WARN Act, but employees may sue individually or in a class action. Their only remedies are payment of lost wages for the period of the violation and reimbursement of their attorney's fees.

Unemployment Insurance Laws

Each state provides for the payment of unemployment benefits to workers who lose their jobs due to no fault of their own. This might be due to a layoff, reduction in hours, or business closure. Each state's rules and benefit calculations are different, but many have the same general features:

- All employers are required to contribute to the funds to pay claims through a payroll tax or surcharge.

- Payment of benefits is administered by a state agency with authority to decide disputed cases and to impose penalties for non-compliance.

- Benefits are calculated as a portion of the worker's average pay, with set minimum and maximum amounts.

- Workers who are employed for only a few weeks or months are not entitled to benefits.

- People are disqualified from benefits if they are terminated from employment for a legitimate reason or if they leave the employment voluntarily.

Knowledge Check

1. How can terminated workers prove a case for unlawful discrimination?

2. Which former employees are not entitled to unemployment insurance benefits?

3. List three examples of why an employee would qualify for unemployment insurance.

13.6 PROTECTING AGAINST EMPLOYMENT LAW LIABILITIES

Employment Practices Liability Insurance

The evolution of employment practices liability insurance (EPLI) offers another example of industry adaptation. In 1991, only five carriers in the United States offered the coverage and only large employers purchased it. By 2020, hundreds of insurance companies offered such policies. The policy protects against nearly all claims arising from the employer–employee relationship. EPLI provides coverage for wrongful employment acts, wrongful termination, sexual harassment, wage and hour violations, and discrimination.[18] The insurance can be expensive, so many employers opt to devote additional resources to prevention and training. Larger firms with thousands of workers are more likely to buy the insurance.

Mandatory Arbitration Agreements

Many U.S. employers have adopted a practice of requiring all employees to agree to submit any legal claims they have against the company to private arbitration rather than government agencies or courts. Some employers have found that the agreements can reduce the costs of litigation and prevent unreasonable jury verdicts. But for some employers, the practice can have the opposite effect.[19]

Legal challenges to this practice have resulted in some restrictions; but within those limitations, the agreements are enforced in court and can prevent workers from suing the employer. But even in arbitration, employees are entitled to the same legal rights and remedies available in court. It is essential to write any such agreement with the assistance of legal counsel. If the agreement violates any established legal restriction, it will be void and will not prevent litigation.

Independent Contractors

Businesses use independent contractors for a variety of services, from plumbing and elevator repair to linen supply, landscaping, and commercial food preparation. Some hospitality companies even "outsource" their security, maintenance, human resources, or service operations. They often find that paying a contractor to perform operational services is more cost efficient than hiring employees.

Independent contractors are not employees, so employment laws don't apply to them. In fact, one of the main advantages to using independent contractors is to avoid responsibility for compliance with employment laws. But calling someone an independent contractor does not make them one. It is not always clear whether a person is or is not an employee, but any company is well advised to seek legal advice to ensure the company is protected. If a person is paid as a contractor but is later found to legally be an employee, the company will be liable for any employment law violations, which may include workers' compensation, minimum wage and overtime, unemployment insurance, income tax withholding, employee benefits, and discrimination.

That risk is complicated by the uncertainty that may arise under the applicable law. There is no clear and definitive way to determine whether a person is an independent contractor. Rather, courts and administrative regulations establish a list of factors used to make the determination. They include:

- The amount of control the company exercises over the person's work, such as supervision, inspection, scheduling, and direction. This is often the most important factor.

- The worker's financial independence, as in a separate company or business.

- The permanency of the relationship.

- The method of payment since contractors are typically paid a sum for the job while employees are paid hourly or by a regular salary.

- Responsibility for providing tools and supplies. Employees are usually not required to provide their own tools, supplies, and uniforms, while independent contractors typically are.

- Whether the work is a part of the employer's normal operations, like valet parking, or sporadic like elevator repairs.[20]

Best Practices

Certain best practices can help protect employers from employment law infractions. These include:

- Evaluate applicants and employees honestly and consistently. The key to avoiding lawsuits for discrimination is to treat everyone equally. Inaccurate performance evaluations are frequently used in court to discredit managers.

- When you recognize a potential liability, document everything you see, hear, and say. Lawsuits go on for years and might not even begin until a couple of years after the employee has left. Nobody's memory is that good, especially managers of hundreds of workers. The notes you keep at work won't just help you remember; they can be used by the company in court.

- Be mindful that employees may be entitled to unpaid leaves of absence and other accommodations for many reasons, and most employees have rights to reinstatement when they are ready to return. Always consult with an HR specialist or legal counsel before refusing a request for leave or for an accommodation for religious, medical, or disability reasons.

- The most common sort of employment legal claim is for retaliation, which is another form of illegal discrimination. Rather than race or age, the action is taken because a person exercised their legally protected rights. This chapter identifies many of those legal rights, including reporting a safety violation, testifying in court, filing a complaint of discrimination or harassment, joining a union, objecting to unsafe working conditions, and so on. Whenever an employee has taken such an action, it is critical to monitor the workplace to ensure the employee is protected from unlawful retaliation.

- Seek assistance when you are unsure. No manager can memorize every employment law, but a good manager can sense a potential for a legal problem and contact HR professionals or legal counsel for advice before creating a liability.

Knowledge Check

1. What is employment practices liability insurance (EPLI)?

2. What are factors used to determine independent contractor status?

3. Identify three best practices that can protect employers from employment law infractions.

IN THIS CHAPTER, YOU LEARNED:

- Employees have many legal rights.

- Employment laws are made by both federal and state governments.

- Employment lawsuits can be filed by individuals, large groups, and government agencies.

- Unlawful discrimination can be proven in court without direct evidence.

- The law prohibits many forms of job discrimination, with very few exceptions.

- Unlawful discrimination can occur at any stage of the employment cycle; the most common are hiring and firing.

- The consequences for violating employment laws can be severe.

- There are many legally protected reasons for needing a leave of absence.

- Improper interview questions can violate many employment laws.

- Employers are required to accommodate workers who are disabled up to a limit.

- Managers who are aware of the law can recognize and actively avoid employment law liabilities.

KEY TERMS

at will—An employment relationship under which an employer may terminate an employee, or an employee may quit with or without notice, at any time, for any reason.

back pay—The amount of money and benefits employees would have earned if they had remained employed; this is typically part of the remedy for illegal employment termination.

bona fide occupational qualifications (BFOQs)—Discriminatory job requirements that are essential to the performance of the job.

business necessity—A legal reason for a policy or action that has a discriminatory effect.

class action—A type of lawsuit brought by one or more individuals on behalf of a much larger group.

constructive discharge—Occurs when an employee resigns due to illegal action or working conditions that are so severe that a reasonable person would have no alternative but to quit.

essential functions—The job tasks required to successfully perform the job.

I-9 form—Written record used to verify an applicant's legal authorization to work.

respondeat superior—A legal principle that holds the employer responsible for the acts of its employees while they are acting in the course of their employment.

right-to-sue letter—A document from the EEOC certifying that the person has complied with the administrative requirements for processing claims of unlawful employment discrimination.

whistleblower—An employee who reports illegal workplace activity to the proper authorities.

wrongful discharge—Illegal termination of an at-will employee.

REVIEW QUESTIONS

1. What are the federal laws that prohibit discrimination in the workplace?

2. What are the potential remedies for violation of federal discrimination laws?

3. What is an example of a bona fide occupational qualification?

4. What are three reasons an employee would be entitled to an unpaid leave of absence?

5. What is the difference between wrongful discharge and constructive discharge?

6. To win a case for employment discrimination, what does the employee have to prove?

7. What are some direct actions every manager can take to protect their company from employment lawsuits?

8. What accommodations are required for employees who are disabled, pregnant, or have religious conflicts with work?

Sex Discrimination

Randy has a new job as an HR manager of a large hotel chain. On Randy's first day of work, Jane, the vice president of human resources, gives him a special project to work on. She explains, "We've had some reports of sex discrimination lately and I need you to look into them and do something before they become big legal problems for us. I'm going to present your recommendations at the next executive meeting."

She continues, "We've had three types of sex discrimination complaints. First, some women believe men are being paid more than them for no good reason. Second, our complaint hotline has received some recent complaints of sexual harassment. Third, some women have reported that they were treated unfairly when they were pregnant."

Randy begins by reviewing the records of the complaints. He finds some job classifications where it does appear that most of the men are paid more than most of the women, but they don't all have the same job duties and some men have been there longer.

He also learns that almost all the sexual harassment complaints are about harassment by customers, not coworkers. The hotline receives about 20 anonymous messages reporting harassment each year, but only two or three actually make a formal complaint to HR a year.

Finally, Randy finds a company policy that housekeepers and servers are temporarily transferred to other less physically demanding jobs when they become pregnant.

DISCUSSION QUESTIONS:

1. Which of these three problems should Randy focus on first?

2. Which one is the greatest legal risk?

3. What additional information will Randy need to know about each problem?

4. What specific recommendations can Randy make to reduce the risk of legal liability for each problem?

ENDNOTES

1. National Conference of State Legislators (April 15, 2008), At-Will Employment – Overview, https://www.ncsl.org/research/labor-and-employment/at-will-employment-overview.aspx.

2. Donald D. Carter, Geoffrey England, Brian Etherington, and Gilles Trudeau, *Labour Law in Canada*, 5th Edition (The Hague, Netherlands: Kluwer Law International, 2002).

3. Society for Human Resource Management (2018). "Employment at will" is not a blank check to terminate employees you don't like. https://www.shrm.org/resourcesandtools/hr-topics/employee-relations/pages/employment-at-will-isnt-a-blank-check-to-terminate-employees-you-dont-like.aspx.

4. U.S. Equal Employment Commission (February 26, 2021 press release), EEOC Release Fiscal Year 2021 Enforcement and Litigation Data, https://www.eeoc.gov/newsroom/eeoc-releases-fiscal-year-2020-enforcement-and-litigation-data.

5. U.S. Equal Employment Opportunity Commission (April 10, 2019 press release), EEOC Releases Fiscal Year 2020 Enforcement and Litigation Data, https://www.eeoc.gov/newsroom/eeoc-releases-fiscal-year-2020-enforcement-and-litigation-data.

6. U.S. Equal Employment Opportunity Commission (July 30, 2018 press release), SLS Hotel to Pay $2.5 Million to Settle EEOC Race, Color, National Origin Lawsuit, https://www.eeoc.gov/newsroom/sls-hotel-pay-25-million-settle-eeoc-race-color-national-origin-lawsuit.

7. U.S. Equal Employment Opportunity Commission (July 19, 2018 press release), Two IHOP Restaurants to Pay Nearly $1 Million to Settle EEOC Sexual Harassment Suit, https://www.eeoc.gov/newsroom/two-ihop-restaurants-pay-nearly-1-million-settle-eeoc-sexual-harassment-suit.

8. *Bostock v. Clayton County, Georgia*, 140 S. Ct. 1731 (2020).

9. EEOC, Religious Accommodations Tips. Retrieved 12/21/2020, https://www.eeoc.gov/employers/small-business/religious-accommodations-tips.

10. Equal Employment Opportunity Commission (July 2, 2018 press release), LA Louisanne Restaurant Settles EEOC Pregnancy Discrimination Lawsuit, https://www.eeoc.gov/newsroom/la-louisanne-restaurant-settles-eeoc-pregnancy-discrimination-lawsuit-82500.

11. Equal Employment Opportunity Commission (May 3, 2018 press release), Seasons 52 to Pay $2.85 Million to Settle EEOC Age Discrimination Lawsuit, https://www.eeoc.gov/newsroom/seasons-52-pay-285-million-settle-eeoc-age-discrimination-lawsuit.

12. Equal Employment Opportunity Commission (March 31, 2017 press release), Texas Roadhouse to Pay $12 Million to Settle EEOC Age Discrimination Lawsuit, https://www.eeoc.gov/newsroom/texas-roadhouse-pay-12-million-settle-eeoc-age-discrimination-lawsuit.

13. Equal Employment Opportunity Commission, The ADA: Your Responsibilities as an Employer, https://www.eeoc.gov/publications/ada-your-responsibilities-employer.

14. U.S. Citizen and Immigration Services, I-9, Employment Eligibility Verification, https://www.uscis.gov/i-9.

15. Consolidated Appropriations Act, 2018, Public Law No. 115-141 (03/23/2018), https://www.congress.gov/115/plaws/publ141/PLAW-115publ141.pdf.

16. The U.S. Department of Labor, Family and Medical Leave Act, https://www.dol.gov/agencies/whd/fmla.

17. The U.S. Department of Labor Occupational Safety and Health Administration, State Plans, https://www.osha.gov/stateplans.

18. Stephanie Gironda & Kimberly Geisler (2017). Employment practices liability insurance: A guide to policy provisions and challenging issues for insureds and plaintiffs. *ABA Journal of Labor and Employment Law*, 33(1), 55-68.

19. William Werner, Christian E. Hardigree, & Shannon Okada (2005), Phantom benefits: Mandatory employment arbitration reconsidered, *Cornell Hotel and Restaurant Administration Quarterly*, 46(3), 363-375.

20. U.S. Department of Labor, Final Rule: Independent Contractor Status Under the Fair Labor Standards Act (January 6, 2021), https://www.dol.gov/agencies/whd/flsa/2021-independent-contractor.

INDEX

third-party reference checks, 67
360-degree appraisals, 153–155
time and motion analysis, 14
tip
        credits, 211–212, 216, 326
        pooling, 211, 212, 216
Title VII (Civil Rights Act of 1964), 59,
    319–320, 321, 322
top-down (or engineering) forecasting,
    33
total reward programs, 194
training, 108–126, 140
        basic skills, 122, 229
        computer-based, 117
        conference, 118
        costs, 174
        criteria, 110, 116
        cycle, 109–110
        evaluation, 110, 124–126
        in-basket, 118
        job instruction, 119
        lecture method, 119
        for managers, 117–119
        objectives, 110, 115–116
        off-the-job, 119
        online, 118–119
        on-the-job, 119
        for performance appraisals,
           155–156
        recordkeeping, 156
        sensitivity, 121–122
        simulation, 121
        team, 122
        the trainer, 118
        vestibule, 121
        virtual, 125–126
trait-based ratings, 144–145
trend
        analysis (of employee demand),
           33–36
        line forecasting, 21–22
turnover, 14, 88, 172–176
        causes of, 174–175
        desired, 172
        intangible costs, 173–174
        rate, 172–173
        remedies for, 175–176
        reports, 113
        tangible costs, 173–174
        undesired, 173–174
two-career/income families, 266
two-tier wage systems, 209–210
type A people, 259–260
type B people, 260

U

unconscious bias, 72
undesired turnover, 172–173
undue burden, 323
unemployment compensation
    insurance, 234, 332–333
unfair labor practice strike, 302–303
unfair labor practices, 279–281, 286,
    288, 296–297, 303
*Uniform Guidelines on Employee
    Testing*, 59
Uniformed Services Employment
    and Reemployment Rights Act
    (USERRA), 324
union
        benefit plans, 240
        security systems, 304
        stewards, 283, 306–308
unions
        certification of, 285
        compensation rates and,
           196–197
        contracts and, 37, 196–197, 286
        decertification of, 285
        density of, 276–277
        elections and, 285–286
        future of, 287–288
        grievances and, 305–307
        in hospitality, 276–278
        job analysis/design and, 10
        legislation affecting, 278–286
        negotiations and, 296–301
        organizing drives and, 285–286
        strikes and, 301–303
        trends of, 276–278
UNITE HERE, 277, 278, 285, 297, 303,
    304, 308. *See also* HERE
United Auto Workers, 278
U.S. Department of Homeland
    Security, 318
U.S. Department of Justice, 323
U.S. Department of Labor, 8, 62, 156,
    196, 203, 215–216, 234, 267, 317,
    318, 327, 329
U.S. Drug Enforcement Agency, 62
U.S. Equal Employment Opportunity
    Commission. *See* EEOC
U.S. National Guard, 278
U.S. Securities and Exchange
    Commission, 232
U.S. Supreme Court, 253, 254, 280,
    319
unstructured interviews, 69

V

valence, 200–201
validity, 56–58
variable labor expenses, 18
vertical job expansion, 16
vestibule training, 121
virtual
        training, 125–126
        workers, 156, 157–158, 267
vocational training, 235
voluntary
        bargaining issues, 297
        benefits, 235–243
        plans, 239
        recognition, 285
Vroom, Victor, 200

W–Z

wage
        compression, 213–214
        expansion, 213–214
        and hour audits, 215
Wagner Act, 276, 279–280, 286, 288,
    296
WARN Act, 332
Watson Wyatt Consulting, 154
weighted application blanks, 59
Welch, Jack, 147
welcoming activities for new
    employees, 97
wellness programs, 261, 265
whistleblowing, 317
wildcat strikes, 302
work
        jurisdiction provisions, 304
        sample tests of job applicants,
           62–63
        sampling of employees,
           112–113
work life/home life balance, 266–267
Worker Adjustment and Retraining
    Notification Act of 1991, 332
workers' compensation, 234–235, 261,
    329–330
workplace
        fatalities, 254, 267
        injuries, 235
        smoking, 265, 266
        violence, 254, 267
written warnings, 179
wrongful discharge, 317, 331–332